POLITICAL TRUST *in* KOSOVO

Exploring Cultural and Institutional Dynamics

Ermira Babamusta, PhD

NY ELITE PRESS

For my parents, Neki and Suzana,
Eda, Russell, Victoria, and Emily

Table of Contents

APPENDICES

ABSTRACT

In this book I examine political trust perceptions across different political-legal institutions and actors in Kosovo (*Alb: Kosova*). I evaluate the levels of political trust using cultural and institutional performance explanations to investigate the key factors that have an impact on political trust.

The study explores national and international political trust, considering various domains: government, political leaders, political parties, Kosovo Courts, Kosovo Police, NATO, United Nations, European Union, and the Kosovo Specialist Court.

There is growing concern about lower levels of political trust across Europe, especially in post-communist countries. In this book, I make the case that trust in political institutions is vital to the democratic functioning of the state. A certain degree of trustworthiness in institutions is a necessary precondition for the legitimacy, fairness, and democratic governance.

The research findings illustrate that transitional democracies like Kosovo face lower levels of trust due to stability concerns and low government performance. There is a clear difference between the trust levels in the local versus international legal institutions of Kosovo. This explains why local courts in Kosovo are perceived less trustworthy (with only 30% trust), when compared to the high trust scores of the Kosovo Specialist Court, stationed outside of Kosovo in The Hague (70%) in 2018.

Results suggest that Kosovo Albanians living inside the country have the same level of distrust in the government as Kosovo citizens living outside the country. While foreign nationals expressed slightly a higher level of trust in Kosovo's government when compared to ethnic Albanians.

Although levels of trust in government are low in Kosovo, the study found the highest trust in the U.S. Embassy (79%) and in law enforcement, primarily policing institutions such as the Kosovo police.

Out of the three international organizations in Kosovo, NATO ranked the highest level of trust amongst Kosovo elite with 84% generalized trust score, followed by 77% for the European Union, and only 51% for the United Nations.

ACKNOWLEDGEMENTS

First and foremost, I would like to thank the Lord for giving me the strength, knowledge, and the ability to persevere through this ambitious scientific study. I found many blessings along the way in achieving set goals, reminding me about discipline and having faith.

I would like to express great appreciation to my doctoral advisor and my committee chair Professor R. Scott Crichlow, who is an exceptional mentor that brings out the best in you. Dr. Crichlow has always eagerly provided his heartfelt support and has given me invaluable guidance, inspiration, and suggestions in my academic pursuit.

I appreciate the insightful guidance of all committee members, Dr. David M. Hauser, Dr. John C. Kilwein, Dr. Joe D. Hagan, and Dr. Robert D. Duval, whose support and incredible ideas are evidence of excellence and outstanding teaching.

I would like to thank my parents Neki and Suzana Babamusta, my sister Edlira, brother-in-law Russell, my adorable nieces Emily and Victoria, who have given me tremendous positive support and cheered me on. Thank you for your love, continued encouragement and inspiring me to follow my dreams. You are the reason I keep pushing myself to make a difference in the world.

Sincere thanks to the great people of Kosovo (*Kosova*) and my dear friends for their hospitality and warm welcome: Hyrie Gashi family, Gëzim Kunoviku family, Valbona Hajredini, Emine Emini, Halil Gashi, Arben Gashi, Assemblyman Mehmet Hjarizi, Lt. Col. Enver Dugolli, Judge Bekim Sejdiu, Minister Glauk Konjufca, Minister Edita Tahiri and Ambassador Teuta Sahatqija.

I would like to thank all the amazing people I met along the way in my cultural-diplomatic field trips in Kosovo (2008, 2012, 2017) to make this study possible. I am grateful to the experts for their in-depth interviews, namely: Dr. Brahim Avdyli, Prof. Neki Babamusta, Vebi Kosumi, Sami Kurteshi, Hafize Elshani, Arbana Xharra, Admir Molla, Besfort Rrecaj, Hyzri Salihu, Xhemajl Shatri, and many more who are listed on Appendix 3 "Kosovo Field Trip Agenda."

Special thanks to former British Defense Attaché to Albania Mark D. Vickers, Aaron Nething, Daniel Wienecke and my dear friend Jeanne Buster for their continued love and support over the years. I wholeheartedly appreciate everything you have done for me.

I am most grateful for the wonderful support and the positive encouragement of family, friends and community that surrounds me. I have been blessed with countless beautiful experiences with the Albanian-American community and my colleagues in politics, art, and media. The people around me always believe I will find success and achieve greater things.

LIST OF FIGURES

LIST OF TABLES

LIST OF GRAPHS

ABBREVIATIONS

AAK	"*Aleanca për Ardhmërinë e Kosovës*"/Alliance for the Future of Kosovo
ADT	Anti-Discrimination Team
ANES	American National Election Studies
BPK	Banking and Payment Authority of Kosovo
CCFR	Chicago Council on Foreign Relations
CRT	Children's Rights Team
DfEE	British Department of Education and Employment
ERA	European Reform Agenda
ESS	European Social Survey
EU	European Union
EULEX	European Union Rule of Law Mission in Kosovo
GEU	Gender Equality Unit
ICJ	International Court of Criminal Justice
ICO	International Civilian Office
ICTY	International Criminal Tribunal for the former Yugoslavia
IMF	International Monetary Fund
KFOR	NATO-led Kosovo Force
KLA	Kosovo Liberation Army
KSC	Kosovo Specialist Court/Kosovo Specialist Chamber
KSF	Kosovo Security Force
KSIP	Kosovo's Standards Implementation Plan
LDK	"*Lidhja Demokratike e Kosovës*"/Democratic League of Kosovo
MUP	Special Police Force unit of the Ministry of Internal Affairs of Serbia
NATO	North Atlantic Treaty Organization
Nisma	The Social Democratic Initiative
NGO	Non-governmental organization
OIK	Ombudsperson Institution in Kosovo
OSCE	Organization for Security and Co-operation in Europe

SAA	Stabilization and Association Agreement
SC	Kosovo Specialist Chambers
SITF	Special Investigative Task Force
SPO	Specialist Prosecutor's Office
TRC	Truth and Reconciliation Commission
UK	United Kingdom
UN	United Nations
UNDP	United Nations Development Programme
UNESCO	United Nations Educational, Scientific and Cultural Organization
UNSC	United Nations Security Council
UNMIK	United Nations Interim Administration Mission in Kosovo
USA	United States of America
USAID	United States Agency for International Development
VJ	Armed Forces of Yugoslavia
VV	"*Vetëvendosje*"/Self-determination Party
WHO	World Health Organization

CHAPTER 1

Introduction

1.1 The puzzle: Determinants of Political Trust

Since the 1960's political science theorists have asserted that developing political trust is important to the democratic and political order of governments.[1] Scholars have debated the importance of declining political trust as a crisis of democracy,[2] increased corruption,[3] weakening of state legitimacy,[4] with "severe consequences for the quality and stability of representative democracy, its institutions, and its actors."[5] Scholars agree that low political trust has broader implications for society. This raises the following questions: Is political trust influenced by political actors or political institutions? Do socio-cultural factors have an impact on trust perceptions? Or does political trust depend on the evaluations of the institutional performance as institutional theorists claim? I examine how both cultural and institutional performance factors influence political trust, focusing on Kosovo as a case study. Specifically, I focus on examining political trust indicators such as national and ethnic identification, interpersonal trust, trustworthiness, and perceived government performance.

Since Kosovo (*in Albanian: Kosova*) declared its independence in 2008, the Kosovo government, with the help of United States, United Kingdom, European Union, NATO, and United

---

[1] Schneider, I. (2017). Can We Trust Measures of Political Trust? Assessing Measurement Equivalence in Diverse Regime Types. *Soc Indic Res*, 133(3), 963–984. doi: 10.1007/s11205-016-1400-8

[2] Huntington, S. P. (1968). *Political Order in Changing Societies*. New Haven: Yale University Press.

[3] Wang, C. (2016, June). Government Performance, Corruption, and Political Trust in East Asia. *Social Science Quarterly*, 97, 211-231. doi: 10.1111/ssqu.12223

[4] Easton, D. (1975). A re-assessment of the concept of political support. *British Journal of Political Science*, 5(4), 435-457.

[5] Van Der Meer, T. (2018, December). Political Trust and the "Crisis of Democracy." *Oxford University Press*, 2. doi: 10.1093/acrefore/9780190228637.013.77

Nations, has made great efforts to strengthen rule law.[6] Specifically, the judicial structure of the prosecution services and courts in general, has been one of the main rule of law pillars in Kosovo, under the EULEX Monitoring Pillar, where E.U. judges and prosecutors are working jointly with Kosovo judges and prosecutors.[7] The European Union is making sure that Kosovo adopts E.U. rules and norms based on legitimacy, accountability, fairness, and credibility.[8] On the other hand, the Kosovo leadership is concerned with creating an image of legitimacy and democracy, as a condition to becoming a European Union member.[9] For instance, Kosovo President Hashim Thaçi's initiative established the Truth and Reconciliation Commission (TRC) in December 2017 to address Kosovo's wartime past, as a step forward to peace for the future generations.[10] The TRC team in charge of preparing the legal and the technical infrastructure, has been supported by international experts, mainly OSCE, the Swiss Embassy, and the United States Embassy.

The process of reconciliation requires bringing forth the truth about the atrocities and war crimes committed during the conflict. It also requires an open dialogue between Kosovo and Serbia facilitated by Brussels, on the issue of missing persons, which has not happened yet. According to the Kosovo Memory Book, there is evidence regarding mass graves' existence at several sites:

> "More than 1,665 persons from all communities are still missing. Mass graves with a majority of Albanian victims have been found on Serbia's territory, and there are thought to be more in Serbia that have not yet been found. More than 300 bodily remains found in previously discovered mass graves are still in the Institute of Forensic Medicine, and whose DNA analyses do not match with the blood samples collected from family members of missing persons."[11]

[6] USAID. (2018, February 12). Kosovo: Rule of Law and governance. Retrieved from: https://www.usaid.gov/kosovo/democracy-and-governance

[7] EULEX. (2018). Monitoring. Retrieved from: http://www.eulex-kosovo.eu/?page=2,58

[8] Lluka, L. (2017). Europeanizing Kosovo: Role and impact of EU-funded non-governmental and civil society organizations (NGOs/CSOs) on policies and institutions of state-building. *University of Agder, Department of Political Science and Management*, 1-84. Retrieved from: http://brage.bibsys.no/xmlui/bitstream/handle/11250/2455884/Lluka%2C%20Lyra.pdf?sequence=1

[9] Visoka, G. (2018, February 16). Becoming Kosovo: Independence, Legitimacy, Future. *Kosovo 2.0*. Retrieved from: http://kosovotwopointzero.com/en/becoming-kosovo-independence-legitimacy-future/

[10] President of the Republic of Kosovo. (2017, December 13). The President established the Preparatory Team for the Truth and Reconciliation Commission. *Office of the President*. Retrieved from: http://www.president-ksgov.net/en/news/the-president-established-the-preparatory-team-for-the-truth-and-reconciliation-commission

[11] Haxhibeqiri, N. (2018, February 14). Transitional justice in Kosovo, 10 years after independence. *Prishtina Insight*, 3. Retrieved from: http://prishtinainsight.com/transitional-justice-kosovo-10-years-independence/

Although Kosovo has taken initiatives to address atrocities committed during the 1998 war, achieving transitional justice in Kosovo, 12 years after independence and 22 years after the war, has proved to be a challenge, due to the slow progress.[12] Kosovo's citizens are demanding the fighting of corruption and exposing wrongdoing by public officials,[13] greater fairness, transparency, efficiency, and accountability from the government institutions.[14] The government of Kosovo has been working closely with USAID to strengthen judicial independence and rule of law, to combat corruption, to strengthen the implementation of the law, to increase professional skills, to provide free legal aid to meet the needs of the citizens, to implement reforms that lead to greater transparency and accountability, and to increase public trust in the public institutions.[15]

This book examines how perceived interpersonal trust and perceived effectiveness of the government is related to levels of institutional trust. Specifically, I focus on examining perceptions of political elite towards the fairness and impartially of legal institutions, with emphasis on the Kosovo Specialist Court. This is for the purpose of evaluating the impact of international efforts on transitional justice to understand how salient politic trust is in local legal institutions, such as Kosovo courts.

The creation of the Kosovo Specialist Chambers (KSC) and the Specialist Prosecutor's Office (SPO) is unique in itself and evidence of a "hybrid court."[16] In other war crime chambers as in Croatia, Bosnia and Herzegovina, and Serbia, the war crime chambers are domestic courts, part of the national judiciary, with a physical state court in the respective country.

In Kosovo however, the Kosovo Specialist Court,[17] although part of the judicial system in Kosovo, the detention facility itself is located in the "host state" – the Netherlands. It also has a

---

[12] Ibid.

[13] Gashi, K. (2017). Kosovo: Transitional Government. *Freedom House Report,* 1-13 Retrieved from: https://freedom-house.org/sites/default/files/NIT2017_Kosovo.pdf

[14] In his opening remarks U.S. Ambassador Delawie addressed the need to strengthen rule of law in Kosovo, by proposing that both civil society and justice institutions work together to promote rule of law norms that include, accountability, accessibility and inclusion in the justice sector. For more see Statement of United States Ambassador Greg Delawie. (2017, September 21). Ambassador Delawie's Opening Remarks Demand for Justice Closing Event. *U.S. Embassy in Kosovo.* Retrieved from: https://xk.usembassy.gov/ambassador-delawies-opening-remarks-de-mand-justice-closing-event/

[15] USAID. (2018, February 12). Kosovo: Rule of Law and governance. Retrieved from: https://www.usaid.gov/kosovo/democracy-and-governance

[16] Warren, M. J., Koliqi, K., Maksimović, N., & Stappers, M. (2008). The War Crimes Chamber in Bosnia and Herzegovina: From Hybrid to Domestic Court. *The International Center for Transitional Justice,* 1-58. Retrieved from http://www.ictj.org/sites/default/files/ICTJ-FormerYugoslavia-Domestic-Court-2008-English.pdf

[17] While the Kosovo Specialist Chambers (KSC) and Specialist Prosecutor's Office (SPO) are two separate institutions, this dissertation applies the terminology commonly used in Kosovo, referring to the "Kosovo Specialist Court"

seat in The Hague, is staffed with international judges and prosecutors, and is not overseen by the International Criminal Tribunal for the former Yugoslavia (ICTY). This makes the Kosovo Specialist Court very unique in nature as it is characterized by both domestic and international elements: (1) Negotiated by the Kosovo Government and the European Union. (2) Adopted by legislation passed by the Kosovan parliament in 2016. (3) Attached to each level of the court system in Kosovo – Basic Court, Court of Appeals, Supreme Court and Constitutional Court, but with a seat in The Hague. (4) funded by the European Union, and other contributing countries such as, Canada, Norway, Switzerland, Turkey, and the United States of America. (5) Staffed with international judges and prosecutors. And (6) Acting in accordance to the Kosovo laws, as well as international law and international human rights law.[18]

Most of my field research was conducted in the cities of Prishtina and Mitrovica in Kosovo, with ethnically mixed communities of both Albanian and Serb, to get a better understanding of what the different perceptions and levels of trust between "in-group" and "out-group" members. Additionally, the research focused on understanding the different levels of trust in various national and international institutions in Kosovo. The aim of the research is to identify factors that affect levels of political trust and to find out whether there is a variation of political trust at the individual country level and the international level. The study adds to the broader understanding of how democracy affects political trust and how international efforts of transitional justice are perceived by the local population, pertaining to institutional performance: level of trust in fairness, accountability, and security in the public institutions.

Specifically, this project will analyze key international actors such as the role of the United Nations and the European Union by comparing differences of perceptions prior to the declaration of independence and post-independence. The starting point is the establishment of UNMIK in 1999 by the U.N. Security Council Resolution 1244, which extended to a EULEX mission in 2008 to operate under the UNMIK umbrella. The unilateral declaration of Kosovo on February 17, 2008 is the first successful act of diplomacy by the Kosovar leadership, and for the purpose of this research is considered as the mid-point of comparison: pre-independence declaration (1999-2008) and post-independence declaration (2008-2014).

The evaluation of the rule of law in Kosovo, presented as a case study here, reveals a disconnect between the ideal democratic standards of rule of law, highly promoted by the international community, and the local reality of distrust and corruption in the political and legal institutions. This research will analyze the political trust factors that influence the disconnect between the two.

---

as a single entity. For more information visit the specialist court's official website available at http://www.scp-ks.org.
[18] Kosovo Specialist Chambers and Specialist Prosecutor's Office. (2018). Specialist Chambers Background: KSC at a glance. Retrieved from: http://www.scp-ks.org/en/background

1.2 Problem Statement

For the past two decades the Kosovo government has been subject to intensive institutional reform, legal restructuring, and a peaceful democratic transition in the post-conflict period. The Kosovo government has worked together with the European Commission to implement the EU related reforms, as per United Nations Security Council Resolution 1244 in June 1999, the European Rule of Law Mission in Kosovo (EULEX) in 2008, the EU-Kosovo Stabilization and Association Agreement (SAA) in April 2016, and the European Reform Agenda (ERA) in November 2016.[19] After the 2008 Kosovo declaration of independence, recent attempts have focused on strengthening rule of law, the prosecution of post-war crimes, crimes against humanity, and crimes against Kosovan law.[20]

Following the allegations of war crimes and crimes against humanity, reported in the Council of Europe Parliamentary Assembly Report of January 7, 2011,[21] the European Union established the Special Investigative Task Force (SITF) in September 2011.[22] The SITF was tasked, "To conduct an independent criminal investigation into the allegations contained in the Report, as well as other crimes connected to those allegations."[23] On July 19, 2014, Chief Prosecutor of the European Union Special Investigative Task Force (SITF), Ambassador Clint Williamson, announced in Brussels that the SITF had found sufficient compelling evidence to file an indictment against the former senior leaders of the former Kosovo Liberation Army (KLA).[24] In his statement Ambassador Williamson addressed the following SITF findings:

---

[19] European Commission. (2018, April 17). Kosovo 2018 Report: Communication on EU Enlargement Policy. *Commission to the European Parliament, the Council, the European Economic and Social Committee and the Committee of the Regions*. Strasbourg. Retrieved from: https://ec.europa.eu/neighbourhood-enlargement/sites/near/files/20180417-kosovo-report.pdf

[20] Koenders, B. (2016, January 15). Betreft Nederland gastland voor de Kosovo rechtbank. *Government of the Netherlands*. Retrieved from: http://www.rijksoverheid.nl/binaries/rijksoverheid/documenten/kamerstukken/2016/01/15/kamerbrief-over-nederland-gastland-voor-kosovo-rechtbank/kamerbrief-over-nederland-gastland-voor-kosovo-rechtbank.pdf

[21] The Special Investigation Task Force (SITF) conducted an independent criminal investigation in 2011 against the allegations contained in the Council of Europe (CoE) report of January 2011 by Senator Dick Marty entitled: "Inhuman treatment of people and illicit trafficking in human organs in Kosovo."

[22] Republic of Kosovo. (2015, August 3). Law on Specialist Chambers and Specialist Prosecutor's Office. *Assembly of Republic of Kosovo*. Law No.05/L-053. Retrieved from: http://www.kuvendikosoves.org/common/docs/ligjet/05-L-053%20a.pdf

[23] Kosovo Specialist Chambers and Specialist Prosecutor's Office. (2018). Specialist Chambers Background: KSC at a glance, 1. Retrieved from: http://www.scp-ks.org/en/background

[24] Williamson, C. (2014, July 29). Statement of the Chief Prosecutor of the Special Investigative Task Force. *Special Investigative Task Force*, 1-7. Retrieved from: http://www.hlc-rdc.org/wp-content/uploads/2014/07/Statement_of_

"We believe that the evidence is compelling that these crimes were not the acts of rogue individuals acting on their own accord, but rather they were conducted in an organized fashion and were sanctioned by certain individuals at the top levels of the KLA leadership. The widespread or systematic nature of these crimes in the period after the war ended in June 1999 justifies a prosecution for crimes against humanity. Accordingly, we anticipate that such charges can be filed in this matter against several senior officials of the former KLA, and that an indictment would also likely include charges for war crimes, and certain violations of domestic Kosovo law, including murder.

Some other domestic offenses – including torture – cannot be prosecuted because these crimes have time expired due to the 15-year statute of limitations on prosecutions. With no court in place at that time, and thus an inability to file an indictment, we were not in position to interrupt the running of the prescriptive period. That said, I do not believe that this will have a detrimental effect on this case, particularly since many of these criminal acts can likely be charged in the context of international humanitarian law violations for which there is no statute of limitations."[25]

Regarding addressing the international humanitarian law violations, the concern then became which court is equipped to bring forth trials of the alleged war crimes. The initial dilemma was whether an already existing state court in Kosovo or the International Criminal Tribunal for the former Yugoslavia (ICTY) was better equipped to prosecute the war crimes allegations and other domestic offenses that occurred during the 1998 war. For this purpose, the Kosovo Specialist Court was created in January 2017, officially called the Kosovo Specialist Chambers (KSC) and Special Prosecutor's Office (SPO).[26] For the purpose of this research I will refer to the commonly used name in Kosovo, "The Kosovo Specialist Court" as one entity.

The Kosovo Specialist Court in The Hague has jurisdiction to prosecute crimes that happened during the Kosovo conflict of 1998 to 2000, including war crimes, crimes against humanity such as kidnapping, torture, organ harvesting, rape, enslavement, deportation, extermination, imprisonment, murder and other crimes such as destruction of civilian property, towns, villages, and

---

the_Chief_Prosecutor_of_the_SITF_EN.pdf

[25] Ibid, 2.

[26] Warren et al. (2008), 7.

religious buildings.[27] In 2017 the Kosovo parliament passed with great opposition and much delay the legislation to put on trial former high-ranking KLA (Kosovo Liberation Army) members.

The majority of people in Kosovo believe that the creation of the special court is an unfair creation.[28] My research reveals that in general people are unhappy with the selective approach of the international efforts to achieve justice for the war crimes in Kosovo, targeting only ethnic Albanians (mainly the KLA veterans), while the Serb criminals who committed atrocities, rape and genocide against ethnic Albanians during the Kosovo war roam free in the streets of Serbia today. In an interview with journalist Hafize Elshani she expressed the need to prosecute all crimes:

"The proposal for a special court is the fastest way for Kosovo to move beyond the Marty report. This can ultimately improve the reputation of Kosovo. Every crime committed means breaking the law, thus all crimes must be persecuted. By allowing the investigation of the victims of the 'other party,' we do not in any way humble our 'victims.' On the contrary, we can build a stronger commitment, based on the expectations that the fate of all victims should be clarified, missing persons should be found, and wounds should be healed. Even today 1,712 people are counted missing in Kosovo since the end of the 1999 war. The missing are Albanians.

There are countless of witnesses and testimonies from hundreds of Albanian women who have been raped during the war. But no one is listening. No wants to reveal the truth. Serbia has yet to apologize for the crimes committed: genocide, rape, and the murdered children. The responsible criminals should be punished. The patience of the Kosovo people has exceeded every norm, considering 20 years after the war there is no justice for Albanian war victims and survivors. UNMIK failed as a mission, now the Special Court raises the question whether it will fail and be corrupt like other missions, or if it will work properly. The reality of the atrocities committed against ethnic Albanians remains in the shadows. While Serbia has the backing of Russia, Kosovo remains hostage to the suffering in the country."[29]

[27] See Statement of the Chief Prosecutor of the Special Investigative Task Force by Ambassador Clint Williamson, 2.
[28] Gashi, S. (2017, November 14). Special Court must bring Kosovo's criminals to justice. *Balkan Insight*. Retrieved from http://www.balkaninsight.com/en/article/special-court-must-bring-kosovo-s-criminals-to-justice-11-13-2017
[29] Elshani, Hafize. (2018, September 20). Personal Communicating. Interview.

Serbia has yet to admit that the genocide in Kosovo occurred. Few members of the Serbian forces have been prosecuted and tried only for war crimes during the 1998-99 Kosovo conflict, but not for genocide.[30] When President Slobodan Milosevic was tried at the International Criminal Tribunal for the former Yugoslavia for crimes committed during the Yugoslav war, he was charged with genocide in Bosnia, but not for genocide and ethnic cleansing in Kosovo. In 2016, Kosovo President Hashim Thaçi announced he was to bring a genocide lawsuit against Serbia at the International Court of Justice for atrocities during the Kosovo war.

The general perception is that no court in Serbia or Kosovo is qualified to prosecute war crimes that occurred during the Kosovo war, and no domestic judge or prosecutor in Kosovo "has dared to prosecute or punish individuals from the KLA who committed war crimes and crimes against humanity."[31] The special court has received much opposition when considering prosecuting Kosovo Liberation Army veterans of the alleged war crimes, since at home they are considered national heroes,[32] who fought to liberate all Albanians from Serbia's oppression.[33]

1.2.1 Contributions and Original Study

This book set out to examine the role that cultural and institutional performance factors play on political trust. The topic of this book informs several areas of the trust literature within the different sources, types and influences of trust, respective to the nascent state of Kosovo. The following are the main theoretical and methodological contributions of this research.

- **Theoretical contribution** – this study aims at contributing to the literature of political trust by incorporating substantive knowledge of the elites within Kosovo. This research uses expert interviews and surveys with political leaders as primary original data to better assess the elite perceptions of political trust across various trust domains. The research focuses on the political elite and experts in Kosovo and examines the country case of Kosovo due to its highly unusual complex government environment with a national and international intertwining nature.

---

[30] Brown, K. (2016, August 09). Kosovo Genocide Suit Against Serbia 'Likely to Fail'. *Balkan Insight*. Retrieved from: http://www.balkaninsight.com/en/article/kosovo-genocide-suit-against-serbia-likely-to-fail--08-08-2016

[31] Gashi, S. (2017).

[32] Poggioli, S. (2016, December 12). Kosovo War Crimes Court Established in The Hague. *National Public Radio*. Retrieved from: http://www.npr.org/2016/12/12/505227820/kosovo-war-crimes-court-established-in-the-hague

[33] Mulaj, K. (2008). Resisting an Oppressive Regime: The Case of Kosovo Liberation Army. *Studies in Conflict & Terrorism*, 31(12), 1103-1119.

- **Kosovo is a unique case study** of deep involvement of international actors, building and strengthening the local institutions in a transitional democracy. Kosovo, as a case study, represents a valuable case to look at the effect of cultural and institutional factors of trust visa vie the domestic-international actors and institutions. Kosovo is considered a unique case of an emerging democracy because of the nature of the conflict, NATO's unilateral intervention, the U.N. Administration of Kosovo, and Kosovo's unilateral declaration of independence. The nature of events that led to the involvement of the international actors was unprecedented.

  Additionally, the nature and the creation of the Kosovo Specialist Court is another unique example where the national and international merge together in an unusual way. Because Kosovo is not recognized by all members as a sovereign state, this case study is particularly valuable for post-conflict transitional democracies literature. The Kosovo case study shows that at the macro level the functioning of democracy and political institutions matter to political trust.

  The study also investigates the role of media on political trust in a post-conflict transitional society in Southeast Europe such as Kosovo. In the Kosovo case the media exposure promotes trust under some conditions when the source is foreign western media or a foreign organization such as the E.U. but discourages political trust under other conditions based on ethnicity.

- **Re-conceptualization of political trust**, adding on to the macro and the micro definitions by taking into account international organizations as another important source of trust (Chapter 2). This research provides a redefined political trust concept, where international organizations become a source of legitimacy and credibility.

  Trust in international organizations or "international trust" matters because it adds to the understanding of the political trust of the state at the international level. By adding international trust to the definition of political trust, this new idea shows the importance of the influence of organizations on people's attitudes.

- **Methodological contribution** – the research is driven by gaps in the existing empirical literature of emerging democracies in Southeast Europe, specifically Kosovo. In particular, lack of data from other cross-national European countries exclude Kosovo or have limited data on the country. Although these types of studies provide general statistics on trust in Western democratic European countries, they do not provide in-depth insight to particular countries of emerging democracies, such as Kosovo.

This book attempts to address this gap by making a contribution to the elite empirical literature of Kosovo using two original datasets, conducted from field research of the political elite and experts, dating from 2012-2013 survey (220 participants) and 2017-2018 survey (40 participants). Other studies usually employ either the American National Election Studies (ANES) or the European Social Survey (ESS).

This research uses a holistic approach by using both ANES and ESS measures of political trust to examine the multiple effects of performance of the government evaluations and cultural explanations of political trust. The originality of the methodology by combining both measures of trust is of interest to the cultural versus institutional debate of political trust.

- **Building an integrative model of political trust** (Chapter 2). The integrative model is built on three levels of the target-based political trust, where the study proposes to add mezzo level to the macro and micro levels of the political trust literature. In the context of mezzo level, the study introduced to add the target-based group-oriented category and call it "mezzo level" or "international trust" to account for citizens' trust in international organizations and in other nations.

Additionally, the study also introduces a third order to the motivation-based political trust. Specifically, the study introduces "third-order trust", information about information about trust, as an addition to the "rational political trust" (first-order trust) and the "psychological political trust" (second order trust). As Table 1 shows, the third-order trust, understood as being informed about your trust label (i.e. high or low trust) can have an effect on actual trust within the ingroup based on knowledge of the same information.

Examining political trust in seven different domains provides a comprehensive and an in-depth analysis of the dimensionality of political trust across various institutions in Kosovo.

1.2.2 Book Structure

This book looks at the elite perceptions of the local and international institutions in including the government, political leaders, Kosovo police, international missions, and the Kosovo Specialist Court. The study develops an integrated model of political trust based on institutional performance and cultural theories. The main research question is a threefold: (1) It addresses what the level of trust is in various national and international institutions in Kosovo; (2) Identifies the factors that affect the levels of political trust; and (3) Looks at the difference of political trust at the country level and international level.

The study first presents the general topic and context for the research conducted in Kosovo. Chapter two provides the literature review and the theoretical framework including concepts and definitions of political trust and the relevance of socio-political factors. The discussion offers a redefined concept of political trust to include "international political trust" to account for trust in international organizations and in other nations. Two major approaches are discussed, cultural and institutional explanations.

Next in chapter three I provide a historical background and review of the Kosovo case study, the legal framework, the establishment of the Kosovo Specialist Court, and Kosovan-Serbia relations. Chapter four presents the research methodology, outlining the main research questions, five hypotheses, operationalization of the variables, and the design of the research. This chapter also identifies the models and structure of political trust. Chapter five presents the main results followed by a discussion of the findings in chapter six. I explain the levels of trust in various institutions and the role of cultural and institutional factors. The final chapter concludes with policy recommendations to increase political trust and to improve public support for the state.

This book uses the English term "Kosovo" for the country name, while also including the country name in the Albanian language – "Kosova." Kosova is a term majority of Kosovo Albanians identify with, which is adopted in many scholarly publications by Kosovan authors in English, while rejecting the term "Kosovo." The term "Kosovo" was adopted from the Serbian language to English.

As of 2020, "Kosovo" is the English term used by the official institutions of Kosovo. However, the general public opinion is that the term "Kosovo" is of Slavic origin (Serbian) and it was imposed by the international community to Kosovans (*Alb: Kosovars*). Majority Albanians in Kosovo prefer "Kosova" instead of "Kosovo"; others prefer "Dardania"; while some others have adapted the current English term "Kosovo," because phonetically, for the non-Albanian speakers, especially in the United States, the term "Kosova" in English would sound with "ei" [Kosovɛ],different from Albanian sound [Kosova] with "a."

Historically there have been a number of countries that have changed country name and flag colors, such as Canada, South Africa, Iraq, Montenegro, etc. For instance, Macedonia agreed to change its name from "Macedonia" to "Republic of North Macedonia" (*Severna Makedonija*) in order to resolve the dispute with Greece. This change was adapted after the two countries reached an agreement in the Treaty of Prespa on June 2018. Kosovo can follow similar steps if it chooses to do so, for any change in the name, flag, or names in the map, to appease the growing dissatisfaction from its citizens after the country receives full recognition internationally.

CHAPTER 2

Literature Review

2.1 The Cultural Versus Institutional Debate

In this section, I will review the major theoretical perspectives to explain levels of political trust in light of transitional democracies. There are two main camps that examine political trust and offer competing ideas how trust in democratic institutions is formed and measured. The cultural versus institutional performance debate has dominated the political science field in answering the question of how trust can be built up in politics. Next, I will focus on three political measures: interpersonal trust, trustworthiness, and legitimacy.

2.1.1 Political Trust in Transitional Democracies

The scholarly debate focusing on conceptualizing trust in transitional democracies is based on the idea that political trust is integral to the functioning of democracy.[34] In a transitional democracy there is evidence of instability, particularly in post-communist societies, as parties with different policy agendas emerge and potentially form new political coalitions.[35] Duch (2001) argues that information and trust in nascent democratic institutions are important to the transitional democracy process for electoral decision-making.[36] As citizens become more informed about the democratic functioning of institutions, "they gain increasing confidence or trust in the responsiveness

---

[34] Dalton, R. J. (2004). *Democratic challenges, democratic choices: The erosion of political support in advanced industrial democracies.* Oxford: Oxford University Press.

[35] Duch, R.M. (2001). A development model of heterogeneous economic voting in new democracies. *American Political Science Review,* 95, 895.

[36] Ibid, 896.

of these institutions to public preferences."[37] As voters become more knowledgeable about the political process, they want to learn and engage in the democratic process.[38]

Inglehart (1977) points out that political information levels in emerging democracies are less developed than in mature democracies.[39] Voters in emerging democracies who are less informed rely more on personal financial circumstances and are less likely to correctly perceive the trends in political performance.[40] However, as citizens become more enthusiastic and learn about the new political system in the transitional democracy process, they adapt to the information opportunities, thus increasing political awareness of the citizens and "cognitive participation."[41]

A second element that is important to emerging democracies is trust in political actors and institutions.[42] Political trust is traditionally conceptualized as an indicator of ethical qualities of public officials,[43] the efficiency of government and the correctness of its decision-making.[44] Therefore, the level of trust for political officials and government institutions depends on ethics and government efficiency. Jamal and Nooruddin (2010) maintained that a good and effective democratic government is based on trusting relationships, where trust is a predictor of more democratic political cultures.[45] As citizens are more content with the democratic nature of the regime, they are likely to support democracy in the country.[46]

According to Mabillard and Pasquier (2015) for a transitional democracy to succeed there needs to be transparency, access to information and trustworthiness.[47] They argued that transparency is a moral imperative for democratic institutions, and it leads to "solid bottom-line benefits in terms of reputation, possibly gaining more trust on the people's side."[48] This also fits with the

---

[37] Ibid, 896.

[38] Susila, I. (2014). Conceptualizing trust in electoral behavior in a transitional democracy: an intergenerational perspective. *University of Hull*, 19.

[39] Inglehart, R. (1977). *The Silent Revolution Changing Values and Political Styles Among Western Publics*. Princeton, NJ: Princeton University Press.

[40] Duch. (2001), 897.

[41] Ibid, 897.

[42] Duch. (2001), 897.

[43] Hosmer, L. T. (1995). Trust: the connecting link between organizational theory and philosophical ethics. *The Academy of Management Review*, 20(2), 379-403.

[44] Hetherington, M. J. (1998), 791.

[45] Jamal, A., & Nooruddin, I. (2010). The democratic utility of trust: A cross-national analysis. *Journal of Politics*, 71, 45. doi:10.1017/S0022381609990466

[46] Ibid, 46.

[47] Mabillard, V. & Pasquier, M. (2015). Transparency and Trust in Government: A Two-Way Relationship, *Yearbook of Swiss Administrative Sciences*, 23. Retrieved from https://www.researchgate.net/publication/314286219_Transparency_and_Trust_in_Government_A_Two-Way_Relationship

[48] Ibid, 24.

rational choice theory which takes into account the cost-benefit analysis of choices. In this context, a rational voter would consider the advantages of the benefit and cost of the decision, whereas an irrational voter would be driven by emotional factors.[49] On the other hand, Riker (1980) maintained that political trust is an attitude "based on non-rational affects rather than an action of rational choice" such as non-rational party identification or non-rational loyalty to the political party.[50] He argued that the notion of trust is fundamental to cooperation and people forming groups that operate private and public activities.[51]

Socio-psychological research has focused on interpersonal trust and the relationship between the individuals,[52] with recent emphasis on the relationship between an organization and citizens.[53] The trust relationship between citizens and institutions depends on the type of trust, in reference to perceived trustworthiness defined by some scholars as ability, benevolence and integrity,[54] and as reliability and fairness by others.[55] Mabillard and Pasquier (2015) argued that most institutions such as the European Union do not take all dimensions of trust into account, but rather consider trust as a unidimensional variable – the citizens' general trust in government.[56]

The contemporary literature sees trust as a fundamental component of democracy (Hardin, 1999; Levi, 1996), focusing primarily on the levels of citizens' trust in government, considering satisfaction with the government performance.[57] The literature differentiates between trustworthiness and trust. Trustworthiness relies on the belief that trusters will not betrayed by the trusted party,[58] while trust "refers to a judgment which reflects beliefs about the trustworthiness of the government, measured through a rate of confidence in government."[59]

---

[49] Susila, I. (2014), 3.

[50] Riker, W. H. (1980). Political Trust as Rational Choice. In: Lewin L., Vedung E. (eds) Politics as Rational Action. Theory and Decision Library (An International Series in the *Philosophy and Methodology of the Social and Behavioral Sciences*), 23, 1. Springer, Dordrecht. https://doi.org/10.1007/978-94-009-8955-9_1

[51] Ibid, 2.

[52] Giddens, A. (1984). *The constitution of society: Outline of the theory of structuration.* Berkeley and Los Angeles: University of California Press.

[53] Bouckaert, G. & Van de Walle. S. (2003). Comparing measures of citizen trust and user satisfaction as indicators of 'good governance': difficulties in linking trust and satisfaction indicators. *International Review of Administrative Sciences*, 69(3), 329-343.

[54] Mayer, R. C., Davis, J. H. & Schoorman, D. F. (1995). An integrative model of organizational trust. *Academy of Management Review*, 20(3), 709-734.

[55] Zaheer, A., McEvily, B. & Perrone, V. (1998). Does trust matter? Exploring the effects of interorganizational and interpersonal trust on performance. *Organization Science*, 9(2), 141-159.

[56] Mabillard & Pasquier (2015), 4.

[57] Ibid, 7.

[58] Levi & Stoker, 2000.

[59] Mabillard & Pasquier. (2015), 7.

At the individual level, culture offers an alternative explanation that suggests that "traditional predispositions" might shape the "democratic utility of trust."[60] Inglehart and Baker (2000) argue that traditional values characterized from a traditional society form a different worldview held by modern values in industrial societies.[61] Their study found a correlation between interpersonal trust and economic development in countries with similar cultural patterns and values.[62] This was true in Protestant European countries, because it allowed for open self-expression, and the creation of democratic social structures that boosted large-scale economic activity. On the contrary, their study found that countries with a communist historical legacy limited the formation of interpersonal trust and tolerance.[63] This view is also supported by Jamal and Nooruddin (2010) who argue that trust is constrained by "traditional predispositions" in authoritarian regimes, corresponding in lower levels of support for democracy.[64]

Understanding the quality of governance is recognized as critical to support for democracy, with respect to the level of corruption.[65] Lewicki et al. (1998) suggest that distrust in politicians and political parties is related to perceptions of not meeting public expectations.[66] Berman (1997) identified three conditions to restoring political trust: (1) government responding to peoples' needs; (2) citizens' participation in the decision-making process; and (3) government pursuing policy that meets public expectations.[67] In his study, Van Der Meer (2018) found that Nordic countries as well as countries in Northwestern Europe with long democratic traditions and low levels of corruptions saw higher levels of trust; whereas trust in government and satisfaction with democracy declined in Southern European democracies.[68] Van Der Meer (2018) points out that the long-term trends are based on "a scarcity of data with often many gaps or rather indirect measures of political trust."[69] Kosovo is one of the countries in Southeastern Europe with limited to nearly none on the Eurobarometer data. This study aims to bridge the gap by providing data ranging from 2008-2018.

---

[60] Jamal & Nooruddin. (2010), 48

[61] Inglehart, R. F., & Baker, W. E. (2000). Modernization, Cultural Change, and the Persistence of Traditional Values. *American Sociological Review*, 65, 21.

[62] Ibid, 35.

[63] Ibid, 39

[64] Jamal & Nooruddin. (2010), 48-49.

[65] Ibid, 49.

[66] Lewicki, R. J., McAllister, D. J. & Bies, R. J. (1998). Trust and distrust: new relationships and realities. *The Academy of Management Review*, 23(3), 438-458.

[67] Berman, E. M. (1997). Dealing with cynical citizens. Public Administration Review, 57(2), 105-112.

[68] Van Der Meer, Tom, W. G. (2018, December). Political Trust and the "Crisis of Democracy". Oxford University Press, 1-23. doi: 10.1093/acrefore/9780190228637.013.77

[69] Ibid, 10.

As the literature has shown, trust in important to transitional democracy. A healthy democratic environment requires increased trust in the political system, engaging of citizens in the democratic processes, transparency, and trustworthiness in the government. According to Huntington (1991) democratic ideas and participation are important to democracy because it relates to citizens' involvement in political life and it reflects the transition from authoritarian to democratic governing. In terms of transitional democracy in Kosovo, the idea of democracy grew with the comprehensive proposal of the Ahtisaari package for the status of Kosovo based on democratic standards and human rights.[70] The proposal called on establishing an Assembly, "consistent with the principles of openness and transparency in democratic decision-making."[71]

In 2001, Kosovo held its first official parliamentary elections, administered by OSCE.[72] On July 2019, Prime Minister Ramush Haradinaj resigned after being summoned for questioning by the Kosovo Specialit Chambers (KSC) in the Hague. After the 2019 parliamentary election, the newly elected Prime Minster Albin Kurti formed a coalition government between *Vetëvendosje* (Self-Determination) and LDK on an anti-corruption platform, with focus on development and employment.

2.1.2 The Theoretical Debate

Cultural theories assume that institutional trust is the exogenous factor, shaped outside of the political sphere, stemming instead from the cultural values and normative beliefs, such as interpersonal trust and national identification.[73] The cultural argument is that the national identification, understood as "a sense of feeling of community amongst the members," facilitates institutional trust by "making people more willingly to cooperate with each other, to unite themselves under the same government."[74] In this case, institutional trust is seen as "an extension of interpersonal trust projected onto the political institution, thereby creating a civic culture. People who have more trust in each other are also more likely to support both formal and informal institutions."[75]

---

[70] Kosovo Assembly. (2007, February 2). Comprehensive Proposal For the Kosovo Status Settlement, 1-59. Retrieved from https://www.kuvendikosoves.org/common/docs/Comprehensive%20Proposal%20.pdf

[71] Ibid, 14.

[72] OSCE. (2001, November 19). First official results in Kosovo election announced. Retrieved from https://www.osce.org/kosovo/54005

[73] Godefroidt, A., & Langer A., Meuleman, B. (2015). Developing political trust in a developing country. The impact of cultural and institutional factors on political trust in Ghana. *Centre for Research on Peace and Development (CRPD) KU Leuven*, 22, 1-19.

[74] Ibid, 4.

[75] Ibid. 5.

Alternatively, *institutional theories* suggest that institutional trust is a function of government performance rather than cultural values,[76] emphasizing the politically endogenous determinant.[77] Based on rational choice perspective, trust in the legal and political institutions is based on the rational evaluations of the institutions' performance.[78] Therefore, the expectation is that "the better the performance of institutions, the higher the level of trust in those institutions."[79] Institutions that perform well, generate trust. In this context, trust is a consequence of institutional performance.[80]

Cultural and institutional traditions are concentrated on two variations: macro[81] and micro[82]. The macro theories argue that the response of the individuals toward the institutions is solely based on the institutions' performance (such as fighting corruption, administration effectiveness, economic growth).[83] Whereas, micro theories are based solely on "the individual's experiences and tastes," suggesting that trust/distrust in institutions might vary according to the individual's experiences in the past.[84]

2.1.3 Measuring Political Trust

Cultural and institutional theories, both micro and macro, have been challenged on many grounds.[85] The issues touch upon the measurement and conceptualization of political trust.[86]

---

[76] Newton, K. (2001). Trust, Social Capital, Civil Society, and Democracy. *International Political Science Review*, 22(2), 201–14.

[77] Pula, E. (2017, October). Determinants of Trust in Institutions in Kosovo: An empirical perspective. *Group for Legal and Political Studies*, 4, 6. Retrieved from http://www.legalpoliticalstudies.org/wp-content/uploads/2017/10/Policy-Report-04-Trust-in-Institutions.pdf

[78] Huseby, B. M. (2000). *Government Performance and Political Support. A Study of How Evaluations of Economic Performance, Social Policy and Environmental Protection Influence the Popular Assessments of the Political System.* Trondheim Norges teknisknaturvitenskaplige universitet.

[79] Pula, E. (2017), 6.

[80] Hetherington, M. J. (1998). The political relevance of political trust. American Political Science Review, 92, 791-808.

[81] Mishler, W., & Rose, R. (1997). Trust, Distrust and Skepticism: Popular Evaluations of Civil and Political Institutions in Post-Communist Societies. *The Journal of Politics*, 59 (02), 418–51. doi:10.2307/2998171.

[82] Rolef, S.H. (2006). Public Trust in Parliament: A comparative study. *The Knesset Information Division*. Jerusalem, 1-60.

[83] Pula, E. (2017), 6.

[84] Ibid, 6.

[85] Mishler, W., & Rose R. (2001), 35.

[86] Parker, S. L, et al. (2014). Rethinking the Meaning and Measurement of Political Trust. *Political Trust and Disenchantment with Politics*, 59-82. DOI: 10.1163/9789004276062_005

Even the basic questions used as measures of the popular political trust indicators are under contestation.[87] Despite the contradictions, the growing literature identifies many measures of trust and causal linkages between the concepts of trust in government and the trusting attitudes.

Numerous scholars have examined political trust by asking: do trust indicators measure specific support for the elected officials,[88] satisfaction with the performance of the political leaders[89] or the institutions,[90] or the diffuse support for the political system?[91] David Easton was one of the early scholars to point out the difference between two levels of trust: (1) trust in authorities (specific support), directed at political leaders, and (2) trust in the regime (diffuse support), directed at institutional structure of the government.[92] Subsequent research has focused on the many factors that cause changes in political trust, depending on the citizens' satisfaction with policy and institutions, political scandals and corruption, foreign policy concerns, social capital, and evaluations of institutions.[93] The overall assumption is that the public is more trusting when they are pleased with the policy outcomes and the elected officials, satisfied with government performance, and when social capital is high.[94]

A second area of research on the measures of political trust has focused on the consequences of trust on other attitudes and behaviors. Many studies have found the president's performance to have a direct effect on trust, in such a way that the higher the dissatisfaction with the political leader's performance, the higher level of public distrust exists.[95] In this case, the causal path from trust to presidential performance is expected to be strong.[96] Another causal path looks at institutional trust and performance. Institutional trust is integral to the functioning of democracy,

[87] Ibid, 85.

[88] Miller, A. H. (1974, September). Political Issues and Trust in Government, 1964-1970. *American Political Science Review*, 68(3), 951–972.

[89] Citrin, J. (1974). Comment: The Political Relevance of Trust in Government. *American Political Science Review*, 68(3), 973–988.

[90] Godefroidt, A., Langer A., Meuleman, B. (2015). Developing political trust in a developing country The impact of cultural and institutional factors on political trust in Ghana. *Centre for Research on Peace and Development (CRPD) KU Leuven*, 22, 1-19.

[91] Miller, A. H. (1974, September). Political Issues and Trust in Government, 1964-1970. American Political Science Review, 68(3), 951-972.

[92] Easton, D. (1975). A re-assessment of the concept of political support. British Journal of Political Science, 5 (4): 435-457.

[93] Parker, S. L, et al. (2014), 87.

[94] Ibid, 87.

[95] Miller, A. H. (1974b). Rejoinder to 'Comment' by Jack Citrin: Political Discontent or Ritualism? *American Political Science Review*, 68(3), 989–1001.

[96] Parker, S. L, et al. (2014), 88.

"enhancing the legitimacy, efficiency, and sustainability of governments by linking citizens to the institutions created to represent them."[97] The expectation is that increased levels of institutional trust can facilitate democratic consolidations, and low levels of institutional trust could result in a democratic breakdown.[98]

Some empirical research has looked at specific dimensions of political trust, emphasizing the difference between various objects of trust (legal and political actors/institutions), versus generalized trust in government (no separation between the political drives). Other scholars argue that trust in the particular objects (diffuse support in the larger system or specific support in the elected officials) drive political behavior more than generalized trust in government.[99]

According to Schneider (2017), "trust perceptions in central political institutions differs from (1) trust in regional and local political institutions, (2) trust in protective institutions like the armed forces and police and (3) trust in order institutions like the courts and police."[100] The study found no relationship between political trust and trust in the police and armed forces across Europe, but a strong relationship in former Soviet countries, suggesting "the effects of corruption and stronger central controls over these institutions."[101] Moreover, the study found "citizens of former Soviet countries do not always perceive courts to be independent of political influence."[102]

Despite the differences, scholars largely agree on trust being important to the legitimacy and the effectiveness of the democratic regimes.[103] Trust is an essential element to the functioning of democracy and to democratic governments because "they cannot rely on coercion to the same extent as other, more authoritarian, regimes."[104] Recent research shows that low political trust levels are associated with "low compliance with the law,"[105] as well as "low generalized trust and social capital."[106] Although there is considerable agreement on the importance of political trust especially to democracy and democratic governance, researchers don't agree on the definitions of

---

[97] Godefroidt et al. (2015), 1.

[98] Ibid, 1.

[99] Levi, M., & Stoker, L. (2000, June). Political Trust and Trustworthiness. *Annual Review of Political Science*, 3(1), 475-507. doi: 10.1146/annurev.polisci.3.1.475.

[100] Schneider, I. (2017), 963.

[101] Ibid, 984.

[102] Ibid, 984.

[103] Mishler, W., & Rose, R. (1997).

[104] Godefroidt et al. (2015), 3.

[105] Hooghe, M., & Marien, S. (2010). Does political trust matter? An empirical investigation into the relation between political trust and support for law compliance. *European Journal of Political Research*, 50(2), 267–291.

[106] Rothstein, B. (2003). Social capital, economic growth and quality of government: The causal mechanism. *New Political Economy*, 8(1), 49–71. doi: 10.1080/1356346032000078723.

political trust.[107] Often times, political trust is taken as a proxy for political legitimacy,[108] interpersonal trust,[109] or trustworthiness.[110]

2.1.4 Interpersonal Trust

Cultural theories assume that institutional trust is "exogenous to the political sphere rooted in cultural values and normative beliefs, such as national identification and interpersonal trust."[111] *Interpersonal trust* is defined as "trust we place in other individuals,"[112] or as "the confidence that other people will not willfully cause harm and will, insofar as possible, consider the interests of others."[113] At the level of the individual, interpersonal trust is key to forming social relationships. At the group level, it contributes to lowering tension, formation of group identities, cooperation, tolerance, stability, as well as support for government institutions and their policies.[114] The rationale behind this notion is that a common *national identity*, or a cohesive sense of feeling of community among members, will supersede subgroup interests.[115]

The general expectation is that national identity or the "we feeling" will increase institutional trust by facilitating cooperation with each other and uniting under the same government.[116] Another expectation is that "people who have more trust in each other are also more likely to support both formal and informal institution."[117] Cultural theories also emphasize social relations formed through early-life socialization, where political beliefs are passed on. It implies that early-life experiences and socializations patterns will vary across gender and socio-economic groups.[118] Institutional trust can differ based on these individual characteristics.

---

[107] Schneider, I. (2017). Can We Trust Measures of Political Trust? Assessing Measurement Equivalence in Diverse Regime Types. *Soc Indic Res*, 133(3), 963–984. doi: 10.1007/s11205-016-1400-8

[108] Almond, G.A., & Verba, S. (1963). The Civic Culture: Political Attitudes and Democracy in Five Nations. Princeton: Princeton University Press.

[109] Blind, P. K. (2006), 6.

[110] Schneider, I. (2017), 964.

[111] Godefroidt, A., Langer A., Meuleman, B. (2015), 2.

[112] Arancibia, C. S. (2008), 8.

[113] Kuchenkova, A. V. (2017). Interpersonal Trust in Russian Society. Sociological Research, 56(1), 82. https://doi-org.www.libproxy.wvu.edu/10.1080/10610154.2017.1338403

[114] Ibid, 82.

[115] Mill, J. S. (1861). Considerations on Representative Government. London: Parker, Son, and Bourn.

[116] Putnam, R. D. (1993). Making democracy work. Princeton, NJ: Princeton University Press. Mishler, W., & Rose, R. (1997), 2.

[117] Godefroidt, A., Langer A., & Meuleman, B. (2015), 3.

[118] Ibid, 3.

Cultural theories of democracy emphasize high levels of institutional and interpersonal trust in civic culture as "vital to making democracy work."[119] Cultural theories hypothesize that interpersonal trust is important to social capital, "which culturalists consider to be critical to effective democratic governance,"[120] and contributing to citizen involvement in political life.[121] Some scholars have looked at the effect of political trust on support for *political participation*.[122] The conventional forms of participation, in stable democracies is characterized by personal participation (voting or donating money to a campaign), or collective participation (membership in a political party).[123] The expectation is that political trust has an effect on political participation because it (1) promotes the "quality and quantity of political involvement," (2) trust strengthens citizens' beliefs that "government is responsive and encourages citizens to express their demands via participation in activities from voting to joining organizations."[124]

Non-conventional forms of participation include "protest" type of participation such as signing a petition, joining demonstrations or strikes.[125] In her study, Arancibia (2008) found a positive correlation between the two types of participation (conventional and non-conventional), "confirming that participation in one type of action makes other types of participation easier."[126] The study also found much higher levels of non-conventional participation than membership in political parties, "showing how these forms of participation have been successfully incorporated with the choices that people face nowadays."[127]

Crepaz and Polk (2012) argue that in-group trust (trust between similar types of people) and out-group trust (trust between those that are different), despite being highly correlated with one-another, they affect conventional (voting) and non-conventional participation (demonstrations, boycotting) differently.[128] A person belonging to the in-group trusters is likely to take part in conventional political participation because he or she perceives the traditional channels of participation as "legitimate and sufficient for the individual voting preferences."[129] Moreover, in-

---

[119] Putnam, R. D. (1993), 11.

[120] Mishler, W., & Rose, R. (1997), 2.

[121] Fukuyama, Francis. (1996). Trust: *The Social Virtues and The Creation of Property*. Free Press Paperbacks.

[122] Arancibia, C. S. (2008), 118.

[123] Ibid, 121.

[124] Mishler, W., & Rose, R. (2005). What Are the Political Consequences of Trust? A Test of Cultural and Institutional Theories in Russia. *Comparative Political Studies*, 38(9), 1053.

[125] Arancibia, C. S. (2008), 131.

[126] Ibid, 132.

[127] Ibid, 132.

[128] Crepaz M, L., & Polk, J. (2012). Democracy in crisis? An analysis of various dimensions and sources of support for democracy. *Joint Research Project*, University of Georgia and University of Gothenburg, World Values Survey, 1-30.

[129] Ibid, 3.

group trusters perceive voting as "an obligation - something that one has to do in order to generate a sense of political identity and belonging to the nation."[130]

On the other hand, when it comes to non-conventional political participation the relationship is reversed, where "the presence of higher levels of out-group trust makes it more likely that an individual will take part in these less conventional actions, whereas high levels of in-group trust actually make this type of participation less likely."[131] This supports Putnam's work on the link between interpersonal trust and political participation, finding a positive link between social trust and political participation.[132] Crepaz and Polk (2012) look deeper at the relationship by confirming that political trust and unconventional political activity are strongly and positively related. They suggest that "more trusting individuals also have greater trust in political institutions and electoral turnout is significantly and positively related to the level of trust in political institutions."[133] Others have observed the relationship between trust and trustworthy government (trustworthiness).[134]

2.1.5 Trustworthiness

Political trust – trust in legal-political institutions and actors – enhances the legitimacy and stability of democratic government.[135] Political trust "links citizens with governments and the institutions that represent them."[136] For citizens, trust reduces the need to monitor government institutions and actors, and for government, trust is beneficial by reducing the need to use coercive force and providing the certainty that the citizens will obey.[137] A measure of political trust carries "implicit information about what constitutes a trustworthy institution for citizens."[138] However, what makes citizens trust or distrust the political institutions? And what makes institutions and political actors trustworthy? Arancibia (2008) argues that there is a link between trust and *trustworthiness*, and that trust "is related and originated in the perceived trustworthiness of institutions."[139]

---

[130] Ibid, 3.

[131] Ibid, 3.

[132] Putnam, R. (1993, 2000).

[133] Crepaz, M, L., & Polk, J. (2012), 4.

[134] Levi, M., & Stoker, L. (2000), 476.

[135] Levi, M., & Stoker, L. (2000), 479.

[136] Arancibia, C. S. (2008), 2.

[137] Ibid, 2.

[138] Schneider, I. (2017), 964.

[139] Arancibia, C. S. (2008), 2.

Trustworthiness is defined as "the capacity and willingness of the other to fulfill trust."[140] Arancibia (2008) proposes that trust is a function of two components of trustworthiness: *fair* and *competent*.[141] An individual is more likely to trust a political institution, if the institution is perceived fair, "both in the process of policy making and in the outcomes those policies have," and competent.[142] *Fairness*, is related to procedures in decision making and to the outcomes of the actions of institutions, "assuring that the process would provide the same opportunities for all those involved on it."[143] A trusting citizen expects institutions to be fair, based on the perceptions and the relevant interests that the "game is not rigged."[144] The expectation is that citizens can trust institutions that are fair and have a fair set of procedures, "that guarantee equal access and equal opportunities of positive outcomes."[145]

Fairness and policy outcomes, although not always uniform, are also important, because of the "different benefits for different groups at different times."[146] The expectation is that the individuals who are disappointed in policy outcomes are likely to have lower levels of trust than those who benefited.[147] This relationship is particularly relevant in legal authorities and legal institutions, because the unsatisfactory outcomes cannot not guarantee public compliance "with the decisions and directives."[148] In this context, even if the individual did not benefit from the policy outcome, the institution can still be perceived as fair by evaluating the outcome "in terms of what is more important for a society to achieve."[149]

Evaluation of trustworthiness is also dependent on *competence* – what institutions can do.[150] The expectation is that trustworthy institutions and actors "should be able to do what they are expected to do."[151] One of the factors that impacts institutional trustworthiness is *corruption*.

---

[140] Ibid, 3.

[141] Ibid.

[142] Ibid, 3.

[143] Arancibia, C. S. (2008), 34.

[144] Levi, M. (1998). *A State of Trust. In Trust and Governance*, edited by V. Braithwaite and M. Levi. New York: Russell Sage Foundation, 90.

[145] Arancibia, C. S. (2008), 36.

[146] Ibid, 36.

[147] Ibid, 36.

[148] Tyler, T. R., & Yuen, J. H. (2002). *Trust in the Law. Encouraging Public Cooperation with the Police and Courts.* New York: Russell Sage Foundation, 6.

[149] Arancibia, C. S. (2008), 37.

[150] Ibid, 37.

[151] Ibid, 37.

Corruptions worsens institutional competence,[152] and it reduces the fairness of institutional activity, by "giving some people or groups of people more access to institutions or to better outcomes resulting from the institutions' activity."[153] Studies find that corruption in democracies "lowers confidence in the political system and political legitimacy."[154] According to Della Porta (2000) "political corruption worsens governmental performance reducing trust in the government's capacity to address citizens' demands."[155] Anderson and Tverdova (2003) support the negative impact of corruption on trust, asserting that trust is lower in cases where corruption is perceived to be widespread.[156]

Other scholars don't agree with the negative impact of corruption and have argued that corruption is necessary in government, in the redistribution of economic resources,[157] and the maintenance and the functioning of the political system.[158] According to Huntington (1968) "corruption provides immediate, specific, and concrete benefits to groups which might otherwise be thoroughly alienated from society. Corruption may thus be functional to the maintenance of a political system."[159] In this context, corruption can increase or maintain political trust and support in governing institutions.[160] According to Manzetti and Wilson (2007), corrupt governments can maintain the levels of the citizens' support,[161] in cases where "government institutions are weak and patron-client relationships are strong."[162] However, most of the research supports the idea that corruption weakens rule of law, lowers quality of services, and has negative economic consequences (Della Porta, 2000; Seligson, 2002; Arancibia, 2008).

---

[152] Della Porta, D. (2000). *Social Capital, Beliefs in Government, and Political Corruption*. In Disaffected Democracies. What's Troubling the Trilateral Countries?, edited by S. J. Pharr and R. D. Putnam. New Jersey: Princeton University Press.

[153] Arancibia, C. S. (2008), 38.

[154] Della Porta, D. (2000).

[155] Ibid, 54.

[156] Anderson, C. J., & Tverdova, Y. V. (2003). Corruption, Political Allegiances, and Attitudes Toward Government in Contemporary Democracies. *American Journal of Political Science*, 47(1), 91-109.

[157] Nye, J. (1967). Corruption and Political Development: A Cost-Benefit Analysis. *American Political Science Review*, 61: 417-427.

[158] Huntington, S. P. (1968). *Political Order in Changing Societies*. New Haven: Yale University Press.

[159] Huntington, S. P. (1968), 64.

[160] Arancibia, C. S. (2008), 38

[161] Manzetti, L., & Wilson, C. J. (2007). Why Do Corrupt Governments Maintain Public Support? *Comparative Political Studies,* 40(8), 949-970.

[162] Ibid, 38.

2.1.6 Legitimacy

Another main body of research suggests that institutional trust is reflective of government performance, instead of the cultural values.[163] *Institutional performance theories* are based on the assumption that institutional trust is endogenous to the political sphere.[164] Trust in legal-political institutions and in actors is based on the rational choice perspective, "the rational evaluation of the design and the performance of the institutions."[165] According to Godefroidt et al,. (2015) institutions that are successful in delivering services and goods, are expected to have higher institutional trust, whereas failing institutions have low levels of trust among citizens.[166] In this context, institutional performance is positively correlated with the level of trust in political institutions.

Institutional theorists emphasize that political trust and distrust are "rational responses by individuals to the performance of institutions,"[167] and that the institutional structure "is a function of rational choice or intentional design,"[168] with "real consequences for government performance and thus for public trust in institutions."[169] In new democracies, the institutional design, in terms of *perceived fairness, transparency, efficiency,* and *accountability,* matters as much as the policy outputs.[170] Improving institutional design will increase institutional trust quickly.[171]

In summary, several studies have analyzed the influence of cultural and institutional determinants of institutional trust. Focusing on cultural factors, Kuchenkova (2017) claimed that interpersonal trust facilitates formation of group identities, cooperation, as well as support for government institutions and policies.[172] Berg and Hjerm (2010) concluded that national identity has a positive impact on institutional trust, but a reverse relationship is seen in strong ethnic national identity, found to have a negative impact on institutional trust.[173] The assumed linkage

[163] Newton, K. (2001). Trust, Social Capital, Civil Society, and Democracy. International Political Science Review, 22(2): 201–214.

[164] Mishler, W., & Rose R. (2001), 35.

[165] Godefroidt et al. (2015), 3.

[166] Ibid, 3.

[167] Mishler, W., & Rose R. (2001), 36.

[168] Shepsle, K. A. (1995). Studying institutions: some lessons from rational choice. In James Farr, John S. Dryzek, & Stephen T. Leonard (Eds.), Political science in history (pp. 276-285). Cambridge, UK: Cambridge University Press.

[169] Mishler, W., & Rose R. (2001), 36.

[170] Godefroidt et al. (2015), 3.

[171] Miller, A. H. (1974, September). Political Issues and Trust in Government, 1964-1970. *American Political Science Review,* 68(3), 951-972.

[172] Kuchenkova, A. V. (2017), 82.

[173] Berg, L., & Hjerm, M. (2010). National Identity and Political Trust. *Perspectives on European Politics and Society,* 11 (4): 390–407. doi:10.1080/15705854.2010.524403.

between interpersonal trust and institutional trust, including the causal direction, has been largely criticized by scholars.[174] In support of this view, Putnam (1993) argued that interpersonal trust increases political trust,[175] whereas other scholars did not find a relationship between the two.[176]

Cultural theories also claim that social relations formed through early-life socialization, and socializations patterns will vary across socio-demographic variables, such as gender, age, education, and occupation.[177] The relationship between institutional trust and the individual characteristics of the socio-economic groups can differ, in some cases seen to have positive effect on institutional trust, and some others have found negative effect or non-significant.[178]

With respect to institutional performance and trustworthiness of institutions Arancibia (2008) has demonstrated that political trust is tied to government performance, where fairness and competence are the two main components of trustworthiness.[179] Based on the rational choice perspective, the design and the performance of the institutions matter significantly.[180]

2.2 Theoretical Framework

In this section, I will discuss the concept of political trust and its definitions. The literature review will focus on the main theoretical explanations of political trust, with emphasis on the cultural versus institutional performance debate. Studies that examine confidence in political institutions, although not in agreement about the level of trustworthiness in politicians or institutions, reflect these dynamics in various domains and activities. By looking at particular domains within the institutional structure of Kosovo, this book hopes to examine the different levels of political trust, respective of domestic and international actors present in Kosovo.

Next, I will focus on the role and relevance of two key socio-political factors – *interpersonal trust*, and *institutional trustworthiness* as key determinants of trust to base the main arguments of the book. By bringing in two aspects of culturalist and institutionalist views, I hope my research will provide a more comprehensive analysis and deeper understanding of the levels of trust, to explain differences across institutions and time periods in the Kosovo case study.

---

[174] Godefroidt, et al. (2015), 3-4.

[175] Putnam, R. D. (1993), 11.

[176] Newton, K. (2001). Trust, Social Capital, Civil Society, and Democracy. *International Political Science Review*, 22 (2): 201–214.

[177] Godefroidt et al. (2015), 3.

[178] Ibid, 4.

[179] Arancibia, C. S. (2008), 38.

[180] Godefroidt et al. (2015), 3.

Defining Political Trust

2.2.1 Political Trust and its Origin

The scholarly debate has primarily focused on the importance of trust for both social and political reasons.[181] Trust is usually fragmented across disciplines, with applications in political science, sociology, psychology, anthropology, management, and economics to name a few. In academia, scholars generally agree on two specifications of trust: *social trust* and *political trust*.[182] "Social trust" also known as "interpersonal trust" is defined as "interpersonal or horizontal trust between citizens, based on first-hand experiences of others."[183] Whereas, "political trust" is concerned with the "vertical or the political trust between citizens and political elites, or citizen confidence in political institutions, learned indirectly and at a distance, usually through the media."[184] Social trust can be detrimental to civic social life,[185] and it is at the center of social science theories. Political trust can be detrimental to the democratic and a stable political life,[186] and it is at the center of political science studies. Critics argue that the concept of trust as applied in the social science context, lacks the idea of accountability,[187] and there is a need for a review of the history of the political conceptualization of trust to correct the deficiencies.[188]

These studies all pointed to two central questions: what are the origins of political trust and what determines public trust in political institutions? Researchers in Western political literature have searched for the origins of political trust by looking at the relevance of trust in the past, presence and future (Fukuyama, 1995; Cook, 2001; Maloy, 2009); the relationship of trust and social capital (Wilson, 1997; Brehm and Rahn, 1997; Putnam, 2000); the social roots of trust (Krishna 2000; Arrow 2000); political trust in established democracies (Kaase and Newton, 1995; Norris, 1999; Pharr and Putnam, 2000; Godefroidt et al., 2015); public confidence in government and democratic institutions (Mishler and Rose, 2001; Catterberg and Moreno 2006; Yang, 2012); and

---

[181] Choi, E., & Woo, J. (2016). The origins of political trust in east Asian democracies: Psychological, cultural, and institutional arguments. *Japanese Journal of Political Science*, 17(3), 410-426.
doi: http://dx.doi.org.www.libproxy.wvu.edu/10.1017/S1468109916000165

[182] Newton, K. (2013). Social and Political Trust. *Norwegian Social Science Data Services*, 1-13. Retrieved from http://essedunet.nsd.uib.no

[183] Ibid, 1.

[184] Ibid, 3.

[185] Ibid, 3.

[186] Maloy, J. S. (2009, April). Two concepts of trust. *The Journal of Politics*, 71(2), 492-505. doi: 10.1017/s0022381609090410 http://www.jstor.org/stable/10.1017/s0022381609090410

[187] Aylmer, G. (1975). *The Levellers in the English Revolution*. Ithaca, NY: Cornell University Press.

[188] Maloy. (2009), 492.

cultural explanations of trust (Mill, 1861; Berg and Hjerm 2010; Richards, 2013; Choi and Woo, 2016). However, the scholarly literature differs on the origins of trust,[189] questioning if there is a link between interpersonal and political trust, and how other determinants of trust, such as political, economic, and socio-cultural conditions play a role.[190] Although scholars differ on the origins of trust and on the causal direction of different types of trust,[191] they agree that trust matters (Easton, 1975; Cooper, Knotts, and Brennan, 2008; Arancibia, 2008; Godefroidt et al., 2015).

Studies on the origins of trust view trust in a three-dimensional approach: social-psychological, social-cultural, and institutional.[192] The first dimension, the *social-psychological approach* suggests that interpersonal and political trust is largely shaped by the individual's personal characteristics (personality type), the knowledge to trust (the tendency to trust others), and institutional contexts (political institutions or lack of).[193] This approach argues that the personal experience shapes the individual's owns behavior, and their expectations toward other people's behavior.[194]

From the psychological perspective, every individual defines their own behavior based on how they think, feel and act, also known as "moral identity."[195] The expectation is that a positive experience motivates individuals to foster more trust towards other people and institutions. Additionally, when the institutional context improves in such a way that it provides positive experiences, individuals are more likely to encourage others to act more honestly, which leads to higher levels of trust towards them.[196] Tamilina and Tamilina (2017) argue that in order to trust others, other people's motives and intentions must be taken into account. Intentions and motives are important to determine if the institutional context will provide a safety net, reducing the risk involved in trusting someone else, or increase the cost of betrayal in cases when individuals are wronged.[197]

The second dimension of the origins of trust studies, *the social-cultural approach* focuses on the role values and norms play in shaping people's choices,[198] as well as the influence of the

---

[189] Arancibia, C. S. (2008). Political trust in Latin America. *University of Michigan*, 1-197.

[190] Choi and Woo. (2016), 411.

[191] Ibid, 411.

[192] Ibid, 411.

[193] Tamilina, L., & Tamilina, N. (2017). Explaining the impact of formal institutions on social trust: A psychological approach. *Munich Personal RePEc Archive*, Paper No. 84560. Retrievable from https://mpra.ub.uni-muenchen.de/84560/ Also see Choi and Woo. (2016).

[194] Ibid, 5.

[195] Shao, R., Aquino, K., & Freeman, D. (2008). Beyond moral reasoning: A review of moral identity research and its implications for business ethics. *Business Ethics Quarterly*, 18(4), 513–540.

[196] Tamilina & Tamilina (2017), 10.

[197] Ibid, 4.

[198] Shi, T. (2001). Cultural Values and Political Trust: A Comparison of the People's Republic of China and Taiwan. *Comparative Politics*, 33(4), 401-419. doi:10.2307/422441

individual's early socialization process on trusting others, civic associations, and political institutions.[199] The main argument is that values and norms, when shaped by early socialization, are likely to remain stable in the same environment. Whereas, attitudes and beliefs are shaped by external stimuli outside the environment, brought by institutional changes, thus causing change in these orientations.[200]

Culturalists believe that the inner layer of culture is deeply rooted in values and norms "that are resistant to change," while the outer layer, consists of attitudes and beliefs, that "frequently interact with the outside environment and are relatively easy to change."[201] Institutionalists are against the independent status of culture because they believe that structural changes will alter people's attitudes and beliefs.[202] The third dimension, *the institutional approach* argues that political trust is influenced by the performance of government institutions, in such a way that poor performance leads to decreasing trust, and well-performing governments see increased levels of citizens' trust.[203]

2.2.2 Definitions of Political Trust

Trust is a complex interpersonal and organizational construct[204] that is the foundation of all human relationships and institutional interaction.[205] A trusting person, group or institution will hold favorable perceptions of each other that allow for expected outcomes[206] and are free from worry to monitor other's behavior.[207] The literature defines trust in four different ways: in terms of risk of uncertainty, willingness to accept vulnerability, the perception of other's expected dependency, and the shared value.[208] Fukuyama (1996) defined trust as the expectation that arises in the community based on shared norms, honest and cooperative behavior. In this context, high

---

[199] Choi, E., & Woo, J. (2016), 411.

[200] Shi, T. (2001), 402.

[201] Ibid, 402.

[202] Ibid.

[203] Godefroidt et al. (2015), 5.

[204] Duck, S. (1997). *The Handbook of Personal Relationships: Theory, Research, and Interventions*. New York: Wiley.

[205] Mistzal, B.A. (1996). *Trust in Modern Societies: The Search for the Bases of Social Order*. Cambridge: Polity Press.

[206] Wheeless, L.R., & Grotz J. (1977, March). The Measurement of Trust and Its Relationship to Self-Disclosure, *Human Communication Research,* 3(3), 251.

[207] Levi, M., & Stoker, L. (2000, June). Political Trust and Trustworthiness. *Annual Review of Political Science,* 3(1), 496.

[208] Cai, R. (2004). Interaction between trust and transaction cost in Industrial Districts. *Virginia Polytechnic Inst.,* 1-64.

level of trust allows for social relationships to emerge,[209] and widespread distrust will impose a kind of "tax" on all forms of economic activity.[210] According to Fukuyama's definition, trust is an efficient means for "lowering transaction costs in any social, economic and political relationship."[211] And in cases where there is lack of trust amongst people or organizations, contractual safeguards, such as the legal apparatus, become the substitute of trust, where cooperation has to be negotiated, agreed or enforced.[212]

As mentioned previously, there are two main theoretical concepts of trust: *social trust* and *political trust*. Social trust refers to the interpersonal trust between citizens, while political trust is between citizens and the political elite, or the citizens confidence in political institutions.[213] Another definition of political trust refers to the "judgment of the citizenry that the system and the political incumbents are responsive, and will do what is right even in the absence of constant scrutiny."[214] Trust comes into play when a new policy is adopted,[215] because there needs to be some level of legitimacy for the policy to be accepted by the citizens.[216] According to Blind (2006), political trust occurs "when citizens appraise the government and its institutions, policymaking in general and/or the individual political leaders as promise-keeping, efficient, fair and honest."[217] This is based on rational and psychological models of reasoning which treat political trust as a rational attitude.[218]

While social trust and political trust are not mutually exclusive of each other, scholars disagree on the direction of the causal relationship and whether such causal relationship exists.[219] Is political trust a result of social capital, or can trustworthy governments create an environment for active civic engagement? Different schools of thought will provide different answers.

---

[209] Ibid, 25.

[210] Fukuyama, F. (1996). Trust: *The Social Virtues and The Creation of Property*. Free Press Paperbacks.

[211] Blind, P. K. (2006). Building Trust in Government in the Twentieth Century: Review of Literature and Emerging Issues. UNDESA, 3. Retrieved from http://unpan1.un.org/intradoc/groups/public/documents/un/unpan025062.pdf

[212] This is known as the "transaction cost" by economics. See Cai, R. (2004), 23.

[213] Newton, K. (2013), 3.

[214] Miller, A. H., & Listhaug, O. (1990, July). Political Parties and Confidence in Government: A Comparison of Norway, Sweden and the United States. *British Journal of Political Science*, 20(3), 358.

[215] Ocampo, J. A. (2006, September). Congratulatory Message. The Regional Forum on Reinventing Government in Asia. Seoul, Korea: UN DESA and the Ministry of Government Administration and Home Affairs, Republic of Korea.

[216] Robinson, E.S, Stoutenborough, J. W., & Vedlitz, A. (2017). *Understanding Trust in Government: Environmental Sustainability, Fracking, and Public Opinion in American Politics*. New York: Routledge.

[217] Blind, P. K. (2006), 4.

[218] Rational political trust is interest-based, where citizens evaluate the behavior of the government and leaders.

[219] Blind, P. K. (2006), 6.

Neo-institutionalists believe that "it is not the social capital that produces political trust, but a trustworthy government, which then generates interpersonal trust."[220] Modernization theorists, on the other hand, argue that increased social trust is associated with increased political participation, (i.e. voting), [221] which is accepted as a sign of political trust and democratization.[222]

2.2.3 Variances of Political Trust

It is important to emphasize that this study is primarily concerned with political trust – meaning the citizens' sense of trusting the political actors, and their trust of governmental institutions.[223] The study presumes that *political trust* is the individuals' opinion towards the political system, the political organizations, and the individual political officials. The individual's opinion is seen as the measurement of the person's evaluation of the performance of political institutions, such as the *government*, *political parties*, *political leaders*, protective institutions like *the police* and the armed forces, as well legal institutions like *the courts*. The aim of the study is to test the political trust model, to find if trust perceptions differ across institutions and actors, and search for explanations to explain the variations of political trust. This section will look at the different categories of political trust and the direction of political trust relationships.

According to the literature, political trust, also referred to as *vertical trust*, and is grouped into two different categories, based on the object toward which trust is directed: (1) "macro level" or *organizational trust*, and (2) "micro level" or *individual political trust*.[224] At the macro level, organizational political trust is issue-oriented,[225] based on the "satisfaction or dissatisfactions of the citizens with the policy alternatives."[226] This variant of political trust is "diffuse" or *system-based trust* (directed to the overall political system and regime), and *institution-based trust* (directed to certain institutions such as police or local municipality).[227] The macro foundation of trust looks at the links between trust and government performance. At the micro level, individual political trust,

---

[220] Ibid, 6.

[221] Almond & Verba. (1963).

[222] Blind, P. K. (2006), 6.

[223] Some scholars make a distinction between "trust" and "confidence" where trust is closely related to the beliefs and commitments of the people, and confidence is the passive emotion associated with the overall sociopolitical system (Blind, 2006). This study uses these two terms interchangeably.

[224] See Figure 1: An integrative model of political and social trust sources, types, and influences.

[225] Matebesi, S. (2017). *Civil strife against local governance: Dynamics of community protests in contemporary South Africa*. Toronto: Barbara Budrich Publishers, 24.

[226] Miller, A. H. (1974, September). Political Issues and Trust in Government, 1964-1970. *American Political Science Review*, 68(3), 951.

[227] Blind, P. K. (2006), 4.

is a person-oriented perspective, based on the approval or disapproval of the political leaders.[228] The micro foundation of trust looks at trust towards individual political leaders, where perceptions of a trustful or distrustful government will depend on the citizens' approval or disproval of the political leaders, instead of the political regime.[229]

Besides the object of trust, other variants of political trust are based on the different types of motivations when trusting political leaders or institutions. *Rational political trust*, also known as "the first order" or "encapsulated trust" involves "an interest-based calculation whereby citizens evaluate whether the government and/or the political leaders act in accordance with their partisan agenda."[230] Based on the rational model of reasoning, the first order of trust "dictates the choice of a dominant strategy that yields larger payoff regardless of how the co-player will choose the strategy."[231] This means that A (i.e. the voter) will attribute an amount of trust to B (i.e. political party or Congress) on a particular ground, such as an issue, C (i.e. rule of law), where B has control over C, and A has an interest on C. In this case, trust is justified because A's interests are encapsulated in B's interests also, making B trustworthy.[232]

Blind (2006) believes that trust will change according to the party that controls the issue, based on the ideological or partisan attachment. He argues that "citizens who follow the tenets of rational political trust, tend to trust the political party or the political leaders with whom they identify."[233] This has placed importance on government trust itself, as an independent determinant for support of government policies.[234]

Another type of motivation that explains political trust (as illustrated in Figure 1) is derived from the *psychological political trust* or the "second-order political trust." The psychological political trust refers to the perceptions of the individuals on the trustworthiness of their political leaders, where truth and sincerity in personality and in behavior are preferred.[235] It involves an "assessment of the moral values and attributes associated with a certain government, political institution and/or individual political leaders."[236] Second-order trust differs from first-order trust,

[228] Matebesi, S. (2017), 24.

[229] Blind, P. K. (2006), 4.

[230] Ibid, 5.

[231] Rapoport, A. (1998). *Decision Theory and Decision Behavior*, 2nd edition. London: Macmillan Press, 248.

[232] Blind, P. K. (2006), 5.

[233] Blind, P. K. (2006), 5.

[234] Hetherington (2005) argues that political trust is more important than ideology or partisanship. See Hetherington, M.J. (2005). *Why Trust Matters: Declining Political Trust and the Demise of American Liberalism*. Princeton: Princeton University Press.

[235] Blind, P. K. (2006), 5.

[236] Ibid, 5.

because in the former benevolence is ascribed to the political representative, and in the later, the citizen assumes that the leader will be guided by rationality instead.[237]

According to psychological political trust view, institutions can influence cooperation by influencing beliefs.[238] How much people trust each other will have an effect on the rational responses to the institutions.[239] Bryan Skyrms (2003) proposes the idea that it is not only important to trust others before cooperating, but it is also important to believe "that one is trusted by others."[240] In other words, "I believe that you can be trusted if I also believe that you believe that I can be trusted."[241] The idea that "I believe that you believe that…" is also known as the third-order belief.[242] Thomas Schelling (1957) suggests that beliefs about what the other person will do, and what the other person believes I will do, will be crucial to successful coordination.[243] In this scenario, cooperation depends on mutual trust, or in third-order trust.

2.2.4 Political Trust Redefined

As proposed by Peri Blind (2006) the trust model indicates that the target based political trust is divided into two categories: *macro* meaning organizational or issue oriented, and *micro* meaning individual or person oriented. However, this model does not account for another trust type, such as international organizations, or relations with other nations as an important source of trust. Fang and Stone (2010) argue that international organizations exert effective influence on the government in such a way that it will condition its domestic policy.[244] Fang and Stone see international organizations such as the United Nations, European Union, the World Trade Organization, as information providers and influencers of domestic mechanisms.[245] International organizations can persuade governments to adopt policy recommendations, based on private information.[246]

---

[237] Rapoport, A. (1998), 248.

[238] Jansson, F., & Eriksson, K. (2015). Cooperation and Shared Beliefs about Trust in the Assurance Game. *PLoS One*. 2015; 10(12): e0144191. Retrieved from https://www.ncbi.nlm.nih.gov/pmc/articles/PMC4671566/

[239] Jansson & Eriksson. (2015), 2.

[240] Ibid, 2.

[241] Rothstein, B., & Eek, D. (2009). Political Corruption and Social Trust: An Experimental Approach. *Rationality and Society,* 21, 81–112. doi: 10.1177/1043463108099349

[242] Jansson & Eriksson. (2015), 4.

[243] Schelling, T.C. (1957). Bargaining, Communication, and Limited War. *Conflict Resolution.*11:19–36. doi: 10.1177/002200275700100104

[244] Fang, S., & Stone, R. W. (2010). Trust and International Organizations. *Political Science*, University of Rochester. 1-41. Retrieved from http://www.sas.rochester.edu/psc/stone/working_papers/Trust%20and%20IO_7.5.pdf

[245] Fang & Stone. (2010), 2.

[246] Ibid, 1.

According to Fang and Stone (2010) persuasion is a two-level game, based on the credibility of the signals and the conditions of the international cooperation:

> "First, the international institution can send a credible signal about a crisis and prompt the government to take an action in response, and second, it can direct the government's attention to domestic experts and make their expertise policy relevant. The condition under which this effect can take place is that there is a preference difference between the IO and domestic experts, and that the institution holds the more moderate policy position.
>
> In such cases, the IO will truthfully reveal its information, thus building trust with the government, and the government will condition its policy on the IO's information. The results suggest that, far from being an obstacle to international cooperation, polarized domestic politics may be a necessary condition for international organizations to exert effective influence."[247]

However, the question then becomes, can international organizations become a credible source of information to influence the country's response to crisis or a certain issue? Major international organizations, including the European Union "find themselves in a crisis of legitimacy" and credibility.[248] Fang and Stone (2010) emphasize that "the effectiveness of international institutions as information providers depends upon trust."[249]

Trust in international organizations matters, as it impacts geographic identification, corruption, and globalization.[250] According to Torgler (2007) a higher level of perceived corruption reduces trust in international organizations in developing countries, and a "stronger identification with the world as a whole" also leads to a higher trust in international organizations.[251] Torgler (2007) investigates state's capacity as a variable of trust, not only how political trust can influence international organizations, but also, the impact of perceived corruption in the country, to look at the institutional functioning and the governance quality.[252]

---

[247] Ibid, 1.

[248] Ibid, 2.

[249] Ibid, 2.

[250] Torgler, B. (2007). Trust in International Organizations: An Empirical Investigation Focusing on the United Nations. *School of Economics and Finance* Discussion Papers and Working Papers Series 213, School of Economics and Finance, Queensland University of Technology. 65-93. Retrieved from https://link-springer-com.www.libproxy.wvu.edu/content/pdf/10.1007%2Fs11558-007-9022-1.pdf

[251] Torgler. (2007), 65.

[252] Ibid, 69.

The general assumption is that a higher perceived corruption may lead to a lower trust in international organizations.[253] Torgler's study found strong effects between the variables of trust in the parliament and in the legal system, as strong externalities, meaning, "political trust at the state level leads to a higher trust at the international level."[254] Brewer et al. (2004) also supports this view that a lower level of government quality reduces trust at the international level, due to the high level of perceived corruption.[255] This supports the notion that trust in international organizations matters.

Since the definition of political trust excludes trust in international organizations or in other countries, I propose to add "international trust" as a variation of political trust, to be added to the integrated trust model illustrated below, in Figure 1. I propose to add target-based group-oriented category and call it *"Mezzo level"* or *"international trust"* to account for citizens' trust in international organizations and in other nations. Political trust is between citizens and the political elite, or the citizen confidence in political institutions and in international trust.[256]

Additionally, what is absent in Blind's trust model, specifically in the motivation-based political trust design, is the *third-order trust*, information about information about trust. The *first-order trust*, known as *rational political trust*, assumes that trust will change based on the ideological or the partisan attachment of the political leader or the institutions. Trust is rational, based on the common interests, where citizens are expected to follow the rational political trust of their leaders, or the political leaders with whom they identify. The citizen assumes that the political representative will be guided by rationality to make the best policy choices. Whereas, the *second-order trust*, referred to as *psychological political trust*, is based on the perceptions of morality and trustworthiness about the leaders. Moral values and certain attitudes associated with political leaders, government, or institutions, are the motivations behind the citizens' trust, where truth, sincerity and trustworthiness of the political leaders and the institutions are preferred. I propose to add the third-order of trust to the integrated model (*See Table 1*).

Third-order of trust, is described as someone who is informed about your trust label, such as low/high trust. In this case, "information about trust can override both individual differences in actual trust and ingroup effects based on the same information."[257] The assumption is that when someone who might be considered "high" on trust but is told that the other person knows him or

---

[253] Ibid, 69.

[254] Ibid, 79.

[255] Brewer, P. R., Gross, K., Aday, S., & Willnat, L. (2004). International trust and public opinion about world affairs. *American Journal of Political Science*, 48, 93–109.

[256] See Figure 7 for a conceptual model of political trust structures in political, legal, public, & international systems.

[257] Jansson & Eriksson. (2015), 10.

her as a "low truster," then the prediction is to not cooperate.[258] In this case, the informed individual eliminates the effect of the first-order trust (trusting based on party identification), and the second-order trust (perceptions of trustworthiness of the leader or institution). Therefore, individual preferences, which were not assumed to change between conditions in similar alignments, as trust relies on the party affiliation, here preferences are in fact expected to change, depending on the given information about trust labels to the individuals.

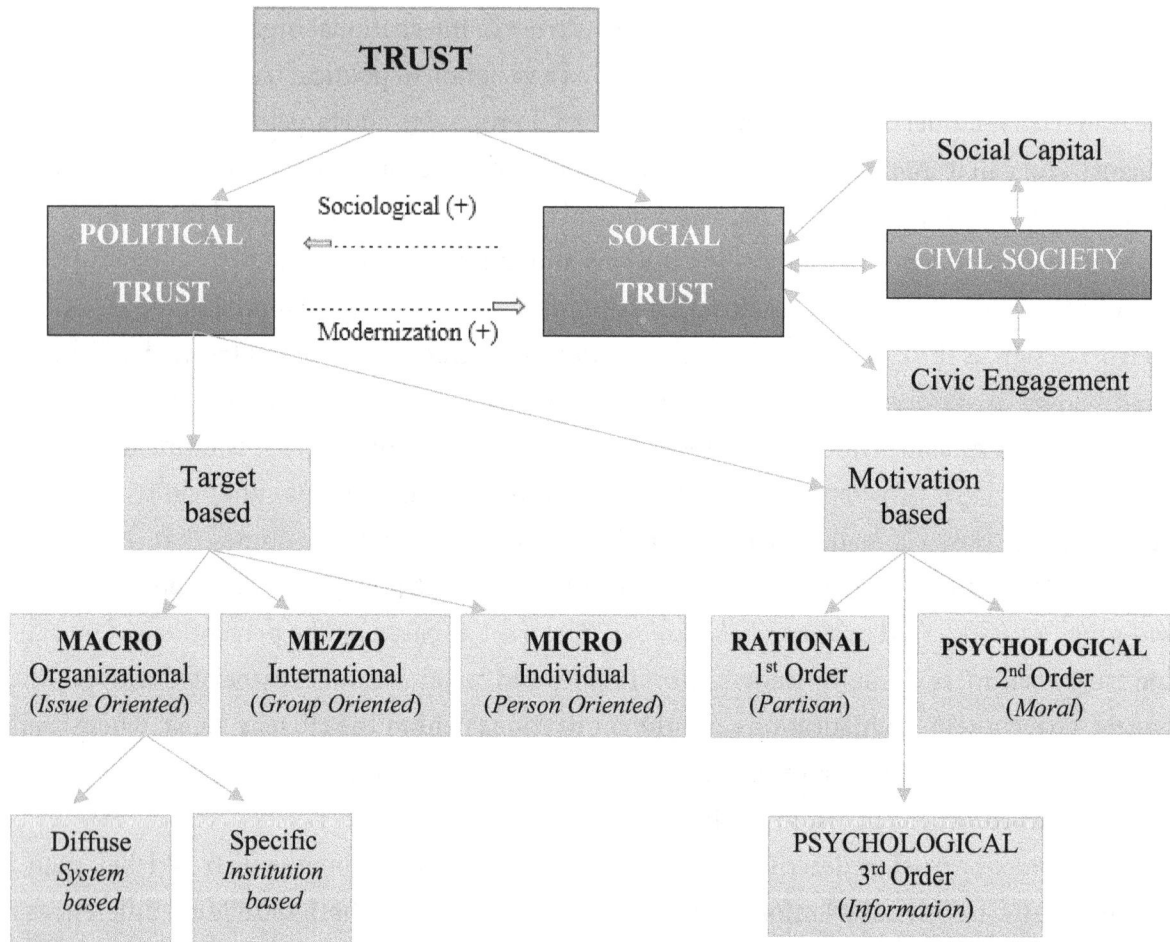

Figure 1: An integrative model of political and social trust sources, types, and influences[259]

---

[258] Ibid.

[259] Based on Peri Blind's determinants of trust, as illustrated in his chapter 2. See Blind, P. K. (2006). *Building Trust in Government in the Twentieth Century: Review of Literature and Emerging Issues.* UNDESA, 7.

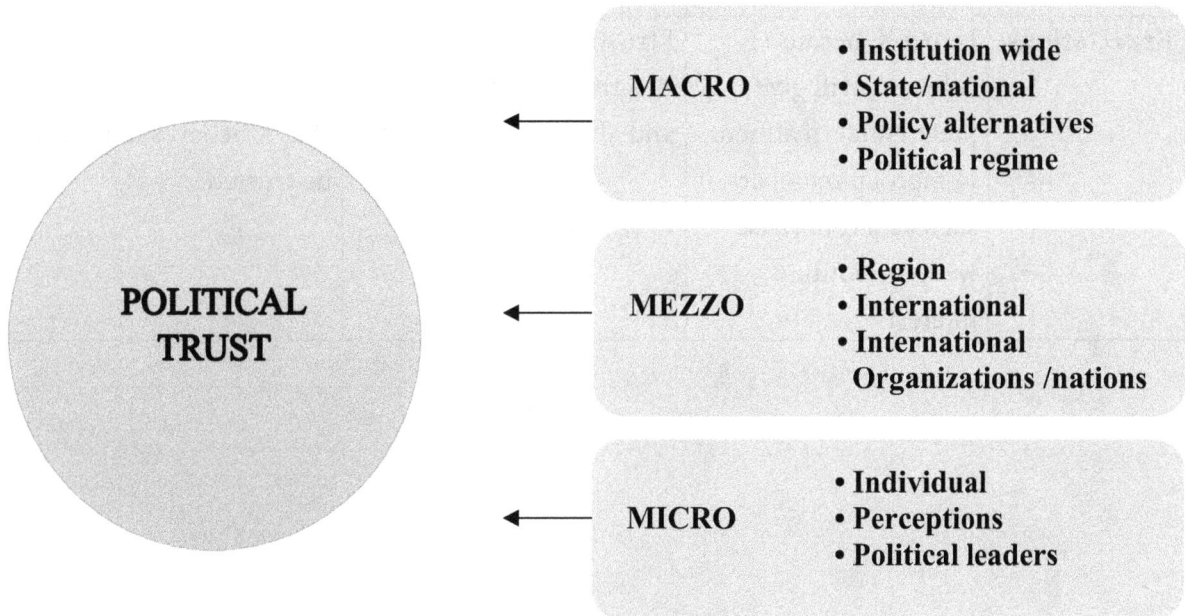

Figure 2: Three Levels of Political Trust[260]

---

[260] The proposed three levels of political trust model incorporate macro, mezzo, and micro, based on political trust literature, adapted from Peri Blind (2006) and social studies. Social studies include mezzo level, in reference to interest groups, working with interest groups, and organizations at the communal level, such as nonprofits, hospitals, business, and neighborhoods. I am applying the same idea, however in the context of the regional relationships, such as citizens' perceptions towards international organizations (such as U.N., E.U., WHO), and/or a country's relation with other countries.

Table 1: Characteristics of First-Order, Second-Order, and Third-Order Political Trust[261]

	First Order Trust	Second Order Trust	Third Order Trust
Influence	Rational Political Trust	Psychological Political Trust	Psychological Political Trust
Main focus	Party / Partisan agenda Ideology	Personality Morals	Information
Expectations	I trust X, because I believe X will give preferential treatment to ingroup members, such as me, because we share similar interests.	I trust X because I believe X is trustworthy, sincere, and always tells the truth.	I believe that X can be trusted if I also believe that X believes that I can be trusted.

---

[261] Adapted from Jansson, F., & Eriksson, K. (2015) and Blind, P. K. (2006).

CHAPTER 3

Background of the Kosovo Case Study

This chapter includes a historical background and a review of Kosovo's independence and statehood, including the political institutional structure, the legal framework, the creation of the Kosovo Specialist Court, and the role of the international community. The foreign policy section focuses on rule of law, relations with Serbia and European Union integration.

3.1 History

Under the Turkish rule of nearly 500 years (1458-1913), Kosovo (*in Albanian: Kosova*) was an administrative unit *"Vilayet of Kosovo"* based on its large Albanian majority.[262] During 19th century, Kosovo was part of Albania's territory, divided by the Ottoman Empire under 4 Albanian provinces or "vilayets": *Kosovo Vilayet* (includes present day Kosovo and part of Macedonia), *Skutari Vilayet* (Shkodër, in present day Albania), *Manastir Vilayet*, and *Janina Vilayet* (given to Greece in 1881).[263] The Kosovo Vilayet[264] included an area of 32,900 km² with a population of 1,038,100, and the capital Skopje (current capital of Macedonia).[265] The League of Prizren in the Kosovo Vilayet,

---

[262] Krasniqi, G. (2015, January). Country Report on Citizenship Law: Kosovo. *European University Institute*, 4. Retrieved from http://cadmus.eui.eu/bitstream/handle/1814/34477/EUDO_CIT_2015_03-Kosovo.pdf%3Bsequence=1

[263] Christo, V. (2008, December). The Four Albanian Vilayets During the Ottoman Empire. *Frosnia*. Retrieved from https://www.frosina.org/the-four-albanian-vilayets-during-the-ottoman-empire/

[264] Major cities included Prishtina (11,000 inhabitants), Prizreni (38.000 inhabitants), Peja (Ipek, 18.000 inhabitants), Tashlixha (3.000 inhabitants). See http://www.njekomb.com/?p=6069

[265] Osmanli Atlasi: XX, Yüzyil Başlar. (1970). Harta zyrtare e Vilajetit të Kosovës nën osmanët gjatë viteve '70 të shek. XIX! Retrieved from http://www.njekomb.com/?p=6069

created to resist Turkish rule, became the cradle of Albanian national identity and Albanian national awakening.[266] In Albania, national hero and military commander Skanderbeg, who led the revolt against the Turks, became "a symbol for hope and an Albanian Renaissance."[267]

After the defeat of the Ottoman Empire by Russia during the Russo-Turkish wars (1877-78), the Treaty of San Stefano (singed on March 1878) penalized Albania, because, "it was considered part of the Ottoman Empire."[268] As a result, the Great Powers divided Albania, by giving away more than half of its ethnic territory to Montenegro, Serbia, and Greece.[269] The Albanians created the League of Prizren *"Besëlidhja e Prizrenit"* (June 10, 1878), to defend the rights of the Albanian nation and to consider the creation of an autonomous administration.[270] The Ambassadors of the six Great Powers (Great Britain, France, Germany, Austria-Hungary, Russia and Italy) met in London on December 3, 1912 to decide the fate of ethnic Albania.[271] The Albanian-populated lands were assigned as follows: Vilayet of Shkodra to Montenegro, the Vilayet of Kosova to Serbia, the Vilayet of Manastir to Macedonia, and the Vilayet of Janina to Greece.[272]

In November 1912, Serbian and Montenegrin forces invaded Kosovo, while simultaneously Albania declared its independence on November 28, 1912, which, "helped foster a nationalist movement in Kosovo."[273] After the first Balkan War, Serbia annexed Kosovo (1912-1913), later incorporated into the Kingdom of Yugoslavia.[274] In 1945 Yugoslavia become a federal republic, under Josip Broz Tito's communist regime, ending the monarchy of King Peter II.[275]

Prior to the break-up of Yugoslavia (1992), Kosovo was under the communist regime of Tito (1944-1980). The federation of Yugoslavia comprised of six republics: Serbia, Croatia, Bosnia

---

[266] Skendi, S. (1967). *The Albanian National Awakening.* Princeton: Princeton University Press.

[267] Pahumi, N. (2007). The Consolidation of Albanian Nationalism: The League of Prizren 1878-1881. (Master's Thesis). *University of Michigan*, 4. Retrieved from https://deepblue.lib.umich.edu/bitstream/handle/2027.42/55462/pahumi_history_honors_thesis_2007.pdf?sequence=1&isAllowed=y

[268] Christo, V. (2008), 1.

[269] Elsie, R. (2010). *Independent Albania (1912-1944): Historical dictionary of Albania.* Lanham: Scarecrow Press, 243.

[270] Jelavich, B. (1999). *History of the Balkans: Eighteenth and nineteenth centuries.* Cambridge University: Cambridge University Press, 361.

[271] Vasa, P. (1999). *The Truth on Albania and Albanians: Historical and Critical Issues.* London: National Press Agency, 1879. Reprint introduction by Robert Elsie. Centre for Albanian Studies. London, 1999.

[272] Ibid.

[273] Kaufman, J.P. (1999, September). NATO and the Former Yugoslavia: Crisis, Conflict and the Atlantic Alliance. *Journal of Conflict Studies*, 19(2), 3. Retrieved from https://journals.lib.unb.ca/index.php/JCS/article/view/4355/5009

[274] Jelavich, C., and Jelavich, B. (1986). *The Establishment of the Balkan National States.* Vol. III. London and Seattle: University of Washington Press.

[275] Walter, R. (1973). *Tito, Mihailović, and the Allies, 1941-1945.* Rutgers University Press, 288.

and Herzegovina, Slovenia, Montenegro and two provinces: Kosovo and Vojvodina.[276] In 1968 violent demonstrations boiled over in Kosovo demanding freedoms, the right to education and autonomy.[277]

> "Under Tito's rule, Kosovar Albanians experienced both harsh persecution and glimpses of freedom. The effects of three decades of government-sponsored colonization by Serbs of almost half of Kosovo's arable land were mitigated when Tito returned a third of the land to its Albanian owners after 1945. Also, some of the prewar measures employed to stifle the Albanian language were lifted. The immediate post-war period was, however, a period of repression in Yugoslavia and after Tito broke with Moscow in 1948, Kosovar Albanians experienced particularly harsh repressive measures, since they were suspected of sympathizing with Albanian president and loyal Stalinist, Enver Hoxha."[278]

During the 1980's ethnic Albanians in Kosovo protested against Serbian rule and the Yugoslav government, they demanded autonomy within Yugoslavia. Ethnic tensions between ethnic Albanians and Kosovan Serbs remained high during the decade due to years of repression by the Serb elite against the ethnic Albanian majority.[279] On March 11, 1981, 10,000 Albanians and students protested in the capital of Prishtina about the poor living conditions and inequality, prompting mass demonstrations and civil unrest across Kosovo.[280]

At the end of Second World War, under President Tito's Yugoslavia, Kosovo became one of the two autonomous provinces of Serbia, within Yugoslavia: the *Autonomous Province of Kosovo and Metohija*[281] and the *Autonomous Province of Kosovo and Vojvodina*.[282] From 1945 until 1963, Kosovo had a lower status than Vojvodina, and it was considered an "Autonomous Region"

---

[276] United States Department of State. The Breakup of Yugoslavia, 1990-1992. Retrieved from https://history.state.gov/milestones/1989-1992/breakup-yugoslavia

[277] Independent International Commission on Kosovo. (2006). *The Kosovo Report*, 1-107. Retrieved from https://reliefweb.int/library/documents/thekosovoreport.htm

[278] Ibid, 11.

[279] Dobbs, M. (1981, April 3). Yugoslavs Take Emergency Steps In Face of Ethnic Disturbance. *Washington Post*. Retrieved from https://www.washingtonpost.com/archive/politics/1981/04/03/yugoslavs-take-emergency-steps-in-face-of-ethnic-disturbance/f1d58e1c-0e8b-4198-a8c1-87db8f4f6000/?utm_term=.132763744a71

[280] Ibid.

[281] In 1968 it was only called the "Autonomous Province of Kosovo" and the word "Metohija" was dropped.

[282] Krasniqi, G. (2015, January). Country Report on Citizenship Law: Kosovo. *European University Institute*, 4.

(*oblast*). In 1963 Kosovo was granted the same level of autonomy as Vojvodina, as an "Autonomous Province" (*pokrajina*) of Serbia.[283]

At the beginning of the Cold War (1946-1989) with the Yugoslavia-Soviet Union split (Tito-Stalin), Yugoslavia was expelled from the communist bloc. In 1948 Yugoslavia broke away from the Soviet Union but maintained a communist regime. In 1989 communism collapsed in Eastern Europe and in 1992 the Federal Republic of Yugoslavia dissolved into its constituent states. Slovenia and Croatia were the first to break away (1995 Dayton Peace Agreement).[284] In 1987 Slobodan Milosevic was elected as President of Serbia, until his overthrow in 2000. Milosvic adopted an extreme Serbian nationalist agenda, which became governmental policy.[285] Milosevic pushed a brutal campaign of ethnic cleansing against ethnic Albanians to force them out of the southern province of Kosovo.[286] In 1989 Milosevic abolished Kosovo's autonomy.[287]

On September 7, 1990, Kosovo declared its first independence, and it was officially recognized only by Albania. Ibrahim Rrugova was elected the first President of Kosovo in 1992. In 1998 the Kosovo War broke out (1998-99) to oppose the oppression from the government of Yugoslavia and Serbia, resolved with NATO's military intervention. In 1999, Kosovo became a United Nations protectorate, policed by 16,000 NATO troops.[288] The same year, Milosevic was charged with war crimes by the ICTY (International Criminal Tribunal for the former Yugoslavia). President Rrugova was reelected as President again in 2002 and in 2005, by the newly formed parliament, while Kosovo was under the administration of the United Nations Mission in Kosovo (UNMIK). On February 17, 2008, Kosovo declared its second independence.

---

[283] Ibid, 4.

[284] BBC. (2006, May 22). Timeline: Break-up of Yugoslavia. Retrieved from http://news.bbc.co.uk/2/hi/europe/4997380.stm

[285] Independent International Commission on Kosovo. (2006), 11.

[286] Chicago Tribute. (1999, March 30). Milosevic increases ethnic cleansing. Retrieved from https://www.chicagotribune.com/news/ct-xpm-1999-03-30-9903300077-story.html

[287] Judah, T. (2011, February 17). Yugoslavia: 1918-2003. BBC. Retrieved from http://www.bbc.co.uk/history/worldwars/wwone/yugoslavia_01.shtml

[288] Bilefsky, D. (2008, February 18). Kosovo Declares Its Independence from Serbia. *New York Times*. Retrieved from https://www.nytimes.com/2008/02/18/world/europe/18kosovo.html

3.2 The Road to Independence

Kosovo (*Alb: Kosova*) gained independence in 2008, but it has not been recognized by some 36 states, including the United Nations (U.N.) and the Holy See.[289] Three out of the five permanent members of the U.N. Security Council (U.S.A., U.K., France) have recognized Kosovo, but China and Russia have not. Kosovo is a member of IMF (International Monetary Fund) and World Bank group, however it is not a member of United Nations. To acquire U.N. membership, Kosovo must be recognized by two-thirds of the 192 members of the organization. As of April 2020, 115 countries have officially recognized Kosovo as an independent state, out of which 15 have withdrawn (Suriname, Burundi, Lesotho, Comoros, Liberia, etc). Specifically, 97 out of the 193 (50%) are United Nations member states, 22 out of 27 (81%) are European Union member states, and 26 out of 30 (87%) are NATO member states.[290]

The Serbian response to the unilateral declaration of independence was to reject Kosovo's claims, demanding Kosovo be returned. Serbia decided to contest the legality of Kosovo's status at the International Court of Justice (ICJ). In July 2010, ICJ ruled in a 10-4 vote in favor of Kosovo's declaration of independence, announcing that Kosovo's unilateral declaration of independence from Serbia in February 2008 did not violate international law.[291]

The immediate international response to the Kosovo conflict, led by the Contact Group composed of United States, France, Germany, Italy, and Russia in 1998, was unsuccessful.[292] United Nations Security Council adopted several resolutions, imposing an arms embargo on Yugoslavia to withdraw its special police force from Kosovo.[293] After failed diplomatic efforts, NATO declared

---

[289] Senèze, N. (2018). Diocese for Kosovo. *La Croix*. Retrieved from http://www.la-croix.com/Religion/Catholicisme/Pape/diocese-Kosovo-2018-09-05-1200966477?fbclid=IwAR2lP2LiKxurh0Qlprg1BUu5r4tqgp8ZPdXgFKnAPXA-PoSLoHMyKxQGCOnY

[290] Radio Free Europe. (2008, February 18). Kosovo Celebrates A Decade Of Sovereignty. Retrieved from https://www.rferl.org/a/kosovo-marks-10-years-independence/29045295.html

[291] International Court of Justice. (2010, July 22). Accordance with international law of the unilateral declaration of independence in respect of Kosovo. *Advisory Opinion of 22 July 2010*, 1-54. retrieved from https://www.icj-cij.org/files/case-related/141/141-20100722-ADV-01-00-EN.pdf

[292] United Nations. (1998, March 11). Items relating to the situation in Kosovo, Federal Republic of Yugoslavia. Retrieved from http://www.un.org/en/sc/repertoire/96-99/Chapter%208/Europe/96_99_8_European_27F_Kosovo%20and%20Federal%20Republic%20of%20Yugoslavia.pdf

[293] United Nations. (1998, March 31). Security Council imposes arms embargo on the federal republic of Yugoslavia. Retrieved from https://www.un.org/press/en/1998/19980331.SC6496.html

its intentions to intervene militarily in Kosovo and launched an air campaign in 1999 against the Yugoslav army (VJ) and the Special Police Forces (MUP).[294]

The United Nations mission (UNMIK) established in June 1999 by Security Council Resolution 1244, promulgated a constitutional framework for Kosovo and in 2001 established the Provisional Institutions of Self-Government (PISG).[295] However, UNSC 1244 did not settle Kosovo's disputed status. After the declaration of independence UNMIK handed over responsibility to an E.U. led mission, EULEX (the European Union Rule of Law Mission in Kosovo). In December 2008, EULEX assumed most of UNMIK's responsibilities in the areas of rule of law. The Council extended the mandate of the European Union rule of law mission in Kosovo until June 14, 2020 to assist the government in becoming stable and democratic.[296]

Unlike the U.N. led mission (UNMIK), the aim of the E.U. mission (EULEX) is not to govern or rule the political institutions, rather assist Kosovo's authorities in their progress towards sustainability and accountability.[297] This allows for the EU to have an advising and mentoring role, while the local Kosovo leaders are in charge of setting the agenda and implementing the policies. However, Kosovo leaders must comply with the internationally recognized standards as set out in the "Kosovo's Standards Implementation Plan" (KSIP) designed by the U.N. in 2002/03.[298]

The standards for Kosovo prioritize economy as one of the eight goals established by the Kosovo Institutions. If Kosovo fulfills all eight conditions set by the United Nations, then the benefit is stability and development in the country as well as membership at the European Union. By joining the E.U. Kosovo can have a positive sum gain and easily attain its economic goals by cooperating with other E.U. members. There is an incentive for Kosovo to keep its end of the bargain and meet the UN standards, because the payoff (European integration) would give Kosovo a good reputation and legitimacy as a sovereign state. In addition, it would create an environment where Kosovo's leadership can pursue their national interests and domestic affairs at the global level via international organizations such as the European Union and the United Nations.

[294] NATO. (2018). NATO's role in relation to the conflict in Kosovo. Retrieved from https://www.nato.int/kosovo/history.htm

[295] Resolution 1244. (1999, June 10). *United Nations Security Council.* S/RES/1244 (1999). Retrieved from https://documents-dds-ny.un.org/doc/UNDOC/GEN/N99/172/89/PDF/N9917289.pdf?OpenElement

[296] European Union. (2008, June 11). Council Decision on amending Joint Action on the European Union Rule of Law Mission in Kosovo. *Official Journal of the European Union*, L 146/5. Retrieved from https://www.eulex-kosovo.eu/eul/repository/docs/CouncilDecision-203336.pdf

[297] European Rule of Law Mission. (2018). EULEX Kosovo, ¶ 2. http://www.eulex-kosovo.eu/

[298] United Nations Interim Administration Mission in Kosovo. (2003). Standards for Kosovo. Retrieved from http://www.unmikonline.org

According to the IMF report since the establishment of Standards for Kosovo, Kosovo's economy has been independent from Federal Republic (FR) of Yugoslavia and its economic policy has been an experiment "in economic institution-building from the ground up."[299] IMF has played a crucial role by providing advice on macroeconomic policy to UNMIK. The Fund and the World Bank have been the driving force for donors and foreign investments in Kosovo.

At the request of UNMIK, IMF has assisted in economic policy implementation and has been successful in establishing the economic institutions. For instance, because of the joined efforts of UNMIK, IMF and the World Bank, the Banking and Payment Authority of Kosovo (BPK) has been established as the central banking and financing institution. Kosovo leaders and U.N. representation have appealed to private enterprises, commercial banks, insurance companies and other donors to ensure prospects for Kosovo. The economic policy has focused on making the economic institutions accountable, setting up tax systems, budgetary and treasury institutions and is working towards a modern payment system.[300] According to the IMF report, these new economic policies have substantially reduced illegal practices, extortions and criminality.

In addition to economic and political development, multi-ethnic movement in education has been given a priority in Kosovo. In efforts to aid reconstruction of higher education in Kosovo the British Department of Education and Employment (DfEE) funded the University of Prishtina in Kosovo, transforming it into a multi-ethnic institution with multi-language teachings in Albanian and Serbo-Croat.[301] The British Council funded projects that increased the number of departments at the university, including Political Science, Public Administration, Media, Sociology and Journalism. These departments were being developed for the first time and some underwent fundamental reform after ten years of isolation during Serbian rule.

However due to the low level of economic development in Kosovo many of the graduate students do not find employment after graduation. Bache and Taylor (2003) believe that the high level of public discontent is due to the high graduate unemployment numbers.[302] Many are forced to pursue employment or further education opportunities in Western Europe, especially Austria and Germany.[303] During the Serbianization strategy of Milosevic regime, ethnic Albanian students were not allowed to study in their mother tongue, Albanian, and demonstrations were suppressed

[299] Demekas, D.G., Herderschee, J., & Jacobs, D. (2001). Progress in Institution-Building and the Economic Policy Challenges ahead. *IMF Report*,1-35. Retrieved from https://www.imf.org/external/np/eu1/kosovo/2001/eng/120601.pdf

[300] Ibid, 11.

[301] Ian, B., & Taylor, A. (2003). The Politics of Policy Resistance. Reconstructing Higher Education in Kosovo. *Journal of Public Policy*, 23(3), 280.

[302] Ibid, 286.

[303] Ibid, 287.

resulting in students being expelled or arrested. Today, the DfEE found the Prishtina University students to be very vocal in political issues and participated in peaceful demonstrations without being dismissed from their academic studies. The Kosovo parliament rejected the Serbianization (Serbian only institutes) and today allows multi-ethnic access to education.

In terms of political institutions, the Kosovo government is composed of the *executive branch* (the government "Qeveria") led by the Prime Minister (currently Ramush Haradinaj since 2017); and the *legislative branch* (the parliament "Kuvendi"). The Kosovo Assembly is comprised of 120 members, who serve a four-year term. The judiciary is independent of the executive and the legislative powers. The Supreme Court is the highest judicial authority, where 15 percent of the judges represent minority groups.[304] After the 1998-99 war, UNMIK established emergency judiciary with local judges and prosecutors, that inherited the previous system used under the Milsevic regime.[305] After the independence, the Ahtisaari packet was key to the state-building process and to the legal reforms in Kosovo's justice system, but the local institutions lacked a comprehensive strategy to establish new mechanisms and procedures.[306]

European Union officials have expressed concerns of political interference in the judiciary.[307] The U.S. State Department favors a domestic shift in the Kosovo judiciary that is fully independent and protected by due process.[308] Although Kosovo authorities respect court orders and the constitution provides for an independent judiciary, the challenge is that "the judiciary at times exhibited bias, was subject to external and political influences, and did not always provide due process."[309] Due to international pressure, there has been a big push to build the capacities of the Kosovo judiciary, independent of political influences.

Bringing justice and human rights were top priority for the U.N. In 2000, UNMIK established the Ombudsperson Institution in Kosovo (OIK) to investigate claims of human rights violations.[310] OIK legal advisors issue special reports with recommendations addressed to Kosovo Assembly

[304] Republic of Kosovo. (2018). Justice System. Retrieved from https://www.rks-gov.net/EN/f45/judiciary/justice-system

[305] Gashi, A., & Musliu, B. (2013). Justice System Reform in Kosovo. *Kosovo Law Institute,* 1-37. Retrieved from https://kli-ks.org/wp-content/uploads/2015/05/Justice-reform-in-Kosovo-RAPORTI-FINAL-ANGLISHT.pdf

[306] Ibid, 4.

[307] OSCE. (2012, January). Independence of the Judiciary in Kosovo: Institutional and Functional Dimensions, 1-29. Retrieved from https://www.osce.org/kosovo/87138?download=true

[308] US Department of State. (2018, April). Kosovo Report. *Bureau of Democracy, Human Rights and Labor,* 1-35. Retrieved from https://www.state.gov/j/drl/rls/hrrpt/2017/eur/277181.htm

[309] United States Department of State. (2013). Kosovo 2013 Human Rights Report. Country Report for Human Rights Practices for 2013. *Bureau of Democracy, Human Rights and Labor, Washington DC,* 10.

[310] See Republic of Kosovo Ombudsperson (2018). The Mission of Ombudsperson Institution. Retrieved from https://oik-rks.org/

"aiming to harmonize the human rights practice with the local and international human rights standards."[311] Specifically, to better improve human rights practices in Kosovo in accordance with the international human rights norms, the Ombudsperson has established three special groups: Children's Rights Team (CRT), Gender Equality Unit (GEU) and the Anti-Discrimination Team (ADT).

Kosovo has been successful in incorporating the multi-ethnic standards and rights of minorities to its local policies, as a condition set by the European Union and the United Nations. The decentralization agenda intents to establish a sustainable government at the local level. However, corruption is still a major issue and poses a challenge to development.[312] There is lack of public trust on the part of the locals regarding government institutions, since Kosovo is not quite 'independent' yet. Kosovo has to undergo the scrutiny of the international community, to make sure that it is following the standards set by the United Nations. This conditionality limits the role of the local political institutions to an extent, since they have to comply with external forces.

In terms of security, Kosovo is still guarded and protected by NATO with 4,000 troops deployed (KFOR). The initial Kosovo Police Service (KSF), was international police called UNMIK police, established by the U.N. Security Council Resolution 1244. OSCE mission in Kosovo took responsibility for training and opening the police school.[313] After the 2008 independence the police force became an agency of the government. The present NATO trained KSF of 2,500, is a lightly-armed and multi-ethnic force, with "no heavy weapons, such as tanks, heavy artillery or offensive air capability."[314] In October 2018, the Kosovo parliament voted on an upgraded mandate to transform the Kosovo Security Force to a 5,000-strong national army.[315]

3.3 Kosovo a Success Story

Kosovo has been successful in the initial *institution-building* phase, with the assistance of the United Nations and the European Union, in building from "ground zero" entirely new institutions.[316]

---

[311] Ibid.

[312] Maliqi, R. (2016, June). Corruption, the Challenge for Kosovo Institutions. *European Journal of Multidisciplinary Studies*, 1(2), 204-209.

[313] Kosovo Police. (2018). History. Retrieved from http://www.kosovopolice.com/en/history

[314] NATO. (2009, April 9). NATO's role in Kosovo. Retrieved from https://www.nato.int/summit2009/topics_en/04-kosovo.html

[315] President of the Republic of Kosovo. (2018). The KSF a professional force ready for every challenge. Retrieved from https://www.president-ksgov.net/en/news/president-thaci-the-ksf-a-professional-force-ready-for-every-challenge

[316] Devenport, M. (1999, July 1). Analysis: UN Faces Kosovo Challenge. *Global Policy Forum*. Retrieved from: https://www.globalpolicy.org/component/content/article/192-kosovo/38785.html

Other major milestones with respect to Kosovo include: (1) the establishment of the *constitution* and (2) *free press*, (3) membership in *international organizations*, (4) recognition of *independence* by 115 countries as of April 2020 (97 out of 193 United Nations member states),[317] (5) *institutional reform*, with U.N. Support to the Security Sector, and the UNDP establishment of core justice capacities, (6) *free and fair elections* with peaceful transitions, (7) improving the rule of law system by reducing the backlog in Kosovo's basic courts, and by introducing mediation within courts, (8) *integration of Serb* judicial authorities into Kosovo's government, (9) the operation of the *judiciary* in the entire country,[318] and (10) rebuilding the *police*[319] with the help of the international community, by developing "an indigenous Kosovo police service that could maintain the rule of law in the long term."[320]

Kosovo is a success story considering the successful intervention of NATO and the creation of the state from scratch.[321] Kosovo's *diplomatic success* is attributed to the combined efforts undertaken by Kosovo's own diplomatic efforts with the support from its international partners, namely: United Sates, United Kingdom, Germany, European Union and the United Nations.[322] Successful public diplomacy and lobbying by Kosovo's Ministry of Foreign Affairs and the Ministry of Diaspora have increased domestics interests and support for initiatives abroad.[323] Kosovo has

---

[317] Pajaziti, M. (2018, February 14). Kosovo's achievements and challenges on the 10th anniversary of independence. *Balkan EU*. Retrieved from: https://balkaneu.com/kosovos-achievements-and-challenges-on-the-10th-anniversary-of-independence/

[318] USAID. (2018, February 12). Kosovo: Rule of Law and governance. Retrieved from: https://www.usaid.gov/kosovo/democracy-and-governance

[319] Bernard Kouchner, who served as the second UN Special Representative and Head of the United Nations Interim Administration Mission in Kosovo (UNMIK), assigned NATO during the transition period post-war Kosovo in 1999, with the task of creating a Kosovo Protection Corps (KPC), consisting of 5,000 active and reserve personnel recruited from the demobilized military. KPC was established as a civilian emergency service agency, headed by General Agim Ceku, former Chief of Staff of the Kosovo Liberation Army, as Commander of the Kosovo Protection Corps. For further information see the UN Interim Administration Mission in Kosovo available at http://unmik.unmissions.org.

[320] Green, M., Friedman, J., & Bennet, R. (2012, July 18). Rebuilding the Police in Kosovo. *Foreign Policy*. Princeton University, p. 1. Retrieved from: http://foreignpolicy.com/2012/07/18/rebuilding-the-police-in-kosovo/

[321] The Independent, UK. (2018, February 17). Leading article: Kosovo: a triumph for intervention https://www.independent.co.uk/voices/editorials/leading-article-kosovo-a-triumph-for-intervention-783279.html

[322] Visoka, G. (2018, February 16). Becoming Kosovo: Independence, legitimacy, Future. https://kosovotwopointzero.com/en/becoming-kosovo-independence-legitimacy-future/

[323] Ministry of Foreign Affairs. (2018). Kosovo's New Foreign Policy Roadmap. http://www.mfa-ks.net/?page=2,209,2540

lobbied for American support and has mobilized the Albanian diaspora in United States for its independence and international support.[324]

The work of the Consulate General of Kosovo in New York has been integral to diplomatic and consular relations for the Albanians in United States and abroad. The New York Consulate has been a vital part of international relations, promoting economic prosperity and building cultural partnerships in U.S. and around the world. In an interview with Ambassador Teuta Sahatqija, General Consul of the Republic of Kosovo in New York, the ambassador pointed out the effective engagement of public diplomacy and the successful transformation of Kosovo.

> "Kosovo is not only building a country, it is building a society as well, that promotes respect and harmony of communities and religions. Recently, Kosovo achieved very good results in economy. Our budget raised 15%, GDP reached 4%, MCC confirmed Kosovo as the one of the 4 best reformers in economy. The World Bank's last report showed significant performance of the index of Doing Business in Kosovo, taking 40th place in the world. Through IPA Funds, EU pledged to invest 635 million in 3 years through different programs. Agriculture, IT and mining are becoming our strong economic leverage.
>
> In 2015 Kosovo signed the Stabilization and Association Agreement with the European Union that opened the door of 400 million consumers of EU market for our companies, preparing Kosovo for further steps toward the EU Integration. We proudly can say that Kosovo is the success story of transforming itself from the war torn, burned land to developing country with growing economy, becoming a provider of the stability and security to the region."[325]

Kosovo is a leading example of state-building success despite its many challenges. United Nations Security Council Resolution 1244 of 10 June 1999 established a transitional government in Kosovo (UNMIK)[326] under international U.N. supervision and NATO presence.[327] However, UNSC 1244 (1999) did not set any time limit for the creation of the "provisional democratic

---

[324] Krasniqi, G. (2016). Rising up in the world: Kosovo's quest for international recognition. *Prishtina Insight*.

[325] Sahatqija, Teuta. (2018, December). In Person Interview.

[326] United Nations. (1999). UNMIK background. United Nations Interim Administration Mission in Kosovo. http://www.un.org/en/peacekeeping/missions/unmik/background.shtml

[327] United Nations Security Council, *UN Resolution 1244 (1999)*. June 10, 1999, S/RES/1244, Security Council official minutes of its 4011th meeting in New York, issued by United Nations. Retrieved from http://www.un.org/ga/search/view_doc.asp?symbol=S/RES/1244(1999)

self-government institutions" in its mandate.[328] Thus, during nearly one decade of U.N. international administration, Kosovo experienced eight years of political vacuum. The frustration of a failed international diplomacy led to Kosovo's unilateral declaration of independence from Serbia in February 2008, adopting the framework of the Ahtisaari Plan.[329]

Within four years since the independence declaration, the international community ended the "supervised independence" on September 10, 2012.[330] German Foreign Minister Guido Westerwelle marked the end of supervised independence as "a step and success for international efforts," and stated that "Kosovo met significant democratic commitments and made progress in the protection of minorities."[331] U.S. President Donald Trump congratulated Kosovo on the significant progress it made over the past 10 years, "in strengthening its sovereignty and multiethnic democracy."[332]

The need for development and the integration has steered Kosovo in an interesting direction, prioritizing policy that *supports local women and gender* balances.[333] The role of gender has been crucial in both economic development, peace, and security issues. For instance, in the case of Kosovo, after a long period of eight years of unfruitful negotiations between the world leaders of the United Nations, and the leaders of the two conflict parties, Kosovo and Serbia, progress was made when local women from both ethnic groups took the initiative and organized the Women's Conference for Peaceful Resolution in 2007. Given that the Albanians and Serbs have a long history of violence and conflict, this animosity was reflected in the leaders' positions regarding the final solutions of the status.

In Kosovo, the role of women proved to be useful by trying to bridge the cultural gaps between the two Albanian and Serb communities and pushed for human rights protection and development. This was highly successful because the conference got the attention of the international

---

[328] The UN peace mission in Kosovo (UNMIK), followed by the EU-led operation is the biggest, longest and the most expensive mission ever.

[329] Full text of the Ahtisaari Plan http://www.unosek.org/docref/Comprehensive_proposal-english.pdf

[330] Supervised independence gave official governing duties to the international representatives in Kosovo alongside Albanian local authorities. Since 2008, Kosovo was overseen by the International Steering Group (ISG), established by US and 23 EU countries. The Group includes Austria, Belgium, Britain, Bulgaria, Croatia, the Czech Republic, Denmark, Estonia, Finland, France, Germany, Hungary, Ireland, Italy, Latvia, Lithuania, Luxembourg, the Netherlands, Norway, Poland, Sweden, Switzerland, Slovenia, Turkey and U.S.

[331] Deutsche Welle. (2012, September 12). International Steering Group passes sovereignty to Kosovo. http://www.dw.de/international-steering-group-passes-sovereignty-to-kosovo/a-16230752-1

[332] President of the Republic of Kosovo. (2018). President Thaçi received a letter of congratulations from the US President, Donald Trump. Retrieved from https://www.president-ksgov.net/en/news/president-thaci-received-a-letter-of-congratulations-from-the-us-president-donald-trump

[333] Corrin, C. (2003). Developing Policy on Integration and Reconstruction In Kosovo. *Development in Practice*, 13(2), 189-207. doi: 10.1080/09614520302946

community members, who supported the women's movement in Kosovo and pledged financial support to rebuild the country and ensure the protection of all ethnic groups in the region.

> "It is very important to realize that institutions, municipalities, government, parliament are all products of political parties. And we cannot change the representation of women and women's role inside institutions if we do not work inside the political parties. That's why the Women's Caucus started a campaign *inside* parliament. The beauty of this is that women of different parties, different ethnicities, and different religions have worked together."[334]

Although Kosovo's *judicial system* is at an early stage, progress has been made in implementing the 2015 justice package laws.[335] The integration of Kosovan Serb judges and prosecutors in the Kosovan judicial system was a big achievement in 2017.[336] Another area of progress includes fight against corruption, especially the investigation and prosecution of high-level corruption and organized crime.

> "The situation in Kosovo prior to independence, had a great need for international support, in order to beef up its security, guarantee its territorial sovereignty and save the lives of Albanians living within its territory. Immediately after acquiring the independence, the Republic of Kosovo, has shown and undoubtedly introduced a new level of stability in the Balkans. Kosovo's Independence has brought stability, brings its people closer to the European Union and NATO Integration. Prishtina's politicians are more responsible and strive to eradicate corruption, poverty and to improve relations with Serbia and other countries in the region."[337]

Kosovo continues to remain engaged in the *dialogue with Serbia*, in efforts to normalize relations. In May 2016, the European Commission proposed visa liberalization for Kosovo citizens, due to the fulfillment of two required benchmarks, migration and security.[338] The first benchmark

---

[334] Sahatqija, T. (2014, October 2). Beyond "soft" issues: The Women's Caucus of Kosovo speaks up. *Chicago Policy Review*. Retrieved from http://chicagopolicyreview.org/2014/10/02/beyond-soft-issues-the-womens-caucus-of-kosovo-speaks-up/

[335] European Commission. (2018, April 17). Key findings of the 2018 Report on Kosovo. Brussels, 1-3. Retrieved from europa.eu/rapid/press-release_MEMO-18-3404_en.pdf

[336] Ibid, 1.

[337] Avdyli, Brahim. (2015, January 14). Personal Communication. Interview.

[338] European Commission. (2018, July 18). Visa Liberalization: Commission confirms Kosovo fulfils all required benchmarks europa.eu/rapid/press-release_IP-18-4562_en.htm

was met on March 21, 2018 when the Kosovo Assembly ratified the border demarcation agreement with Montenegro with an affirmative vote by 80 representatives. The second benchmark met was Kosovo's track record in the fight against crime and corruption, monitored by the E.U. technical mission in Kosovo for the past 2 years.[339] The Kosovo government continues its efforts to improve its rule of law system and the performance of the justice sector.

3.4 Rule of Law

It has been twenty-one years since NATO intervened to save ethnic Albanians from the brutal Serbian ethnic cleansing campaign. Today, Kosovo faces the new reality of statehood and independence recognition. NATO (KFOR), the U.N. (UNMIK) and the E.U. (EULEX) have been the primary missions to provide governance, institution building, security, and rule of law in the country. Kosovo is a unique case of international administration, where international institutions have executive and administrative power, in other words acting as legitimate state structures with certain powers. An example is the Kosovo Specialist Chambers (KSC) and Specialist Prosecutor's Office (SPO), which are part of the judicial system in Kosovo, adopted by the Kosovo Assembly, with a seat in The Hague.[340] Commonly referred to as the *Kosovo Specialist Court*," the KSC is independent, constituted through Kosovan legislations, and is financed by the E.U.[341]

The commitment to rule of law was embedded in the institutional framework created by the U.N. and E.U. In 2001 UNMIK created Pillar I "Police and Justice" during the institutional transformation phase to unify three components of the judicial system, police, justice, and prisons under one umbrella.[342] Under the 15 May 2001 Constitutional Framework most government functions were transferred to the provisional institutional of Kosovo, however the justice and police sector were administered by the international community under Pillar I. UNMIK, KFOR and OSCE collaborated to enhance law enforcement and the development of the local police force, but "the division of responsibility was not always clear and coordinated."[343]

During the institution building phase UNMIK's leadership created a joint Kosovo-International Administration, employed international judicial personnel, and rejected the creation of Kosovo

[339] European Commission Report. (2018, July 18). Update on the implementation of the remaining benchmarks of the visa liberalization roadmap by Kosovo. Brussels, 18.7.2018 COM (2018), 543, 1-12. https://ec.europa.eu/home-affairs/sites/homeaffairs/files/what-we-do/policies/european-agenda-migration/20180718_com-2018-543-report_en.pdf

[340] The Kosovo Specialist Court consists of two institutions: KSC and SPO. See Kosovo Specialist Chambers & Specialist Prosecutor's Office. (2018). Background. Retrieved from https://www.scp-ks.org/en/documents

[341] Ibid.

[342] Call, C. (2007). *Constructing Justice and Security After War*. Washington DC: United States Institute of Peace, 284.

[343] Ibid., 284.

War Crimes and Ethnic Crimes Court.[344] By year 2000 the Judicial system under the United Nations consisted of the Supreme Court, district courts (5), municipal courts (22), the commercial court, the High Court for Minor Offences, minor offenses courts (22) and offices of the Public Prosecutor (13).[345]

In 2008, the European Union Rule of Law Mission (EULEX) was deployed in Kosovo under the framework of U.N. Resolution 1244 to improve the standards of two pillars: police and justice.[346] It is considered "the largest civilian mission under the Common Security and Defense Policy of the European Union."[347] The mission's primary focus is to strengthen three areas of rule of law: judiciary, police and customs. EULEX exercises some executive power in the justice component and prioritizes institutional reform and transformation in rule of law.[348] The European Union has been reluctant to give Kosovo officials full ownership and has promoted "learning by doing" tactic using the MMA (Monitor, Mentor and Advise) approach.[349] The applicability of the law has been a major issue as there are UNMIK regulations still in place.[350] Furthermore, EULEX "has failed in establishing a functioning judicial system in the north," where judges make decisions based on two different laws: the Serbian judges follow Serbian law, while the Kosovan judges follow Albanian laws.[351]

In 2012 the police, justice and customs were restructured into executive departments.[352] The EULEX judges and prosecutors retained executive responsibility focusing on cases of war crimes, organized crimes and high level of corruption.[353] The Law on Courts that entered into force on January 1, 2013 introduced a new court structure with three tiers: the Basic Courts (7 first instance basic courts organized by territory), the Court of Appeals (second instance court, in Prishtina)

---

[344] Baskin, M. (2001, June 5). Lessons Learned on UNMIK Judiciary. *Pearson Peacekeeping Center,* 2. Retrieved from http://siteresources.worldbank.org/INTLAWJUSTINST/Resources/lessonsKosovoJudiciary.pdf

[345] Ibid., 2.

[346] EULEX. (2018). About EULEX: Mission and Mandate. Retrieved from https://www.eulex-kosovo.eu/?page=2,60

[347] Ibid., 1.

[348] Keukeleire, S. Kalaja, A., & Çollaku, A. (2011, February). The EU and Kosovo: Structural Diplomacy in Action, but on the basis of one-sided paradigm? *The Center for the Study of International Governance,* 4.

[349] See EULEX. (2018). EULEX's two objectives: 1. Monitoring, Mentoring, Advising (MMA) 2. Executive Function. Retrieved from http://www.eulex-kosovo.eu/?page=2,44

[350] Betts, W. S., Carlson, S. N., & Grisvold, Gregory. (2001). The Post-Conflict Transitional Administration of Kosovo and the Lessons-Learned in Efforts to Establish a Judiciary and Rule of Law. *Michigan Journal of International Law,* 22(3), 1-20. Retrieved from http://repository.law.umich.edu/mjil/vol22/iss3/1

[351] Cierco, T., & Reis, L. (2014). EULEX's Impact on the Rule of Law in Kosovo. *Revista De Ciencia Politica,* 34(3), 657.

[352] Ibid., 656.

[353] European Union Mission in Kosovo. (2018). Executive Division. Retrieved from http://www.eulex-kosovo.eu/?page=2,2

and the Supreme Court (in Prishtina).[354] EULEX's mandate has been extended until June 2020. Under the new mandate "EULEX judges and prosecutors are embedded in Kosovan institutions" with mixed panels, until the transition is made for all the rule of law institutions to be headed by Kosovan officials.[355] Kosovo has made efforts to harmonize its national legislation with the EU *Acquis* to meet the required standards in becoming a European Union member. Kosovo's Constitution has incorporated international rule of law obligations; however, the challenge has been implementation of the new laws.[356]

According to Rule of Law Index, maintaining order and security is one of the defining aspects of rule of law.[357] Specifically, the fight against organized crime is a required norm for political leaders, law enforcement and judicial authorities, as part of the of the feasibility study for EU enlargement package.[358] An increased level of crime in the country would prevent public officials from achieving their goal of strengthening rule of law. In the case of Kosovo, public officials have worked in partnership with EULEX to fight three important factors of order and security: organized crime, narcotics, and terrorism. The Compact of Joint rule of law was signed in November 2012 between Kosovo, EULEX and the European Union of Special Representative (EUSR) to help Kosovo align its legislation with the *Acquis*. The E.U. acquis is "the body of common rights and obligations that are binding on all EU countries, as EU Members," giving the European Union primacy over national law.[359]

In an interview with Judge Bekim Sejdiu, Judge of the Constitutional Court of Kosovo and former Consul General of the Republic of Kosovo in New York, he stated that the new justice system in Kosovo has been brought in line with the E.U Acquis and international standards.[360]

"With the ending of the war in Kosovo and deployment of international administration, a new legal system was erected from scratch. This huge enterprise involved two fundamental dimensions: First, creation of the new legal order through

---

[354] Assembly of Republic of Kosovo. (2010). On Courts. Law No. 03/L-199, *Republic of Kosovo*. Retrieved from http://www.assembly-kosova.org/common/docs/ligjet/2010-199-eng.pdf

[355] European Commission, *Kosovo Progress Report*, (2014), 5.

[356] Justice and the People. (2013,30 October). *Delivering Justice*, Expert Roundtable Report, Prishtina.

[357] Rule of Law Index is launched by World Justice Project (WJP) and audited by European Commission Joint Research Center (JRC). See European Commission Joint Research Center https://ec.europa.eu/jrc/en/news/jrc-assesses-rule-law-index and World Justice Project http://worldjusticeproject.org/rule-of-law-index

[358] European Commission. (2013), 13.

[359] European Parliament, Council of the European Union. (2009, July 7). Regulation (EC) No 662/2009 of the European Parliament and of the Council. Retrieved from https://eur-lex.europa.eu/legal-content/EN/TXT/?qid=1548891307441&uri=CELEX:32009R0662

[360] See Appendix 3 for the full interview.

adopting of new legal acts. Second, establishment of the new justice system, which entails organization of the court system, public prosecutorial system, correction service, etc.

From 1999/2000, when the UNMIK was deployed, and up to 2008 when Kosovo became an independent country, the entirely new legal system was established. This, in itself, is a remarkable success of the joint efforts of the Kosovar institutions and the international missions (EU, UN, NATO). Furthermore, the legal order created in Kosovo has been shaped within the normative framework of the EU standards. In other words, the Constitution and the laws adopted in Kosovo, particularly after the independence in 2008, reflect the legal standards generated from the EU acquis communautaire as well as the highest international standards on human rights and protection of ethnic minorities."[361]

The international community, particularly the missions of the United Nations and the European Union, have been instrumental in setting out the constitutional framework of Kosovo's judiciary in accordance with the international standards. The European standards are in the framework of the European Union's Stabilization and Association Process. Based inter alia on the Copenhagen criteria, these standards "describe a multi-ethnic society where there is democracy, tolerance, freedom of movement and equal access to justice for all people in Kosovo, regardless of their ethnic background."[362]

Although the role of the international organizations in Kosovo has been viewed positively as institution-building, they haven't escaped criticism and conflict.[363] Specifically, the lack of a coherent and consistent legal system in Kosovo has been a result of the United Nation's poor decision to use different legal frameworks: one legislation deriving from the Yugoslavian, and the UNMIK rule of law pillars.[364] Adding to this confusion is the ambiguity of what legal concepts apply. Despite the legal system in Kosovo undergoing numerous reforms under EULEX, there is still lack of a uniform system. This poses a challenge for Kosovo in harmonizing its legislation with

---

[361] Sejdiu, Bekim. (2018, November 28). Personal Communicating. Interview.

[362] Security Council Report. (2003, December 10). Standards for Kosovo, 1-16.

[363] Scorgie, L. (2003). Kosovo and the International Community: The Prolonging and Exacerbation of a Crisis. A worldwide journal of politics, 1-40. Retrieved from http://citeseerx.ist.psu.edu/viewdoc/download?-doi=10.1.1.581.3608&rep=rep1&type=pdf

[364] National Council for European Integration. (2015). National Strategy for European Integration: Kosovo 2020, 1-64. Retrieved from http://www.kryeministri-ks.net/repository/docs/National_Strategy_for_European_Integration_Kosovo_2020_ENG.PDF

the E.U. Acquis. UNMIK's failure to change the political culture in Kosovo has contributed to the decline in public opinion, "reflected in the Kosovar population's increasing level of dissatisfaction with UNMIK's performance."[365]

The IMF report that polled public perceptions regarding the effectives of UNMIK and EULEX showed that Kosovars favored a more voluntary policy driven mission such as EULEX, rather than a coercive type such as UNMIK.[366] Since UNMIK's tasks started from the ground in establishing the institutions it had a more direct and managing role. On the other hand, EULEX referred the leadership to the Kosovo institutions and maintained an advisory role. During EULEX mission, Kosovan policymakers are free to adopt policy and practices, which the local citizens are holding them accountable for (no longer UNMIK) the poor performance in bringing promised economic growth.

During UNMIK, Kosovan leadership was not the policy-making body, rather the U.N. All policy formation and implantation during UNMIK required approval of the external forces (in this case the U.N./International community) with little governing function in the hands of the Kosovar politicians. This constrained the possibility of effective policy implementation given that the locals did not trust the external actors.

According to Lemay-Hébert (2009) the degree of trust between the international presence in Kosovo and the local citizens is related to the lack of accountability to assure success of the international administration.[367] He argues that on the broader social dimension, the legitimacy aspect of state-building has been overlooked in Kosovo, focusing on the institutional aspects instead.

"The social dimension of state-building is a crucial aspect to take into account in any state-building attempt. Lacking the social bond necessary to instill a relationship of trust between a given government and its citizens, international rule is almost certain to be resented by the local population and to be seen as a blow to their dignity.

The political response, namely direct governance, seems unfit to correctly address the social challenges of postwar state-building. Hence, the idea of "neo-trusteeship" of war-torn territories, at least in their contemporary form in Kosovo, seems hardly compatible with the objective of fostering and nurturing legitimacy in

---

[365] Lemay-Hébert, N. (2009). State-building from the outside-in: UNMIK and its paradox. *JPIA*, 66. Retrieved from https://jpia.princeton.edu/sites/jpia/files/2009-4.pdf
[366] IMF Report. (2001). Progress in Institution-Building and the Economic Policy Challenges Ahead. Prepared by Dimitri G. Demekas and Johannes Herderschee (EUI) and Davina Jacobs (FAD).
[367] Lemay-Hébert, N. (2009), 75.

an externally-led state-building project. Cultural sensitivity, along with robust accountability mechanisms and a greater local ownership of the process can help the mission garner a certain degree of legitimacy."[368]

3.5 Kosovo Specialist Court

Pressures from the European Union and standards for E.U. membership have forced post-communist Eastern European states to adopt human rights standards, evident in the Kosovo case as well.[369] Kosovo is part of the Stabilization and Association Process (SAP), which is the E.U.'s policy framework for Kosovo towards European integration.[370] SAP outlines human rights as one of the requirements of the standards for Kosovo.[371] Kosovan and E.U. leaders meet on a regular basis to assess Kosovo's development with regard to fulfilling E.U. partnership requirements. OSCE has created two institutions to handle human rights and rule of law: the Kosovo Judicial Institute (Academy of Justice)[372] and the Ombudsperson's Office. Both institutions have full local ownership and investigate claims of human rights abuses or violations by officials. Another institution came into force in July 2018 and was given jurisdiction over crimes against humanity and war crimes – the *Kosovo Specialist Court* (KSC), consisting of two distinct institutions: the Specialist Chambers (SC) and the Specialist Prosecutor's Office (SPO).

The European Union along with the Kosovo government established the Kosovo Specialist Chambers and the Specialist Prosecutor's Office to investigate war crimes in Kosovo. The request came from Brussels in 2014, when the European Union was seeking to extend the mandate of EULEX mission and to continue investigating serious and politically sensitive crimes.[373]

---

[368] Ibid, 79.

[369] Samuels, K. (2005). Sustainability and Peace Building: A Key Challenge. *Development in Practice,* 15(6), 734. Retrieved from https://doi.org/10.1080/09614520500296278

[370] European Union Office in Kosovo. (2017, July 3). Stabilization and Association Agreement between EU and Kosovo. Retrieved from https://eeas.europa.eu/delegations/kosovo/29175/stabilisation-and-association-agreement-between-eu-and-kosovo_en

[371] United Nations Interim Administration Mission in Kosovo. (2003). Standards for Kosovo. Retrieved from http://www.unmikonline.org

[372] In 2017 it transformed to the "Academy of Justice". See Academy of Justice. (2017). Kosovo Judicial Institute has been transformed into Academy of Justice. Retrieved from https://ad.rks-gov.net

[373] Human Rights Watch. (2014, April 11). Kosovo: Approve Special Court for Serious Abuses. Retrieved from http://www.hrw.org/news/2014/04/11/kosovo-approve-special-court-serious-abuses

3.5.1 A rocky start: Opposition for the creation of the Special Court

After persistent international pressure for creation of the Specialist Court, the new court was set to try wartime abuses and crimes against humanity.[374] This came as a shock for the public opinion, as Kosovo Albanians expected Serbia to answer for the war crimes committed during the genocide of ethnic Albanians that claimed over 11,000 lives, 4,000 declared missing,[375] and 1,650 still missing today 22 years after the war.[376] The international community warned that if Kosovo did not establish such special court then the United Nations Security Council would create one, leaving the Kosovar leadership with no option but to conform to international pressure.[377]

Kosovo's Prime Minister at the time, Isa Mustafa stated that "it is not easy for the government to take such decisions," and urged the members of the parliament to vote in order to "fulfill this international obligation."[378] Visar Ymeri of the opposition party (VV) spoke against the creation of the special tribunal saying it would undermine the state of Kosovo and there are many uncertainties about "who and how the court will be created, who will nominate the judges, who will finance it and to who will this court be accountable to."[379]

The legal framework that would allow for the creation of the special court was put on hold due to the six months of political deadlock following the June 2014 elections. Kosovo was unable to form a new government until December 2014 when Isa Mustafa, leader of the centre-right Democratic League of Kosovo (LDK) made a coalition agreement with Hashim Thaçi,[380] former Prime Minister and leader of the Democratic Party of Kosovo (LKD).[381] The European Union was constrained by the legitimacy of the domestic institutions. The domestic political structures lacked capability to form the institutions needed in passing the new law at Kosovo's National Assembly.

[374] Visoka, G. (2017, September). Assessing the potential impact of the Kosovo Specialist Court. *PAX*, 1-48. Retrieved from https://www.impunitywatch.org/docs/IW_PAX_REPORT_Specialist_Court_ENG.pdf

[375] Gazeta Express. (2015, April 16). The 16th Anniversary of Kosovo Albanians Exodus. Retrieved from http://www.gazetaexpress.com/en/news/today-marks-the-16th-anniversary-of-kosovo-albanians-exodus-94440.

[376] Saracini, K. (2015, April 21). Kosovë, aktivitete në kuadër të "Javës për Personat e Zhdukur." *Agjencia Telegrafike Shqiptare*. Retrieved from http://www.ata.gov.al/kosove-perkujtohet-java-per-personat-e-pagjetur-253208.html

[377] Bota Sot. (2015, March 3). Hapet rruga nga Qeveria për themelimin e Gjykatës Speciale. VV-ja, kjo Gjykatë është mbi shtetin e Kosovës. Retrieved from http://botasot.info/kosova/379293/hapet-rruga-nga-qeveria-per-themelimin-e-gjykates-speciale-vv-ja-kjo-gjykate-eshte-mbi-shtetin-e-kosoves

[378] Ibid.

[379] Gazeta Express. (2014, April 20). Vetëvendosje përsëri kundër EULEX'it dhe Gjykatës Speciale. Retrieved from http://www.gazetaexpress.com/lajme/vetevendosje-perseri-kunder-eulexit-dhe-gjykates-speciale-9182/?archive=1

[380] Hashim Thaçi at the time was the Minister of Foreign Affairs and had expressed interest in the Presidency when Atifete Jahjaga's mandate terminated in 2016.

[381] Gardner, A. (2014, December 9). Kosovo Forms New Government. *Politico*. Retrieved from http://www.politico.eu/article/kosovo-forms-new-government

"The creation of the special court requires a number of amendments to Kosovo's legal code," and the National Assembly put it to the vote on May 7, 2015.[382] In addition to rejection from the opposition (three parties, VV, AAK and Nisma), members of the ruling coalition announced that they would not vote for the amendments to enable the creation of KSC.[383]

The European Union and United States favored the creation of the special court based abroad arguing that "it would help Kosovo build 'international credibility'" and "if Kosovo's parliament rejects the special court, the United Nations will address the issue."[384] Based in the Netherlands, the Specialist Court is expected to prosecute alleged war crimes committed by senior Kosovo Liberation Army members (KLA). Former head of the UNMIK legal office, Alexander Borg Oliver stated that the selection approach on war crimes is one-sided and unprecedented:

> "Kosovo has no obligation to accept or to assist in the establishment of the special court for crimes allegedly committed by the Kosovo Liberation Army. The special court is directly and exclusively aimed against the Kosovo Liberation Army for alleged war crimes committed by Kosovars during the Kosovo conflict. Such a selective approach on war crimes that focuses only on alleged crimes committed by one side in the conflict is unprecedented. The United Nations Security Council can decide to establish the court even without Kosovo's consent according to Chapter 7 of the UN Charter, but this idea lacks support and it cannot be implemented."[385]

MP Rexhep Selimi of the opposition Party "Vetëvendosje" stated that he would vote against the draft law questioning the creation of a court only for Kosovo: "there is no special court for Serbia to punish the crimes caused in the Balkans by the Serbian state. The creation of such special court would delegitimize all the international court rulings by Hague, UNMIK and EULEX," that previously ruled innocent and not war criminal members of the Kosovo Liberation Army (KLA).[386]

Serbian authorities announced the potential arrest of President Hashim Thaçi (former KLA commander and current President of Kosovo) if he entered Serbia to take part in the NGO

---

[382] Ibid.

[383] Blakaj, L. (2015, January 5). Opozita Nuk e Voton Gjykatën Speciale. *Zëri*. Retrieved from http://www.zeri.info/aktuale/13784/opozita-nuk-e-voton-gjykaten-speciale

[384] Human Rights Watch. (2014, April 11). Kosovo: Approve Special Court for Serious Abuses.

Retrieved from http://www.hrw.org/news/2014/04/11/kosovo-approve-special-court-serious-abuses

[385] Koha Ditore. (2014, April 14). Borg Oliver: Special Court Against KLA will Damage Kosovo. Retrieved from http://koha.net/?id=27&l=6264

[386] Blakaj, L. (2015, January 5).

conference on European Integration in Belgrade on April 24, 2015.[387] The arrest warrant of 10 years period was issued by a Serb court during Milosevic's leadership. In 2000, the District Court in Belgrade also issued an arrest warrant for the former British Prime Minister Tony Blair for war crimes, along with other Western leaders, later cancelled. Former E.U. Special Envoy to Kosovo, Wolfgang Petritsch stressed that "Serbia lost a chance to be constructive, especially in the phase where an important dialogue is taking place between the countries."[388] The European Union has made it clear to Serbia that "Serbia's progress toward accession depends on Belgrade improving its relations with Kosovo."[389]

The White House has been pushing for a deal between Kosovo and Prishtina. In early 2020, Washington requested from the Kosovan government to remove the 100% imposed tariffs on Serbian goods, "as part of efforts to normalize relations between the countries."[390] The European Union has been pursuing accession negotiations for both countries,[391] but has been skeptical of the US-backed land-swap plan to redraw the borders of Kosovo.[392] These tensions resurfaced ahead of the no-confidence vote on March 25, 2020, which overthrew the government of Prime Minister Albin Kurti.

3.5.2 Turning Over a New Leaf in Justice

In 1993, United Nations established the International Criminal Tribunal for the former Yugoslavia (ICTY) to investigate and prosecute violations of human rights, war crimes, genocide, and crimes against humanity. The Hague Tribunal ceased to exist on December 31, 2017 after intervening in serious international crimes for more than two decades.[393] As the U.N. tribunal for former

---

[387] Focus News Agency. (2015, April 22). Hashim Thaçi to Be Arrested If He Enters Serbia. Retrieved from http://www.focus-fen.net/news/2015/04/21/370050/politika-hashim-thaci-to-be-arrested-if-he-enters-serbia.html

[388] RTK Live. (2015, April 22). Serbia Lost a Chance of Reconciliation with Kosovo. Retrieved from http://www.rtklive.com/en/?id=2&r=1679

[389] Lehne, S. (2012, March). Kosovo and Serbia: Toward a Normal Relationship, 1-16. Retrieved from https://carnegieendowment.org/files/Kosovo_and_Serbia.pdf

[390] Nahzi, F. (2020, April 7). Applauding Kurti's Fall, the US is Testing Kosovo's Loyalty. *Balkan Insight*. Retrieved from https://balkaninsight.com/2020/04/07/applauding-kurtis-fall-the-us-is-testing-kosovos-loyalty/

[391] Walker, Sh. (2020, March 26). Kosovans look on aghast as government falls while coronavirus bites. *The Guardian*.

[392] Walker, Sh., MacDowall, A. (2018, September 3). US-backed Kosovo land-swap border plan under fire from all sides. *The Guardian*. Retrieved from https://www.theguardian.com/world/2018/sep/03/us-backed-kosovo-land-swap-border-plan-under-fire-from-all-sides

[393] Ristic, M. (2017, January 4). Hague Tribunal Prepares for Shutdown in 2017. *Balkan Insight*. Retrieved from http://www.balkaninsight.com/en/article/the-last-year-for-the-icty-01-02-2017-1

Yugoslavia was preparing to close, a new E.U.-backed court was being established[394] to manage alleged war crimes that occurred between January 1998 and December 2000 during the Kosovo war.[395]

Kosovo's parliament approved the creation of the Specialist Chambers in 2015. In April 2015, the Kosovo Constitutional Court found the constitutional amendment, proposed by the Kosovo government, to be in compliance with the Constitution. The constitutional amendment was adopted by the Kosovo Assembly in August 2015 under Article 162 of the Kosovo Constitution, providing the legal framework to establish Kosovo Specialist Chambers (KSC) and the Specialist Prosecutor's Office (SPO).[396] The Law on the Specialist Chambers and the Specialist Prosecutors Office 05/L-053 (2015) (Special Law) enabled the mandate of the chambers to "ensure secure, independent, impartial, fair and efficient criminal proceedings in relation to the allegations of grave trans-boundary and international crime committed during and in the aftermath of conflict in Kosovo."[397]

The President of the Kosovo Specialist Chambers, Judge Ekaterina Trendafilova, stated that the experience of building the Kosovo Specialist Chambers includes "elements unprecedented in international or internationalized courts, [and] will in turn contribute to future mechanisms of accountability and justice."[398] The functioning arrangements of the chambers and the cooperative relationship on administrative matters make the two institutions highly unique in nature.

In January 2016, Kosovo and the Netherlands signed an interim Host State Agreement, allowing for the function of the KSC in the Hague. The agreement entered into force in January 1, 2017 allowing KSC to conduct criminal proceedings in the territory of the Netherlands. Nineteen international judges were appointed to the Roster of International Judges in February 2017 and the Specialist Chambers became judicially operational in July 2017.[399]

The Kosovo Specialist Chambers (KSC) and the Specialist Prosecutor's Office (SPO) are two independent institutions established within the Kosovo justice system, with a seat outside Kosovo.

[394] McLaughlin, D. (2017, November 24). New EU-backed court for Kosovo war crimes awaits its first case. *Irish Times*. Retrieved from https://www.irishtimes.com/news/world/europe/new-eu-backed-court-for-kosovo-war-crimes-awaits-its-first-case-1.3304389

[395] Kosovo Specialist Chambers and Specialist Prosecutor's Office. (2018). Specialist Chambers Background: KSC at a glance. Retrieved from: http://www.scp-ks.org/en/background

[396] Kosovo Specialist Chambers. (2018, March). Kosovo Specialist Chambers and Specialist Prosecutor's Office – First Report 2016-2018, 1-64. Retrieved from https://www.scp-ks.org/sites/default/files/public/content/ksc_spo_first_report_en.pdf

[397] Ibid, 6.

[398] Ibid, 6.

[399] Ibid, 9.

The Kosovo Specialist Chambers are comprised of two organs: the Chambers, which follow the structure of the justice system of Kosovo, and the Registry. The SPO is also part of the judicial system in Kosovo and it "has the authority, *inter alia*, to request the presence of and to question suspects, victims and witnesses."[400] The KSC and SPO are funded by the E.U. member states and Third Contributing States, with large contributions from Norway and the Swiss Confederation. KSC are responsible in dealing with trials of individual criminal responsibility. The existence of KSC is temporary until Kosovo is notified by the European Union Council on the concluding of the investigations and proceedings.[401] The mandate and jurisdiction of KSC are specific to the international crime violations that occurred between 1998-2000 in Kosovo.

The KSC jurisdiction covers crimes commenced or committed in Kosovo by or against persons of Kosovo or FRY citizenship.[402] KSC President, Trendafilova stated that the new court will not be ethnically biased and that it is mandated to try crimes committed on Kosovo territory:

> "The Specialist Chambers will not prosecute any ethnic group. They will not prosecute any organization. The Specialist Chambers will only prosecute and hold accountable individual persons. The Law [on the Specialist Chambers and Specialist Prosecutor's Office] clearly provides for individual criminal responsibility, which means that persons may only be held accountable for crimes they committed as individuals, not as representatives of an ethnic group, of communities, or any other groups."[403]

Article 31 of the Kosovo Constitution ensures the right to fair and impartial trial, adopted in March 2017 by the Specialist Chambers Judges in the Rules of Procedure and Evidence. The rules also provide protection of witnesses, victims and at-risk individuals who cooperate with the KSC. The Witness Protection and Support Office (WPSO) is responsible for the robust protection and support system for the witnesses and participants giving testimony for the KSC.[404]

The statutory mandate of the Kosovo Specialist Chambers stipulates for independent, impartial, efficient and fair criminal proceedings, with the capacity to manage complex cases of international humanitarian and human rights violations.[405] KSC President Trendafilova asserted that the

---

[400] Ibid, 53.

[401] Ibid, 12.

[402] Ibid, 13.

[403] Ristic, M. (2017), 1.

[404] Kosovo Specialist Chambers. (2018), 43.

[405] Ibid, 6.

Kosovo Specialist Chambers remain committed to the effective administration and management of trials, as well as being transparent to ensure efficient proceedings.[406]

> "We are determined to ensure that the Kosovo Specialist Chambers will be seen as a beacon of independence, impartiality and fairness, not tainted by any influence, interference or political agenda, and a sterling safeguard not only of the fundamental rights of the accused, but also the security and safety of victims and witnesses."[407]

Three years after its creation, the Specialist Chambers initiated its first legal invitations in 2018, followed by the first round of witness interviews in January 2019.[408] The first indictments against Kosovo officials were filed in 2020 and they remain confidential.[409] On February 2020, the Special Prosecutor requested a Pre-Trial Judge and notified the Kosovo Specialist Chambers of his intent to initiate proceedings.[410] The pre-trial judge has "a maximum of six months to either confirm or dismiss the indictments."[411]

> "The Kosovo Specialist Chambers did not identify the suspects but several former high-level officials from recent years have previously been summoned for questioning by the tribunal... The KLA's war veterans' organization has said that more than 100 ethnic Albanian fighters had been called for questioning so far."[412]

On March 2020, two Judges of the Kosovo Specialist Chambers (KSC) have resigned from their posts: Judge Keith Raynor of United Kingdom and Judge Andres Parmas of Estonia. On

---

[406] Ibid.

[407] Ibid, 7.

[408] Mušanović, M. (2020, March 31). Kosovo Specialist Chambers: Providing compensations for victims. *European Western Balkans*. Retrieved from https://europeanwesternbalkans.com/2020/03/31/kosovo-specialist-chambers-providing-compensations-for-victims/

[409] AFT. (2020, February 24). First indictments are filed before the Kosovo Specialist Chambers. *Justice Info*. Retrieved from https://www.justiceinfo.net/en/tribunals/mixed-tribunals/43880-first-indictments-are-filed-before-the-kosovo-specialist-chambers.html

[410] Kosovo Specialist Chambers. (2020, February 24). Specialist Prosecutor formally notifies of intent to initiate proceedings. Retrieved from https://www.scp-ks.org/en/specialist-prosecutor-formally-notifies-intent-initiate-proceedings

[411] AFT. (2020), 1.

[412] Ibid, 1.

November 2019 Judge Ann Power-Forde of Ireland also resigned, following her appointment to the Court of Appeals of the Republic of Ireland.[413]

3.6 Kosovo-Serbia Relations

Since the end of the 1999 conflict Serbia and Kosovo have reached many milestones, including the Martti Ahtisaari Plan of 2008 and the 2013 Brussels Agreement.[414] The Ahtisaari Plan provided for a transition plan for a handover of responsibilities and capacities to Kosovo institutions and leadership over time.[415] On April 19, 2013 the governments of Kosovo and Serbia reached an agreement on their normalization of relations, under the auspices of the European Union in Brussels.[416] The Brussels deal was the first step toward normalizing relations between the two countries. The reached agreement opened the way to the European Union membership.

Both Serbia and Kosovo are on the road toward European Union membership. On January 21, 2014 Serbia received full candidate status for E.U. membership,[417] while Kosovo is a potential candidate.[418] On July 25, 2014, the European Union and Kosovo chief negotiators initialed the Stabilization and Association Agreement (SAA) between the E.U. and Kosovo in Brussels.[419] Normalization of relations between Kosovo and Serbia is a precondition to the European Union membership.[420]

[413] Kosovo Specialist Chambers. (2019, November 4). Judge Ann Power-Forde resigned. Retrieved from https://www.scp-ks.org/en/judge-ann-power-forde-resigned

[414] European Western Balkans. (2018, October 10). Getting to an Agreement between Serbia and Kosovo. Retrieved from https://europeanwesternbalkans.com/2018/10/18/getting-agreement-serbia-kosovo

[415] Kosovo Assembly. (2007, February 2). Comprehensive Proposal For the Kosovo Status Settlement.

[416] Smolar, P. (2013, April 30). Serbia and Kosovo sign historic agreement. *The Guardian*. https://www.theguardian.com/world/2013/apr/30/serbia-kosovo-historic-agreement-brussels

[417] European Commission. (2014). Serbia membership status, candidate country. Retrieved from http://ec.europa.eu/enlargement/countries/detailed-country-information/serbia/index_en.htm

[418] Ibid.

[419] SAA is an agreement that guides the process of establishing relations between Kosovo and EU-Western Balkans, including negotiations on political and economic cooperation between Kosovo and EU, provisions on many policy areas such as justice, security, trade, political dialogue, etc. European Union Office in Kosovo (2014, May 5). Stabilization and Association Agreement negotiations successfully completed. Retrieved from http://eeas.europa.eu/delegations/kosovo/press_corner/all_news/news/2014/20140502_03_en.htm

[420] Radosavljevic, Z. (2018, September 10). Kosovo-Serbia talks break down as tensions mount again. EURACTIV. http://www.euractiv.com/section/enlargement/news/kosovo-serbia-talks-break-down-as-tensions-mount-again/

Kosovo's relations with Serbia are impeded by the fragile coalition between Belgrade and Prishtina, facilitated by the European Union.[421] Kosovo's primary vulnerability is the unresolved status issue. Five out of twenty-eight EU members do not recognize Kosovo as a state, undermining its sovereignty.[422] However, they do recognize Kosovo's integration process in the E.U. Serbia opposes Kosovo's independence, but it has begun to normalize relations with Kosovo's government by reaching the first bilateral agreement between the two governments in 2013.[423] Normalization talks have made little progress since they began in 2013.

On April 19, 2013 Serbia's Prime Minister Ivica Dacic and Kosovo's Prime Minister Hashim Thaçi (currently president) signed an historic agreement at NATO headquarters in Brussels, titled "First Agreement of Principles Governing the Normalization of Relations."[424] The 15-point document outlined the basic framework of negations and the normalization process, with key point being the creation of the Association of the Community of Serb Majority municipalities. Uncertainty of the status and uncertainty regarding the implementation of the Brussels Agreement are key challenges Kosovo faces in its current process of E.U. integration. They also have policy implications in the larger regional security and foreign policy framework. Since the implementation process is overseen by the European Union and NATO, the effectiveness of these international institutions affects the relations between the stakeholders.

Tensions rose again in September 2018, when Serbia's President Aleksandar Vucic proposed a territorial swap along ethnic lines with Kosovo, in particularly North Kosovo (majority Serb) to be handed over to Belgrade in exchange for Presevo Valley (majority ethnic Albanian).[425] Kosovo's President Thaçi opposes the idea of division along ethnic lines but is open to border correction or a peaceful border adjustment. German chancellor, Angela Merkel opposed the idea of division

---

[421] International Crisis Group. (2013, February 19). Serbia and Kosovo: The Path to Normalization. *Europe Report 223, Brussels*, ii. Retrieved from http://www.crisisgroup.org/~/media/Files/europe/balkans/kosovo/223-serbia-and-kosovo-the-path-to-normalisation

[422] "EU 5" refers to the five EU countries that have yet to recognize Kosovo as an independent state, namely: Cyprus, Greece, Romania, Slovakia, and Spain. Kosovo is formally recognized by the other 23 member-states of the European Union. The E.U. views Kosovo as a potential candidate for membership.

[423] See full text of the 2013 Brussels Agreement. (2013, April 19). Kosovo-Serbia Agreement Text. *Tribuna*. Retrieved from http://www.gazetatribuna.com/?FaqeID=2&LajmID=5226

[424] The agreement was facilitated by the European Union, led by EU foreign policy chief Catherine Ashton. NATO also played an important role in this agreement and is responsible for its implementation, as per the request of both Serbia and Kosovo. NATO. (2014, January 14). *Secretary General's Annual Report 2013*, 1-45. Retrieved from http://www.nato.int/cps/en/natohq/opinions_106247.htm?selectedLocale=en

[425] Presevo Valle in Albanian "*Lugina e Preshevës*." See MacDowall, A. (2018, August 22). Could land swap between Serbia and Kosovo lead to conflict? *The Guardian*. Retrieved from https://www.theguardian.com/world/2018/aug/22/serbia-kosovo-could-land-swap-between-lead-conflict

for fear of instability in the region and it might cause a domino effect in Bosnia-Herzegovina and in Macedonia. United States and France are reconsidering their position toward the potential partition of Kosovo, saying "different options are on the table."[426]

In November 2018, Kosovo placed trade tariffs on Serbian goods from 10% to 100%, in retaliation to Belgrade's efforts to block Kosovo's accession to Interpol.[427] Prime Minister Ramush Haradinaj considered Kosovo's failure to join the international police organization "due to Serbia's aggressive stance."[428] Serbia has repeatedly blocked Kosovo's attempts to join the United Nations. Serb Mayor of North Mitrovica Goran Rakic resigned because of Prishtina's decision to increase the tariffs and the four Serb-majority communities ended communication with Kosovo state institutions.[429] The territorial swap proposal reflects the desire of both Serbs and Albanians to be united with ethnic co-nationals, but it leaves out, "securing the well-being of citizens, enhancing security and freedom, and building relations of trust between and within communities."[430]

---

[426] Ibid.

[427] DW. (2018, November 21). Kosovo slaps 100 percent tariff on Serbian goods after Interpol bid failure. Retrieved from https://www.dw.com/en/kosovo-slaps-100-percent-tariff-on-serbian-goods-after-interpol-bid-failure/a-46400277

[428] Ibid.

[429] Zivanovic, M. (2018, November 27). Serb Mayors in Kosovo to Resign Amid Tensions. Retrieved from http://www.balkaninsight.com/en/article/serbian-mayors-in-kosovo-to-resign-11-27-2018

[430] Gordy, E. (2018, October 10). Why Borders Are Not the Problem or the Solution for Serbia and Kosovo. Foreign Affairs Magazine. Retrieved from https://www.foreignaffairs.com/articles/kosovo/2018-10-10/why-borders-are-not-problem-or-solution-serbia-and-kosovo

CHAPTER 4

Research Methodology and Methods

This chapter includes the main research questions and hypotheses. In more details, this part outlines the data and the research design, the methods of data collection, the sample selection, and the type of data analysis.

4.1 Research Questions and Hypothesis

The main three research questions that this study addresses are:

(1) **What is the level of trust in a series of national and international institutions in Kosovo?**

(2) **What are the factors that affect the levels of political trust?**

(3) **Is there significant variation in political trust at the individual country level and international level?**

The contribution is threefold. First, it creates an integrated model, based on institutional performance and cultural theories literature. Second, it tests the theories that are vital for a liberal democracy and political trust, in the context of post-conflict Kosovo (*Alb: Kosova*). And finally the discussion offers analysis of important institutional and cultural factors such as interpersonal trust, national and ethnic identity, perceived government performance, perceived trustworthiness, analysis of determinants of political trust, and broader implications of the institutional performance approach. Moreover, the study adds to the conceptualization of political trust, by redefining political trust to include *international trust* – trust in international organizations and other nations, not just individuals and national institutions. The study concludes with suggestions for further research.

Cultural and institutional theories have analyzed political trust at the *macro level* – by looking at the performance of institutions, and *micro level* – based on individual's experiences. Macro level theories argue that political trust is based on citizens' the satisfaction or dissatisfaction towards the performance of the institutions[431] and the policy alternatives.[432] In this context, political trust is strongly linked to the performance of institutions.

Alternatively, micro theories argue that political trust is formed by the varying individuals' experiences with the institutions, based on the approval or disapproval of the political leaders.[433] In this scenario, perceptions of trustful or distrustful government will depend on the citizens' approval or disproval of the political leaders, not the political regime.

This research distinguishes between system-based trust (the political system), the national political trust (government, leaders, police, courts), and international political trust (EU, UN). I expect citizens' perceptions for the Kosovo Specialist Court to align with their expectations toward the international community (such as the UN, EU, NATO), since the specialist court has been created in the same European standards and democratic framework.

Based on the macro – institutional theory, this study expects to find a strong link between government performance and the citizens' perceptions towards trust in institutions. The higher the government performance, the higher the political trust.

According to the institutional theory, political trust depends on the efficiency and outputs of institutions. Kosovo as a newly independent country, has undergone many political transformations and democratic developments. Studies have shown that political trust is vital to democracy and have emphasized that "institutional legitimacy is strongly linked with the democratic legitimacy."[434]

As Kosovo leaders face criticism over transparency and corruption, it is important to explore how legitimacy and trustworthiness of government and leaders affect political trust. In accordance to the cultural and institutional performance theories of political trust, I develop the following five hypotheses:

---

[431] Mishler, W., & Rose, R. (2001), 36.

[432] Miller, A. H. (1974, September). Political Issues and Trust in Government, 1964-1970. *American Political Science Review*, 68(3), 951.

[433] Matebesi, S. (2017), 24.

[434] Pula, E. (2017), 8.

H1: *Interpersonal trust is expected to have a positive influence on the levels of political trust. (a) National identification is expected to strengthen institutional trust. (b) Ethnic identification is assumed to weaken trust in institutions.*

H2: *Trustworthiness is expected to have a positive influence on the levels of political trust. a) The higher the individuals' satisfaction with the fairness and competence of the political leadership, the higher the political trust in government. b) The more individuals believe trials are fair and impartial, the more trust they have in the legal institutions.*

H3: *Media is expected to have a positive relationship with political trust. The more trust individuals have in media as the primary source of information, the more trust they have in institutions.*

H4: *Perceived efficiency of the government to meet objectives is positively related to the levels of political trust. The higher the individuals' satisfaction with the government's performance, the higher the individuals' level of trust in institutions.*

H5: *Perceived democratic functioning of the government is positively related with the individuals' level of trust in the institutions. The higher the individuals' perceptions towards the level of democracy, the higher the individuals' level of trust in institutions.*

With respect to the socio-democratic characteristics, used as indicators of socialization, because previous findings of these variables (gender, age, religion, ethnicity, education, profession) have contradictory and inconclusive findings,[435] I refrain from formulating a hypothesis. The theoretical model about the relationship between socialization, cultural and institutional factors, and political trust, is conceptualized in Figure 6. All determinants of political trust included in the conceptual model of this study are illustrated in Figure 6.

---

[435] Godefroidt et al. (2015), 5.

4.2 Models of Political Trust

Most authors use a one-dimensional model of political trust where all the indicators and factors are summed to represent political trust.[436] A few others have argued recently for a multi-dimensional structure of political trust across three dimensions: political institutions (political parties, government, parliament, leaders); neutral and order institutions (police and legal system); and power-checking institutions (press and television).[437]

The macro-level perspective only identifies two variants of political trust: (1) diffuse or system-based trust (directed to the overall political system); and (2) institutional based trust, (directed at certain institutions, such as police, legal system, government). However, what is absent is another variant of political trust at the *mezzo level*, (3) international trust (directed to international organizations and other countries). As discussed in chapter 2, this study proposes the addition of international trust to the political trust model, to incorporate international institutions, such as the United Nations, European Union, NATO, International Courts, and relationships with other countries (which can be represented by their embassy in the respective country).

Thus far, most of the literature has analyzed political trust, as generalized trust, with an 'everything in the kitchen sink' approach, or a one-dimensional perspective (*see Figure 3*). I argue that, a multi-dimensional approach is needed, to better understand the effects of the two levels of trust: *national political trust* and *international political trust* (*See Figure 4*). In this study, national political trust is characterized by trust in national institutions, such as government, parliament, politicians, political parties, as well as order or neutral institutions such as the legal system (courts) and the police. Whereas, the international political trust is characterized by trust in international organizations such as the United Nations, the European Union, NATO, International Courts, and relevant foreign country/embassy.

Since political trust is expected and found to vary cross-nationally, it is important to investigate political trust measurements across national trust and international trust. This study considers cultural and institutional performance expectations to be complementary, not mutually exclusive. To explore changes in political trust, this study has considered the multi-dimensional models of political trust, instead of a single-factor or a one-dimension model. It would be difficult to understand political trust in any isolated institutions alone, without having any "compared to

---

[436] Andre, S. (2014). Does Trust Mean the Same for Migrants and Natives? Testing Measurement Models of Political Trust with Multi-group Confirmatory Factor Analysis. *Soc Indic Res*, 968. DOI 10.1007/s11205-013-0246-6

[437] Rothstein, B., & Stolle, D. (2008). The state and social capital. An institutional theory of generalized trust. *Comparative Politics*, 40(4), 441–467.

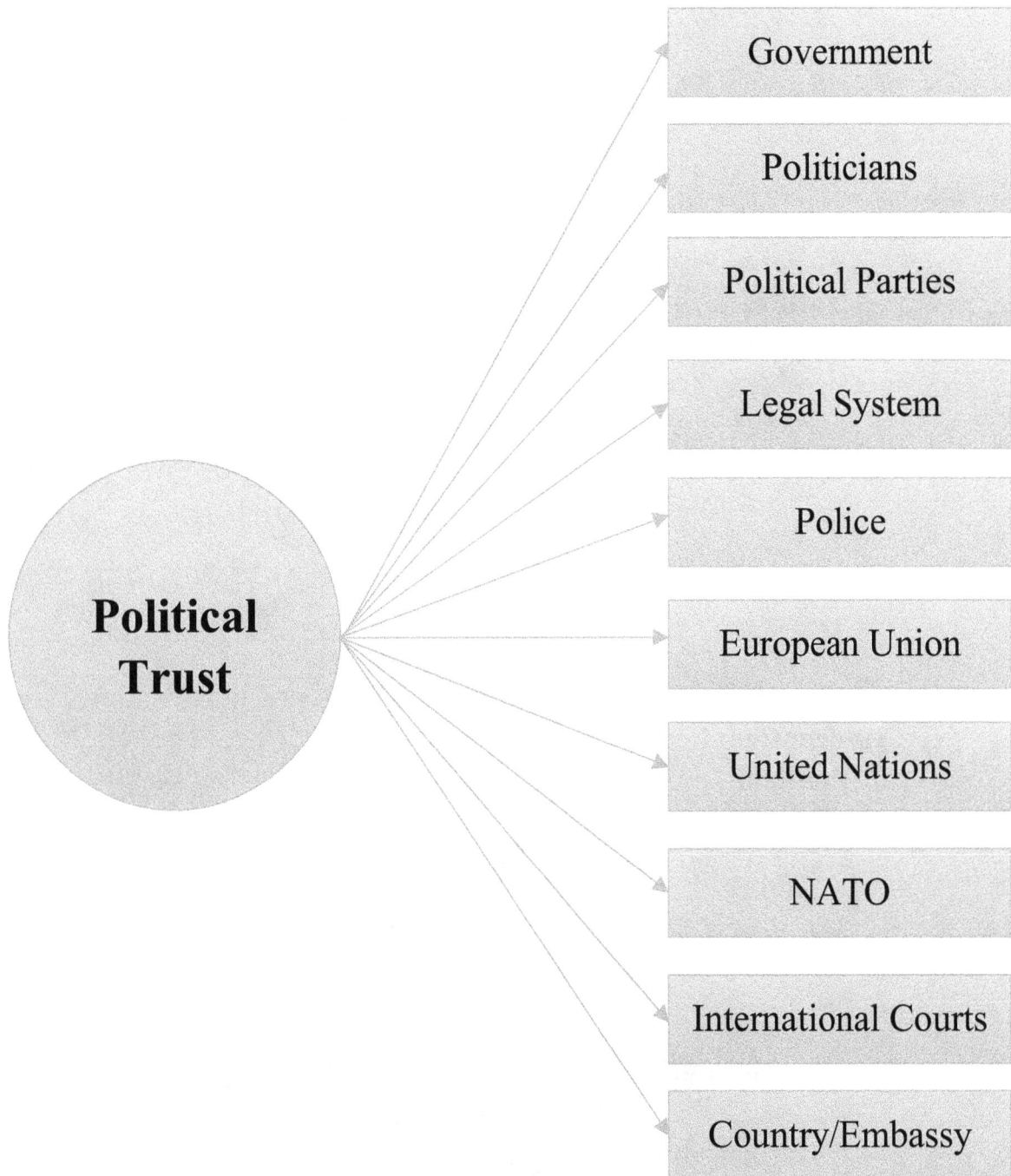

Figure 3: One-Factor Model of Political Trust[438]

---

[438] Adapted from the Stefanie Andre (2014) model of political trust.

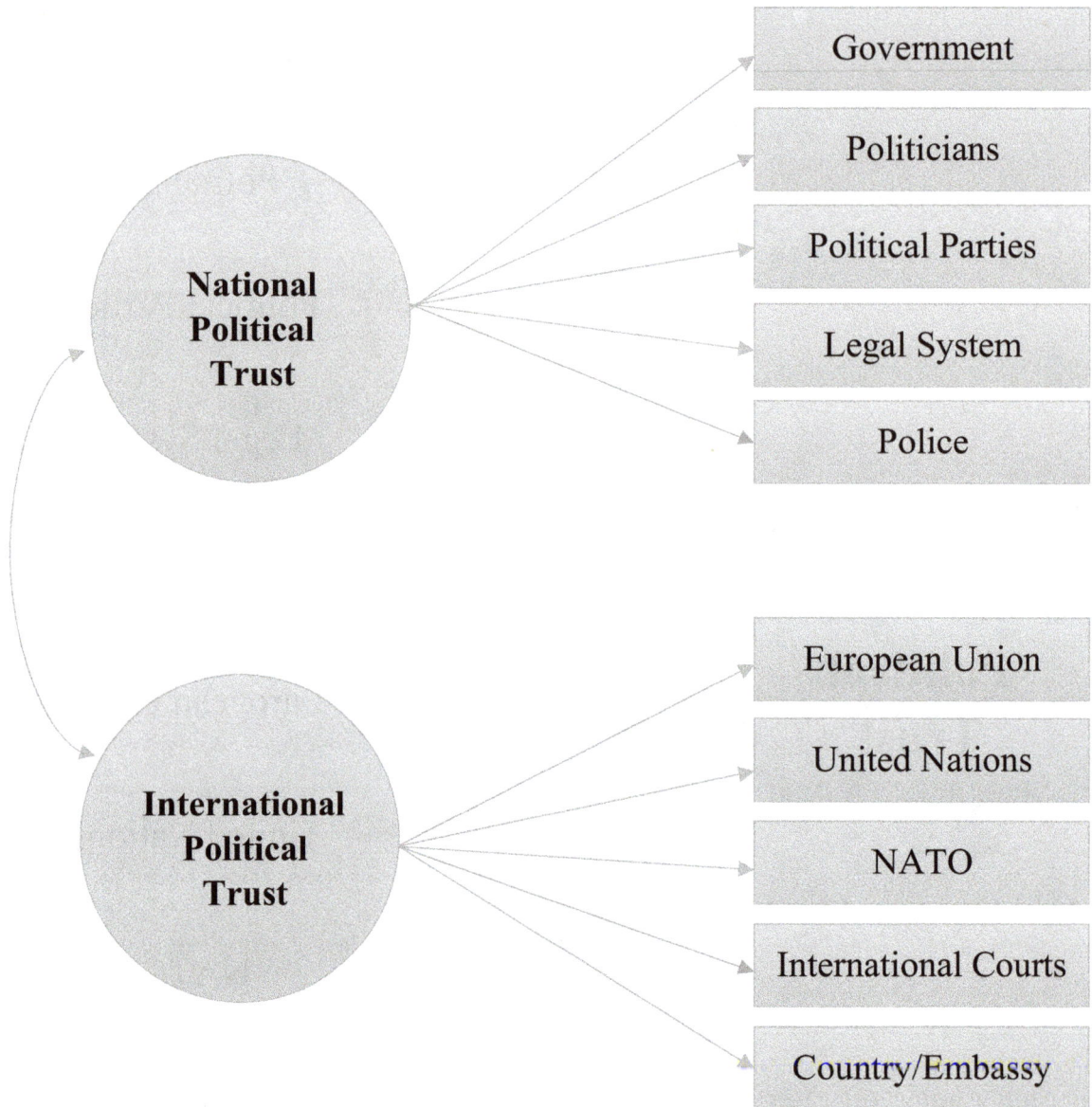

Figure 4: Two-Factor Model of Political Trust[439]

---

[439] Figure 3 and Figure 4 are adapted from the Stefanie Andre (2014) model of cross-cultural comparisons of political trust. The model has been revised to fit the Kosovo case study, with respect to the international community involvement. See Andre, S. (2014). Does Trust Mean the Same for Migrants and Natives? Testing Measurement Models of Political Trust with Multi-group Confirmatory Factor Analysis. *Soc Indic Res.*, 115:963–982. doi: 10.1007/s11205-013-0246-6

what" type of criticism.[440] For instance, the Chicago Council on Foreign Relations 2004 study was designed to replicate earlier surveys used in previous years, 1990, 1994, 1998 and 2002 to compare changes in American foreign policy perceptions across different time periods.[441] This study compares attitudes of Kosovo's political elite pre- and post-independence, from the survey conducted in Kosovo in 2012-2013, replicated again to some extent in 2018, to account for recent years changes, if any, in political trust.

The results section will examine two approaches of political trust: (1) the *institutional explanations* based on the performance of the government and (2) the *socio-cultural explanations* from the perspective of individual norms and beliefs. The discussion section will interpret and describe the significance of trust in light of the two alternative models of trust:

(1) Blind/Godefroidt, Langer & Meuleman's social vs. political integrative model of sources of trust, influenced by cultural theories (*national & ethnic identity, interpersonal trust*) and institutional performance theories (*government performance*). (*See Figure 1 and Figure 6*)

(2) Andre's two-factor structure model with trust in the *national political trust* (government, politicians, police, legal system) and *international political trust* (E.U., U.N). (*See figure 4*)

As noted earlier, there are many domains of political trust, including institutions and actors: government, politicians, political parties, the legal system (courts), police, international organizations, and media/TV.[442] I will compare the two different models to see if certain factors (social versus political) or certain dimensions of structures institutions (national versus international) will be more significant in the levels of political trust. The model proposed by Godefroidt, Langer, and Meuleman (2015) is helpful in understanding the impact of institutional and cultural factors on political trust (*Figure 6*). The multi-factor structure model by Andre (2014) is important in making the distinction between the many domains of political trust across the varying institutions, national and international. Both models give a complete picture of the factors and determinants of political trust.

---

[440] Cook, T. E., & Gronke, P. (2001, April). The Dimensions of Institutional Trust: How Distinct is Public Confidence in the Media? *Midwest Political Science Association*, Chicago, 2.

[441] Chicago Council on Foreign Relations. (2006, March 30). *Global Views 2004: American Public Opinion and Foreign Policy*. Ann Arbor, MI: Inter-university Consortium for Political and Social Research.

[442] Andre, S. (2014), 970.

Social Capital (Social trust, Network)

Interpersonal Trust (National Identity, Socialization)

Political Participation (Electoral, Institutional, Non-institutional)

Other Political Factors (Partisanship, Policy Issue, Media Exposure)

Trustworthiness (Fair, Competence, Corruption)

Government Performance (Legitimacy, Efficacy, Accountability)

Socioeconomic Background (Gender, Age, Education, Religion, Ethnicity)

Political Trust (Trust in Politicians, Institutions, IO)

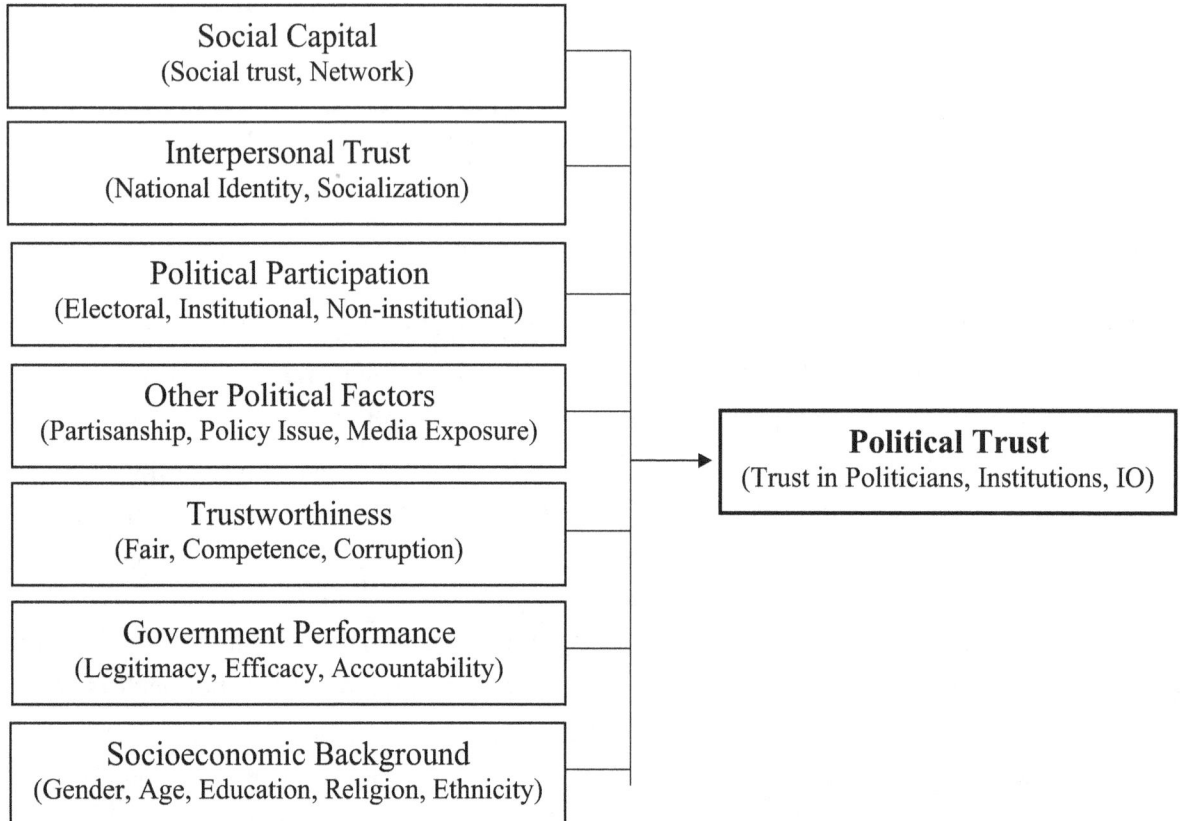

Figure 5: Conceptual Model about Determinants of Political Trust

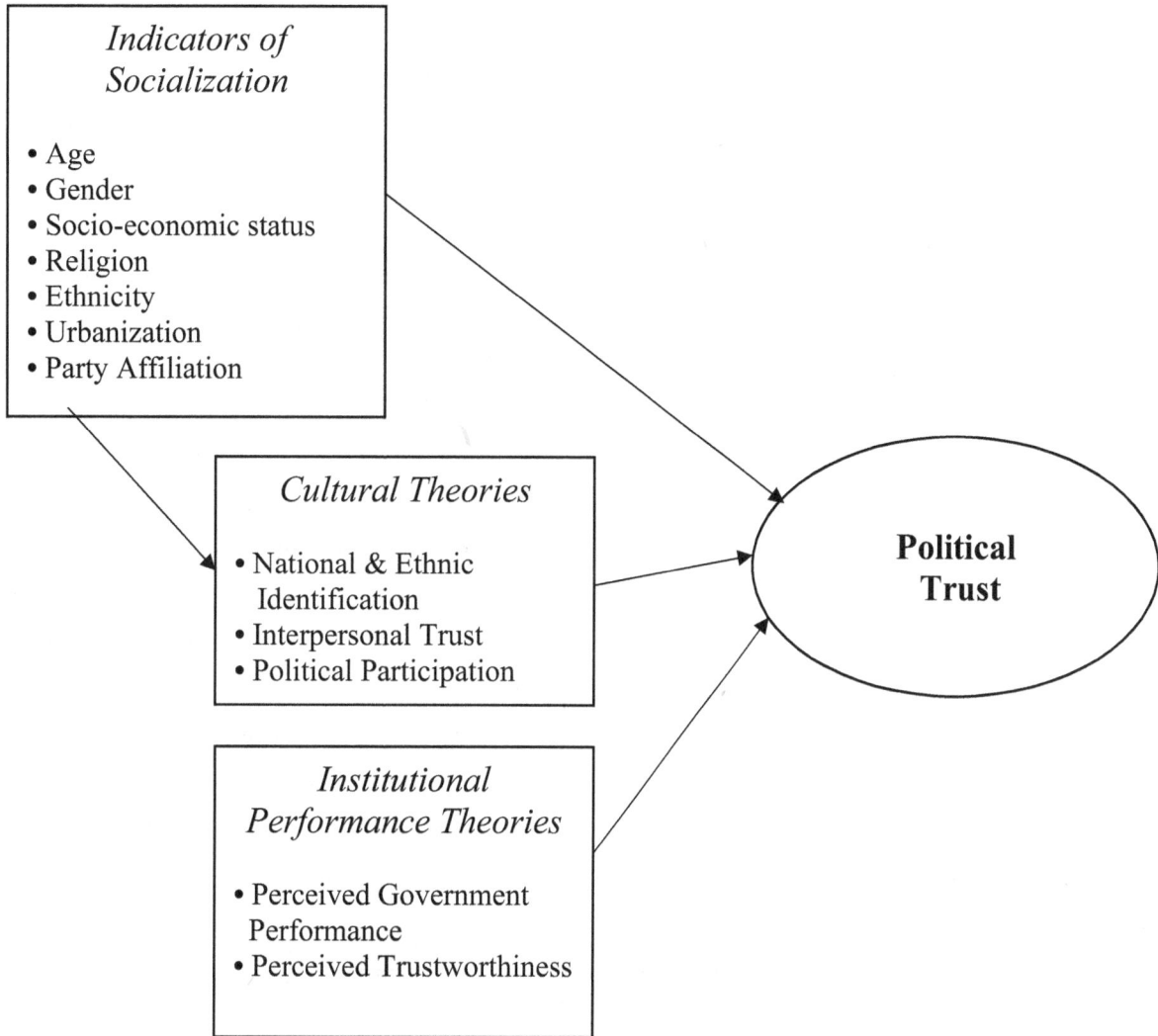

Figure 6: Theoretical Model about the Relationship between Socialization, Cultural and Institutional Factors and Political Trust[443]

---

[443] The conceptual model of the origins of institutional trust, proposed by Godefroidt, Langer, and Meuleman (2015). See Godefroidt, A., Langer, A., & Meuleman, B. (2015). Developing political trust in a developing country. *Centre for Research on Peace and Development* (CRPD). KU Leuven, 6. Political Participation and Perceived Trustworthiness have been added to reflect the recent suggestions of the literature on the cultural vs. institutional performance debate.

4.3   Data and Research Design

4.3.1 Nature of the Study

This research uses a mixed methods research, by using quantitative and qualitative tools in a single study. The design of the research methods is related to the research questions and the research problems.[444] The basic advantage is that both qualitative and quantitative methods generate primary and secondary research results. The mixed methods approach is best when addressing research questions more comprehensively, in particular those that are broad, complex and multi facets.[445]

In this study, a quantitative approach was taken in order to prove or disprove the proposed five hypotheses. Furthermore, the statistical analysis of the results provides a comprehensive answer to the posed three research questions pertaining to political trust. The qualitative methods contribute to filtering out the external factors that have an effect on the variables. Another advantage of the qualitative research is that it offers a complete description and analysis of the research topic, "without liming he scope of the research and the nature of participant's responses."[446] The present study is a quantitative, descriptive comparative study, employing sampling and data collection procedures. Considering the approach being both quantitative and qualitative in nature, this study is guided by the goal to validate the assumptions raised in the hypotheses and add to the knowledge of origins and determinants of political trust.

4.3.2 Research Strategy

The main purpose of this research is to understand the levels of political trust and to investigate if cultural and institutional performance factors have any positive or negative affect on the growth of trust. To achieve this objective, data was collected using primary sources that included the collection of responses through first-hand research, using surveys and interviews with the political elite and experts in Kosovo. Secondary research involved the collection of key information published by reliable important sources such as United Nations documents, European Union progress reports, U.S. State Department documents, and annual reports from Kosovo's Ministry of Foreign Affairs.

---

[444] Silverman, D. (2005). *Doing qualitative research: a practical handbook* (2nd ed.). London: Sage.

[445] Tariq, S., & Woodman, J. (2013). Using mixed methods in health research. *JRSM short reports*, 4(6), 2042533313479197. doi:10.1177/2042533313479197

[446] Collis, J., & Hussey, R. (2003). *Business Research: A Practical Guide for Undergraduate and Postgraduate Students*. Palgrave Macmillan Houndmills: Basingstoke, Hampshire.

The research findings are based on a ten-year project, aiming (1) to understand the political situation in Kosovo (*in Albanian: Kosova*), including the legal framework and the role of the international community, and (2) to explore the various factors that influence political trust in Kosovo, across many institutions (national and international), as well as in different periods of time – pre- and post-2008 independence declaration being a key temporal marker for comparison purposes. Research have collected data from Western and European countries, in recently-established democracies, however data from post-conflict Kosovo is lacking or non-existent with major gaps in-between years.

In this research primary data were collected through quantitative and qualitative methods, using surveys and interviews conducted on field trips in Prishtina, Kosovo: two main original datasets, conducted from field research of the political elite and experts, dating from 2012-2013 survey (220 participants) and 2017-2018 survey (40 participants). In this study the data set was designed to look at three dimensions of institutional trust – government institutions, legal institutions and actors (the international community, the European Union, the United Nations, NATO), as an attempt to understand the different levels of political trust across various institutions, in different time periods. The purpose is to understand what drives trust in government and what influences levels of trust in different channels of government. Table 2 includes a summary of the research strategy, the aim, data collection and implementation tools.

Table 2: Research Strategy and Methods

Stage	Method	Aim	Implementation
1	Preliminary travel to research sites in Kosovo.	To construct a more comprehensive understanding of the areas of concerns: United Nations role, multilateral diplomacy, and international negotiations. To complete thesis research with intent to continue pursuing advanced graduate research during doctoral studies.	Began independent work study through the course work of Master's thesis, via Long Island University in New York. (2007) Field trip in Prishtina, Kosovo under the auspices of UNMIK and UNHCR (April 05-19, 2007), conducted 30 structured interviews with public officials. Thesis: *Kosovo Status Talks: A Case Study on International Negotiations*, LIU. (2007) Presented at the 2009 NPSA Conference (Northeastern Political Science Association) in Philadelphia, Pennsylvania, "*Kosovo the Balkan Dilemma: Multilateral Diplomacy in Nation-Making.*" (November 19-22, 2009)
2	Literature review, travel to European Union research sites in Europe, Strasbourg, France.	Understand the research problem from the European perspective. To identify relevant research topics: European Union law and institutions.	WVU Study Abroad Program in Political Science and International Studies, in Strasbourg, France. Site visits to German, French, and EU institutions in Brussels and Luxembourg: European Court of Justice, European Commission, European Parliament, the Council of Europe, the European Court of Human Rights. (May 17 – June 03, 2010) Began independent research study through the course work of doctoral program at West Virginia University. (Fall 2010)

3	Travel to Prishtina and Mitrovica in Kosovo, key expert interviews and survey: structured interviews and semi-structured interviews, unstructured observation.	Understand the research problem from the local Kosovan perspective. To identify related variables and factors. To examine the state's characteristics in policy-oriented behavior and to identify foreign policy objectives and priorities. To understand national identity, security concerns and ethnic relations between ethnic Serbs and Albanians. Testing of hypotheses.	Field trip in Kosovo (November 09 – December 23, 2012), conducted key expert interviews and survey, lived in Prishtina, Kosovo and made connections with high level officials, U.N. and E.U. authorities, legal experts and local scholars. Site visits included Ministry of Diaspora, Ministry of Foreign Affairs, the Prime Minister's Office, Ombudsman's Office, Ministry of Culture, Assembly of Kosovo, Ministry for the Kosovo Security Forces. Traveled to Mitrovica's ethnic Serbian and Albanian communities, and in Mitrovica's Trepca mining company site. Conducted quantitative survey (220 participants) and semi-structured interviews. (November 2012-March 2013)
4	Travel to London, United Kingdom, unstructured observation.	To understand the role of U.K. and the role of the Albanian diaspora in United Kingdom.	Lived in London, U.K., made connections, participated in cultural diplomacy events with the Embassy of Kosovo and the Embassy of Israel in London, met with Ambassador Mal Berisha. (February 21, 2015 – May 23, 2016) Successfully defended the Ph.D. prospectus. (July 16, 2016)

| 5 | Travel to New York, expert interviews | To understand the role of United States, and the role of Albanian diaspora in U.S.A. | Lived in New York, met with the diplomatic core at the Consulate General of Kosovo in New York, attended cultural diplomacy events, with speakers U.S. Ambassador to U.N. Nikki Haley and Ambassador Teuta Sahatqia, met with the Kosovo delegation to United Nations. (March 15 – May 30, 2018) |
| 6 | Travel to Prishtina and Prizren in Kosovo, expert interviews and survey: structured interviews and semi-structured interviews. | Operationalization of factors and variables, build rapport with the community.

Further testing of hypotheses for comparative purposes. | Third field trip to Kosovo, (October 31 –November 07, 2017), conducted key expert interviews, lived in Prishtina, visited Prizren and made connections with the political elite, prosecutors, EULEX, and the KSC.

Conducted quantitative survey (40 participants) and semi-structured interviews. (September 19 – November 24, 2018)

Defended Dissertation (December 18, 2018) |

4.3.3 Research Scope

My initial idea was to evaluate the role of the government and the international community from a local perspective using gained insight from expert interviews and the quantitative surveys conducted during the first field trips in Kosovo from November 09 to December 23, 2012. I kept this purpose for the second field trip in November 2017 but narrowed it down to trust in political-legal institutions. The 2018 survey was specifically crafted to assess trust in government and elite perceptions of the joint EU-Kosovo work on rule of law, with the creation of the Kosovo Specialist Court.

Before I started my doctoral research project, my research and preparation began during my master thesis at Long Island University (LIU) in 2007. At the time I was working as a Project Manager, during an internship at the Department of Peace-Keeping Operations and Logistics, at the United Nations Headquarters in New York. Simultaneously, I was also pursuing a master's program in political science at LIU, and an advanced graduate program in United Nations Diplomacy.

This sparked my interest in human rights, democracy, good governance, and diplomacy in Kosovo. I had the opportunity to attend U.N. Security Council meetings and high-level General Assembly meetings discussing the security and political agenda for Kosovo.

During the master's research, I traveled to Kosovo on April 05 – 19, 2007 to interview the political elite to understand the role of United Nations, multilateral diplomacy, and international negotiations. Due to the increased security concerns, I took special interest in inter-ethnic relations in Kosovo between ethnic Serbs and ethnic Albanians. The site visits and the unstructured observations proved to be very useful to my doctoral research, particularly to the operationalization of one of the cultural variables "interpersonal trust" with respect to *national identity* and *ethnic identification*. The cultural theories expect that national identity will be related to political trust and perceptions of the political system.[447] Albanian cultural traditions in Albania and Kosovo emphasize a strong sense of feeling patriotic and national pride to unite Albanians into a unitary linguistic and cultural nation. Geopolitically speaking, Albania[448] is the only country in the world that is surrounded by its own people and land, due to the partition after WWII: Montenegro[449] in northwest (Albanians living in Podgorica, Ulqin, Plave, Guci, Tivar, Rozhaje), Kosovo[450] and Serbia[451] in the northeast (Presheva, Bujanoc, Medvegje, Novi Pazar), Macedonia in the east (Tetove, Gostivar, Struge, Skopje, Kumanove, Kercove, Diber),[452] and Greece in the south (Chameria).[453] More recently, Belgrade and Prishtina have been discussing the "border adjustments" idea or an agreed upon territorial exchange to diffuse ethnic conflict. The bargain, opposed by E.U. leadership, includes border changes involving the Serb-populated territories in

---

[447] Almond, G., & Verba, S. (1963). *The Civic Culture: Political Attitudes and Democracy in Five Nations*. Princeton, NJ: Princeton University Press.

[448] 40 % of Albanians live outside of Albania, with current population of 2.8 million (2017). It is estimated that over 15 million Albanians live around the world. See AIK. (2012, February 24). Sa Shqiptare ka në botë? *Presheva Jonë*. Retrieved from https://www.preshevajone.com/sa-shqiptare-ka-ne-bote-sipas-presheva-jone-jemi-15-milione-pajtoheni-ju/

[449] According to the 2011 census there are 30,439 ethnic Albanians that live in Montenegro.

[450] More than 1 million Albanians fled the country during the 1998 Kosovo war, who have returned after the conflict. According to the 2015 census the total population of Kosovo is 1,870,981, excluding North Kosovo, comprised of four ethnic Serb communities (North Mitrovica, Leposavić, Zvečan and Zubin Potok), estimated 2015 population of 79,910. See "Agjencia e Statistikave të Kosovës," Retrieved from http://ask.rks-gov.net

[451] According to the 2011 census there are 60,809 Albanians that live in Serbia. See "Становништво према националној Припадности." Statistics of Serbia.

[452] According to the 2002 national census there are 509,083 Albanians that live in the north-western part of Macedonia, making it the largest ethnic minority to live in the country.

[453] According to the 2001 census there are 650,000 Albanian immigrants living in Greece, out of which 443,550 are Albanian citizenship holders. See Martin, Philip L., Martin, Susan Forbes, Weil, Patrick. (2006*). Managing Migration: The Promise of Cooperation*. New York: Lexington Books.

northern Kosovo and the Albanian-populated territories in southern Serbia, pushed by Serbian President Aleksandar Vucic and Kosovo President Hashim Thaçi."[454]

After extensively analyzing Track I (official government diplomacy), Track II (informal diplomacy), and Track III talks (people to people diplomacy), my master's thesis research findings of January 2008 called for independence declaration, subsequently followed by Kosovo's unilateral declaration of independence in February 17, 2008.[455] My research on Kosovo continued while pursuing the doctoral program in Political Science and International Relations program at West Virginia University in Morgantown, WV.

The initial doctoral study (2012-2013) raised questions about how to measure government performance in terms of legitimacy, fairness and competence, focusing on attitudes towards the leadership, the institutions, and the international community, such as the United Nations, the European Union, NATO, OSCE, and Red Cross. The biggest challenge that I faced with the study was lack of data on the country, therefore I had to rely on collecting original data. When I visited Kosovo in 2012, most of the institutions newly formed under the E.U. framework, had not published any annual statistics. This made it difficult to run analysis on large samples, and I had to rely on collecting my own small samples: 220 in the first survey and 40 in the second survey. Because I was collecting data first-hand, I wanted to use in-depth semi-structured interviews and quantitative surveys as my primary and only method to collect data. The 2012 survey ended up being very lengthy, 25 pages, with 170 total questions (*See Appendix 2*). To ensure participation I scheduled meetings ahead of time, confirmed and re-confirmed several times, lasting to two hours or more for each in-depth interview. Meetings were scheduled back to back in both formal and informal settings, during the timeframe from 7:00 a.m. until 9:00 p.m. Building local connections and engaging in lengthy conversations was needed to gain trust and fully understand the local perspective.

4.3.4 Field Trips in Kosovo

I carried out three field trips to Kosovo, in 2007,[456] 2012 and 2017, traveling to neighboring Macedonia and Albania as well. Most of my time was spent in Kosovo to gain a local perspective on the community's perspectives on the local leadership, the role of the international community,

---

[454] Vajdich, D. P. (2018, October 11). Let Serbia and Kosovo define their own peace. *Washington Post*. Retrieved from https://www.washingtonpost.com/news/global-opinions/wp/2018/10/11/let-serbia-and-kosovo-define-their-own-peace/?noredirect=on&utm_term=.c98444bb444d

[455] Babamusta, E. (2008, January). *Kosovo Status Talks: A Case Study on International Negotiations.* (Master's Thesis). Long Island University, NY, 1-254.

[456] During the 2007 field trip, I was hosted by the lovely families of Gëzim Kunoviku and Valbona Hajredini.

rule of law, and foreign policy issues. To get a deeper understanding of each community in terms of its own culture and social structure, I visited both Serb and ethnic Albanian communities in Kosovo. I also visited ethnic Albanian communities in Macedonia to understand their experiences in terms of treatment as a minority and access to the integrated services. This aspect is important to the national and ethnic identification variables of this research, to better understand whether and if cultural identities influence people's trust in the political and legal state institutions.

According to Almond and Verba (1963) and Easton (1965) the cultural explanations of political trust, which include interpersonal trust and group identification,[457] provide for a "cohesive cement" in the sense of feeling as a community amongst the members.[458] Berg and Hjerm (2010) argue that "collective identities" is related to national borders, not just the formation of "we-feelings" in people.[459] The idea is that "interpersonal trust is supposed to help make political institutions work because it can 'spill over' into political trust", providing support for functioning and legitimate institutions.[460] Therefore, to better understand the representation of national identity in the sense of "we-feelings" as well as geographical territory I travelled to different urban and rural areas, as well as cities with large ethnic minority populations, such as Mitrovica and Prizren.

Mitrovica in particular has received significant attention for ethnic conflict. As a result of the North Kosovo crisis, the city has been divided into two administrative units (divided by the Ibar River): North Mitrovica, the Serb-majority municipality, and South Mitrovica, the Albanian-majority municipality, both operating within the Kosovo legal framework. Kosovo's Albanian leadership is concerned with North running "parallel" political and economic institutions with financial support from Belgrade. The Serb parallel institutions exist within Kosovo, and are recognized by Kosovo's constitution, but they take orders from Serbia, rather than Kosovo.[461] I visited the Mitrovica bridge in 2007, also known as the Ibar River Bridge, where the crossing over Ibar river separates North Mitrovica with a 29,460 Serb population, and South Mitrovica with 80,000 Kosovan Albanians in the south.[462]

I revisited Mitrovica again in 2012, and the atmosphere was quite different from the 2007 trip in terms of safety. During the 2007 trip, we were told to stay inside the vehicle at all times, to

---

[457] Almond, G.A. & Verba, S. (1963). *The Civic Culture: Political Attitudes and Democracy in Five Nations.* Princeton: Princeton University Press.

[458] Easton, D. (1965). A System Analysis of the Political Life. Chicago, IL: The University of Chicago Press, 176.

[459] Berg, L., & Hjerm, M. (2010), 392.

[460] Ibid, 392.

[461] Rossi, M. (2018, September 19). Partition in Kosovo Will Lead to Disaster. Foreign Policy. Retrieved from https://foreignpolicy.com/2018/09/19/partition-in-kosovo-will-lead-to-disaster-serbia-vucic-thaci-mitrovica-ibar/

[462] OSCE. (2018, October 10). Profile of Mitrovica/Mitrovicë North. *Organization for Security and Co-operation in Europe.* Retrieved from https://www.osce.org/mission-in-kosovo/122119

avoid looking people in the eye who were walking in the streets, and show only my U.S. passport if stopped, not my Albanian passport if I didn't want any problems. At checkpoint, two KFOR French soldiers requested to see my passport and asked questions about the purpose of my trip. I identified myself as a student from America.

In 2007 there was a heightened tension and sense of fear and insecurity when traveling to Mitrovica. One ethnic Albanian accompanying me in the car during the trip, asked to be dropped off in South Mitrovica, a predominantly Albanian majority population, for fear of being arrested if crossing over to the Serbian North side. He told me that Mitrovica was one of the many places in Kosovo where ethnic cleansing and murders of ethnic Albanians occurred in April 1999. His uncle had been imprisoned by the Serb paramilitary police, and he feared it would make matters worse for him and his family if he stepped foot in the Serb side of Mitrovica and was found out that he was ethnic Albanian. So, we dropped him at a local cafe in South Mitrovica where he waited until we returned from the North. On my return trip in 2012, I was able to roam freely in Mitrovica, and didn't go through any checkpoints. The atmosphere was more relaxed, and you could see everywhere American flags, Albanian red and black flags along with European Union flags.

During the 2012 field trip, (November 09 - December 23, 2012), I stayed with two wonderful and generous host families of Gëzim Kunoviku and Hyrie Gashi. I lived in Bregu i Diellit "the Sunny Side" neighborhood in Prishtina, the capital of Kosovo (*Alb: Kosova*), located near the Kosovo Assembly and the Government of Kosovo building. The aim of the trip was to identify relevant factors and variables important to my research's hypotheses, and to understand the state's characteristics in policy-oriented behavior and foreign policy priorities. This is important in understanding the research problem from the local Kosovan perspective. I conducted semi-structured interviews and quantitative survey questionnaire with 220 participants.

During the two months stay I was able to make connections with high level officials, from the U.N., E.U. and NATO commanders, as well as meet with legal experts and local scholars from the University of Prishtina and the Institute of Albanology. Site visits included Ministry of Diaspora, Ministry of Foreign Affairs, the Prime Minister's Office, Ombudsman's Office, Ministry of Culture, Assembly of Kosovo, Ministry for the Kosovo Security Forces, the European Union Office in Kosovo and UNMIK headquarters in Prishtina. I also traveled to Mitrovica's ethnic Serbian and Albanian communities, and in Mitrovica's, the Trepca mining company site. Along with site visits to Peja, Rrugova, Gjilan, Mitrovica, Shpella e Gadimes "The Marbe Cave" in Lipljan, and the Mother Teresa Memorial House in Skopje, the capital of Macedonia.

The third field trip to Kosovo took place from October 31 to November 07, 2017, hosted by the amazingly kind and generous Hyrie Gashi family. The aim of the trip was to understand changes in the perceptions toward political and legal institutions, if any, for comparison purposes, and to assess the local attitudes towards the newly created Kosovo Specialist Court. I conducted key expert interviews and quantitative survey with 40 participants. I made connections with the political elite, prosecutors, lawyers, international staff from EULEX, the Kosovo Specialist Chambers (KSC) and SPC. Site visits included field trip to Gjakova, Prizren, the Albanian League of Prizren Museum, the Kalaja Fortress, Our Lady of Ljevis, (a UNESCO World Heritage Site), the stone bridges, the Church of Holy Savior, and the Church of our Lady of Perpetual Succour.

My mother's origin, "Cani" family, is from Malësia e Madhe in Gjakova, so this area was of great interest to me, and it was the first time I had ever been there. Cani is considered one of the oldest Albanian surnames and clans. Mahmud Cani is the first to be documented[463] they moved from Kosovo to Peqin, Albania in 1810, who fought in Dibër for Albania's independence against the Ottoman oppression, along with my great-grandfather Ramazan Cani[464] (Renaissance Patriot) and my grandfather Kastriot Cani (Albanian National Hero).[465]

On August 02, 2004 the honorable U.S. Congressman Mark Kennedy awarded Kastriot Cani, and his family, as collaborators of America to establish democracy through the Resistance Front, and my father Professor Neki Babamusta, for building democracy between Europe and U.S.A. [466] They have fostered a 100-year old relationship of friendship with Albania, USA and UK, a relation that initiated in the 1920s, and strengthened during the WWII war (1940-45), through the anti-communist organization "The Resistance Front" (Fronti i Rezistencës) and still continues today. The Resistance Front was directed by Hamdi Frashëri (chairman), Dill Cani (vice-president), dhe Kastriot Cani (Head Security of Mustafa Gjinishi, politically persecuted), Cen Kruja (politically persecuted), etc.

In addition to understanding the local Kosovan perspective, building democratic institutions and political legitimacy in Kosovo, three additional field trips (France, U.K., NY) were crucial in understanding the European perspective. On May 17 to June 03, 2010 I took part in the study abroad program in political science and I.R. studies in Strasbourg, France. The program was titled "Comparative Law and Institutions: Europe and the European Union" and was led by Dr. John

---

[463] Gripshi, G. (2014). *Historia e Peqinit. Tiranë*, Albania: Shtëpia Botuese "8 Nëntori," 263.

[464] Ramazan Cani, historic Albanian figure, Renaissance Patriot, awarded highest honor "Nation's Teacher."

[465] The Babamusta Family and Cani Family have fostered a 100-year old relationship of friendship with Albania, U.S.A. and U.K., a relation that initiated in the 1920s, and strengthened during the WWII war (1940-45), through the anti-communist organization "The Resistance Front" (Fronti i Rezistencës). The Resistance Front was directed by Hamdi Frashëri (chairman), Dill Cani (vice-president), and Kastriot Cani (Head Security of Mustafa Gjinishi, politically persecuted), Cen Kruja (politically persecuted).

[466] On July 04, 2013, U.S. Senate Majority Leader, the honorable Senator Harry Reid, awarded Neki Babamusta for his international advocacy of democracy, and Ermira Babamusta, "Distinguished Humanitarian Award," for her contribution to the international community, U.S. and Kosovo.

Kilwein, Director of Undergraduate Studies of Political Science Department at West Virginia University, in conjunction with Dr. Partrick Dollat, Senior Lecturer at the Institution for Political Sciences at the University of Strasbourg. The program was very helpful in understanding the E.U. and institutions with respect to international law and European affairs. Kosovo has been making progress in its efforts to European Union integration and membership. Understanding the European perspective of the political institutions and international laws involved in the integration process helped me get a better understanding of the factors involved.

The excellent program included site visits and seminars at the European Parliament, European Commission, Council of Europe, EuroCorps, the European Court of Human Rights, the European Court of Justice, the European Economic and Social Committee, EU institutions located in Strasbourg (France), Brussels (Belgium) and Netherland, the Foreign Ministry in Luxembourg, the Police Directorate in Offenburg and regional courts in Karlsruhe (Germany). The course-related trips gave a better insight to the strengths and challenges of the European Union. We met with EU officials at the European Parliament and with foreign ministers who discussed political issues, security, and foreign affairs. Site visits in Germany included the Supreme Constitutional Court "Bundesverfassungsgericht," located in the city of Karlsruhe, and a meeting with the Chief of Police of the Polizeidirektion in Offenburg, who had served in Kosovo to train the local police.

Germany was one of the first countries to recognize Kosovo's independence and establish bilateral diplomatic relations. Kosovans are very thankful to Germany for providing refuge to hundreds of thousands of refugees during the 1998-99 war. Germany also played a key role in the democratization efforts, promotion of regional cooperation and stability, along with training of police officers, judges, public prosecutors and civilian experts.[467] Remittances from diaspora, primarily located in Germany and Switzerland, are the main economic drivers of Kosovo's economy, estimated to account for about 15% of GDP.[468]

Another country which has been crucial in providing support pre- and post-statehood, has been United Kingdom. Specifically, U.K. provided a £110 million program of humanitarian assistance in 1999, and over £17 million for technical assistance in building the governmental institutional framework.[469] I lived in United Kingdom in 2015 for a year (February 21, 2015 - May 23, 2016) and stayed with my family, while engaging in diplomatic and political activities with the

[467] Federal Foreign Office. (2018, November). Kosovo: Political Relations. Retrieved from https://www.auswaertiges-amt.de/en/aussenpolitik/laenderinformationen/kosovo-node/kosovo/228088

[468] Morelli, V. L. (2018, August 13). Kosovo: Background and U.S. Relations. *Congressional Research Service*, 8. Retrieved from https://fas.org/sgp/crs/row/R44979.pdf

[469] Doyle, N., & Morina, E. (2013, October). The United Kingdom's Foreign Policy towards Kosovo - A policy perspective. *Group for Legal and Political Studies and Prishtina Council on Foreign Relations*, 7, 1-22. Retrieved from https://www.files.ethz.ch/isn/172261/Policy%20Report%2007%202013.pdf

Embassy of Kosovo and Embassy of Israel in London. From March 15 to May 30, 2018 I lived in New York, to take part in the United Nations meetings, meeting with a Kosovo delegation visiting the U.S., and meeting with the diplomatic core of the Consulate General of Kosovo in New York. I attended cultural diplomacy events, organized by the Consulate, with renowned political keynote speakers, the U.S. Ambassador to the United Nations, Nikki Haley, and Kosovo Ambassador to the United States, Teuta Sahatqija. The diplomatic engagements helped me get a better understanding of the inner workings of the U.N. and foreign diplomacy.

4.3.5 Data Collection Method and Tools

I carried out formal research following the protocol of the methodology, learning from what other researchers have done in the past in the area of rule of law. Initially, I reviewed United Nations rules of law indicators linked to state-building efforts in constructing effective and credible criminal justice institutions (police, judiciary), namely: *performance, capacity, integrity, transparency* and *accountability*, as well as *treatment of members of vulnerable groups*.[470] After understanding the performance measures, I reviewed the work of other researchers, to see what has been documented in scholarly journals and publications on political science disciplines.

I consulted the work of two previously prepared studies that were very useful in crafting and guiding my survey questionnaires – the Chicago Council on Foreign Relations (CCFR) 2004 survey and Katharine Richards' rule of law 2013 survey. The Chicago Council on Foreign Relations[471] conducts opinion surveys to study policy attitudes and perceptions of United States leaders, international norms, international institutions, and foreign policy goals.[472] This guided my first 2012 survey. Katharine Richards is a professor at the University of Connecticut, who did independent fieldwork in Croatia to understand the local legal perspectives on international human rights trials, focusing on rule of law initiatives and institutional reforms.[473] Richards' (2013) survey used structured interview questions to research the opinion of citizens of Croatia about the effectiveness of war crime trials. This guided my second 2018 survey questionnaire (See Appendix 1.)

---

[470] Department of Peacekeeping Operations. (2011). The United Nations Rule of Law Indicators: Implementation Guide and Project Tools. *United Nations Publication*, 1-137.

[471] In 2006 the CCFR Council changed its name to the Chicago Council on Global Affairs.

[472] Chicago Council on Foreign Relations. (2006, March 30). Global Views 2004: American Public Opinion and Foreign Policy. Ann Arbor, MI: *Inter-university Consortium for Political and Social Research*. http://doi.org/10.3886/ICPSR04137.v1

[473] Richards, K. (2013). International Trials, Rule of Law and Local Legal Consciousness in Croatia: Can International Justice Transform Local Norms? *University of Connecticut*, Storrs, 1-210.

Traditionally, political trust is measured in two ways, the European Social Survey (ESS) using an 11 point-scale[474], asking questions whether or not to trust government institutions, and the American National Election Studies (ANES), asking questions about the performance of the government. The EES measurement, is based on cultural theories where political trust "is expected to be constant through time, whereas the ANES measurement asks more for an evaluation of government at a point in time."[475]

The Chicago Council on Foreign Relations 2004 survey, asked people to rate their feelings toward international organizations on a scale of 0 to 100 from very cold to very warm for 1) the World Trade Organization (WTO), 2) the U.N., 3) the World Bank, 4) Multinational corporations, 5) the European Union, 6) the International Monetary Fund (IMF), 7) the International human rights group, 8) the World Court, and 9) the World Health Organization (WHO). Next, the survey lists Cuba, Iran, North Korea, and China, asking the participant, "Do you favor or oppose having diplomatic relations with the following countries?" Similarly, my 2012 survey asked the participants, "Are you in favor of having 1) trade ties, 2) diplomatic ties with the following countries?" listing: 1) Serbia, 2) Greece, 3) Macedonia, 4) Albania, 6) Montenegro, and 7) Russia as the choices with "in favor" and "against" as the two available responses. ANES and the Chicago Council on Foreign Relations survey provided for a good opportunity to test for specific performances of institutions, where the measurement is based on the trust for the government to do what is right.[476]

Katharine Richards' rule of law 2013 survey asked on a 5-point scale from "no trust" to "complete trust" to rate how much the respondent trusts the following sources about the International Criminal Tribunal for the former Yugoslavia (ICTY). Then it lists A) Newspaper, B) Television, C) Family and friends, D) Croatian government, E) Religious leaders, F) ICTY. Similarly, my 2018 survey asks to rate the following as sources about the Kosovo Specialist Court on war crimes, listing A) Newspaper/TV, B) Albanian Media, C) Serbian Media, D) Foreign Media, E) Kosovo government, F) Kosovo Specialist Court. Richards' (2013) survey provided for a good measure asking the people directly for political trust.

Because this research is looking at both cultural and institutional performance theories, the two surveys conducted in this study employ a combined approach. The questions in both surveys were framed in a manner that led respondents to provide direct "yes" or "no" responses, ranking order questions to prioritize policy issues and problem areas. EES measures, from a 1 to 5 Likert scale, ranging from "no trust" (=1) to "complete trust" (=5) were used asking people to indicate whether they trust several institutions, listing government, legal and international institutions.

---

[474] Other scholars have used other scales, such as a 4-point scale, or a 7-point scale.

[475] Andre, S. (2014), 970.

[476] Ibid, 971.

To evaluate performance of the government and of the leaders, ANES measurements were used, asking people to respond with "very satisfied" (=1) to "very dissatisfied" (=5), or a 1 to 4 scale "strongly agree" (=1) to "strongly disagree" (=4), and "very much" to "not at all" four-point scale. I avoided ambiguous questions, or questions that were too vague, lacked context or were too complex to understand. A lot of effort was put into translating the questions of the two surveys to Albanian and in English, including the interviews with the political elite and legal experts. Additionally, transcribing the voice recorded interviews manually for the verbatim transcript to later be translated to English was time consuming and the work was very rigorous. However, the expert interviews, were very important to the qualitative data collection method, in collecting detailed information about the research questions.

For the purpose of the qualitative research, in-depth interviews were used. The main advantage of in-depth interviews is that it allows the participants to explore the research topic in depth, by offering a more complete picture of the relevant factors that play a role, in this study – rule of law and attitudes of political trust.[477] Qualitative interviews are an essential research method and "the most direct, research-focused interaction between research and participant,"[478] often seen as one of the best ways to "enter into the other person's perspective."[479] In terms of the collection tool for the face-to-face interviews, semi-structured questionnaire was used, where questions were prepared ahead of time to guide the researcher toward the research objectives. Below are some of the sample questions included in 2018 semi-structured interview.[480]

Question 1:	What are your thoughts about the creation of the Kosovo Specialist court on war crimes?
Question 2:	What do you think will be the biggest challenges facing Specialist Court International Judges?
Question 3:	What difficulties do you envision the international judges will encounter when dealing with allegations of war crimes from KLA members, organized crime and other violations from 1998-2005?
Question 4:	What are some of the major problems today facing Kosovo Albanians who have immigrated outside the country?

[477] Boyce, C., & Neale, P. (2006). Conducting In-Depth Interviews: A Guide for Designing and Conducting In-Depth Interviews for Evaluation Input. Pathfinder International Tool Series, 1-16.

[478] Kazmer, M. & Xie, B. (2008). Qualitative interviewing in internet studies: Playing with the media, playing with the method. *Information, Communication, and Society*, 11(2), 258.

[479] Patton, M. Q. (2002). Qualitative research and evaluation methods (3rd ed.). Thousand Oaks, CA: Sage, 341.

[480] A detailed form of the interview guide is included in Appendix 1 for the 2017-2018 interviews and Appendix 2 for the 2012-2013 interviews.

Question 5:	What do you believe are currently some of the major challenges of the Specialist Court?
Question 6:	What about the current and future challenges of Kosovo people/government in dealing with the Specialist Court?
Question 7:	Do you think that the Kosovo Specialist Court has strengthened rule of law in Kosovo? Why? Why not?
Question 8:	How would you describe accountability, fairness, and transparency of the Specialist Court in Hague, Kosovo courts and Kosovo government?
Question 9:	What are some local or international initiatives to strengthen rule of law in Kosovo?
Question 10:	What are the biggest obstacles to achieving justice for the violations of human rights/war crimes that occurred in the 1998 Kosovo war?

4.4 Measures and variables

4.4.1 Measures of Political Trust

The aim of this study is to 1) determine the level of trust in various national and international institutions in Kosovo (*in Albanian: Kosova*), 2) identify the factors that influence levels of political trust, and 3) examine how political trust varies among different government institutions. Data are collected from two key original quantitative surveys conducted in Kosovo in 2012-2013 (220 participants) and 2017-2018 (40 participants). Results will be compared to see whether and how perceptions of political trust might differ pre- and post-2008 independence. Additional qualitative data was coordinated involving face-to-face interviews with the political elite and rule of law experts to gage the social and political attitudes towards political trust.

Indicators

Dependent Variable: Political Trust

The dependent variable is *political trust*. In accordance to the existing literature political trust was operationalized in this study from seven domains of political trust:

(1) trust in government;
(2) trust in politicians;

(3) trust in legal system;

(4) trust in police;

(5) trust in international organizations;

(6) trust in another country/embassy; and

(7) trust in media/TV.

Based on the European Social Survey (ESS) scale, the question on the 2018 survey was worded as follows: "Rate how much trust do you have in the following institutions?" Subsequently, the following national institutions and actors were mentioned: (1) Kosovo government, (2) Kosovo Police, (3) U.N., (4) E.U., (5) NATO, (6) Kosovo Specialist Court, (7) Kosovo courts, (8) U.S. Embassy in Kosovo. Respondents were asked to rate each institution on a 5-point Likert scale ranging from "no trust" (=1) to "complete trust" (=5).

Trust in media in the 2012-2013 survey was worded as follows: "Which media source do you think is the most reliable in Kosovo? List the numbers in each option below, rating them from 1 to 5, 1 being most reliable and 5 the least reliable." Respondents were asked to rate each media source from 1 (most reliable) to 5 (least reliable) during two time periods, "Pre-Independence" and "Post-Independence." Year 2008 is the break off point pre- and post-independence, using Kosovo's declaration of independence on February 17, 2008 as the divisive mark. Five media sources were listed following the question: (1) Albanian, (2) Serb, (3) American, (4) British, (5) Foreign/other. At the time, in addition to Albanian and Serbian media/TV, the majority of the communication to the Kosovo institutions was coming from the U.S. State Department, U.S. Embassy, the British Prime Minister's Office, and the German Counselor, as the key players involved in Kosovo's economic and political development during the time when the survey was conducted in 2012-2013. Instead of having one generalized trust index for media, I used the five separate media sources to see if there is a difference of trust in each sector.

In the 2018 survey, with the creation of the Kosovo Specialist Court, the trust in media question was rephrased to specifically identify participants' perceptions on war crimes, using six institutions as sources about the Kosovo Specialist Court. The question was worded as follows: "Rate how much you trust the following as sources of about the Kosovo Specialist Court on war crimes?" The listed sources were: (1) Newspaper/TV, (2) Albanian media, (3) Serbian media, (4) Foreign media, (5) Kosovo government, and (6) Kosovo Specialist Court. The establishment of the Kosovo Specialist Court set up to prosecute alleged war crimes during and after the war in Kosovo came with much controversy in Kosovo.[481] Therefore, it was important in this study to find out whether trust in the media sources had an effect on the trust levels in the court itself.

---

[481] Pineles, D. B. (2018, August 19). War Crimes Indictments Could Wreck Kosovo-Serbia Talks. *Balkan Insight*.

Independent Variables

In accordance with previous research,[482] political trust is examined as being the function of cultural and institutional performance factors. Therefore, the independent variables capture four measures of political trust: (1) *national identity*, (2) *interpersonal trust*, (3) *trustworthiness* and (4) *perceived government performance*. The cultural category includes national identity (*national and ethnic identification)* and interpersonal trust (*political participation*). The second category, institutional performance includes trustworthiness in government and leaders (*fairness, competence*) and perceived government performance (*legitimacy, effectiveness*).

National Identity

"National Pride" was used as an indicator for national identity or attachment to the nation. The 2012-2013 survey asked participants to rate the national symbols on a 5-point Likert scale from "very satisfied" (=1) to "very dissatisfied" (=5) by asking: "Your view regarding Kosovo's national symbols (flag, emblem, hymn)." Other indicators of national identification included in the socio-demographics variables include *citizenship, place of birth/residence, nationality*. Ethnic identification refers to the ethnic background of the individual.

Two questions were asked to ethnic Albanians and Serbs in Kosovo (*Alb: Kosova*) to gage the attachment to their nation: "How is an Albanian from Kosovo identified?" with four possible answers: "Albanian," "Kosovan," "Kosovan Albanian," and "Other (explain)." The same question was repeated for Serb from Kosovo. Another question asked: "Are you in favor of the unification of Kosovo with Albania?" with a "yes" or "no" answer, to understand if the locals view their national pride and patriotism as part of the motherland, with close ties to Albania, or whether Kosovo Albanians see themselves as a separate nation.

Another question was asked to understand if Kosovo Serbs in the conflict area in the North (Mitrovica) have the same attachment to the nation by asking: "Do the Serbs in the North feel they are Kosovan citizens?" with "yes," "no," and "partially" responses.

Interpersonal Trust

Interpersonal trust is operationalized by three items measuring trust in people in the same ethnic group, different ethnic group, and political participation. The question was asked: "Do Serbs take part in local elections?" with "yes," "no," and "partially" responses. This question was asked

[482] Godefroidt, A., Langer A., & Meuleman, B. (2015).

because of the growing concerns of the Kosovo leaders of the existing parallel structures in the North, where Kosovo Serbs follow orders from Belgrade rather than Prishtina.

To understand trust in the same ethnic group and in different ethnic group two different scales of interpersonal trust were used. First participants were asked to rate their trust in different sources. Secondly, they were asked to choose the best way to address crime based on the different ethnicity of the perpetrator. (1) Operationalized by measuring trust in people with diverse characteristics: people from different ethnic groups and nationalities, and from your region or different regions. The question was phrased: "Rate how much you trust the following as sources of about the Kosovo Specialist Court on war crimes?" The following sources were mentioned: Albanian Media, Serbian Media, Foreign Media. Respondents could rate on a 1 to 5 Likert scale, ranging from "no trust" (= 1) to "complete trust" (= 5). The 2012-2013 survey indicators also list "British Media" and "American Media" in addition to "Foreign other."

(2) The second question asked: "If a Kosovan committed war crimes in Kosovo, what is the best way to address the crime?" The following legal institutions were mentioned: Kosovo court, Serbian court, the Kosovo Specialist Court, ICTY Hague Tribunal, being asked to choose one of the options. The same question was asked for individuals who identify as Serbian. "If a Serbian committed war crimes in Kosovo, what is the best way to address the crime?"

Trustworthiness

Political trust is understood as "an individual's expectation that a political actor will act in their interest," across different targets: the political system, the government, political parties, institutions, and political actors.[483] Trustworthiness is equated with "a trustee's commitment to act in the truster's interest."[484] Researchers have focused on the relationship between democracy and political trust, expecting democratic institutions that are *fair* and *competent* to positively influence trust.[485] Perceptions of trustworthiness are measured on two scales: *fairness* and *competence*.

The American National Election Studies (ANES) distinguishes between regime-based trust, and incumbent-based trust, where the latter captures trust perceptions of the political leaders and officials, and the former captures attitudes toward the broader political system as a whole.[486] This study measures different types of trust, such as the political leaders and the legal institutions, as targets of political trust. For each target the study measures trustworthiness based on the fairness/

---

[483] Bauer, P. C., & Fatke, M. (2014, February 05). Direct Democracy and Political Trust: Enhancing Trust, Initiating Distrust–or Both? *Swiss Political Science Review,* 20(1), 51. doi:10.1111/spsr.12071

[484] Ibid, 51.

[485] See Mishler & Rose (2001) and Catterberg & Moreno (2006).

[486] Parker et al. (2014), 91.

competence scale, as well as the ANES scale of trust (1) honest, (2) know what they are doing, (3) do the right thing, and (4) interest.

In this study trust in *legal system* is linked to *fair* and *impartial* as measures of *"fairness"* and *"competence"* for trustworthy legal institutions. First the participants were asked in the 2018 survey: "How much confidence do you have in the Kosovan courts to conduct fair trials?" followed by 4-point scale answers "very much," "some," "a little," or "not at all." The same question was asked for international courts to see people's perceptions of trust and fairness.

Secondly, the survey asked: "Which judges are better able to make impartial decisions in trials of a) war crimes b) genocide/human rights violations that took place in Kosovo?" in a three-choice answer: 1) international judges, 2) Kosovan judges, and 3) Serbian judges. The study also included *"interest"* as one of the ANES measures to understand the direct political trust with the institution or actor. The question was phrased: "Do you think EU has the best interest of Kosovo in mind when making decisions in the Specialist Court?" with "yes" and "no" responses. The 2012-2013 survey asked participants: "How satisfied are you with the citizens' interests being represented by the political parties?" on a 5-point Likert scale from "very satisfied" (=1) to "very dissatisfied" (=5).

Trustworthiness in *political leaders* in this study was measured by various aspects of the ANES scale on a 5-point scale "very satisfied" (=1) to "very dissatisfied" (=5). Questions were asked whether leaders (1) create a mutual trust atmosphere, (2) demonstrate honesty and are ethical, (3) demonstrate a clear vision, (4) declare their expectations/hopes, (5) provide necessary support, (6) show tolerance, and (7) have good relationships with civil servants regardless of position. These measures provide insight to people's perceptions that are influenced by evaluations and traits of political officials and institutions.

Performance

Perceptions of government performance were measured by asking the participants to rate government *legitimacy, transparency, efficiency,* and *accountability*. Performance measures are used to measure (1) individual-level job performance and (2) institutional performance.[487] The evaluation of the job performance of a political leader, or the president's performance toward a certain policy or objective. Trust in the leadership is as an important component to political trust as presidential popularity can increase people's trust, and poor performance "can sour individuals on the national government, or even the entire political system."[488] The performance category of

---

[487] Godefroidt et al. (2015), 5.

[488] Parker et al. (2014), 92.

variables is composed of measures of (1) quality of institutions, in terms of efficiency, responsiveness, transparency, (2) governance, and (3) government competence.[489]

In this study, *"perceived government performance,"* is measured by quality or the outputs of the institutions, *"satisfaction with the government performance,"* as in government *legitimacy and effectiveness*, derived from institutional features such as accountability, efficiency, transparency, and fairness. Participants were asked to rate on a 5-point scale "very satisfied" (=1) to "very dissatisfied" (=5), about leaders (1) making administrative goals and priorities practical and understandable to the citizens; (2) communicating their decisions and act immediately, (3) communicate effectively and charismatically with carious groups; (4) take responsibility for their actions without blaming others; (5) include others during planning; and (6) use training that teaches skills in leadership.

In addition to evaluations of *quality of government institutions* in general, this study measures evaluations of *policy-oriented government performance* The question was phrased: "Do you think that the minorities in Kosovo are protected?" in 4-point Likert scale "strongly agree," "somewhat agree," "somewhat disagree," and "strongly disagree." Other questions asked to rate the priorities of the Ministry of Foreign Affairs by importance on a scale on 1 to 5, "1" being "most important" and "5" being the "least important," followed by 5 policy choices: create diplomatic relations, promote political interest, promote economic interest, protect citizens' rights (women, minorities) and maintenance of law and order. Another policy domain tested in this study is European Union integration, where the question asked was: "Do you think a) Kosovo, b) Serbia meets the condition for membership in the EU?" on a 4-point scale from "strongly agree" to strongly disagree."

The study provides insight on the *Kosovo police* performance and the role of the *international civil and military presence*. Performance perceptions were measured by asking: "Is Kosovo Police effective in the following tasks?" in five different tasks, (1) protecting life and property, (2) maintaining public order and pace, (3) preventing and detecting crime, (4) protecting people's rights and freedoms, (5) treating people equally regardless of race, color, religion, gender and age. The choices were to rate 1-5 each of the tasks, pre/post-independence. The same question was repeated for the international presence, asking: "Do you think that the international civil and military presence is effective in Kosovo?" On a 5-point scale "very satisfied" (=1) to "very dissatisfied" (=5).

Additional questions were asked to evaluate the role of several international institutions, namely EULEX, UNMIK, NATO, ICO, KFOR, OSCE, pre- and post-independence, on a 5-point scale from "efficient," "efficient and powerful," partially efficient," inefficient" and "poor." Questions about performance satisfaction whether UNMIK fulfilled the conditions of the mission and whether the EU has been efficient were asked on the 5-point scale "very satisfied" to "very dissatisfied."

---

[489] Tendler, J. (1997). *Good Governance in the Tropics*. Maryland: Johns Hopkins University Press.

Another measure of performance used was "*integrity*," where the respondents were asked their performance perceptions regarding three institutions, 1) Kosovo police, 2) EULEX and 3) UNIMK if they think these institutions show responsibility and professional integrity, with a "yes" or "no" answer. This measure is based on the United Nations rule of law indicators, listing "integrity, transparency, and accountability," "competence," "treatment of vulnerable groups" and "capacity" as the main four rule of law indicators. The question was phrased: "Do you think the Kosovo police is competent in achieving the strategic objectives described above?" listing the 5 aforementioned tasks with a "yes" and "no" answer. To understand perceptions of trust in the Kosovo police as an institution the following question was asked, "Do you trust the Kosovo police," with a "yes" or "no" answer.

In terms of the broader political system, the question was framed, "Do you think the government today in Kosovo is?" followed by 5 options: (1) democratic and fair, (2) democratic but not strong, (3) it does not function, (4) corrupted, and (5) not democratic. Based on the research, corruption is expected to have a negative effect on political trust, where higher corruption leads to lower political trust in institutions.[490] Other socio-economic variables included gender, age, education. Table 3 and Table 4 show the complete list of variables.

Table 3: Description of Variables
(Based on 2018 Survey)

Variable	Description
Trust Index in Institutions	
Trust in Kosovo Government	Respondents' level of trust in Kosovo Government
Trust in Kosovo Police	Respondents' level of trust in Kosovo Police
Trust in UN	Respondents' level of trust in United Nations
Trust in EU	Respondents' level of trust in European Union
Trust in NATO	Respondents' level of trust in NATO
Trust in Kosovo Specialist Court (KSC)	Respondents' level of trust in KSC Court
Trust in Kosovo Courts	Respondents' level of trust in Kosovo Courts
Trust in US Embassy in Kosovo	Respondents' level of trust in US Embassy in Kosovo
Trust in Media Sources	
Trust in Newspaper/TV	Respondents' level of trust in Newspaper/TV as source of about the Kosovo Specialist Court on war crimes

[490] Fang & Stone. (2010), 2.

Trust in Albanian Media	Respondents' level of trust in Albanian Media as source of about the Kosovo Specialist Court on war crimes
Trust in Serbian Media	Respondents' level of trust in Serbian Media as source of about the Kosovo Specialist Court on war crimes
Trust in Foreign Media	Respondents' level of trust in Foreign Media as source of about the Kosovo Specialist Court on war crimes
Trust in Kosovo Government	Respondents' level of trust in Kosovo Government a source of about the Kosovo Specialist Court on war crimes
Trust in Kosovo Specialist Court (KSC)	Respondents' level of trust in Kosovo Specialist Court as source of about the Kosovo Specialist Court on war crimes
Performance of legal institutions and actors	
Caring about KSC decisions	Respondents' care about the decisions the Kosovo Specialist Court makes in war crimes trials
Safety	Respondents' perceptions on whether the decisions of the Kosovo Specialist Court affect feelings of safety in Kosovo
Effectiveness	Respondents' perceptions toward the effectiveness of the Kosovo Specialist Court in achieving justice for war crimes

Fairness	Respondents' confidence in Courts to conduct fair trials:
	    a. Confidence in Kosovan Courts
	    b. Confidence in International Courts

Impartiality	Respondents' perceptions towards which judges are better able to to make impartial decisions in trials of (1) war crimes and (2) genocide/human rights violations that took place in Kosovo:
	    a. Kosovo Specialist Court International Judges
	    b. Kosovan Judges
	    c. Serbian Judges

EU	Respondents' perception toward EU if it has the best interest of Kosovo in mind when making decisions in the Kosovo Specialist Court

Achieving Justice	Respondents' perceptions toward the best way to address the crime of (1) genocide, (2) war crimes committed by a (1) Kosovan, (2) Serbian:
	    a. Kosovo Court
	    b. Serbian Court
	    c. Kosovo Specialist Court
	    d. ICTY Hague Tribunal

Socio-Demographic Characteristics	
Age	Respondents' age
Religion	Respondent's ethnicity
Ethnicity	Respondent belongs to an ethnic group
Gender	Respondents' gender
Residence	Respondent resides in Kosovo
Citizenship	Respondent is a citizen of Kosovo
Profession	Respondents' occupation
War Crime Victim	Respondent is a war crime victim

Refer to Appendix 1 and Appendix 2 for the full survey questionnaire conducted in Kosovo in two different time periods. Appendix 1 includes the 2012-2013 survey of 220 participants conducted in Kosovo. Appendix 2 includes the 2017-2018 survey of 40 participants.

Table 4 includes a description of all the indicators of political trust for each sector of government. Followed by Figure 7, illustrating the structure of political trust in four systems: political, legal, public, and international.

Table 4: Indicators for Each Sector

(Based on 2012-2013 Survey)

Sector	Description
Political Leaders	
Mutual Trust	Have the leaders created an atmosphere of mutual trust for the people and government?
Honesty and Moral Behavior	Do leaders in Kosovo demonstrate honesty and moral behavior in accordance with the appropriate ethics in all their actions? (satisfied 5-point scale)
Clear Vision	Do leaders demonstrate a clear vision with known purposes for the administration and the people? (satisfied 5-point scale)
Administrative Goals and Priorities	Do leaders make the administration goals / priorities practical and understandable to the citizens starting from the most important to the least important ones?
Immediate Communication of Decisions	Do leaders communicate their decision and do they act immediately? (satisfied 5-point scale)
Effective Communication of Decisions	Do leaders communicate so effectively and charismatically with various groups? (satisfied 5-point scale)
Tolerance	Do leaders show tolerance? (satisfied 5-point scale)
Training	Do leaders use training that teaches skills in leadership and common work? (satisfied scale)
Kosovo Government	
Democratic and Fair	Do you think the government today in Kosovo is democratic and Fair?
Reform	Do you think Kosovo needs reforms in the (1) legal system, (2) electoral system, (3) economic system?
Change in Governance	Do you think it is necessary to have a change in the governance of Kosovo?
Political Parties	
Cooperation	Is there cooperation between political parties in Kosovo?
Trust	Do you trust political parties in Kosovo?

Political Philosophy	Do you think that the political philosophy of parties is led by (1) Ideology, (2) Ethnic belonging, (3) Regional belonging?
Citizens' Interests	How satisfied are you with the citizens' interests being represented by the political parties? (satisfied 5-point scale)
The International Community	
Serbia	Are you satisfied with the relations between Kosovo-Serbia? After declaring independence in 2008, has Serbian government changed its attitude towards Kosovo? Your opinion on Serbia-Kosovo talks, how do you evaluate them? Your opinion on multilateral talks, how do you evaluate them? (Satisfied scale); (1) pre-independence, (2) post-independence.
UN Role	Do you think the UN has played a positive role in Kosovo? How do you evaluate the role of UNMIK (1) pre-independence? (2) post-independence? (Efficient to poor 5-point scale)
UNMIK	Do you think that UNMIK has fulfilled the conditions of the mission for Kosovo? (Satisfied Scale)
EU Role	Do you think that the role of the European Union has been efficient in Kosovo? How do you evaluate the role of the EULEX? (Efficient to Poor scale)
NATO Role	How do you evaluate the role of NATO? (1) pre-independence? (2) post-independence? (Efficient to Poor scale) Do you think that NATO's intervention stopped the genocide in Kosovo? Do you think that NATO's intervention is the cause of independence?
Overall Role of International Community	How do you evaluate the role of international community including here UNMIK, EULEX, ICO, KFOR, OSCE, (1) pre-independence, (2) post-independence? (Efficient to Poor scale)
Foreign Policy Decisions	
Decisions of Leaders by state in Foreign Policy	How do you evaluate the decisions of the leaders of these states in foreign policy towards Kosovo, Serbia, Russia, USA, UK, France, Germany, Albania (1) pre-independence, (2) post-independence? (very poor to the best rank)
Decisions of Leaders in domestic politics	(very poor to the best 7-point scale)

EU Integration	Is Kosovo in the path towards EU? (Yes/No)
	Is Serbia in the path towards EU? (Yes/No)
	Do you see Kosovo in the future as a member of the EU? (Yes/No)
	Rate the steps the leaders have taken towards the EU membership (1-5)
Kosovo Police and International Civil/Military Presence	
Military Presence	Do you think the military presence of the international community is needed in Kosovo? (Yes/No)
Effectiveness	Do you think that the Kosovo Police is effective in implementing its strategic objectives? (Satisfied 5-point scale)
	Do you think that the international civil and military presence is effective?
	Is Kosovo police effective in the following tasks?
	(1) Protecting life and property, (2) Maintaining public order and peace, (3) Preventing and detecting crime, (4) Protecting people's rights and freedoms, (5) Treating people equally regardless of race, color, religion, gender, age.
Management	How do you evaluate the management of the Kosovo Police? (efficient scale)
	How do you evaluate the management of EULEX? (efficient 5-point scale)
Trust	Do you trust the Kosovo police? (Yes/No)
	Do you trust the foreign military forces in protecting Kosovo? (Yes/No)
Competency	Do you think Kosovo police is competent in achieving the strategic objectives? (Yes/No)
Responsibility & Integrity	Do you think the following show responsibility and professional integrity? (1) Kosovo Police, (2) EULEX, (3) UNMIK. (Yes/No)
Coordination	Do you think there is sufficient coordination between the Kosovo Police and EULEX?
Role of Media and TV	
Role of Media	What role did the media / TV play? (1) Albanian, (2) Serb, (3) Foreign.
Reliable Source	Which media source do you think is the most reliable in Kosovo? (Albanian, Serb, American, British, Other) (Pre /Post Independence)

Influence	Has media /TV had an influence in the image of (1) Kosovo, (2) Serbia?
Support	Which side do you think has the (1) Albanian media, (2) Serbian supported?
Propaganda	Do you think there is anti-Albanian propaganda in the Serb media? (Yes/No)
	Do you think there is anti-Serb propaganda in the Albanian media? (Yes/No)
Safety	
Safety	Do you think Kosovo was safer (1) Pre-Independence, (2) Post Independence?
	The tension between Albanians and Serbs in North has (increased/ decreased scale).
	Do you think there is safety currently in Kosovo? (Agree 4-point scale)
	Do you think the issue in the North has a solution? (Agree 4-point scale)
	How do you consider the Situation in the North pre- and post-independence? (stabilization scale)
Return of Minorities in Kosovo	(increase to decrease 5-point scale)
Return of Albanians in Kosovo	(increase to decrease 5-point scale)
Free movement of minorities in Kosovo	(increase to decrease 5-point scale)
National Identity	
National Identity & Pride	How is an Albanian from Kosovo identified?
	How is a Serb from Kosovo identified? (Albanian, Kosovan, Kosovan Albanian, Other)
	Do the Serbs in the north feel they are Kosovan citizens?
	Do Serbs take part in local elections?
National Symbols	Your view regarding Kosovo's national symbols (flag, emblem, hymn) (satisfied 5-point scale)

National Image	Do you consider Kosovo today: Multiethnic State (Yes, No, Somewhat agree) Stabilized State (Yes, No, Somewhat agree) Democratic State (Yes, No, Somewhat agree) Independent State (Yes, No, Somewhat agree)
Ethnic Minority	Do you think that the minorities in Kosovo are protected? (agree scale)
Feelings of Discrimination	Rate cases of violations against property (for all citizens): Property rights Rate cases of violations of minority rights: physical abuse, discrimination Rate cases of violation of women's rights: abuse/ domestic violence, rape, discrimination (1-5 scale; pre/post-independence)
Support of Government for Women	(increase to decrease 5-point scale; pre/post-independence)
Socio-Demographic Characteristics	
Gender Age Nationality	Place of Birth & Residence Education Profession Leadership Position

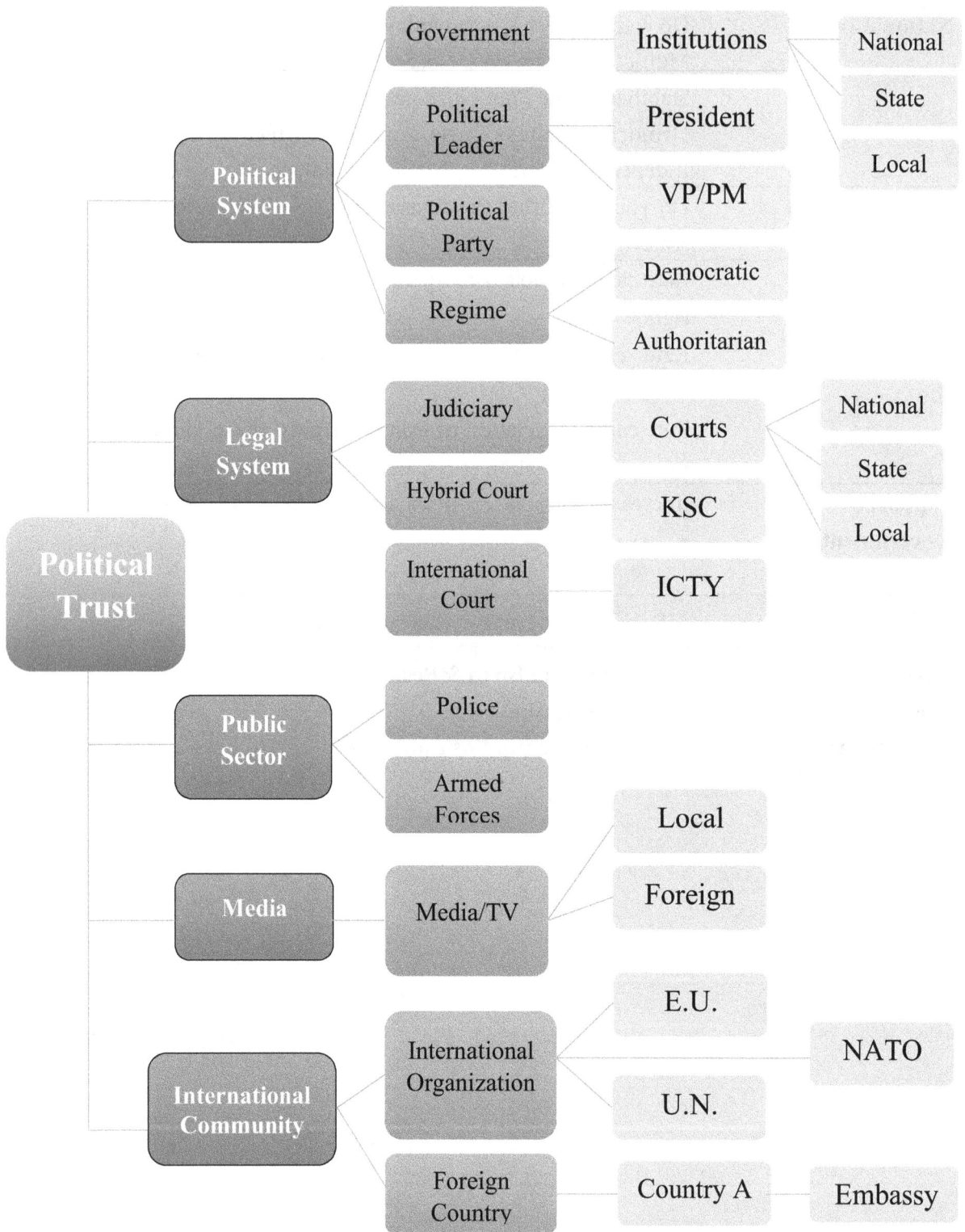

Figure 7: Structure of Political Trust in Political, Legal, Public, and International Systems

4.4.2 Sample Selection

For this study I employed the case study approach with a single case analysis of political trust in Kosovo (*Alb: Kosova*) by comparing elite perceptions of political trust pre/post-independence, towards government institutions, political leaders, and the international community. A second survey was conducted in 2018 to get an in-depth understanding of Kosovo's level of trust change over time, by focusing on rule of law and the creation of the Specialist Kosovo Court. Case studies allow for exploration and understanding of complex issues, by providing "a holistic and in-depth investigation"[491] of the research problem in many areas and fields, particularly in government, management, and law.[492]

The method of *purposive sampling* was used to develop the research sample of political trust in Kosovo. According to the purposive sampling technique, sample members are selected based on the expertise, knowledge and relevant work experience in the field that is being researched.[493] In the current study, the sample members who were selected are political leaders, foreign affairs, legal, and rule of law experts, who have knowledge and work experience in Kosovo. Within this context, the selected participants were diplomats, executives in government post, ministers and assembly members, lawyers, police officers, administrative staff employed in international organizations such as the United Nations, European Union, NATO, and university professors particularly in the fields of political science, law, history and sociology to get a full understanding of the cultural and institutional performance factors that influence political trust.

The 2012-2013 survey conducted in Kosovo was a sample of 220 participants of experts and the political elite. The 2018 survey included the sample of 40 experts from various agencies and offices dealing with foreign affairs, rule of law and legal affairs in Kosovo.

Participants of this study were officials and experts of 10 key agencies and offices operating in Kosovo, and specifically in Prishtina, namely:

1) Assembly of Kosovo,
2) Government of Kosovo building,
3) Kosovo's Security Force,
4) The Ministry of Diaspora,
5) Ministry of Culture, Community and Youth,
6) United Nations,

---

[491] Zainal, Z. (2007, June 9). Case study as a research method. *Jurnal Kemanusiaan,* 9, 1-6. Retrieved from http://psyking.net/htmlobj-3837/case_study_as_a_research_method.pdf

[492] Stake, R.E. (1995). *The Art of Case Study Research: Perspective in Practice.* London: Sage.

[493] Freedman, D. A., Pisani, R., & Purves, R. A. (2007*). Statistics.* 4th ed.. New York: W. W. Norton & Company.

7) European Union,

8) NATO,

9) Media/TV,

10) University of Prishtina and Institute of Albanology.

The survey questionnaires were printed and handed out to the participants in person or via email, later collected to discuss part II of the survey, which included expert interviews. On some occasions from the 2012 survey, a group of 20-30 participants were gathered in a room, were explained the scope of the study and were handed the survey. Quantitative and qualitative data collected from the 2012 and 2018 surveys were used to build five conceptual models of political trust, illustrated by: (1) sources of trust in Figure 1; (2) trust levels in Figure 2; (3) characteristics of motivation-based trust in Table 1; (4) trust determinants, based on the cultural and institutional factors in Figure 5; and (5) the structure of political trust in Figure 7.

4.4.3 Interviews

Purposeful qualitative research methodology was used as the main approach for the interviews conducted for this study. The survey, in addition to the quantitative data, used open-ended structured questions where the participant could not deviate from the topic, allowing the respondent room to discuss the topic in great details. This approach is favored by researchers to provide a more complete picture of the research topic.[494]

The expert interviews were semi-structured questions, allowing the political official to provide an in-depth analysis of the research topic in different areas, namely: (1) situation in Kosovo pre/post-independence, (2) Kosovo leadership under local leaders; (3) international and diplomatic relations with other countries; (4) role and function of the international community; (5) Kosovo toward European Union; (7) Kosovo police and the international civil/military presence (8) Role and function of Media/TV; (9) leadership and the future of Kosovo; and (10) strengthening rule of law and challenges of the Kosovo Specialist Court.

The 2012 interviews were carried out from November and December of that year in Kosovo. The initial contact was made by telephone or email whilst I was living in Prishtina, Kosovo. The meeting locations were arranged in Kosovo after confirming the appointments. The locations were chosen in a quiet place free from distractions to allow for accurate recording of the information.[495]

---

[494] Weiss, R. (1994). *Learning from Strangers; The Art and Method of Qualitative Interview Studies*. New York, The Free Press, 222.

[495] Creswell, J. (1998). *Qualitative Inquiry and Research Design; Choosing Among Five Traditions*. London, New Delhi, Thousand Oaks, Sage Publications, 372.

The interviews lasted for one to two hours per person, using a digital voice recorder. The majority of interviews were conducted in the Albanian language, and then translated into English by the author.

The quantitative survey was conducted in person or via email from November 2012 to March 2013, using closed-ended questions. The group surveys conducted at the police academy or the university, where 20 to 30 participants were gathered at once, were done according to a structured academic procedure, to explain the scope, the research questions and provide instructions about the survey. The survey was very lengthy (25 pages, 125 questions), so this ensured the successful completion of the survey. Interviews on the other hand (45 questions), were conducted by leading the process of building trust and rapport with the interviewee, to have the feel of a conversation, rather than a structured academic process. According to Weiss (1994) this allows for the responded to feel more at ease, to provide more valuable information and to ensure that all the questions were being answered.[496]

The 2017-2018 interviews (20 questions) were conducted in Prishtina, London, and New York with diplomats and key experts as illustrated in this section. The quantitative survey was conducted via email during September and November 2018, while I was still in the United States. The survey was much shorter compared to the 2012-2013 survey, only 2 pages long, with 15 questions excluding the additional socio-demographic questions. The focus of the 2018 survey was primarily to understand the level of political trust in various institutions, to identify the level of confidence in the Kosovo Specialist Court, and to compare local preferences of international judges versus local judges and prosecutors.

Participants of this study included interviews with the political elite and experts from various offices, namely:

(1) the Prime Minister's office in Kosovo (*in Albanian: Kosova*);
(2) Consulate General of Kosovo in London and New York;
(3) UNMIK, EULEX, and KFOR;
(4) the Ombudsman Institution of Kosovo;
(5) senior staff working at the Government building and the Assembly of Kosovo;
(6) various ministries: Ministry of Justice, Ministry of Diaspora, Ministry of Culture, Ministry for Kosovo Security Force, and the Ministry of Local Government and Administration;
(7) UNDP;
(8) Kosovo Chambers of Commerce;
(9) Institute of Albanology; and
(10) the International Red Cross.

---

[496] Weiss, R. (1994), 222.

The respondents were free to express their views during the in-depth interviews and the conversations flowed smoothly, naturally, and pleasantly. In both surveys the participants were assured that their answers were being treated confidential and used only for the academic purpose of research. Ensuring that the surveys were truly confidential is important to the survey response rate and the honest nature of the answers.[497]

The qualitative interviews were conducted with the consent of the participant, within the parameters of The Data Protection Act.[498] The interview participants were given the choice to remain anonymous or to have their identity revealed with a short bio included, to ensure comfort. Overall, it was an enjoyable and great experience meeting with the high-ranking officials and learning about rule of law and diplomacy.[499]

4.4.4 Analytical Constrains

Case studies are limited because results can't be generalized to the wider population.[500] The size of the sample was small, 220 and 40. A larger sample would enhance the reliability of the research.[501] This project was taken on specifically as a case study since data for Kosovo are almost non-existing and not available, with several years missing in many studies. Schneider (2017) found varying results of political trust in Western and Easter Europe, making the application of trust models difficult to apply across Europe.[502] Thus, case studies are important to understand the effects of political trust factors over the political institutions in each country.

Data produced from surveys "are likely to lack details or depth on the topic being investigated."[503] Therefore a combined qualitative and quantitative method was employed to overcome this constrain. The analysis of the role of the cultural and institutional factors on political trust maybe be influenced by other determinants not mentioned here. In the qualitative findings, bias may affect the validity, consequently affecting political trust determinants.[504] However, informa-

---

[497] Kelley, K., Clark, B., Brown, V., & Sitzia, J. (2003, May 1). Good practice in the conduct and reporting of survey research. *International Journal for Quality in Health Care, 15(3)*, 261–266. https://doi.org/10.1093/intqhc/mzg031

[498] SRA & MRS. (2005, October). Data Protection Act 1999: Guidelines for Social Research. *Social Research Association*,1-63. Retrieved from http://the-sra.org.uk/wp-content/uploads/sra_data_protection.pdf

[499] See Appendix for a complete list of activities, interviews, meetings and site excursions.

[500] Stake, R.E. (2005). Qualitative case studies. In N.K. Denzin & Y.S. Lincoln (Eds.) The Sage handbook of qualitative research (3rd ed.), 443-466. Thousand Oaks, CA: Sage.

[501] Lameck, W. U. (2013, July). Sampling Design, Validity and Reliability in General Social Survey. *International Journal of Academic Research in Business and Social Sciences, 3(7)*, 212-2018. doi: 10.6007/IJARBSS/v3-i7/27

[502] Schneider, I. (2017), 963.

[503] Kelley et al. (2003, May 1).

[504] Easterbrook, P. J., Berlin, J. A., Gopalan, R, et al. (1991). Publication bias in research. *Lancet, 337,* 867–72.

tion obtained from government officials is reliable because it represents the target population of the research. The political elite represents the interests and the voice of the people; thus, it should be applicable to the wider population. But in reality, "the nation and the public are not homogenous."[505] To overcome this limitation, the research focused on perceptions of political, public, legal, and international institutions for a complete view.

---

[505] Griffiths, P. (2015). The "Necessity" of a Socially Homogeneous Population: The Ruling Class Embraces Racial Exclusion. *Labour History*, (108), 123-144. doi:10.5263/labourhistory.108.0123

CHAPTER 5

Results

This chapter presents the findings of the study based on quantitative information gathered from two surveys conducted in Kosovo in 2012-2013 and 2018. The findings relate to the research questions that guided the study, followed by discussion of the research findings. Data was analyzed to the levels of political trust in Kosovo across different institutions in Kosovo, including government, political leaders, political parties, police, courts, and the international community.

5.1 Levels and Structure of Political Trust in Kosovo

5.1.1 Trust in Government

Trust in government primarily captures "attitudes toward the entire political system," including the national and local government.[506] In the 2018 survey the study asked, "Rank how much trust do you have in the Kosovo government?" and majority response shows no trust. Notably, 67.5% responded that they have "no trust," and only 7.5% felt that they have "complete trust" (*See Graph 1*). This shows that in Kosovo (*in Albanian: Kosova*) there is lack of trust in the overall political system.

Additionally, 60% of men and 77.7% of women answered that they have no trust in the Kosovo government, and only 9% of males and 0% of females have complete trust in the government. Graph 1 shows a higher amount of distrust in the Kosovo government among women.

---

[506] Parker et al. (2014), 89.

How much trust do you have in the KOSOVO Government?

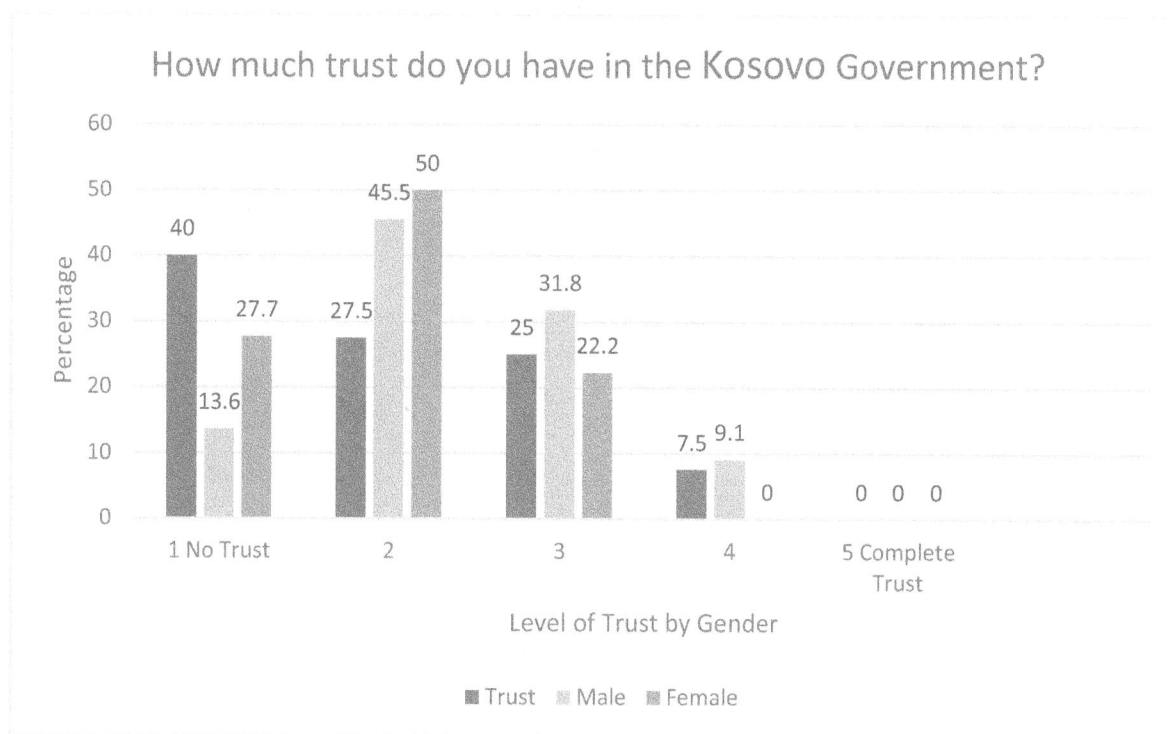

Graph 1: Trust in Kosovo Government by Gender (2018)

To better understand the socio-demographic factors that influence trust, this study asked the participants in the 2012-2013 survey to, "Rate the support of government for women" pre/post-independence. They answered that pre-independence it was lower (40%), neither higher nor lower (39%), and higher (24%). However, perceptions of support of government for women post-independence increased significantly: 67% (higher), 17.2% (neither higher no lower) and only 1.5% (lower).

The results suggest that higher support of government for women does not affect positively women's overall trust in government. This means that another factor accounts for the higher number of women distrusting the Kosovo government. This is in line with the findings of another study which finds that women in Kosovo generally tend to have less trust in institutions compared to men, "specifically in parliament and politicians."[507]

This study also found different levels of trust towards the Kosovo government between Kosovo Albanians and other nationals. The findings show that ethnic Albanians tend to have less trust in the institutions compared to foreign nationals. Respectively, 80% of Kosovo Albanians who are ethnic Albanians have no trust in the Kosovo government, and among the other foreign nationals (non-Albanian) 50% said to have trust level 3 (on a scale of 1 "no trust" to 5 "complete trust") and 12.5% were level 4 of trust (See Graph 2).

---

[507] Pula, E. (2017), 13.

How much trust do you have in the Kosovo Government?

Level of Trust by Ethnicity	1 No Trust	2	3	4	5 Complete Trust
Trust	40	27.5	25	7.5	0
Ethnic Albanian	15.6	65	15.6	3.2	0
Foreign	12.5	25	50	12.5	0

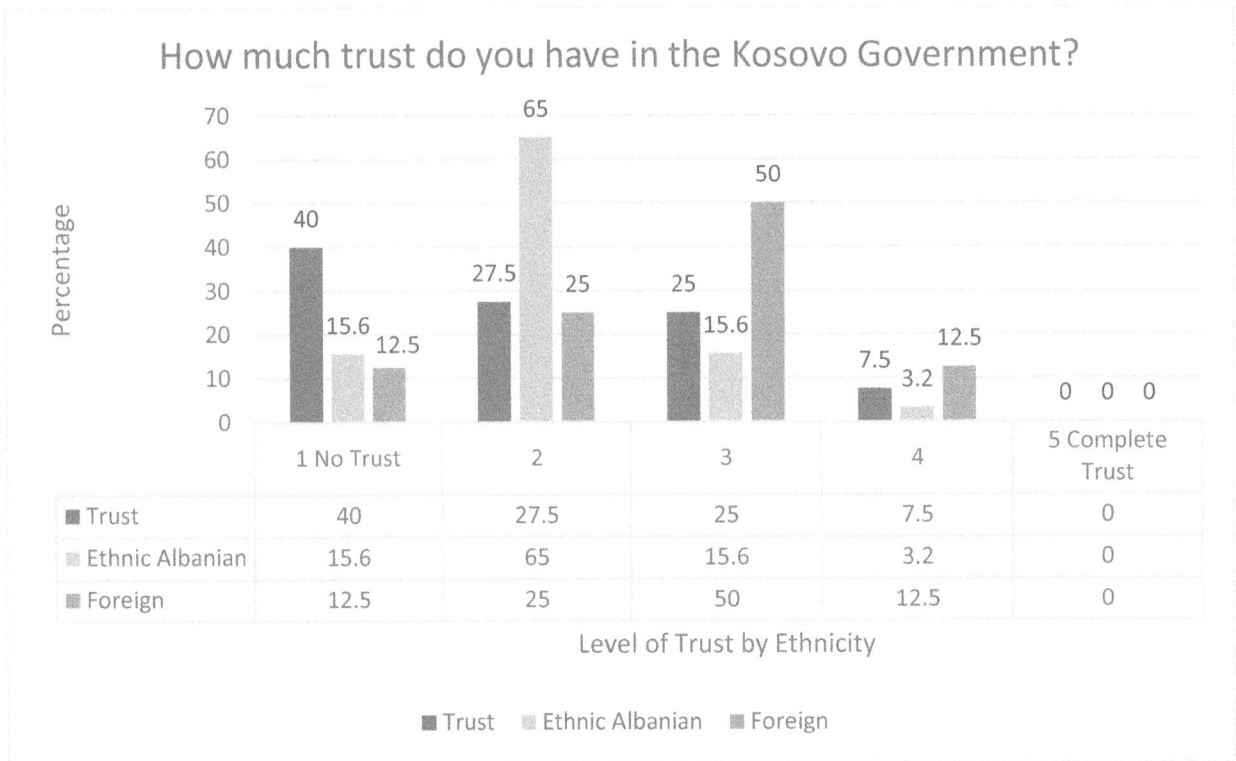

Graph 2: Trust in Kosovo Government by Ethnicity (2018)

Trust in political institutions is vital to democracy, but in post-communist countries, "popular distrust for institutions is widespread."[508] Low levels of public trust undermine the confidence in both institutions and individuals (leadership). Democracies function best when there is a greater confidence in institutions and when the institutions are trustworthy. A strong and stable democracy requires effective trustworthiness dynamics in the democratic institutions. The commitment to democracy (to trust and to be trusted) is a crucial condition between the government and the governed in order to sustain democracy.

The analysis in the next chapter will discuss the cultural and institutional factors that influence political trust in Kosovo. Table 5 shows the demographics of the participants of the study, based on age, gender, ethnicity, nationality, and residence.

---

[508] Mishler & Rose. (2001), 35.

Table 5: Demographics of the 2012 and 2018 Study

	2012-2013 Survey		2018 Survey	
Total Participants	220		40	
Age	*Age* *Participants*		*Age Participants*	
			25-39	14
	18-24	11	40-59	20
	25-34	80	60 plus	6
	35-44	65		
	45-54	42		
	55-64	12		
	65 +	10		
Gender	*Male*	*Female*	*Male*	*Female*
	183	37	22	18
Ethnicity / Nationality	Albanian	134	Albanian	32
	Kosovar (*Alb: Kosovar*)	45	American	3
	Kosovo Albanian	10	British	2
	Albanian-American	10	Jewish	1
	Albanian-Swiss	5	Swedish	1
	Albanian-Swedish	5	Dutch	1
	Albanian-German	5		
	Serb	4	*Only 1 person in Kosovo identified as Kosovo Albanian in the 2018 survey, everyone else identified as "Albanian"*	
	British	2		

Education/ Religion	Employed in Leadership Position Yes (76) No (144)		Religion	
	Education:		Catholic	1
	High School	17	Other Christian	4
	University (BA)	96	Islam	18
	Master (MA)	87	Buddhist	1
	Ph.D.	20	Nonreligious / Agnostic	16
Job	Government	35	Government	6
	Administrative	42	Administrative	7
	Local NGO	15	Local NGO	5
	IO	8	IO	5
	Business	10	Business	5
	University	60	University	9
	Media/TV	20	Media/TV	1
	Police	30	Military/Police	3
Residence	Kosovo (*Alb: Kosova*)	145	Kosovo (*Alb: Kosova*)	17
	USA	10	USA	10
	UK	6	UK	10
	Albania	20	Albania	1
	Sweden	10	Sweden	1
	Macedonia	4	Netherlands	1
	Germany	5		
	Serbia	7	Kosovo citizen living in Kosovo (17)	
	Italy	2		
	Switzerland	5	Kosovo citizen living outside of Kosovo (10)	
	Turkey	1		
	Belgium	5	Foreign national outside Kosovo (13)	

Place of Birth (City, State)	Inside Kosovo (Alb: Kosova):		State:	
	Mitrovice	13	Kosovo (Alb: Kosova)	23
	Prishtine	60	Albania	5
	Prizren	5	UK	3
	Drenas	3	US	3
	Gjakove	6	Italy	1
	Ferizaj	1	Turkey	1
	Peje	5	Netherland	1
	Gjilan	4	Former Yugoslavia	4
	Lipjan	6		
	Kacanik	4	City of Birth:	
	Shtime	2		
	Dragash	4	Vuçitërnë	1
	Kamenice	2	Mitrovice	5
	Istog	2	Prishtine	16
	Outside Kosovo (Alb: Kosova):		Drenas	4
			Peje	4
	Zurich	1	Elbasan	1
	Presheve	1	Tirane	1
	Podujeve	2	Podujeve	1
	Belgrade	2	London	2
	Malisheve	3	Istanbul	1
	Vlore	2	Dito	1
	Shkoder	1	Durres	2
	Tropoje	1	Chicago	2
	Bilisht	1		
	Tirana	4		
	Shkup	2		
	Struge	3		
	Bujan	1		
	Durres	1		
	Rahovec	1		

5.1.2 Trust in Kosovo Police

Although levels of trust in government are low in Kosovo, the study found the highest trust in law enforcement, primarily policing institutions such as the Kosovo police. The results from the 2012-2013 survey indicate 75% of the respondents answered "yes" to the question, *"Do you trust the Kosovo police,"* and 25% said no (*See Graph 3*). When asked again to rate how much trust the respondent has in the Kosovo police in the 2018 survey, moderate scores were found in the overall generalized trust (53% trust), but a 27% decrease from five years ago. The 2018 results from the 5-point scale ranging from "no trust" (=1) to "complete trust" (=5), show that 10% rated "no trust" (=1) in Kosovo Police; 15% as "2," 10% as "3," 45% as "4," and 25% as "5" (=complete trust).

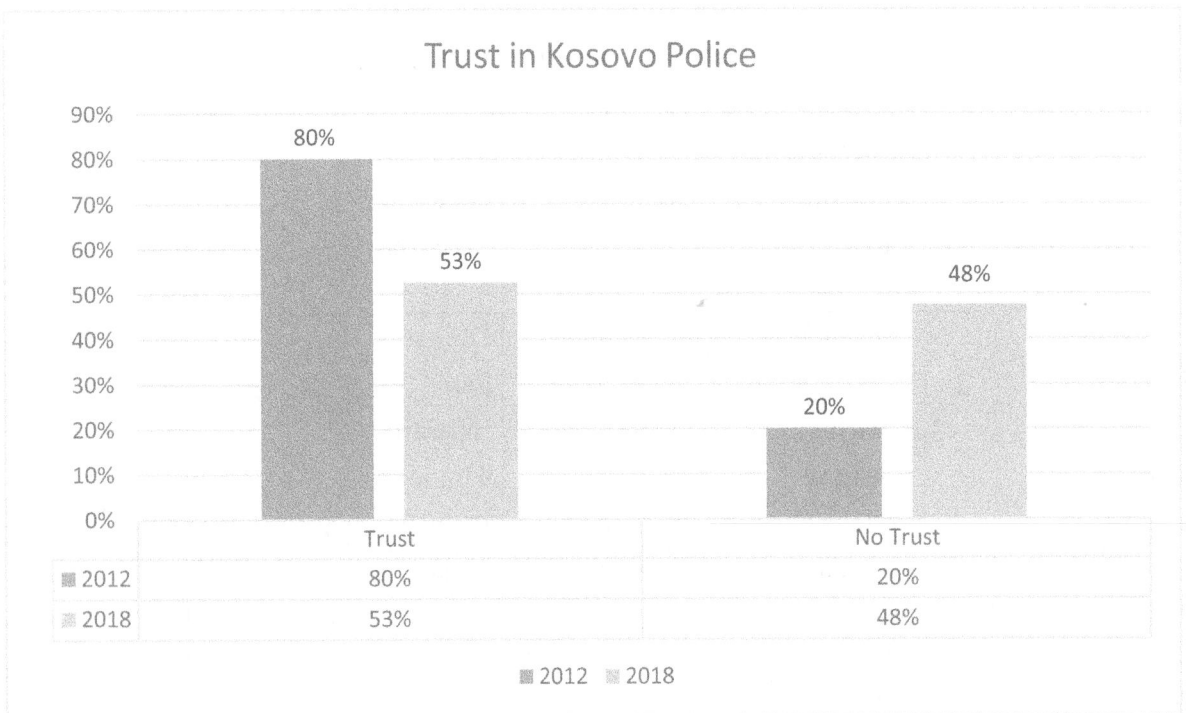

Trust in Kosovo Police

	Trust	No Trust
2012	80%	20%
2018	53%	48%

Graph 3: Comparing Trust Ratings in Kosovo Police (2012-2018)

In general, confidence in the Kosovo police has maintained moderate to high levels due to the legitimacy of law and effectiveness of the legal authorities. Such attitudes may help sustain high rates of trust in government institutions. Overall, the study shows that the participants were satisfied with the Kosovo police doing their job. When asked in 2012-2013, *"Do you think that the Kosovo police is effective in implementing its strategic objectives?"* 79% were satisfied with the *effectiveness* of Kosovo police. Levels of trust were also high regarding the *competence* of Kosovo police.

The results showed that 83% of the respondents believe that the Kosovo Police is competent in achieving the strategic objectives in five rule of law areas, namely: (1) protecting life and property; (2) maintaining public order and peace; (3) preventing and detecting crime; (3) protecting people's rights and freedoms; and (5) treating people equally regardless of race, color, religion, gender and age.

Additionally, the respondents were asked to rank on a 1 to 5 scale from "very satisfied" (=1) to "very dissatisfied" (=5) the effectiveness of Kosovo police in each of the aforementioned areas, pre/post-independence. With respect to *protecting life and property,* 40% were very satisfied pre-independence, with a higher-ranking post-independence to 58% of satisfaction in the effectiveness of Kosovo police. Post-conflict Kosovo in 2008 was faced with the problem of property of the retuning refuges.[509] In 2009, "between 50,000 and 60,000 claims on damaged or illegally occupied property in Kosovo are outstanding, and more than 200,000 people from the country are displaced in Serbia and Montenegro."[510] This suggests that the growing problem of property had an influence on the perceptions pre-independence reflecting lower levels of satisfaction.

In 2019 property rights still remain a problem, however reforms undertaken by the Kosovo Ministry of Justice and Kosovo Protection Agency (KPA) have proposed a new property law, where women too have the right of inheritance, "which contradicts tradition and common usage."[511] The 2018 Country reports highlights the difficult process of introducing new legal mechanisms and addressing individual property rights: "In Kosovo, property rights are poorly defined and enforced, especially those of women and of members of minority communities. The process of establishing clear property relations is still marked by unresolved issues from the pre-conflict and immediate post-conflict era. Return, restitution and reparation remain burning issues."[512] Post-independence, Kosovo's constitution reformed the law on property rights by including women as property owners in real estate, with inheritance rights. However, women make up only 16% of real estate owners:

> "The low percentage proves that implementation of the law is lagging. Complications
> with property rights arise from the unreliable cadastral records, non-harmoniza-
> tion of laws regulating property inheritance, legal uncertainties with regard to the
> functioning of courts, the deficient notary system, a lack of electronic databases,

---

[509] Tawil, E. (2009, February). Property Rights in Kosovo. A Haunting Legacy of Society in Transition." *International Center for Transitional Justice,* 1-69. Retrieved from https://www.ictj.org/sites/default/files/ICTJ-FormerYugoslavia-Kosovo-Legacy-2004-English.pdf

[510] Ibid, 4.

[511] BTI. (2018). *Kosovo Country Report,* 4. Retrieved from https://www.bti-project.org/en/reports/country-reports/detail/itc/RKS/

[512] Ibid, 4.

and claims and allegations that properties were sold more than once by displaced Serbs.

Another problem is that Serbian internal and external refugees can reacquire property, but they are often barred from using it. Municipalities failed to comply with expropriation procedures and to prevent the demolition of properties belonging to displaced people and the construction of illegal structures on their property. EULEX tried to solve these issues, with limited success. The Kosovo Police Service has been responsive to property crimes."[513]

The challenges in dealing with the property rights problem and the increased number of property crimes related to displaced people could be one of the explaining factors why we see a 27% decrease of trust in the Kosovo police post-independence. Maintaining public order and peace ranked #1 in the 2012-13 survey, in satisfaction with the effectiveness of Kosovo police in its tasks, followed by protecting life and property as #2, protecting people's freedoms and rights at #3, preventing and detecting crime coming at #4, and treating people equally as #5.

According to the United Nations indicators of rule of law, the role and importance of administrative and management capacity are indicators for effectiveness of rule of law when measuring performance.[514] To assess whether the Kosovo police has competent leadership, this study asked in the 2012-2013 survey, "*How do you evaluate the management of the Kosovo Police*? "to rank on a 1-5 point-scale, where "efficient" (=1), "efficient and powerful" (=2), "neither efficient nor powerful" (=3), "not efficient" (=4), and "not efficient and poor (=5), during pre/post-independence.

---

[513] Ibid, 4.

[514] Department of Peacekeeping Operations. (2011). The United Nations Rule of Law Indicators: Implementation Guide and Project Tools. *United Nations Publication*, 1-137.

How do you evaluate the management of the Kosovo Police?

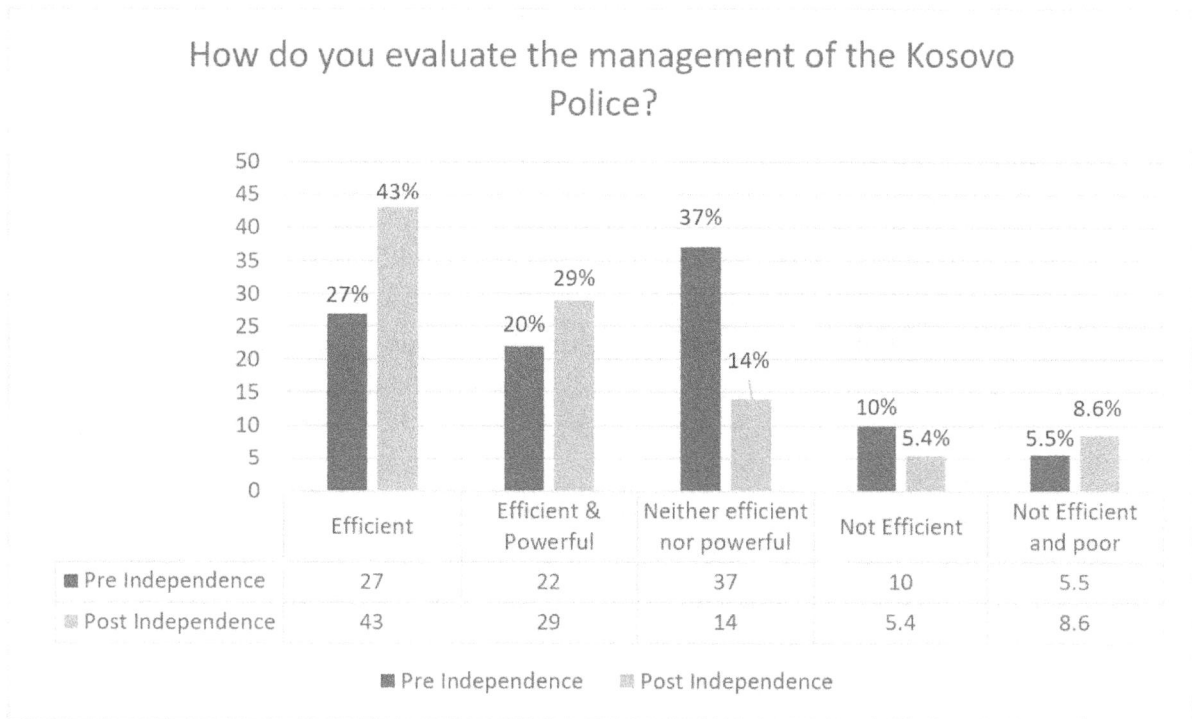

	Efficient	Efficient & Powerful	Neither efficient nor powerful	Not Efficient	Not Efficient and poor
■ Pre Independence	27	22	37	10	5.5
▨ Post Independence	43	29	14	5.4	8.6

■ Pre Independence   ▨ Post Independence

Graph 4: Management of Kosovo Police Pre-Post Independence Comparison

The study shows a higher level of efficiency in the management capacity of the Kosovo police, post-independence, where 43% said "efficient" post-independence compared to "27%" pre-independence; 29% said "efficient and powerful," compared to the 20% prior independence; nearly half said 14% "neither efficient nor powerful" for after 2008 when 37% said so pre-independence; only 5.4% answered "not efficient" for post-independence to the 10% pre-independence; and 8.6% said "not efficient and poor" post-independence, compared to the 5.5% pre-independence (*See Graph 4*).

The findings of this study suggest a positive relationship between perceived effectiveness of the institution to meet objectives with the higher level of trust in that institution, (**confirming hypothesis 4**). In the Kosovo case, perceived satisfaction with the performance of the police, satisfaction with effectiveness, management capacity, and competence to achieving the strategic objectives seem to largely determine the high level of trust in the police institution. The results confirm the existing literature of trust flowing two ways: (1) top-up trust based on competence; and (2) top-down trust, based on manager's organization's ability, benevolence, and integrity.[515]

---

[515] Mayer, R., Davis, J., & Schoorman, F. (1995). An integrative model of organizational trust. *The Academy of Management Review*, 20(3), 709–734.

Generally, institutional theory (efficiency and outputs of institutions)[516] and organizational theory (the external and internal environment of the organizations)[517] relate high levels of political trust with performance and with the institutional environment such as efficiency, legitimacy, and accountability. The relationship between trust in institutions and the perceived institutional effectiveness finds support in this study. As demonstrated by the findings of this study, in Kosovo the political trust in police depends on the efficiency and output of the institution, where the higher the satisfaction with its performance, the higher the individuals' level of trust with the policing institution, as proposed in Hypothesis 4. The next section will discuss if this relationship holds true in another type of policing institution (i.e. NATO, KFOR), regarding the international military and civil presence in Kosovo.

5.1.3 Trust in the International Civil and Military Presence

To investigate whether the same high level of trust exists in the *international civil and military presence*, this study asked the participants whether the international presence is needed in Kosovo, if it is effective and what their trust perceptions are. The 2012-2013 survey asked: "Do you trust the foreign military forces in protecting Kosovo?" 88.6% answered "Yes" and 11.4% said "No." Another question asked: *"Do you think the military presence of the international community is needed in Kosovo?"* to which 91.4% said "Yes" and only 8.6% said "No."

In terms of Kosovo's aspiration to join NATO, 62% of the respondents believed in 2012-2013 that Kosovo is ready from an institutional perspective, and 37% answered "No." Majority of the people were satisfied with the international civil and military presence in Kosovo, 29% were "very satisfied" in its effectiveness, 51.36% answered "more or less satisfied," 10% were "neither satisfied nor dissatisfied," 6.8% were more or less dissatisfied, and only 5% were very dissatisfied in the effectiveness of the international civil and military presence in Kosovo. It makes sense that people who feel that international military presence is *effective*, they are more likely to trust the military forces protecting the country, which in Kosovo showed a strong positive relationship between the two.

The 2012-2013 survey also asked the participants whether they think Kosovo Police, EULEX, and UNMIK show *responsibility and professional integrity,* used as a performance measure of political trust based on United Nations rule of law indicators. The U.N. treats this measure as complementary to perceptions of effectiveness, to provide a better understanding of accountability and institutional performance. The United Nations rule of law indicators and guidelines point

---

[516] Huseby, B. M. (2000).

[517] Raynard et al. (2015).

out that the relevance of the performance indicator will depend on the specific institutional and organizational environment that is being studied: "In the basket on the 'integrity, transparency and accountability of the police, the ability to file complaints of misconduct against the police is an important indicator of accountability. However, it may be irrelevant if there are no effective procedures for alleged incidents of police misconduct or corruption to be investigated. The two indicators are complementary."[518] This study also added "responsibility and professional integrity" as two complementary indicators of accountability.

The study found significantly higher scores indicating *"showing high responsibility and integrity"* for the Kosovo Police, and very low scores for UNMIK, and for EULEX the opinion was nearly split in half (*See Graph 5*). Respondents were asked: *"Do you think the following institutions show responsibility and professional integrity?"* immediately followed by listing: (1) Kosovo Police, (2) EULEX, and (3) UNMIK with a "Yes" and "No" answer.

The results show that 80% overwhelmingly said "Yes" for Kosovo Police, only 56% answered "Yes" for EULEX, and surprisingly 74% said "No" for UNMIK, in terms of not showing high responsibility and integrity in Kosovo (*Alb: Kosova*).

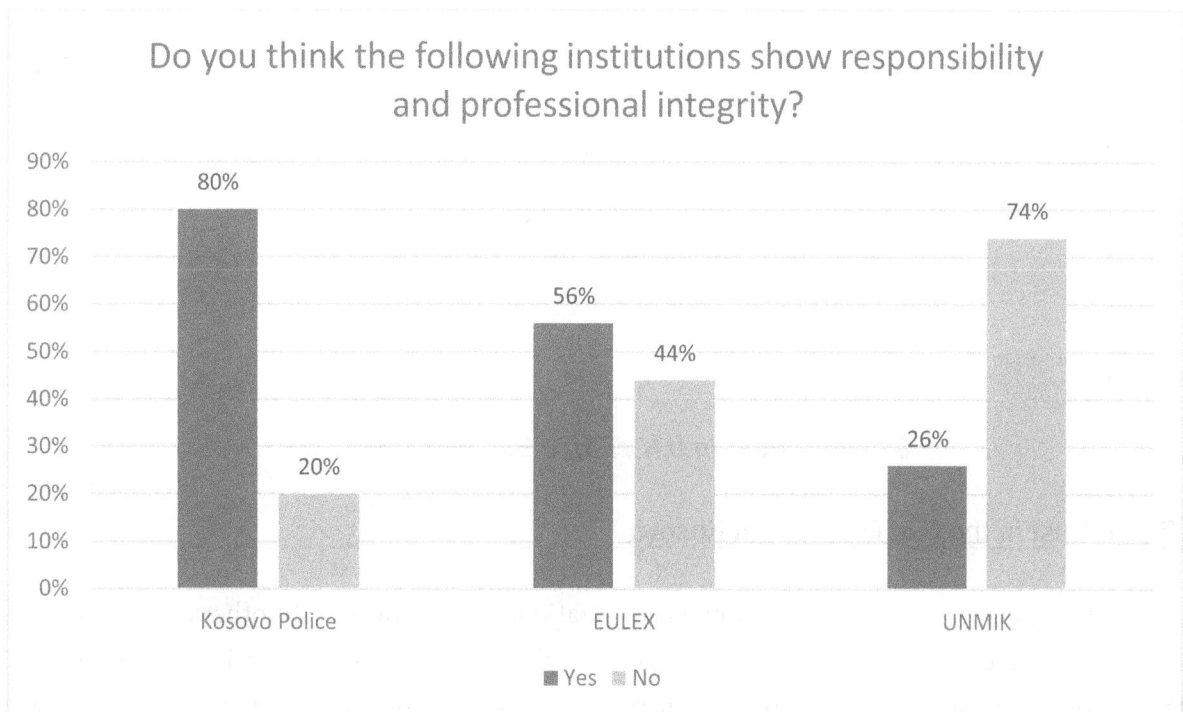

Graph 5: Accountability Indicators, UNMIK, EULEX, Kosovo Police (2012)

---

[518] Department of Peacekeeping Operations. (2011). The United Nations Rule of Law Indicators: Implementation Guide and Project Tools. *United Nations Publication*, 3.

The 2018 survey shows more or less maintaining the same 2012 attitudes towards the U.N., E.U., and NATO. Out of the three international organizations in Kosovo, NATO ranked the highest level of trust amongst Kosovo elite with 84% generalized trust score,[519] followed by 77% for the European Union, and only 51% for the United Nations (*See Graph 6*). The question posed was, "*Rate how much trust do you have in the following institutions?*" On the 5-point scale ranging from "no trust" (=1) to "complete trust" (=5). The results are consistent with the 2012 findings of the study, with no shift in perceptions towards the three organizations. Graph 6 also shows the high trust level for the U.S. Embassy in Kosovo (79% generalized score).

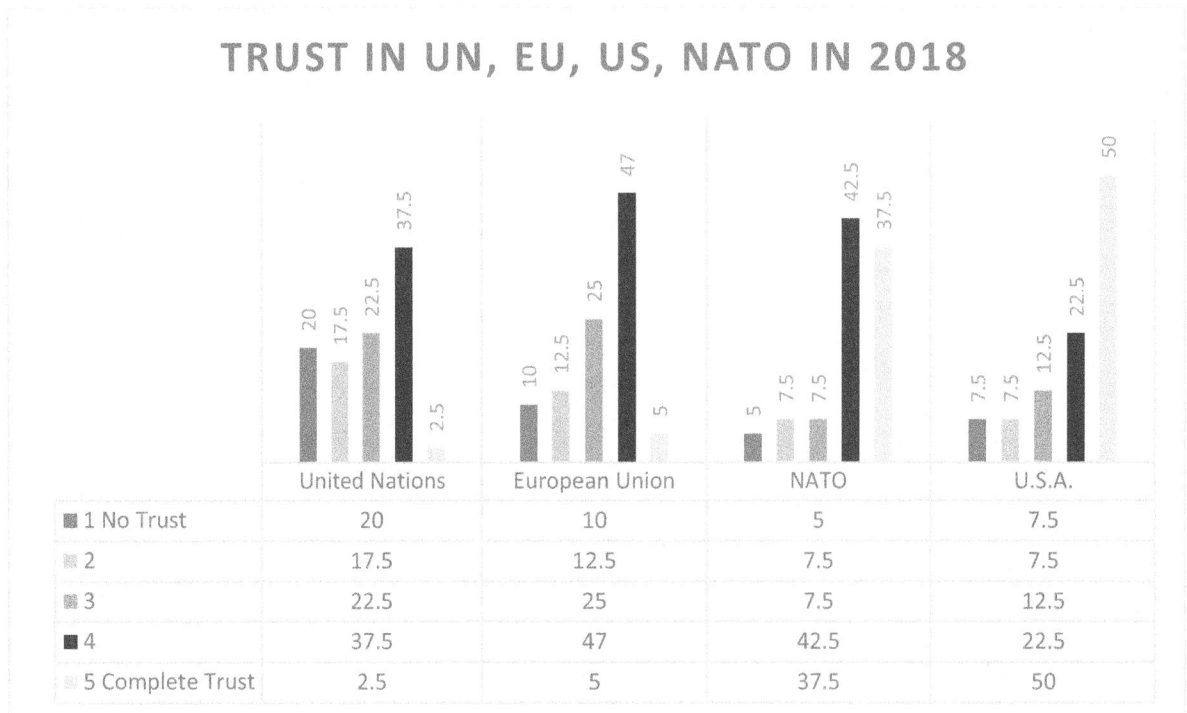

TRUST IN UN, EU, US, NATO IN 2018

	United Nations	European Union	NATO	U.S.A.
1 No Trust	20	10	5	7.5
2	17.5	12.5	7.5	7.5
3	22.5	25	7.5	12.5
4	37.5	47	42.5	22.5
5 Complete Trust	2.5	5	37.5	50

Graph 6: Trust in U.N., E.U, U.S.A., NATO in 2018

5.1.4 Trust in the U.S. Embassy in Kosovo

Most studies don't consider international organizations nor relations with other countries when measuring perceptions of political trust. This study claims that it would be an incomplete view of the political trust structure if neither two elements are taken into consideration. The next chapter will discuss the political trust models, and how cultural and institutional factors affect the direction of trust, and the relationships between them. It is important to consider The United States

---

[519] Generalized trust score for NATO is calculated by taking half of the score "3" (7.5 /2=3.75%) and adding one half to the sum of scores "4" and 5" (3.75+ (42.5+37.5) = 83.75%, and the other half to the sum of scores "1" and "2."

when analyzing political trust in Kosovo (*Alb: Kosova*), since the U.S. has been spearheading many decision-making and dialogue mechanisms for building Kosovo's democracy and institutions and negotiating between Belgrade and Prishtina.

The next chapter will also evaluate the elite perceptions of the decisions of the leaders of several countries and their foreign policy toward Kosovo, including U.S., UK, Germany, France, Albania, and Serbia. This is done to understand whether foreign policy choices influence political trust, as previous studies suggest that citizens appraise policymaking and government in general when they find governments and political leaders trustworthy.[520]

Generally, Albanians have strong ties with United States, given the historic and amicable diplomatic relationship with Albania and the independence efforts in Kosovo. When it comes to Kosovo politics, Kosovo leaders feel the pressure to oblige to whatever the international community (U.N., E.U.) requests, and the local criticisms has been that the international community doesn't always serve the interests of Kosovo, but their own agencies instead, or those of other parties. Often times, if the European Union is not happy with Kosovo, it will threaten its leaders with the E.U. membership block and delays. For instance, on November 22, 2018 Kosovo placed 100% trade tax on all goods imported from Serbia. Serbia on the other hand blamed the European Union "for failing to prevent Kosovo's move."[521] The European Union immediately told Kosovo "To normalize relations as a precondition to entering the bloc."[522]

When asked, *"Do you think the E.U. has the best interest of Kosovo in mind when making decisions in the Kosovo Specialist Court?"* In the 2018 survey, 55% of the responded answer "No." Despite the European Union's efforts to have a successful mission in Kosovo, distrust in the European Union undermines public trust in politics and the effectiveness of the mechanisms already put in place for Kosovo's democratic development.[523] On the other hand, The United States has gone to great lengths relying on diplomacy to support Kosovo in its independence and democratization endeavor. The pro-US sentiment is very evident in Kosovo, with American flags decorating the main square in Prishtina, painted on the walls, and the naming of one of the main roads in Prishtina "Bulevardi Bill Klinton."

> "Kosovo continues to have emotional, political and economic bonds with the country that 20 years ago led a western intervention in its war with the Federal Republic

---

[520] Blind, P. K. (2006).

[521] Associated Press, (2018, November 22). Tensions Soar Between Kosovo and Serbia Over Trade Tax. *New York Times*. Retrieved from https://www.nytimes.com/aponline/2018/11/22/world/europe/ap-eu-serbia-kosovo-tax.html

[522] Ibid.

[523] European Commission. (2018). Kosovo 2018 Report. *SWD*. Strasbourg, 156, 1-86. Retrieved from https://ec.europa.eu/neighbourhood-enlargement/sites/near/files/20180417-kosovo-report.pdf

of Yugoslavia, eventually leading to Kosovo's declaration of independence. Some surveys suggest it has the highest approval of US leadership of any country. Roads, as well as schools and sports centers, are named after Clinton's secretary of state, Madeleine Albright, the US congressman Eliot Engel, the former president George Bush and the leaders of other NATO member countries including the UK's Tony Blair, of whom Kosovo is particularly fond."[524]

Former NATO supreme allied commander Gen. Westley Clark called for continued involvement of the U.S. in Kosovo to foster regional stability in the Balkans, stating: "The United States and Europe must remain committed to the western Balkans, with a particular emphasis on strengthening democratic institutions so that governments can address the needs of their citizens."[525] The 2012 survey asked the respondents, *Do you think that Kosovo still needs support from other countries?*" In a 4-point scale "strongly agree" (=1) to "strongly disagree" (=4). Unanimously there was not a single vote for "strongly disagree." Only 2.2% said "somewhat disagree," and majority 75% said "strongly agree" to needed support from other countries.

Next, the survey asked: *Are you in favor of the U.S. continuing to support Kosovo?*" With the same 4-point "strongly agree" to "strongly disagree" scale, 92% of the respondents said "strongly agree"; 4.9% "somewhat agree"; 3.18% somewhat disagree; and only 0.45% said "strongly disagree." By including this variable "support from U.S." we can distinguish between the levels of political trust when referring to the international community. Although the United States "largely handed over responsibility for the region's political, institutional and economic development to Brussels, believing that the Balkans' democratic future lay in E.U. membership," there is an overwhelming response in support of the U.S. continuing to support Kosovo, with 89% believing that *coordinating with United States is necessary* and 96.09% favor U.S. support (*See Graph 7*). When comparing elite attitudes of 2018 from five years ago, trust in United States remains strong, as well as very high trust scores for NATO, contrary to lower levels of trust in the United Nations, and moderate to high scores in the European Union. Chapter 6 will discuss cultural and institutional factors that could potentially explain the difference in the levels of trust across the international actors in Kosovo (*Alb: Kosova*).

---

[524] Dezfuli, C. (2018, February 16). 51st state: Kosovo's bond to the US. *The Guardian*. Retrieved from https://www.theguardian.com/artanddesign/2018/feb/16/51st-state-kosovos-bond-to-the-us-photo-essay

[525] Clark, W. K. (2018, April. 11). Don't wait for the western Balkans to blow up again. The U.S. and the E.U. must act. *The Washington Post*. Retrieved from https://www.washingtonpost.com/news/global-opinions/wp/2018/04/11/dont-wait-for-the-western-balkans-to-blow-up-again-the-u-s-and-the-e-u-must-act/?utm_term=.58939f2529d9

Do you think coordination with US is necessary?
Are you in favor of the US continuing to support Kosovo?

	Favor US Support (2012)	Coordination with US (2012)	Trust Kosovo Government (2018)	Trust US Embassy (2018)
Yes	96.09	89.6	20	78.75
No	3.91	10.4	80	21.25

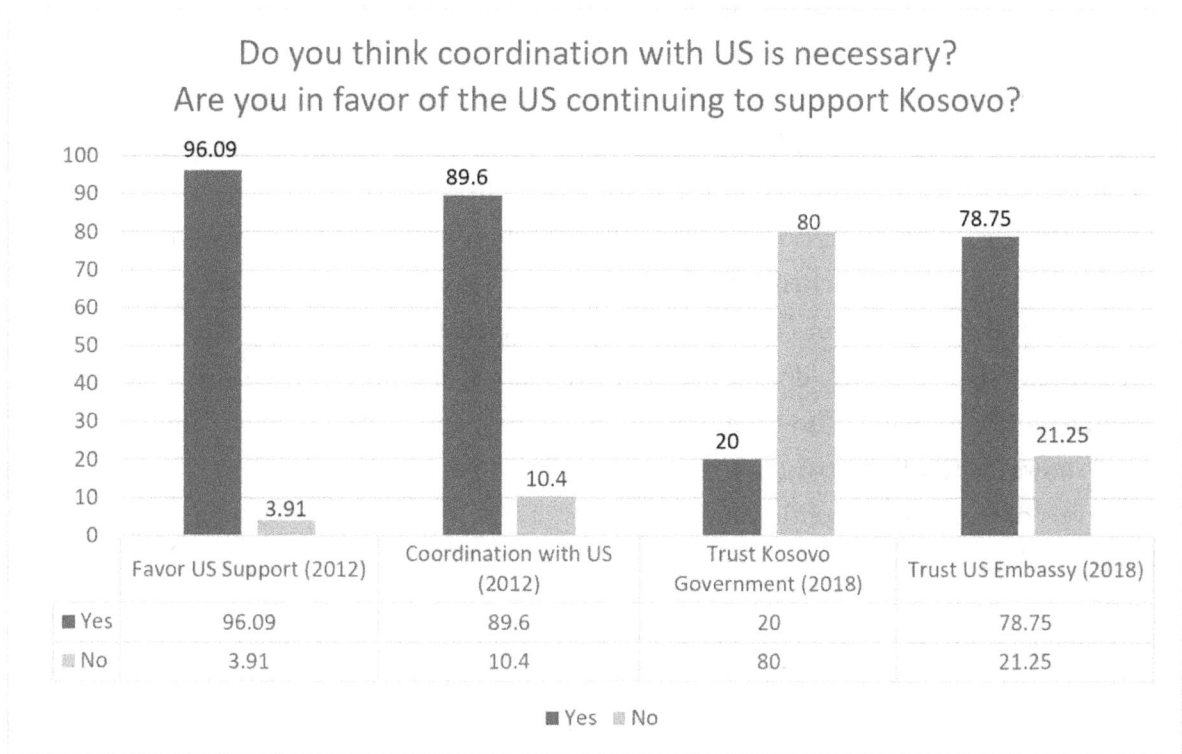

Graph 7: U.S. Support, Trust, and Coordination (2012-2018)

The findings of this study show enormous support of Kosovo Albanians in 2018 for the U.S. and NATO, as their primary most trusted institutions, high trust in E.U., while showing high levels of distrust for Kosovo national political institutions, low trust for the U.N., and decreasing trust in Kosovo police compared to the high trust scores five years prior. In Kosovo (*Alb: Kosova*), the European Union supports rule of law reform using an integrated approach by combining the efforts of police, justice and customs, as mandated by EULEX's Monitor, Mentor and Advise (MMA).[526] The E.U. also has an executive mandate to properly investigate war crimes, including organized crime, corruption, and inter-ethnic crimes. The next section will look at political trust in legal institutions, including local Kosovo courts and the hybrid court established by the joint E.U.-Kosovo efforts, the Kosovo Specialist Court.

---

[526] Derks, M., & Price, M. (2010, November). The EU and Rule of Law Reform in Kosovo. Conflict Research Unit, *Netherlands Institute for International Relations*, 1-62.

5.1.5 Trust in the Kosovo legal system

This study included Kosovo Courts as one of the operationalized seven items measuring the dependent variable, political trust. By including this variable, this study can differentiate between perceptions of trust in the Kosovo political institutions (the government in general) and attitudes towards local legal institutions (local courts). The data show high levels of distrust in local courts. The 2018 survey asked the participants: "*Rate how much trust do you have in the Kosovo courts?*" on a 5-point scale ranging from "no trust" (=1) to "complete trust" (=5).

The results show that 70% do not trust Kosovo courts, and only 30% trust the local courts. Respectively, 35% answered "no trust" in Kosovo courts, and only 2.5% said "complete trust." Graph 8 shows the results for trust in Kosovo courts in 2018 on the 5-point Likert scale. Compared to the levels of trust in the political and civil institutions, the study shows high distrust in the political and legal institutions, such as the government and the courts, and higher trust levels in the police.

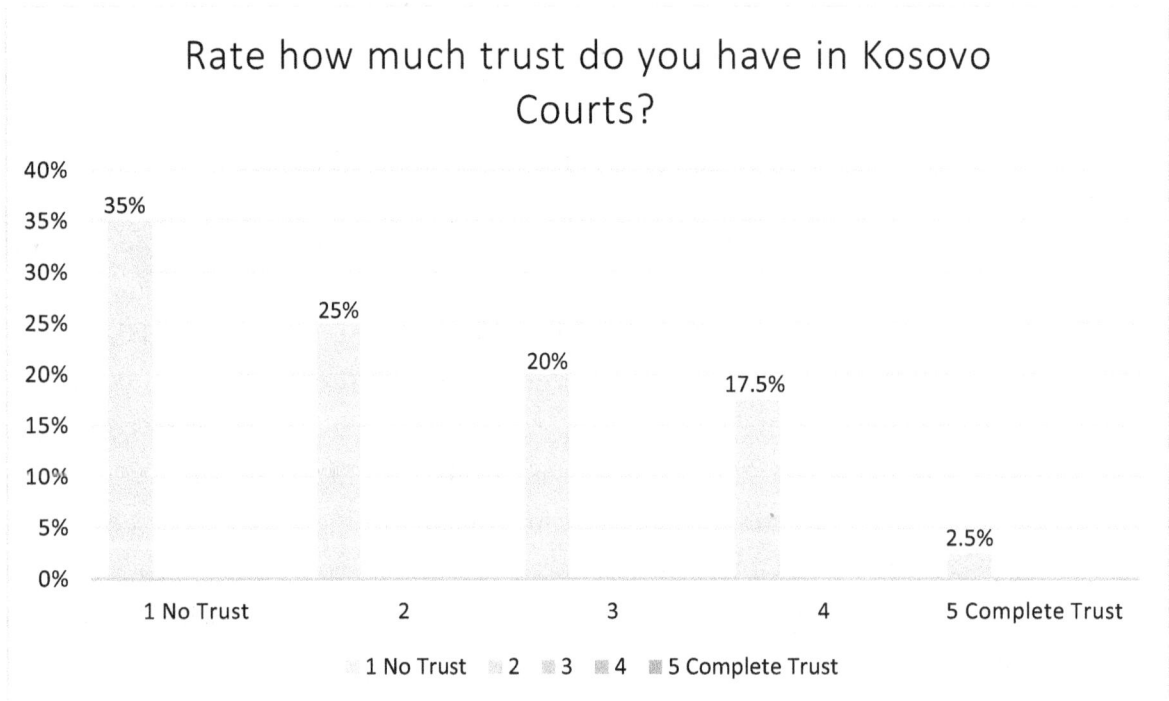

Graph 8: Trust in Kosovo Courts (2018)

5.1.6 Trust in the Kosovo Specialist Court

When looking at the local legal system in Kosovo (*Alb: Kosova*) and the Kosovo Specialist Court, it helps us understand if institutions play a role in the levels of political trust. The *"One-Factor Model"* of political trust, also known as the *one-dimension* perspective, assumes that there is no relationship between each actor and institution, considering political trust as generalized trust (*See Figure 3*). This study argues that a *multi-dimensional* approach is needed to better understand the two levels of trust: *national political trust* and *international political trust* (*See Figure 4*).

The study asked in the 2018 survey: *"Rate how much trust do you have in the Kosovo Specialist Court?"* on a 5-point scale ranging from "no trust" (=1) to "complete trust" (=5). The data show that Kosovo Albanians do not have trust in the local Kosovo legal system, but they do trust the Kosovo Specialist Court, despite the controversy surrounding the creation of this court, and the 2018 failed attempts to revoke the law "that allows for the new Hague war crime court for Kosovo to operate."[527]

The results show that 60% trust the Kosovo Specialist Court (KSC), respectively: 22.5% said that they completely trust the court; 25% rated "4" on the 5-point trust scale; 25% rated "3"; 12.5% rated "2"; and 15% rated "1" (=no trust), as illustrated in Graph 9. Trust in the KSC in 2018 suggests that Kosovo (*Alb: Kosova*) is still in need of support from the international community, as indicated in the 2012 survey, where 75% strongly agreed to support from other countries. To understand the differences of attitudes of political trust in the legal institutions this study investigated public perceptions on the *effectiveness* of the court, *impartiality, fairness,* and *confidence in the decisions of the court* on the war crime trials as performance and trustworthiness measures. These relationships are discussed and analyzed in chapter 6.

---

[527] Morina, D. (2018, January 18). Push to Scrap Special Court Fails Again in Kosovo. BIRN.

RATE HOW MUCH TRUST DO YOU HAVE IN THE KOSOVO SPECIALIST COURT, KOSOVO COURTS AND THE EUROPEAN UNION?

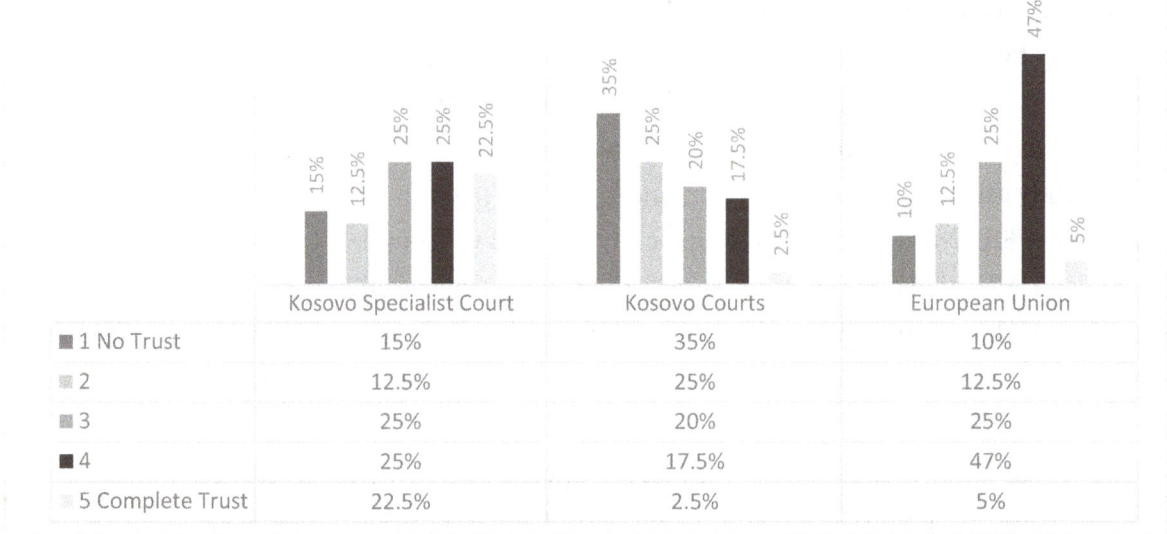

	Kosovo Specialist Court	Kosovo Courts	European Union
■ 1 No Trust	15%	35%	10%
■ 2	12.5%	25%	12.5%
■ 3	25%	20%	25%
■ 4	25%	17.5%	47%
5 Complete Trust	22.5%	2.5%	5%

Graph 9: Trust in the Kosovo Specialist Court, Kosovo Courts and the E.U. (2018)

Graph 9 illustrates the variations of trust among three institutions: the Kosovo Specialist Court, Kosovo Courts, and the European Union. The results suggest that in general, perceptions about the Kosovo Specialist Court are in line with those toward the European Union, where 64.5% trust the European Union and 60% trust the Kosovo Specialist Court, compared to only 32.5% that trust the local Kosovo Courts.[528] This suggests that there is a directional relationship between political trust and international political trust, as seen in the link between trust in the European Union and trust in the Kosovo Specialist Court.

---

[528] These numbers are based on the generalized trust score, by combining "rate 5" and "rate 4" scores on the positive end of "complete trust" of the trust scale, adding half of the "rate 3" responses, to get a generalized score of trust versus no trust. For example, regarding the posed question of the survey, "How much trust do you have in the Kosovo Special Court?" the responses were: 15% said "1 no trust", 12.5% said "2", 25% said 3, 25% said "4" and 22.5% said "5 complete trust". To get a generalized score of "general no trust" scores "1 no trust" and "2" are added together (15% + 12.5% = 27.5%); then for the "general complete trust" score, "5 complete trust" and "4" are added together (22.5% +25% = 47.5%). Then, score '3' is divided in half since the respondent is leaning either way toward trust or no trust (25% / 2 = 12.5). And the half of score "3" is added to each "generalized no trust" and "generalized complete trust" (generalized no trust: 27.5% + 12.5%. = 40%; generalized complete trust: 47.5% + 12.5% = 60%).

5.1.7 Trust in Media/TV

The relationship between trust in media and political trust has been largely overlooked.[529] In this study, media and TV is treated as a complimentary variable to political trust, as an important source of information about the Kosovo Specialist Court, to understand if there is a link between trust in media and trust in the institutions. The 2018 survey posed the question, *"Rate how much you trust the following as sources of about the Kosovo Specialist Court on war crimes?"* Followed immediately by: (1) Newspaper/TV; (2) Albanian media; (3) Serbian Media; (4) Foreign Media; (5) Kosovo government; and (6) Kosovo Specialist Court. A 5-point Likert scale of trust was used, indicating "no trust" (=1) and "complete trust" (=5).

The results show low ratings in trusting media/TV in general, 66.25% stated "no trust," respectively: 17.5% said "1 no trust"; 30% ranked as "2"; 37.5% as "3"; 15% as "4" and 0% said "5 complete trust" (*See Graph 10.1*).

When comparing levels of trust on the six media as *sources about the Kosovo Specialist Court on war crimes*, three sources ranked low: (1) Serbian Media ranking the lowest (84% no trust)[530]; (2) followed by Kosovo Government (75% no trust)[531]; and (3) Albanian Media (69% no trust)[532]. Kosovo Specialist Court ranked as the highest source of trust out of the 6 media, with 64% approval trust ratings,[533] followed by Foreign Media with 63% approval ratings.[534]

---

[529] Ariely, G. (2015). Trusting the Press and Political Trust. A Conditional Relationship. *Journal of Elections,* 25(3), 351-367, doi: 10.1080/17457289.2014.997739

[530] Based on the 2018 Survey, using a 5-point Likert scale from "no trust" (=1) to "complete trust" (=5). The results for trust in Serbian Media as source about the Kosovo Specialist Court on war crimes, were: 50% said "1 no trust; 17.5% said "2"; 32.5% said "3" and 0 % for both "4" and "5 complete trust."

[531] The 2018 results for trust in Kosovo Government as source about the Kosovo Specialist Court on war crimes, were: 37.5% said "1 no trust"; 20% said "2"; 37.5% said "3"; 5% said "4" and 0% said "5 complete trust."

[532] The 2018 results for trust in Albanian Media as source about the Kosovo Specialist Court on war crimes, were: 17.5% said "1 no trust"; 30% said "2"; 42.5% said "3"; 10% said "4"; and 0% said "5 complete trust."

[533] The 2018 results for trust in the KSC Court as source about the Kosovo Specialist Court on war crimes, were: 12.5% said "1 no trust"; 15% said "2"; 17.5% said "3"; 22.5% said "4"; and 32.5% said "5 complete trust."

[534] The 2018 results for trust in Foreign Media as source about the Kosovo Specialist Court on war crimes, were: 17% said "1 no trust"; 5% said "2" 30% said "3"; 45% said "4"; and 2.5% said "5 complete trust."

Do you trust the following as sources about Kosovo Specialist Court on war crimes?

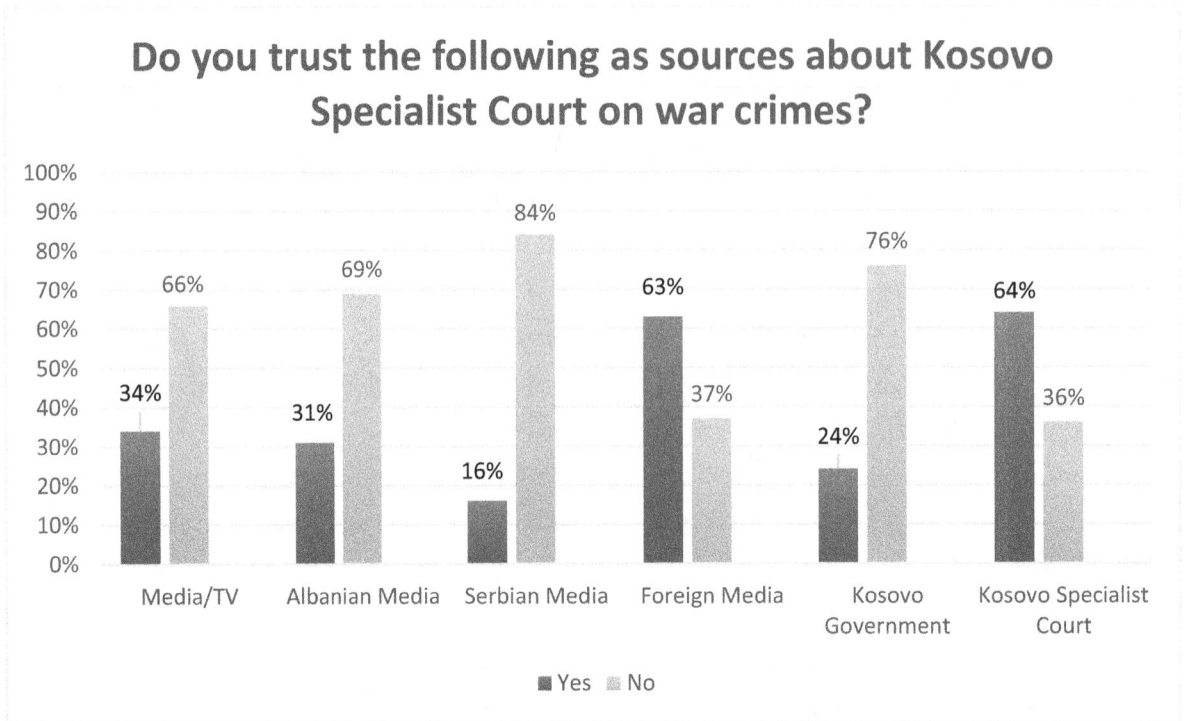

Graph 10.1: Trust in Media Sources about Kosovo Specialist Court on War Crimes (2018)

When comparing trust perceptions in media between men and women, women scores were in line with similar low scores in trust in government. Only 33% of women said they trust media and TV as a source for the Kosovo Specialist Court, and 67% said no; compared to 52.25% of males who trust media, and 47.72% who have no trust in the media.

The results show that men had mixed feelings about trusting media as a source: "17.5% ranked "no trust" (=1); 13.63% ranked as "2"; 59.09% said "3"; 22.72% as "4" and 0% chose "5 complete trust". Women showed low trust scores in general in media: 27.7% ranked "1 no trust"; 22.22% ranked as "2"; 33.33% ranked as "4" and 0% ranked as "5 complete trust" (*See Graph 10.2*). It is interesting that neither males nor females chose the "complete trust" for media as a source for the Kosovo Specialist Court.

Trust in Media by Gender and Ethnicity

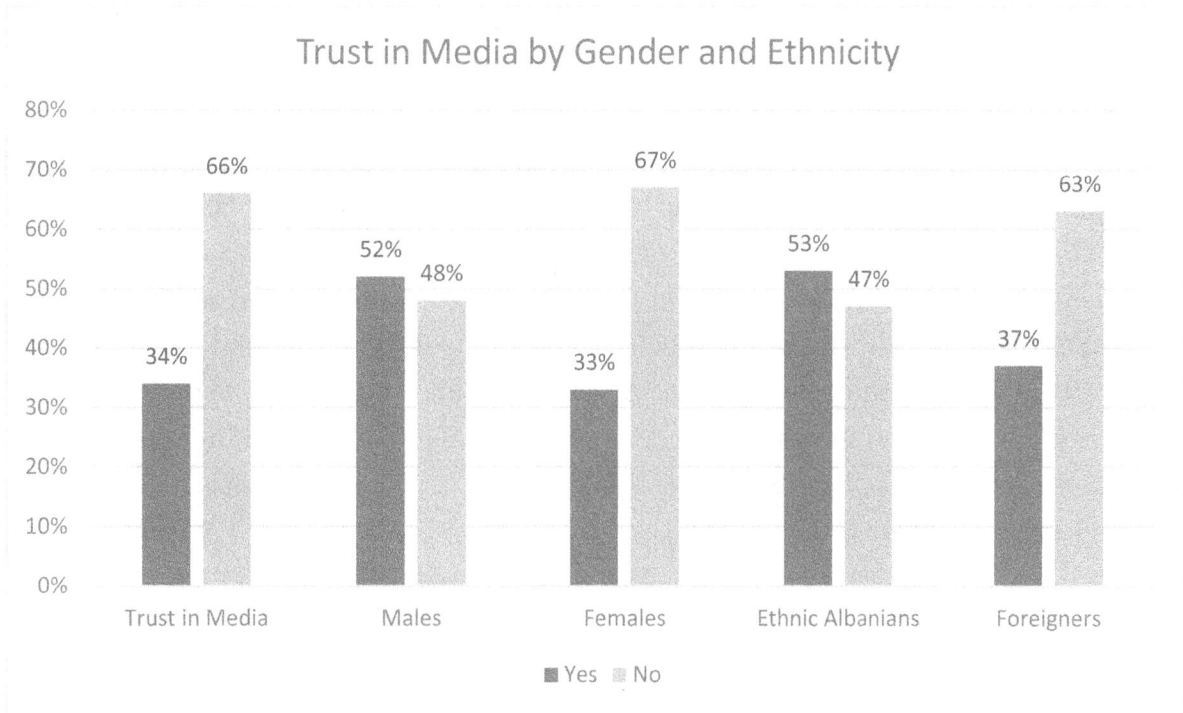

Graph 10.2: Trust in Media about Kosovo Specialist Court by Gender and Ethnicity (2018)

When comparing ethnic Albanians and foreign (non-Albanian ethnicity) scores of trust in media, the data show that foreigners displayed more levels of distrust toward the media, and Albanians were split in the middle, leaning towards trusting the media. Specifically, 53.13% of Albanian ethnicity trust the media, and 46.88% do not; whereas only 37.5% of foreign nationals trust the media, and 62.5% do not trust the media as the source of information about the Kosovo Specialist Court on war crimes. However, when considering Kosovo Albanians living in Kosovo, with the Kosovo citizens living outside Kosovo and the foreign nationals outside of Kosovo, the findings show that Kosovo citizens living inside Kosovo were more trusting of media as a source on the Kosovo Specialist Court on crimes, with 58.82% approval trust ratings; compared to 60% distrust ratings of Kosovo citizens living outside of Kosovo; and 62% of distrust ratings of Foreign nationals living outside of Kosovo (*Alb: Kosova*).

To better understand the role media plays in influencing the image of the state, the 2012 survey asked, "Has Media / TV had an influence in the image of (1) Kosovo, *(2) Serbia?*" with a "yes" and "no" answer. The results show that 95.6% believe Media/TV has influenced the image of Kosovo, while 4.4% said no. While 79% believe that Media/TV has influenced the image of Serbia, and 21% do not. The next question the study asked was: *"Which side do you think has the (1) Albanian*

media, (2) Serb media supported?" pre/post-independence, listing as options: (1) Albanian side;
(2) Serb Side; (3) Both sides.

The results show that pre-independence (1999-2008) *Albanian Media* supported the Albanian
side (85%), 12% said "both sides," and only 3% said Serb side. Post-independence (2008-2013) the
results show a decease on Albanian side and increase of support on both sides: 60% said Albanian
Media/TB supported the Albanian side; only 4% said Serb side; and 36% said "both sides."
Whereas *Serbian Media*, there was no shift in support, it was exactly the same as pre-independence
(1999-2008) and post-independence (2008-2013). The results show that 95% said Serbian media
supported the Serb side; only 3% support the Albanian side; and only 2% said "both side" for both
time periods. The findings suggest an increased support for both sides (meaning both Albanian
and Serb side) of 48% from the Albanian Media after independence, when compared to before the
independence of 2008 (*See Graph 11.1*).

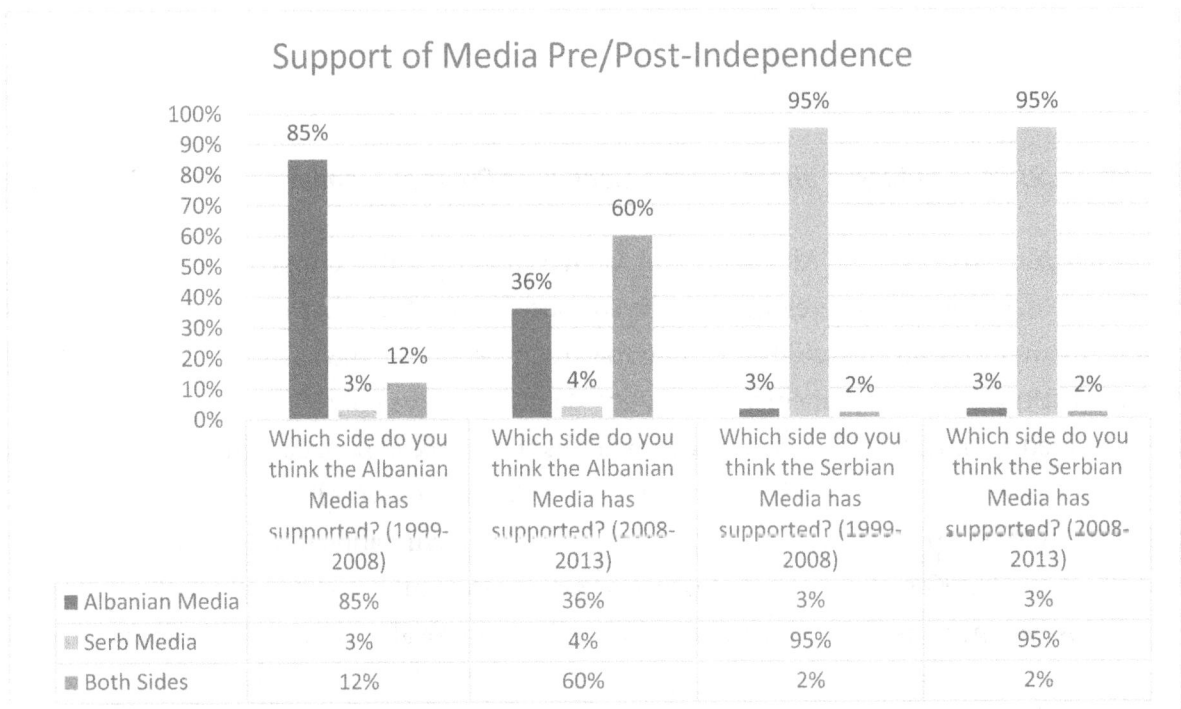

Support of Media Pre/Post-Independence

	Which side do you think the Albanian Media has supported? (1999-2008)	Which side do you think the Albanian Media has supported? (2008-2013)	Which side do you think the Serbian Media has supported? (1999-2008)	Which side do you think the Serbian Media has supported? (2008-2013)
Albanian Media	85%	36%	3%	3%
Serb Media	3%	4%	95%	95%
Both Sides	12%	60%	2%	2%

Graph 11.1: Support of Albanian and Serb Media Pre/Post-Independence in Kosovo

To assess whether the media played a positive or negative role in Kosovo (*Alb: Kosova*) and
to see if there was a shift in perceptions compared to pre- or post-independence, the study asked:
*"What role did the (1) Albanian media/TV, (2) Serbian Media/TV, (3) Foreign Media/TV play, pre/
post-independence?"*, listing "positive" and "negative" as the two possible answers.

The results show that the Albanian Media and the Foreign Media played a positive role in both time periods pre- and post-independence, whereas Serb Media played a negative role during pre- and post-independence. however, there was a 4% increase on positive role post-independence, where foreign media dropped 7% post-independence in positive influence. (Results Pre-independence: Albanian media 94% positive, 6% negative; Serb media 6% positive, 94% negative; Foreign media 93% positive, 7% negative. Results Post-independence: Albanian media 90% positive, 10% negative; Serb media 10% positive, 90% negative; Foreign media 86% positive, 14% negative) (*See Graph 11.2*).

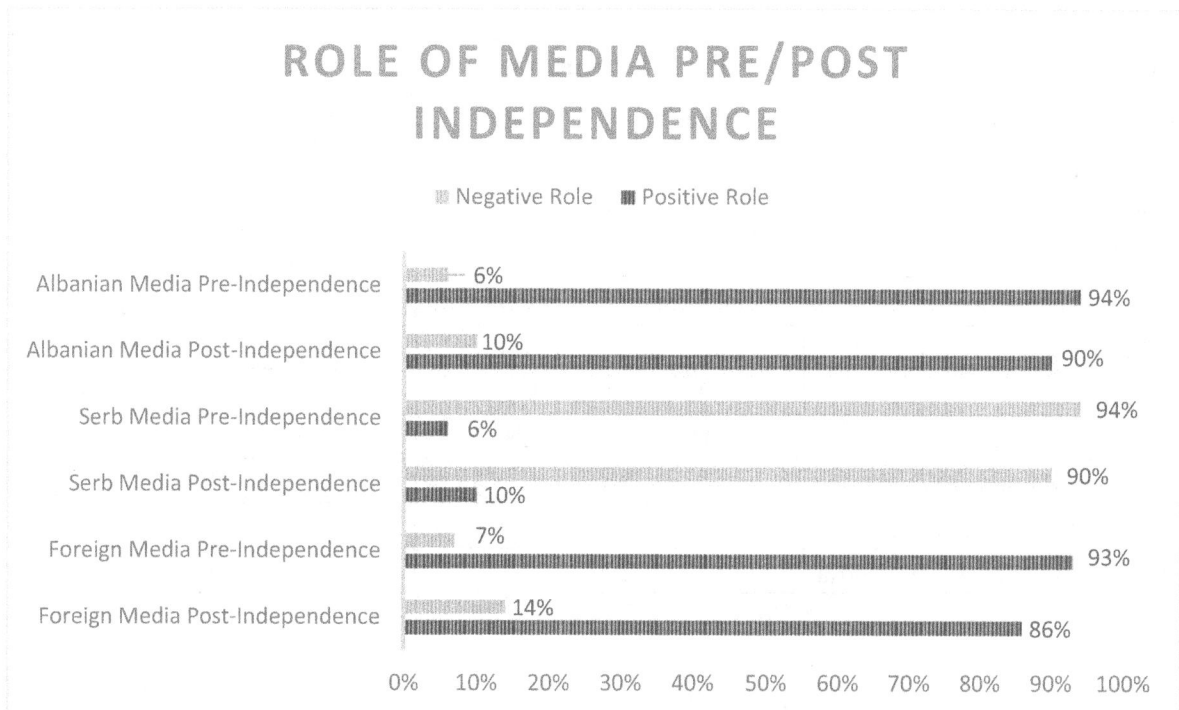

ROLE OF MEDIA PRE/POST INDEPENDENCE

Negative Role   Positive Role

Category	Negative	Positive
Albanian Media Pre-Independence	6%	94%
Albanian Media Post-Independence	10%	90%
Serb Media Pre-Independence	94%	6%
Serb Media Post-Independence	90%	10%
Foreign Media Pre-Independence	7%	93%
Foreign Media Post-Independence	14%	86%

Graph 11.2: Role of Albanian, Serb & Foreign Media in Kosovo Pre/Post-Independence

When the respondents were asked in 2012 to *rank the media sources in Kosovo* from "most reliable" (=1) to "least reliable" (=5), during *pre-independence*, American, and British were the most reliable sources, respectively: American, British, Foreign, Albanian, Serb. During *post-independence*, British Media took No.1 as the most reliable media source in Kosovo, followed by American media at No. 2, then Foreign Media at No. 3 (listing Deutsche Welle News), Albanian Media at No. 4, and Serbian Media taking the last place for "least reliable" media source. In 2018, Kosovo Albanians shared the same attitude in trusting foreign media more (65% trust) and Serb media the least (84% no trust), Albanian media (65% no trust).

The 2012 study also asked: "*Which areas in the media / TV in Kosovo have progressed?*" listing (1) Defamation law, (2) Copyright law, and (3) Public broadcasting law, during pre/post-independence. The results show that all three had higher scores during post-independence, suggesting progress in the three areas. Defamation law had improved post-independent from 66% pre-independence to 77% post-independence. Copyright law had progress from 45% pre-independence to 77% during post-independence. Public Broadcast law improved post-independence, 81% compared to 69% pre-independence (*See Table 6*).

Table 6: Comparison of Media Role and Progress (Pre/Post-Independence)

Country: Kosovo (*Alb: Kosova*)	Pre-Independence		Pre-Independence	
Progress in Law	**YES**	**NO**	**YES**	**NO**
Defamation Law	66%	34%	77%	23%
Copyright Law	45%	55%	77%	23%
Public Broadcasting Law	69%	31%	81%	19%
Role of Media	**Positive**	**Negative**	**Positive**	**Negative**
Albanian	94%	6%	90%	10%
Serb	6%	94%	10%	90%
Foreign	93%	7%	86%	14%
Propaganda in Media	**YES**		**NO**	
Anti-Albanian in Serb Media	95%		5%	
Anti-Serb in Albanian Media	29%		71%	

CHAPTER 6

Explaining Political Trust in Kosovo

In this chapter, I will interpret and describe the significance of the findings considering the research questions and hypotheses posed in the study. The discussion will include comparisons between 2012-2013 and 2018 results, in light of the pre/post-independence timeframe. Additionally, I will focus on the role of cultural and institutional performance factors – *national identification, interpersonal trust, trustworthiness, perceived government performance*, as the key determinants of political trust.

6.1   Variations in Political Trust

6.1.1 International and Country Level

This research identified different sources of political trust stemming from the *individual country level* (political, civil, legal systems) and the *international level* (international institutions and actors). Political trust is vital to democracy, in particular for new democracies – such as post-conflict Kosovo (*in Albanian: Kosova*).[535] Godefroidt et al. (2015) argue that high levels of political trust facilitate democracy, whereas decreased levels of trust act as a barrier to the functioning and the legitimacy of democratic institutions.[536]

The dependent variable *political trust* is operationalized from seven domains of political trust: (1) trust in government; (2) trust in politicians; (3) trust in the legal system; (4) trust in police; (5) trust in international organizations; (6) trust in another country; and (7) trust in media/TV. The research objective is to identify variables that can explain key factors that influence political trust in Kosovo from the cultural and the institutional performance context. The study addresses

---

[535] Godefroidt et al. (2015), 1.

[536] Ibid.

three main research questions: What is the level of trust in a series of national and international institutions in Kosovo? What are the factors that affect the levels of political trust? And, is there significant variation in political trust at the individual country level and international level?

Empirically this study is grounded on the two conceptual models of political trust: (1) *"social vs. political integrative model"* of sources of trust, focusing on the importance of cultural theories and institutional performance theories;[537] and (2) the *"two-factor model"* emphasizing trust in both the national and international political trust.[538] In the first step, the seven aforementioned domains of political trust in the national and international level have been identified to assess the dimensionality of political trust across various institutions. Secondly, the study will analyze which direction trust flows, based on the socio-cultural and institutional explanations.

Graph 12 displays the results for nine institutions in Kosovo to understand the variations in the political trust levels at the country level and international level, namely: (1) Kosovo government, (2) Kosovo police, (3) Kosovo courts, (4) the United Nations, (5) the European Union, (6) NATO, (7) United States Embassy in Kosovo, (8) Kosovo Specialist Court in The Hague, and (9) Media/TV.

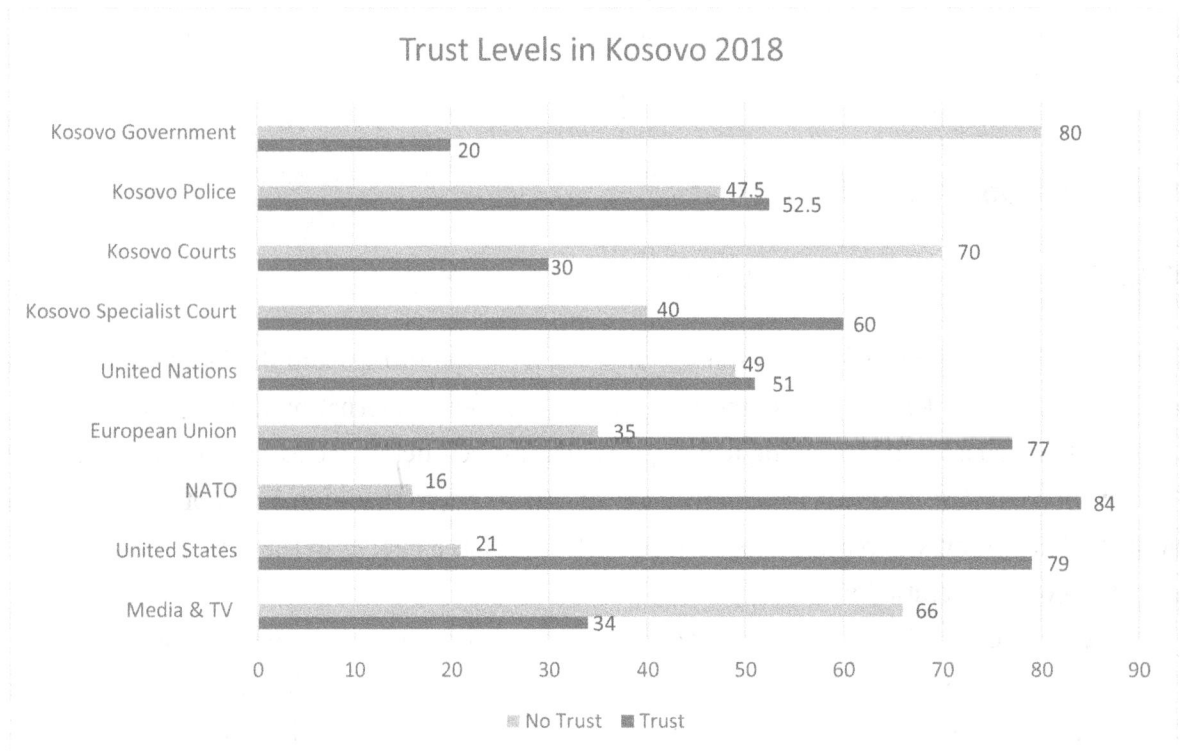

Trust Levels in Kosovo 2018

Institution	No Trust	Trust
Kosovo Government	80	20
Kosovo Police	47.5	52.5
Kosovo Courts	70	30
Kosovo Specialist Court	40	60
United Nations	49	51
European Union	35	77
NATO	16	84
United States	21	79
Media & TV	66	34

Graph 12: Results of Political Trust Levels in Kosovo (2018)

---

[537] Blind, P. K. (2006), 4.

[538] Andre, S. (2014), 970.

Comparing results of political trust between the individual country level and the international level across nine different institutions in Kosovo (*Alb: Kosova*), the data reveals significant differences. The study finds strong differences between international political trust and national political trust, with high distrust levels in government institutions and high trust in the international community. National political trust is significantly less at the political and legal institutions in Kosovo, such as the government and the courts; but with moderate trust in the Kosovo police and media. Whereas, international political trust is significantly higher in NATO, United States, European Union, but with lower trust for the United Nations, and moderate scores for the Kosovo Specialist Court. The results of this study are in line with other studies of political trust that claim lower levels of trust are associated in transitional democracies, attributing distrust in the political system to higher corruption, to well-being and government performance.[539]

Kosovo Albanians significantly distrust the Kosovo government and the Kosovo courts, with 80% no trust in the government, and 70% no trust in the local courts. The opposite is found at the international political level, reporting higher level of trust in NATO (84%), United States (79%), and the European Union (67%). The study also found moderate trust levels towards the media and TV (66%), the Kosovo Specialist Court (60%), Kosovo police (53%), and lower levels for the United Nations (51%).

To investigate the variances between domestic political trust and international political trust the next section will explore the impact of four factors identified from the cultural and institutional performance theories – *national identification, interpersonal trust, trustworthiness*, and *perceived government performance*. To assess the relationship between the cultural factors, this study looks at 1) the impact of feelings of *national identification* on political trust expecting a positive relationship between the two; and a weaker relationship between *ethnic identification* and trust (**hypothesis 1**). The literature suggest that national pride and national identification strengthens institutional trust.[540]

This study will look at the *horizontal trust* between citizens known as *interpersonal trust*, and the *vertical trust* between citizens, known as the political trust between the citizens and the political elite or confidence in the political institutions. *Trustworthiness* is expected to have a positive influence on the levels of political trust, based on fairness, legitimacy, and the competence of the institutions (**hypothesis 2**). Media is also expected to play a role in political trust, since it is a vital source of information about politics[541] (**hypothesis 3**).

---

[539] Catterberg, G., &Alejandro, M. (2006). The Individual Bases of Political Trust: Trends in New and Established Democracies. *International Journal of Public Opinion Research*, 18(1), 32.

[540] Godefroidt et al. (2015), 10.

[541] Ariely, G. (2015), 354.

To study the linkage between the institutional performance factors and political trust this study will look at the *perceived efficiency of government* and the democratic functioning of the state. Both relationships are expected to be positive where, the higher the satisfaction with the government's performance the higher level of trust in institutions (**hypothesis 4**); and the higher the individuals' perceptions towards the level of democracy, the higher the individuals' level of trust in institutions (**hypothesis 5**).

The next section will discuss the determining factors of political trust to understand the trust variances in Kosovo (*Alb: Kosova*) and the relationships that exist between the political trust and international political trust, if any.

6.2 Socio-Cultural Explanations

6.2.1 The Role of National Identification

The scholarly debate on the socio-cultural explanations has primarily focused on the role of national identity and interpersonal trust as two cultural determinates of political trust. Cultural theories emphasize the different socialization experiences, treating national and ethnic identity as an exogenous factor, outside of the political sphere.[542] Berg and Hjerm (2010) argue that a sense of cohesiveness or a sense of community amongst the members is needed in order for political institutions to exist over time.[543] National identity facilities political trust because people who are united under national pride are more willing to cooperate with each other and united under one government.[544] Cultural theories also assume that social relations formed through early socialization will have an impact across genders and different civic groups.[545] The study tests the idea of examining how collective identity – national and ethnic identification affect political trust in Kosovo.

In this study, national identification is operationalized by four measures: *national pride, citizenship, place of birth/residence,* and *nationality*. National pride is viewed as an extension of national identification as in the attachment to the nation. The 2012-13 survey asked 220 participants, "*Your view regarding Kosovo's national symbols (flag, emblem, hymn)*" on a 5-point scale from "very satisfied" (=1) to "very dissatisfied" (=5). The results show that only 45% of the respondents are satisfied with Kosovo's national symbols, and 56% are not. Interestingly, 34% answered "very

---

[542] Godefroidt et al. (2015).
[543] Berg &. Hjerm. (2010), 392.
[544] Godefroidt et al. (2015), 4.
[545] Ibid.

POLITICAL TRUST IN KOSOVO

dissatisfied" (=5). The results suggest that Kosovo Albanians are not happy with the national symbols.

Prior to the 2008 independence, Kosovo identified with Albania's red and black flag, with the eagle being the national pride symbol for all Albanians. However, after the declaration of independence, Kosovo was required to choose new national symbols, to represent the birth of the new state of Kosovo. Kosovo adopted the new gold and blue flag showing six white stars above a golden map of Kosovo, to symbolize Kosovo's six ethnic groups: Albanian (88%), Serb (6%), Bosniaks and Gorani (3%), Roma, Ashkali and Egyptians (2%), and Turks (1%).[546] Based on the findings of 2012-2013 study majority of Kosovo Albanians do not identify with the new national symbols, but with the Albanian eagle instead. This is evident in many celebrations and international events. During the 2018 World Cup, two ethnic Kosovo Albanian players of the Switzerland soccer team, Granit Xhaka and Xherdan Shaqiri celebrated their goal when they beat Serbia 2-1, by making the Albanian double-headed eagle hand gesture. The double eagle sign (interlocking the thumbs and stretching out the fingers to look like the eagle) is considered a nationalist symbol representing the double-headed eagle displayed in Albania's flag.[547] The celebration brought political tension between Serbian nationalists and ethnic Albanians, whereas Serbia called it a provocation.[548]

To better assess the feelings of national pride and the attachment to the nation, the survey also asked: "*How is an Albanian from Kosovo identified?*", listing four options: (1) Albanian; (2) Kosovan: (3) Kosovan-Albanian; and (4) Other (explain). The data shows that majority of the Kosovo Albanians identify as "Albanian" (55%), followed by "Kosovan-Albanian" (35%), and "Kosovar" (10%).[549] The findings suggest that Kosovo Albanians do not have strong attachments to the national symbols of the state, and identify as Albanians not Kosovans (*See Table 8*).

When looking at the perceptions of political trust in the Kosovo government and the satisfaction with the Kosovo's national symbol this study finds a direct relationship between the two. Majority of Kosovo Albanians show dissatisfaction with the national symbols (56%), as well as high distrust levels in the government (80%). The study concludes that a weak national identity has a negative impact on political trust (which **confirms hypothesis 1**). Feelings of national identification have a significant impact on political trust. Strong national identification strengthens institutional trust, and weak national identity decreases political trust.

---

[546] Kosovo National Census (2011). *Agjencia e Statistikave të Kosovës*. Retrieved from http://www.Esk.rks-gov.net

[547] ABC News. (2018, June 22). World Cup: Albanian eagle celebration controversy as Switzerland beats Serbia 2-1. Retrieved from https://www.abc.net.au/news/2018-06-23/granit-xhaka-and-xherdan-shaqiri-goals-help-swiss-down-serbia/9828254

[548] BBC News. (2018, June 23). 'Double eagle' celebration provokes Serbs. Retrieved from https://www.bbc.com/news/world-europe-44586587

[549] "Kosovar" is the Albanian term referring to a Kosovo national.

National Identity and Political Trust in Kosovo

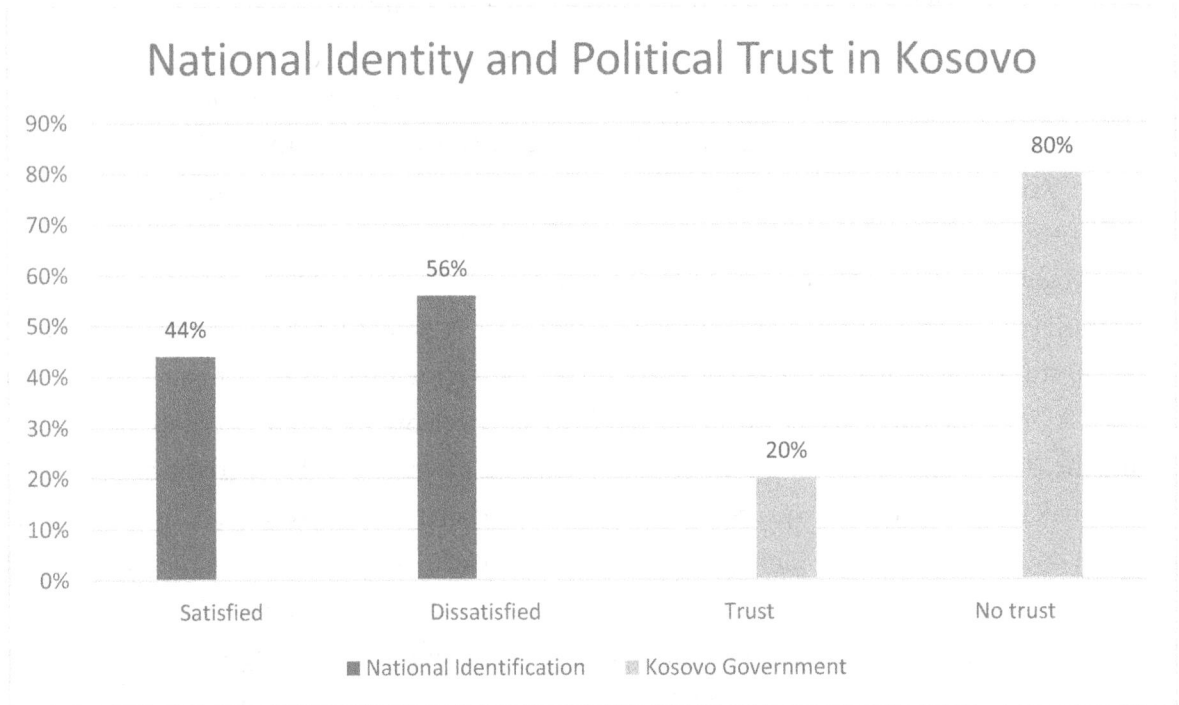

Graph 13: National Identity and Political Trust in Kosovo

Based on my research in Kosovo (*Alb: Kosova*), Kosovo Albanians share the same nationalist bond with Albanians in Albania. In an interview with Hyzri Salihu, Professor of Philosophy and Sociology from the University of Prishtina, he maintained the ethno-national identity as a unifying factor among Albanians and rejected the notion of "Kosovar" identity.

"The term '*Identiteti Kosovar*' (Kosovan Identity), does not exist, it is made up. An ethnic Albanian citizen of Kosovo identifies as '*Shqiptar i Kosovës*' (Kosovo Albanian). Albanians of Kosovo are an inseparable part of the Albanian nation as a whole and its ethnic lands. Although Kosovo and Albania are separated by political borders, they will always be united in the heart of the nation as one. There is no division among Albanians, but there is moral and spiritual unity, which is reflected greatly in the literature, culture, sharing of ideas about family and politics. When we talk about Kosovo, we think about the unfair separation of the ethnic Albanian territories from the motherland."[550]

---

[550] Salihu, Hyzri. (2018, November 26). Personal Communication. Interview.

Historian and Professor of History and Literature, Neki Babamusta, in an interview talked about the two components of national identity: personal identity and common identity, including traditions, citizenship, residence, language, and religious affiliations. He shared that for ethnic Albanians traditions, ancestors and values are of great importance:

> "An Albanian feels proud of being Albanian, for having Albanian blood, and Illyrian origin. National symbols are celebrated and valued by Albania and Kosovo. Scientific symposiums are organized in Kosovo and Albania dedicated to high Renaissance figures in order to preserve the national identity. In my 40-years working as a history teacher, I have spread Albanian language education in Albania and in Kosovo. Meanwhile, in Kosovo, teaching in Albanian was prohibited by the Tito regime, where many professors were dismissed and imprisoned. Teachers who spread the Albanian language in Kosovo were persecuted, ill-treated, imprisoned, by shutting down the schools for the Albanian students, who were forced to learn in secret."[551]

Albanians and Kosovo Albanians feel a sense of community and brotherhood based on the common history, language, ancestry, and Illyrian origin. This supports the findings of the 2013 survey that showed Kosovo Albanians rejecting the newly created national state symbols and aligning their nationalistic feelings with the Albanian nation.

> "The national consciousness and the Illyrian genesis of the population naturally connects the common identity between Albania and Kosova. Another factor that connects the common identity between Albania and Kosova is the creation of a new European and democratic identity. Both countries want to integrate into the European family, with great assistance from America, England, Germany, and the European Union. European and democratic identity means meeting standards, having stability and economic growth, respect for cultures and other minorities, political stability, functioning of the rule of law and the legal state with democratic structures in the service of the people, and not political clans."[552]

Another value that unites Albanians in Kosovo and Albania is the tradition of "BESA," which is a code of honor for all Albanians meaning trust or faith. *Besa* is a tradition passed down through the centuries as a pledge of honor to show generosity and hospitality. The Albanians swore oath and gave their besa to protect and shelter the 2,000 Jews who sought refuge in Albania and Kosovo

---

[551] Babamusta, Neki. (2018, November 26). Personal Communication. Interview. See Appendix for the full interview.
[552] Ibid.

(*Alb: Kosova*) in 1943. Given the historical significance of the strong sense of national identity, it is no surprise that Kosovo Albanians will continue to have strong ties with Albania and identify as Albanians "*Shqiptar*"[553] instead of "*Kosovar.*"

According to Berg and Hjerm (2010) national identity is important to the collectiveness of community, as it develops attitudes and bonds.[554] Creating strong bonds between individuals within a territory increases a stronger internal loyalty and cohesiveness,[555] which in turn shape the political system.[556] To better understand national pride in Kosovo from the local perspective, this study asked the question: "*Are you in favor of the unification of Kosovo with Albania?*", with a "yes" and no" answer.

The 2012-2013 results show an overwhelming support in favor of unification with Albania, with 84% saying yes (184 participants out of 220), and only 16% said "no" (36 respondents). Additionally, 85% of the participants believed that Kosovo (*Alb: Kosova*) is capable of governing itself, however 91% favored a change in leadership (*See Graph 14*).

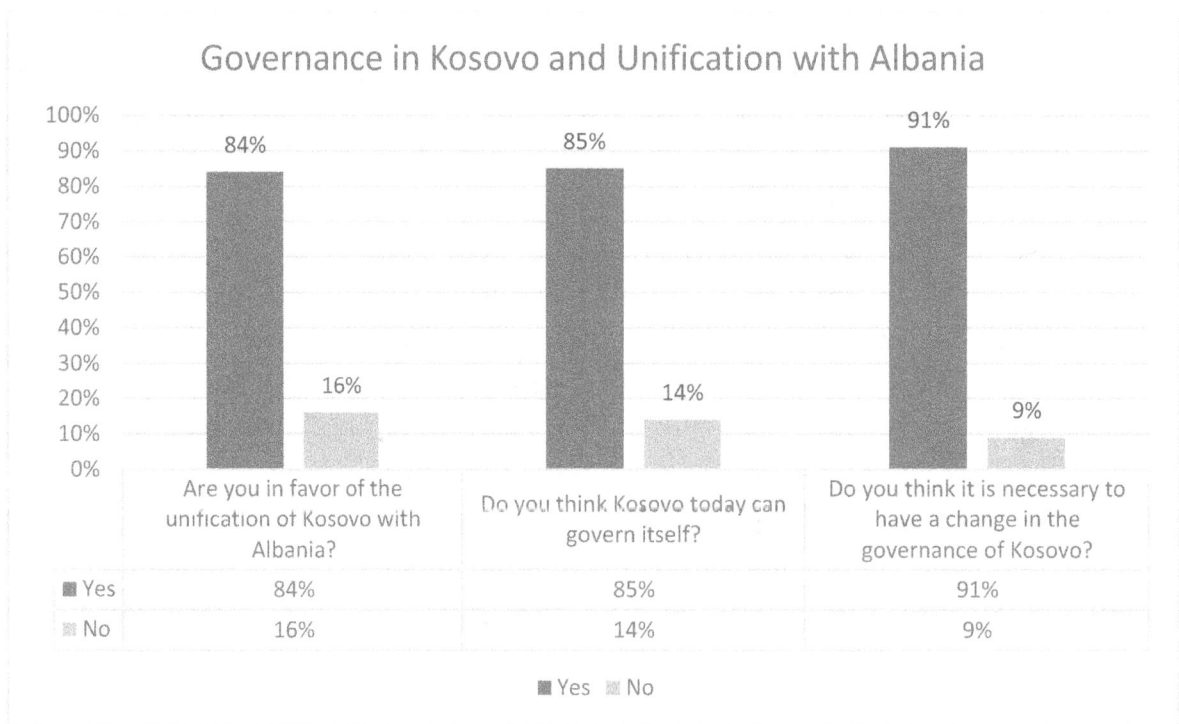

Governance in Kosovo and Unification with Albania

	Are you in favor of the unification of Kosovo with Albania?	Do you think Kosovo today can govern itself?	Do you think it is necessary to have a change in the governance of Kosovo?
Yes	84%	85%	91%
No	16%	14%	9%

Graph 14: Governance in Kosovo and Unification with Albania (2012-2013)

---

[553] "Shqiptar" means Albanian.
[554] Berg & Hjerm. (2010), 393.
[555] Ibid, 393.
[556] Easton, D. (1965), 176.

To analyze the difference in trust perceptions between people from the same group or "in-group trusters," and members from outside the group "out-group trusters," the study looked at two socio-cultural variables: *citizenship* (Albanian vs. foreign nationals) and *residence* (Kosovo citizens living inside the country, outside the country). The data showed that 89.08% of Albanian nationals have no trust in the Kosovo government, compared to the 62.5% of foreign nationals. A slightly higher percentage of foreign nationals (37.5%) trust the Kosovo government compared to only 10.95% Albanians who do (*See Table 7*). This confirms the previous findings of the study showing Kosovan Albanians to have low scores of national identity and political trust. Similarly, the study found the same amount of distrust in the Kosovo government in citizens living in Kosovo (84.67% said no trust) and citizens living outside of Kosovo (85%).

Table 7: Levels of Political Trust in Kosovo Government by Nationality and Residence

	Do you trust Kosovo government?			
	Albanians	Foreign Nationals	Kosovo citizens inside the country	Kosovo citizens outside the country
Yes	10.92%	37.5%	15.33%	15%
No	89.08%	62.5%	84.67%	85%

The study finds a positive connection between national identification and political trust (**Hypothesis 1a**). Weak feelings of national pride or attachment to the nation are associated with low trust in government. Moreover, the study finds that dissatisfaction with the national symbols of the state have a negative impact on national identity and reduce the feeling of cohesiveness in society. The study concludes that in the case of Kosovo, political trust is a consequence not a cause of national identity, because of the pre-existing shared pride and identity with Albania.

6.2.2 Ethnic Identification and Participation

Another component of national identification is *ethnic identity*. The literature suggests that ethnic identification weakens trust in institutions.[557] The 2012 results are supportive of the theory that show weaker trust in institutions due to ethnic identification by undermining collective action. The study looked at the Serb ethnic group in Kosovo (*Alb: Kosova*) to understand if they feel part of the greater national identity or the attachment to the nation. And specifically, if those feelings affect the community's participation in political affairs. The survey posed the question: "*How is a Serb from Kosovo identified?*" Followed by: (1) Serb; (2) Kosovan; (3) Kosovan-Serb; (4) Other

---

[557] Godefroidt et al. (2015), 5.

(explain). The results show that majority of the Kosovo Serbs identify as "Serbian" (72%); where 22.4% identified as "Kosovan-Serb"; 4.6% said "Kosovan"; and 1% said "Other" listing *Serb from Kosovo & Metohijo*" (*See Table 8*).

The survey also asked: "Do the Serbs in the North feel they are Kosovan citizens?" with a "yes," "no," and "partially" answer. The results show majority 59% answer "no"; 33.3% said "partially" and only 7.3% said "yes." There is a great disconnect between the ethnic minority groups in Kosovo and national and ethnic identity. To assess how this relationship has an effect on political trust, the study asked, "*Do Serbs take part in local elections?*" with a "yes," "no," and "partially" answer. The results show that only 8.64% of Kosovo Serbs participate in the local elections; whereas 27.27% do not participate in elections, and 64.09% said "partially." The results show a weak relationship between political trust, in this case participation in the traditional form of voting and ethnic identification (**in support of Hypothesis 1b**).

This is also supported by low scores of perceptions about civil society being active, when the study asked, "*Do you think that the civil society is active in the decision-making process?*" The results show low participation scores, only 8.8% believe that the civil society is active in decision making; 38.18% said "no"; and 53.64% said "partially." Modernists theories associate increased political participation such as voting, as a sign of political trust and democratization.[558] Voting is seen as a legitimate tool for citizens to register their political preferences that affect their well-being.[559] According to Crepaz and Polk (2012) members of the same group or "in-group trusters" perceive voting as an, "Obligation - something that one has to do in order to generate a sense of political identity and belonging to the nation."[560] In Kosovo (*Alb: Kosova*), the relationship between political participation and national ethnic identity is weak as shown by the low participation in both voting and being active in the decision-making process (**Hypothesis 1b**).

---

[558] Blind, P. K. (2006), 6.

[559] Crepaz & Polk. (2012), 4.

[560] Ibid, 3.

Ethnic Identification and Political Participation

	Do Serbs take part in local elections?	Do the Serbs in the North feel they are Kosovan citizens?	Do you think that civil society is active in the decision-making process?
Yes	8.64%	7.30%	8.8%
No	27.27%	59%	38.18%
Partially	64.09%	33.30%	53.64%

■ Yes ■ No ■ Partially

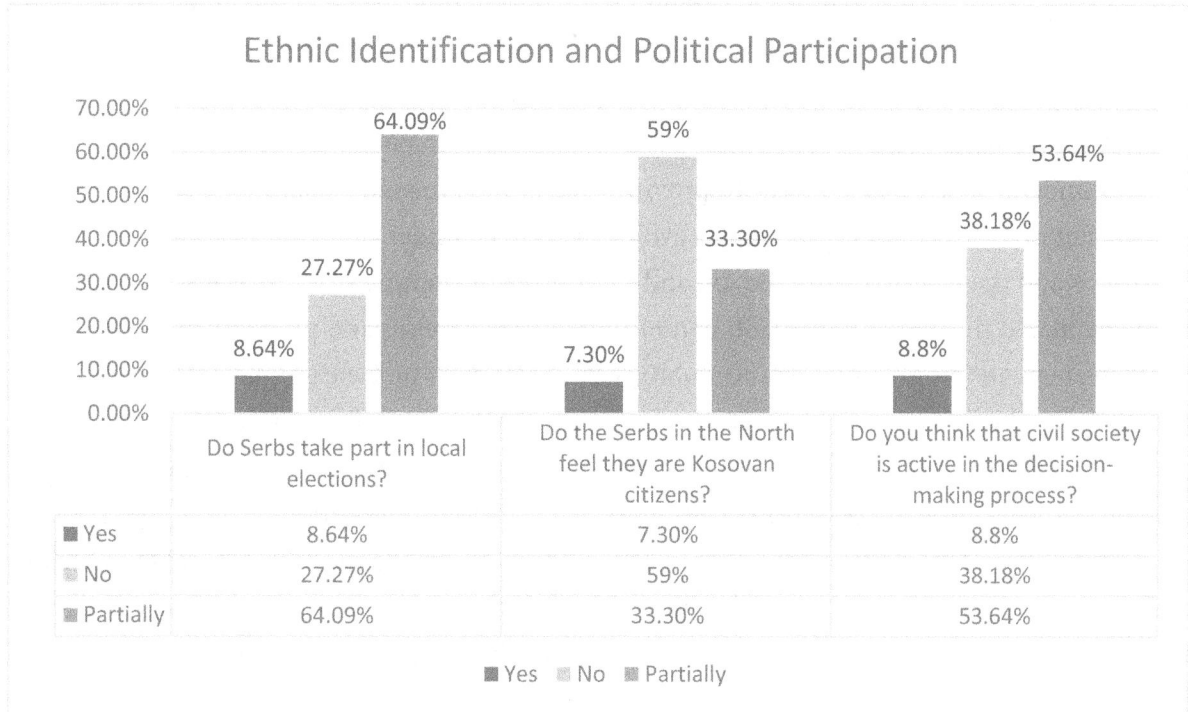

Graph 15: Ethnic Identification and Political Participation in Kosovo

The low participation and attachment to the state scores in this study, for both ethnic Albanians and Kosovo Serbs, are supported by cultural explanations. Cultural theories look at cultural explanations such as group identification of ethnic background and national identity, as well as interpersonal trust as preconditions to political trust.[561] The common ground among cultural theorists is the focus on the "we-feeling" binding people together or the cohesiveness of the society.[562] Berg and Hjerm (2010) argue that national and ethnic identification is a better representation of political trust than interpersonal trust. The idea is that identity is what tends to "glue people together in a society," whereas interpersonal trust relies on the evaluations of the individuals, and not the cohesiveness of the society.[563]

However, I would argue that interpersonal trust could strengthen cohesiveness, if we consider out-group trust, trust between those that are different. Berg and Hjerm (2010) attribute national identification and trust between similar types of people or "in-group" trust. However, the "we-feeling" identity or a sense of togetherness can also emerge from the out-group, if they feel a sense of belonging to the society.[564] In the case of Kosovo (*Alb: Kosova*), the political leaders, with the

---

[561] Berg & Hjerm. (2010), 392.

[562] Ibid.

[563] Ibid, 392.

[564] Crepaz & Polk. (2012), 6

assistance of EULEX, have invested in strengthening inter-ethnic relation and protecting minority rights under rule of law to strengthen unity, participation and belonging to the multi-ethnic state.[565] Some of the government measures included ensuring effective participation, return of property, improving socio-economic life and representation in public services.

Post-independence steps toward improving inter-ethnic relations focused on ensuring equal representation of all communities in Kosovo's institutions, under the protection of Constitution of Kosovo and the Law on the Protection and Promotion of Communities.[566] The Kosovo government facilitated the return of the Serb community to their houses and property in Kosovo, with the implementation of the return and stabilization project, as in the example of the Llapllasella community, where 60 Serb families returned to live.[567] Another priority included decentralization, as a key component of the Ahtisaari's Comprehensive Proposal, to ensure integration of Serbs in Kosovo and spreading of power and decision making to the communities.[568]

Kosovo's President Hashim Thaçi, former Prime Minister, echoed the commitment to the democratic and the multi-ethnic society in Kosovo. In his speech at the "Improving Inter-Ethnic Relations in Kosovo" roundtable, organized by the Project for Ethnic Relations (PER), President Thaçi stated:

> "It is important that we view the achievements and challenges of Kosovo as the shared interest of all the citizens of Kosovo. Democratic Kosovo intends to build a country for all its citizens. Democracy means the active participation of citizens in elections and in government. The government is committed to building and cultivating a democratic and multi-ethnic society. As such, Kosovo is an independent and democratic country and the homeland of all of its citizens. The institutions and citizens of Kosovo have taken great steps toward improving inter-ethnic relations. Even though this may not yet be at the desired level, all communities now participate in Kosovo's institutions. Together, we have fulfilled many promises for issues relating to equal access and rights for all of our citizens."[569]

[565] Baldwin, C. (2006). Minority Rights in Kosovo under International Rule. *Minority Rights Group International*, 1-40. Retrieved from https://www.refworld.org/pdfid/469cbfc20.pdf

[566] Law No. 03/L-047. On the protection and promotion of the rights and communities and their members in Kosovo. *Assembly of Kosovo*. Retrieved from http://www.assembly-kosova.org/common/docs/ligjet/2008_03-L047_en.pdf

[567] Council of Europe. (2010, May 31). Second Opinion on Kosovo. Advisory Committee on the framework convention for the protection of national minorities, 1-52. ACFC/OP/II (2009)004 Retrieved from https://www.ecoi.net/en/file/local/1264460/1226_1279011996_pdf-2nd-op-kosovo-en.pdf

[568] Kosovo Assembly. (2007, February 2). Comprehensive Proposal for the Kosovo Status Settlement, 1-59. Retrieved from https://www.kuvendikosoves.org/common/docs/Comprehensive%20Proposal%20.pdf

[569] Office of the Prime Minister. (2009). Prime Minister Thaçi: Our commitment and our dedication to a multi-ethnic society will not stop – this is for the good of Kosovo. Retrieved from http://kryeministri-ks.net/en/prime-minis-

To better understand perceptions of multi-ethnic and democratic representation in Kosovo (*Alb: Kosova*), the 2012-2013 survey of this study posed the following question: "*Do you consider Kosovo today as a (1) multi-ethnic state, (2) stabilized state, (3) democratic state, and (4) independent state?*" Listing "yes," "no," and "somewhat agree" as the three possible answers. The majority of the participants view Kosovo as a multi-ethnic, democratic and independent state; however, they find the country unstable. The results show that 68.6% believe that Kosovo is a multi-ethnic state, 41% answered "somewhat agree" to the stabilized state question, 55% said "yes" to the democratic state, and 50% believe Kosovo is an independent state (*See Graph 16*).

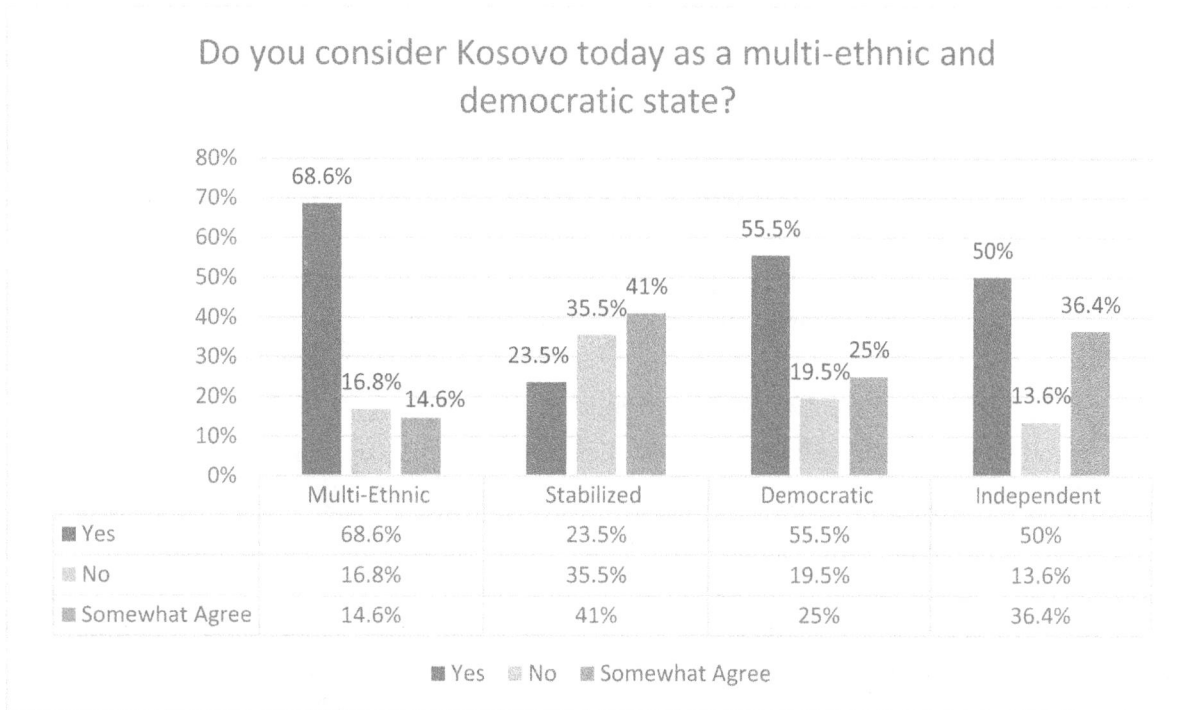

Do you consider Kosovo today as a multi-ethnic and democratic state?

	Multi-Ethnic	Stabilized	Democratic	Independent
Yes	68.6%	23.5%	55.5%	50%
No	16.8%	35.5%	19.5%	13.6%
Somewhat Agree	14.6%	41%	25%	36.4%

Graph 16: Perceptions about Kosovo as a multi-ethnic and democratic state (2012-2013)

Overall, the study found that majority of the Kosovo Albanians do not have a cohesive sense of nationality when it comes to identifying as a "Kosovan." Regarding national and ethnic identification, the study found that in Kosovo exists a strong bond across ethnic lines, not the statehood or nationality. This suggests that Kosovan Albanians and Kosovan Serbs are not connected by a shared sense of national identity and national pride. Only 22% of the respondents identified as "Kosovan" (*Alb: Kosovar*), and an even lower percentage of Kosovan Serbs (4.6%) identified with

ter-thaci-our-commitment-and-our-dedication-to-a-multi-ethnic-society-will-not-stop-this-is-for-the-good-of-kosovo-2/

the same term "Kosovan." Majority ethnic Albanians in Kosovo identified as "Albanian" (55%), whereas ethnic Serbs of Kosovo identified as "Serbian" (72%) (*See Table 8*).

National Identification in Kosovo (2012)							
How is an Albanian from Kosovo identified?				*How is a Serb from Kosovo identified?*			
Albanian	Kosovan/ Kosovar	Kosovan Albanian	Other	Serbian	Kosovan/ Kosovar	Kosovan Serb	Other
Percent 55%	10%	35%	0%	*Percent* 72%	4.6%	22.4%	1%
Participants 121	22	77	0	*Participants* 160	10	49	2
Total 220 participants							

Table 8: National Identification of Kosovo Albanians and Serbs (2012-2013)

While Kosovo Albanians share a great sense of patriotism and nationalism with Albania, Kosovo Serbs, share their patriotic feelings with Serbia, not Kosovo.

"Serbs come from the Carpathian Mountains of Russia, later settled in Kosovo. Throughout different periods in history, they invaded and occupied Kosovo, carrying out genocide against the autochthon Albanians in Kosovo. Serbs do not have anything in common with Kosovo, and they have always felt connected to Belgrade."[570]

In 2018, Serbia's President Aleksandar Vucic suggested the partition of Kosovo or land swap along ethnic lines, rejected by the E.U. and America. Kosovo's President Hashim Thaçi opposed the redrawing of the borders and stated that "Kosovo will remain multi-ethnic."[571] Later in 2019 Thaçi was entertaining the idea of "border correction" that would involve Presevo Valley (*Alb: Lugina e Preshevës*) joining Kosovo. However, neither party is willing to go through with this proposal. The territorial exchange debate has changed the dynamics among European foreign leaders, who see any adjustment of borders as a threat to stability and security in the wider region.

6.2.3 The Importance of Interpersonal Trust

The two main theoretical concepts of trust are – *social trust* and *political trust*. Social trust is characterized by the interpersonal trust between citizens, whereas political trust is between the citizens

---

[570] Salihu, Hyzri. (2018, November 26). Personal Communication. Interview.

[571] KoSSev. (2018, August 27). Thaci: No partition of Kosovo, no land swap. *N1 News*. http://rs.n1info.com

and political leadership, or citizens and government institutions.[572] Cultural and social theories emphasize interpersonal trust as in civic engagement,[573] and in-group visa vie out-group trust.[574] While institutional theorists focus on institutional trustworthiness and trustworthy political leaders.[575]

The theoretical debate has focused on the causal relationship between social and political trust.[576] Does political trust produce social capital (increased interpersonal trust, increased political participation) or is active civic engagement a result of the environment created by the trustworthy government and leaders? Institutionalists attribute political trust to the trust in government institutions, as performance-based evaluations of the political institutions.[577] While culturalist argue that increased social trust is associated with increased engaging of direct action (political participation), which is regarded as a sign of political trust and democratization.[578]

In this study, interpersonal trust is operationalized by measuring trust in three domains: (1) same ethnic group (in-group trust); (2) different ethnic group (out-group trust); (3) and political participation. Other studies have found interpersonal trust to be an important factor that has given rise to political trust.[579]

In-Group vs. Out-Group Trust

The 2018 study asked same ethnic group and in different ethnic groups to rate their perceptions of trust about the sources of information about the Kosovo Specialist Court. The posed question was: "Rate how much you trust the following as sources of about the Specialist Court on war crimes?" on a 5-point trust scale ranging from "no trust" (=1) to "complete trust" (=5). Followed by listing 6 sources: (1) Newspaper/TV; (2) Albanian Media, Serbian Media, Foreign Media, Kosovo Government and Kosovo Specialist Court. The findings show Serbian media with the lowest trust score (84% no trust), followed by Kosovan Government (75% no trust); and Albanian Media (69% no trust) ranked third. The Kosovo Specialist Court rated higher trust scores (64% trust), including Foreign media (63% trust).[580]

---

[572] Schiffman, L., Shawn, T., & Sherman, E. (2010). Interpersonal and political trust: modeling levels of citizens' trust. *European Journal of Marketing*, 44(3/4), 369-381, https:// doi.org/10.1108/03090561011020471

[573] Newton, K. (2013), 3.

[574] Crepaz & Polk. (2012), 3.

[575] Levi & Stoker. (2000), 476.

[576] Blind, P. K. (2006), 6

[577] Godefroidt et al. (2015), 5.

[578] Almond & Verba. (1963), 35

[579] Kuenzi, M. (2008). Social capital and political trust in West Africa. Afrobarometer, 96, 1-32.

[580] The trust rating for Media/TV in general was 66.25% "no trust," and 33.75% said they trust it as a source about the Kosovo Specialist Court on war crimes.

Regarding *Albanian Media* as a trusted source of information, when comparing Albanian nationals with Foreign nationals, the study shows foreign nationals to have less trust in Albanian media (75% said no, 25% yes). Albanian nationals said 60% "no trust," and 40% trust score. However, both Albanian and foreign do not trust Albanian media. Similar results are seen for *Serbian Media*, with 60% Albanian nationals having no trust, (40% yes); and 75% of foreign nationals having no trust, and only 25% having trust. Regarding *Foreign Media*, both Albanian and Foreign nationals have high trust scores, with 78% of Kosovo Albanian nationals having trust, and 75% foreign nationals having trust in foreign media as a source regarding the Kosovo Specialist Court.

When looking at Kosovo Government and the Kosovo Specialist Court as sources: 75% of Albanians do not trust the *Kosovo Government*, while 60% of foreign nationals do trust the Kosovo government as a source. The study shows a higher number of foreign nationals to trust the Kosovo government as a media source for information about the Kosovo Specialist Court. A higher number of Albanians have trust in the Kosovo Specialist Court, with 75% saying they do trust, and only 25% do not trust it. Out of the foreign nationals, 62.5% said they trust the KSC as a source about the Specialist Court, and only 37.5% said they do not trust it (*See Graph 17*).

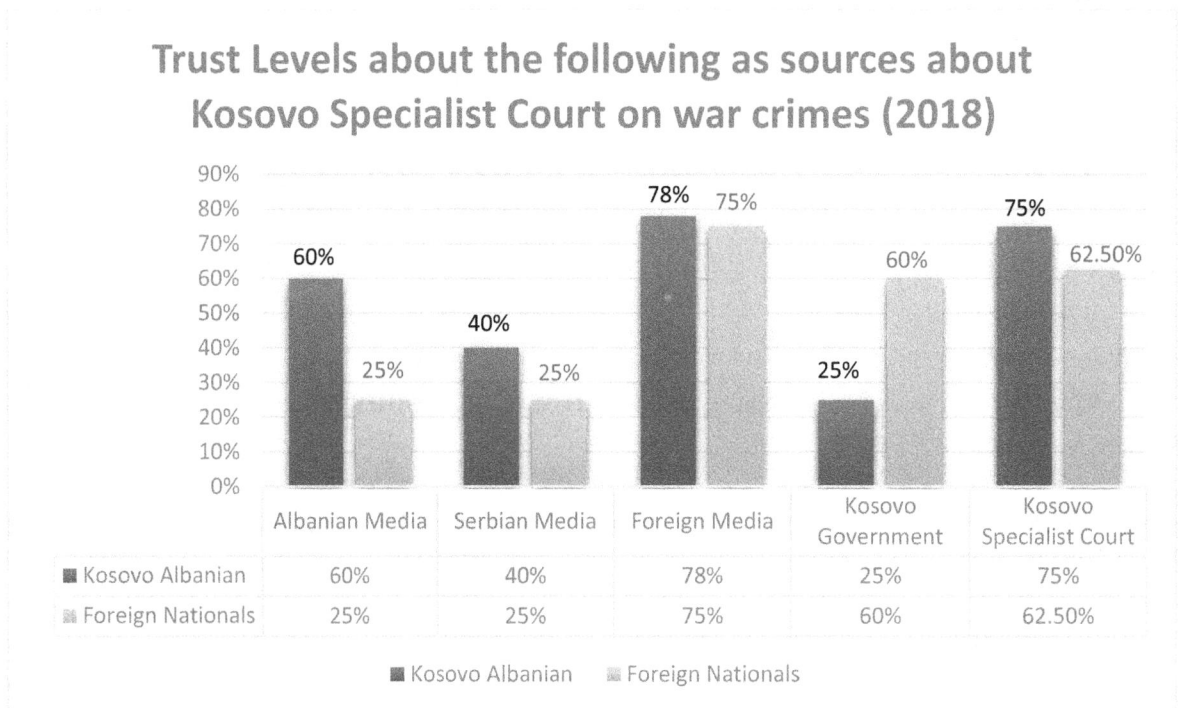

Trust Levels about the following as sources about Kosovo Specialist Court on war crimes (2018)

	Albanian Media	Serbian Media	Foreign Media	Kosovo Government	Kosovo Specialist Court
Kosovo Albanian	60%	40%	78%	25%	75%
Foreign Nationals	25%	25%	75%	60%	62.50%

Graph 17: Trust Levels of Media Sources about the Kosovo Specialist Court based on nationality (2018)

Overall, the study finds that Kosovo Albanian nationals (ethnic Albanians) have high levels of trust for foreign media and foreign institutions also Albanian media, but not for Kosovo government, and not for Serbian media. Whereas, foreign nationals have low trust for Kosovo government and Serbian media, and high scores for Albanian media, Kosovo government and the Kosovo Specialist Court.

The findings suggest that ethnic Albanians do have in-group trust and out-group trust, but it is a positive relationship only in Albanian media (in-group) and foreign institutions (out-group); and a negative relationship of trust with Serbian Media (out-group) and Kosovo government (in-group). This suggests that Kosovo Albanian do identify on the basis of nationalism with Albanian media (**supports Hypothesis 1a**), but this nationalism and support is not shared for the Kosovo government. Although the Kosovo government as a source of information is part of the in-group, the expectation would be that ethnic Albanians and nationals would identify with members of the same group and have a strong trust relationship. It is interesting that foreign national (out-group) have more trust in Kosovo government as a media source (60%) than the in-group members, Kosovo Albanians, only 25%.

When looking at the trust scores of ethnic Albanians towards Serbian media, the general expectation is that ethnic identification is assumed to weaken trust (**hypothesis 1b**). The findings of this study support hypothesis 1b, concluding that ethnic identification weakens political trust.[581] It is interesting that foreign nationals have less trust in Serbian media when compared to Albanian media. This could be due to negative attitudes and propaganda from the Serbian media. Aarts, et al. (2012) argue that the dominance of negative information on the media and TV has a negative effect on political trust and in forming political attitudes.[582] The negativity bias has been present in Serbian media with anti-Albanian sentiment, "with an explosion of hate" and prejudice against ethnic Albanians.[583]

During my trip in post-war Kosovo in 2007, I saw on the walls of burned and destroyed Albanian houses, anti-Albanian ethnic slurs pained on the walls, with the drawings of "plis" a traditional cap worn by ethnic Albanian men. In Northern Mitrovica with majority Serb, I saw the slogan "Kosovo is Serbia," painted on the walls, as a display of Serbian sentiment against Kosovo's independence. The discrimination against ethnic Albanians in Kosovo has carried out throughout

---

[581] In this study, "media" is considered as a one of the seven domains of political trust, namely: (1) trust in government; (2) trust in politicians; (3) trust in legal system; (4) trust in police; (5) trust in international organizations; (6) trust in another country/embassy; and (7) trust in media/TV.

[582] Aarts, K., Fladmoe, A., & Strömbäck, J. (2012). Media, Political Trust, and Political Knowledge: A Comparative Perspective, 98-118.

[583] Rudic, F. (2017, May 16). Rabid Anti-Albanian Sentiment Grips Serbian Media. *Balkan Insight*. Retrieved from http://www.balkaninsight.com/en/article/rabid-anti-albanian-sentiments-grip-serbian-media-05-16-2017

1844, 1912, in the 90s and in the 1998-99 war, where ethnic Albanians have been subject to oppression, ethnic cleansing campaigns and genocide:

> "During their offensives, forces of the FRY and Serbia acting in concert have engaged in a well-planned and coordinated campaign of destruction of property owned by Kosovo Albanian civilians. Towns and villages have been shelled, homes, farms, and businesses burned, and personal property destroyed. As a result of these orchestrated actions, towns, villages, and entire regions have been made uninhabitable for Kosovan Albanians. Additionally, forces of the FRY and Serbia have harassed, humiliated, and degraded Kosovan Albanian civilians through physical and verbal abuse. The Kosovo Albanians have also been persistently subjected to insults, racial slurs, degrading acts based on ethnicity and religion, beatings, and other forms of physical mistreatment."[584]

Anti-Semitism against Albanians is being promoted by Serbia's President Aleksandar Vucic with the ethnic partition talks in 2018, suggesting that Kosovo Serbs should not be citizens of Kosovo, rather Serbia. The partition plan further heightens ethnic tensions between ethnic groups in Kosovo and decreases interpersonal trust amongst different ethnic communities. The conversation should focus on the protection, safety, and the well-being of the multi-ethnic society, both in Serbia and Kosovo.

The decreased levels of interpersonal trust were also evident in civic engagement and political participation of the Serbian minority in Kosovo. The data shows that only 8.64% of Kosovan Serbs participate in local elections. To better understand the factors that influence low political trust within the in-group, the study also factored in "safety" as a possible explanation. When asked in 2012, *"Do you think Kosovo was safer 1) Pre-Independence or 2) Post- Independence?"* 86% said Kosovo was safer post-independence, and only 14% said pre-independence. When asked, *"Do you think there is safety currently in Kosovo?"* On a 4-point scale from "strongly agree" (=1) to strongly disagree (=2), the results show that majority of the respondents felt safe. Respectively, 23% answered "strongly agree"; 52% "somewhat agree"; 17% "somewhat disagree" and 8% answered "strongly disagree." Overall Kosovan Albanians feel safe post-independence (*See Graph 18*).

---

[584] American Public Media. (1999). War Crimes Indictment against Milosevic. Justice For Kosovo. Retrieved from http://americanradioworks.publicradio.org/features/kosovo/more2.htm

PERCEPTIONS ABOUT SAFETY & MINORITIES

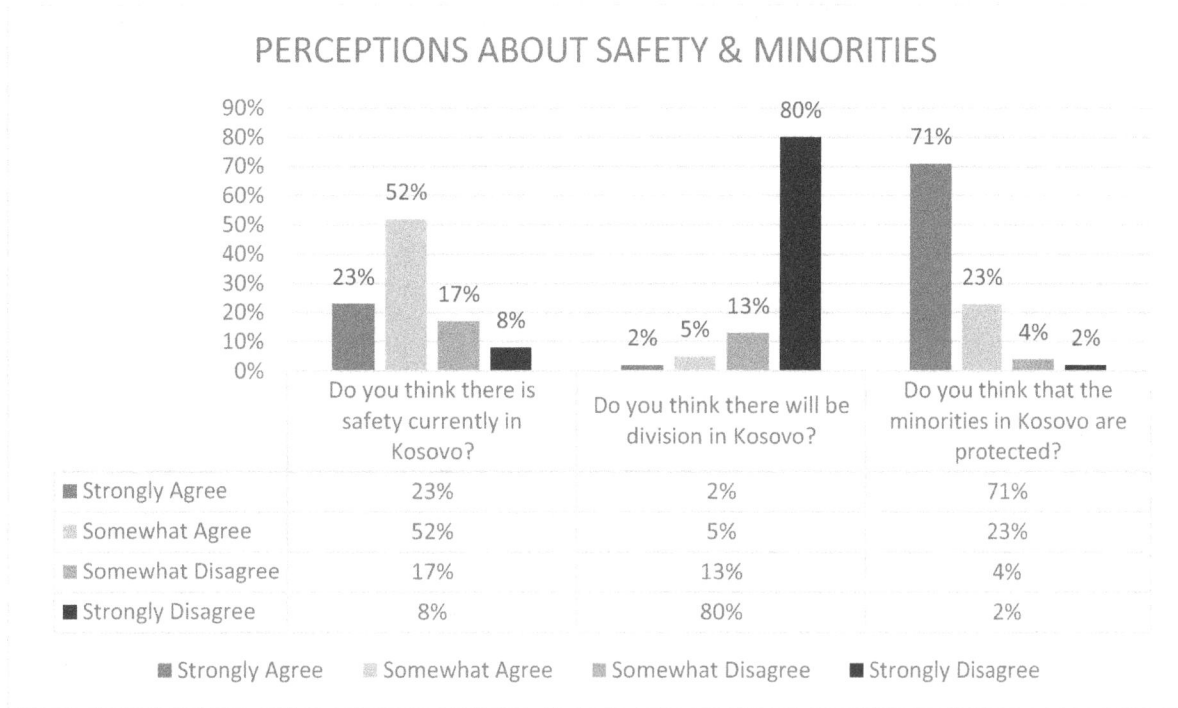

	Do you think there is safety currently in Kosovo?	Do you think there will be division in Kosovo?	Do you think that the minorities in Kosovo are protected?
■ Strongly Agree	23%	2%	71%
▨ Somewhat Agree	52%	5%	23%
▨ Somewhat Disagree	17%	13%	4%
■ Strongly Disagree	8%	80%	2%

■ Strongly Agree   ▨ Somewhat Agree   ▨ Somewhat Disagree   ■ Strongly Disagree

Graph 18: Perceptions about Safety and Minorites in Kosovo (2012-2013)

The study also raised the situation in North, to understand if the attitudes towards the ethnic tension in the North of Kosovo has shifted pre- and post-independence. The posted question was: *"How do you consider the Situation in the North pre- and post-independence?"* On a 5-point scale, from "not stabilized" (=1), to "grave and serious" (=2), "stabilized but delicate" (=3), stabilized (=4), and "needs to improve" (5). The results show that pre-independence, the majority of Kosovo Albanians felt that the situation in the North was not stabilized, as well as grave and serious. After independence, the attitudes had changed slightly to stabilized but delicate, with some also thinking grave and serious, and not stabilized. The results were: Pre-independence: 46% not stabilized; 44% grave and serious; 3% stabilized by delicate; 5% needs to improve. Whereas, post-independence: 27% not stabilized; 27% grave and serious; 37% stabilized but delicate; 2% stabilized; and 7% needs to improve) (*See Graph 19*).

Another question asked: *"Do you think that the minorities in Kosovo are protected?"* On a 4-point scale of "strongly agree" (=1) to "strongly disagree" (=4). The results show overwhelming support: 72% "strongly agree" that the minorities in Kosovo are protected; 23% said "somewhat agree"; 4% "somewhat disagree"; and only 1% answered "strongly disagree." Regarding the division pertaining to the North, the study asked: *"Do you think there will be division in Kosovo?"* On the same 4-point agree to disagree scale. Results show that majority feel that they do not think there will be division in Kosovo in 2012. Specifically, 80% answered "strongly disagree"; 13% "somewhat disagree"; 5% "somewhat agree" and only 2% said "strongly agree" (*See Graph 18*).

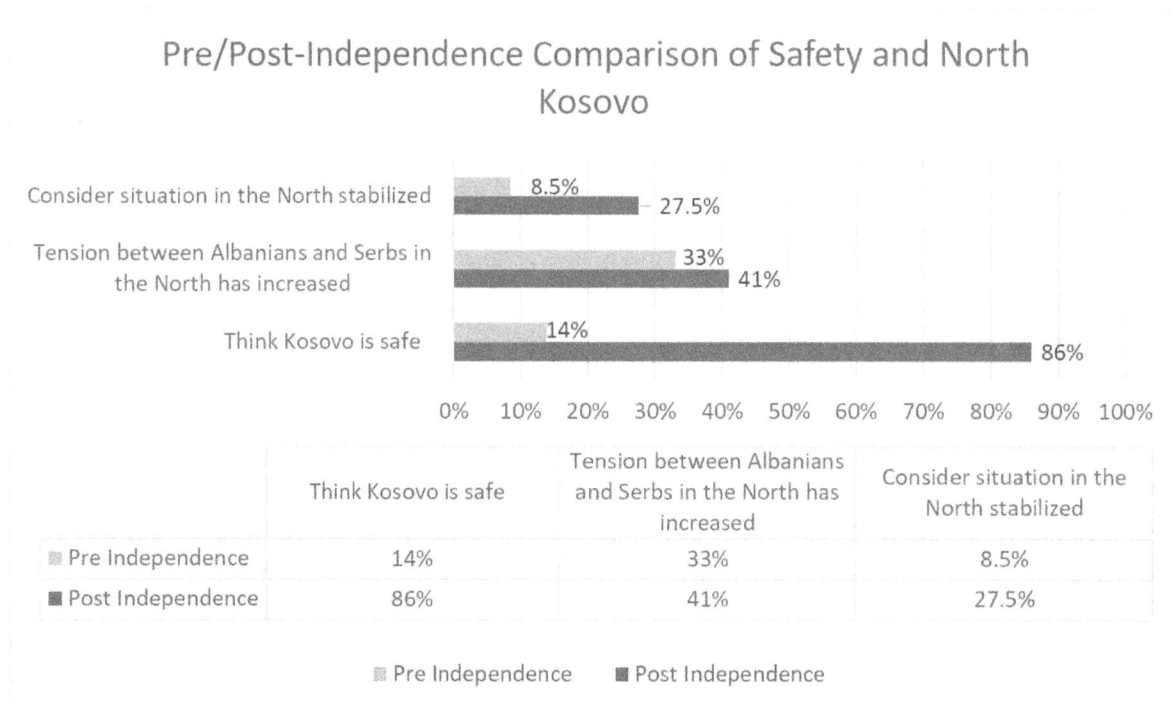

Pre/Post-Independence Comparison of Safety and North Kosovo

	Think Kosovo is safe	Tension between Albanians and Serbs in the North has increased	Consider situation in the North stabilized
Pre Independence	14%	33%	8.5%
Post Independence	86%	41%	27.5%

Pre Independence   Post Independence

Graph 19: Pre/Post-Independence Comparison of Safety Perceptions and North Kosovo

The results of the study are in line with the Kosovan policies for protection of minorities. During my filed research in 2012, I met with the Ombudsperson in Kosovo, Mr. Sami Kurteshi to better understand the ethnic relations and treatment of minorities. During the interview Mr. Kurteshi stated that minorities in Kosovo are treated equally to all Kosovo citizens, regardless of ethnicity. He added that minority rights in Kosovo were advanced in such a way that it had created "positive discrimination." Meaning that Kosovo was giving advantage to minorities, especially the Serbian communities, because it was such as strong requirement from the European Union to improve minority rights, that it affected them positively, in favor of the Kosovan Serbs.[585] He added that the application of the law was a main concern and advocated for further legal reforms.

Overall, majority of the respondents think Kosovo is safer post-independence, however they do not consider the situation in the North stabilized, 8% increase of tension between Albanians and Serbs post-independence. The findings of the study reflect the events happening in Kosovo at the time. The results of study conducted in 2012, show the reality of the civil disruption happening

---

[585] Kurteshi, Sami. (2012, December 26). In Person Interview.

in Kosovo, after Kosovo declared its independence in 2008. In October 2011 violent confrontation between civilians and police in North Mitrovica occurred. The local Serb population put up a wall, as "a political statement and a physical barrier against a government it does not recognize."[586] The Mitrovica area in particular, located in North Kosovo, has experienced the worst level of civil disruption since the 2008 declaration.

Despite the increased tension in 2012, the majority of Kosovan Albanians felt that there would be no division in Kosovo. This is particularly interesting to the current political situation in Kosovo, where partition is on the table as a possible option. The proposal includes an exchange of North Kosovo (majority ethnic Serb) with Presevo Valley in the South Serbia (majority ethnic Albanian). Germany strongly opposes the redrawing of borders between Serbia and Kosovo, concerned about the interethnic conflict and stability in the region. German Foreign Minister, Heiko Mass in an interview with the Wall Street Journal echoed the previous statement of German Chancellor Angela Merkel that the "borders of the region were not subject to change."[587]

> "We don't think that talks on territory exchange between Kosovo and Serbia are particularly constructive. It can tear open too many old wounds in the population there. The move might open the Pandora's Box of interethnic conflict in some of the poorest countries in the region."[588]

The increase of tension between the ethnic Serbs and ethnic Albanians could be one of the reasons that explains the distrust in Serbian Media. As tension between the two communities rose higher post-independence (compared to pre-independence), the level of distrust in Serbian media and media exposure also increased. This suggests that there is a positive relationship between increased level of tension between ethnic groups (out-group trusters) with the level of interpersonal trust towards the ethnic community. The higher the tension, the higher the distrust between the out-group trusters. (*See Graph 20*)

The findings **confirm hypothesis 1(b)** in the study that ethnic identification is assumed to weaken trust in institutions. The study concludes that interpersonal trust has an influence on

[586] Fison, M. (2011, October 30). Tensions between Serbs and Albanians flare up in Kosovo. *The Independent UK*. Retrieved from https://www.independent.co.uk/news/world/europe/tensions-between-serbs-and-albanians-flare-up-in-kosovo-6256499.html

[587] Gray, A. (2018, August 13). Angela Merkel: No Balkan border changes. *Politico*. Retrieved from https://www.politico.eu/article/angela-merkel-no-balkan-border-changes-kosovo-serbia-vucic-thaci/

[588] Norman, L., and Hinshaw, D. (2018, August 31). U.S., Germany at Odds Over Serbia-Kosovo Land Swap. *The Wall Street Journal*. Retrieved from https://www.wsj.com/articles/u-s-germany-at-odds-over-serbia-kosovo-land-swap-1535729377

the levels of political trust, when considering media. The higher the tension between out-group members of different ethnicities, the higher the distrust in institutions.

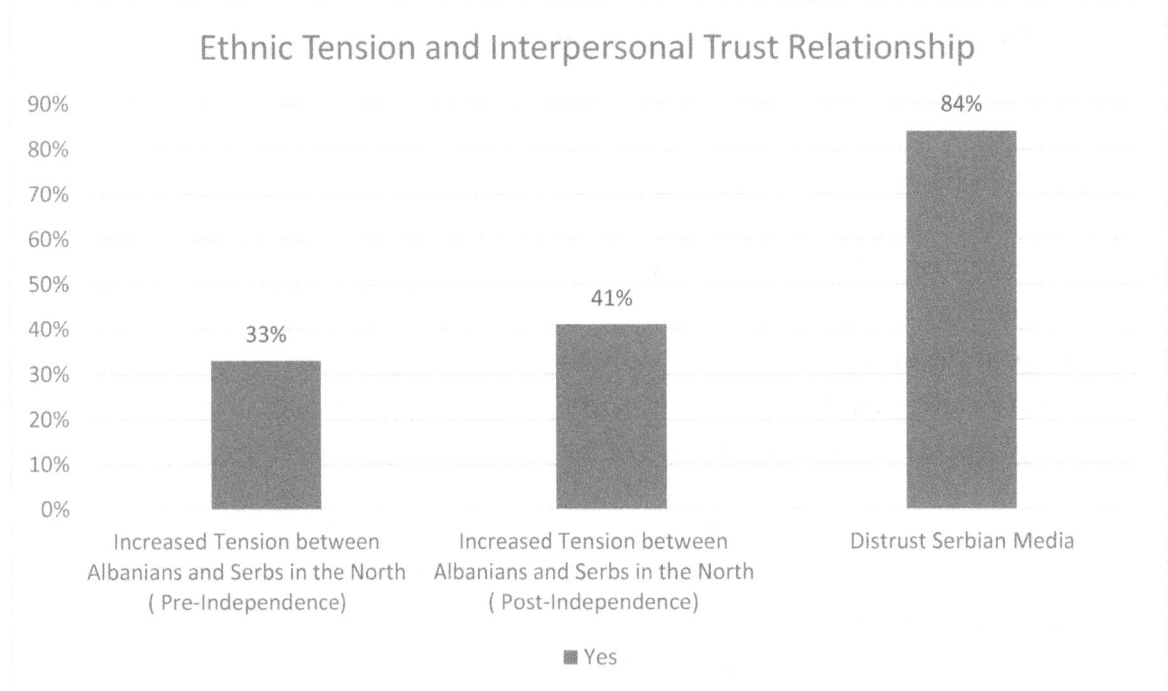

Ethnic Tension and Interpersonal Trust Relationship

33%	41%	84%
Increased Tension between Albanians and Serbs in the North (Pre-Independence)	Increased Tension between Albanians and Serbs in the North (Post-Independence)	Distrust Serbian Media

■ Yes

Graph 20: Ethnic Tension and Interpersonal Trust Relationship (Pre/Post-Independence)

In addition to ethnic tension and how it relates to trust in the media, the study looked at another domain of political trust, the legal system. To understand how ethnic identification and interpersonal trust affect trust in the different courts, including Kosovo courts, Serbian courts, ICTY Hague Tribunal, and the Kosovo Specialist Court, participants were asked questions about war crime and human rights violations suppositions committed by different ethnic groups.

First the study tried to understand the level of trust in each legal institution, by asking: *"If a person committed an act of genocide in Kosovo, what is the best way to address the crime?"* followed by, (1) Kosovo court, (2) Serbian court, (3) Kosovo Specialist Court, (4) ICTY Hague Tribunal. The results show that the ICTY Hague Tribunal was chosen by majority (43%), followed by the Kosovo Specialist Court (39%), and Kosovo court at 18%. Serbian court received 0 votes. Given that Serbian troops carried out genocide against ethnic Albanians during Slobodan Milosevic's regime, it is no surprise that Kosovo Albanians have no trust in the Serbian courts.

The same question was asked for war crimes, to see if there would be a difference in opinion. Respondents were asked: *"If a person committed war crimes in Kosovo, what is the best way to address the crime?"* listing as options, (1) Kosovo court; (2) court in country where criminals came from; (3) Kosovo Specialist Court; and (4) ICTY Hague Tribunal. The study finds similar results for both genocide and war crime cases by choosing the ICTY Hague Tribunal as the best choice. Majority of the people felt that the ICTY Hague Tribunal was the best option (45%), followed by Kosovo Specialist Court (29%), Kosovo court (21%), and 5% chose "court in country where the criminal came from." There is a 10% decrease of trust in war crime cases (29%) in the Kosovo Specialist Court (KSC) when compared to the genocide trials (39%).

KSC is part of the Kosovo judiciary, with a seat in the Hague to prosecute war crimes and crimes against humanity. The Kosovo Specialist Court was set up for the trials of the alleged war crimes committed by high ranking members of the Kosovo Liberation Army, the Albanian paramilitary that fought against the Yugoslav and Serb forces in the Kosovo 1998 conflict. After NATO's intervention in March 1999, KLA was later disbanded and replaced by the Kosovo Police Force. The Albanian public in Kosovo is very unhappy that the court is focusing only on KLA-related war crimes, while ignoring other crimes. This could explain one of the reasons why there is a 10% decrease of trust for the KSC to handle war crime cases, versus the higher ratings for genocide trials within the same court.

> "The Kosovo Specialist Court is a discriminatory court as it is set up to only prosecute only ex-KLA (Kosovo Liberation Army) members for crimes committed during the war and after the war. If the court was prosecuting all individuals that have committed war crimes during the war, including all the nationalities I would consider that as an appropriate court of justice. As such court is in breach of human rights as it discriminates the perpetrators of the war crimes, one party is prosecuted and the other party/ies are not."[589]

> "Public opinion of the European Union in Kosovo is shifting because Kosovo is the only country in Europe which is isolated. Countries like Ukraine, with a population of 50 million and in a civil war are able to travel across Europe VISA free but Kosovo cannot. Kosovar Albanians did not invade or ethnically cleanse Serbia yet the E.U. created a special court only prosecuting Albanian. It is disheartening, it would be as preposterous as creating a special court against Jews during WWII."[590]

To better understand whether ethnic identification plays a role on interpersonal trust, when considering the court as a measure of the political trust, the study asked questions on the basis of ethnicity/nationality to compare the answers. The question asked was: *"If a Kosovan/Serbian*

---

[589] Kosumi, Vebi. (2018, November 14). Personal Communication. Interview.
[590] Molla, Admir. (2018, October 2). Personal Communication. Interview.

committed war crimes in Kosovo, what is the best way to address the crime?" The findings show that the Kosovo Specialist Court is the best way to address the crime for both Kosovan (42.5%) and Serbian criminals (39%). The respondents chose 27% for ICTY for a Kosovan, and 36% for a Serbian; 0 for Serbian Court for Kosovan, and 2.4% for Serbian committed crimes; and 30% for Kosovo court for Kosovan and 21.9% Serbian. There is a slight difference for Kosovo courts (as the second option after KSC) for crimes committed by a Kosovan. In an interview for the study, one respondent expressed the preference of Kosovo courts to try war crimes over the Kosovo Specialist Court:

> "I believe that that the local courts – with some help from the international judges/ attorneys – would have been able to prosecute and try those individuals that are suspected to have committed crimes during the war period. This Special Court feels like it has been established to investigate and prosecute only individuals of one ethnicity."[591]

Another interviewee wished to move beyond the administrative failures of the international missions in Kosovo, and prioritized the well-being of the citizens:

> "Considering the sensitivity of the situation and failure of UNMIK, EULEX and Kosovo courts to deal with these crimes, it is an imperative to deal with the past and close all chapters of the past in order to focus in the future and wellbeing of our citizens."[592]

The findings confirm that ethnic identification weakens trust in institutions (**confirms hypothesis 1b**). In-group trusters, in this case Kosovo Albanians do not trust out-group members (Serbs). Therefore, 0% chose Serbian courts as the best way to address war crimes committed by Kosovars (*Table 9*). The study shows higher scores for international institutions such as the International Criminal Tribunal for the former Yugoslavia (ICTY) and the Kosovo Specialist Court (KSC).

---

[591] Female participant. (2018, September 23). Personal Communication. Interview.
[592] Rrecaj, Besfort. (2018, September 26). Personal Communication. Interview.

Table 9: Perceptions of Local vs. International Courts Addressing War Crimes (2018)

Perceptions of Local vs. International Courts							
If a KOSOVAN committed war crimes in Kosovo, what is the best way to address the crime?				*If a SERBIAN committed war crimes in Kosovo, what is the best way to address the crime?*			
Kosovo Court	Serbian Court	KSC	ICTY	Kosovo Court	Serbian Court	KSC	ICTY
Percent 30%	0%	42.5%	27.5%	*Percent* 21.9%	2.4%	39%	36%
Total 40 participants							

6.2.4 The Cultural Perspective

This study conceptualized political trust as an important exogenous factor of the socio-cultural theory that is relevant to transitional democracies with respect to culture. The cultural explanation in this research conceptualized trust as an indicator of two cultural variables: *national identification* and *interpersonal trust*. The expectation is that culture might shape the democratic utility of trust, to the extent there is a positive influence on the levels of political trust (Jamal and Nooruddin, 2010). In particular, national identification has been linked to strengthening institutional trust (Godefroidt et al., 2015). Berg and Hjerm (2010) argued that national identity facilitates a cohesiveness amongst the community members, making cooperation more likely for people united under national pride, thus expanding networks and trusting relationships.

With respect to national identification the data in this study supports the link between national identification and institutional trust, to the extent that weak national identity decreases political trust. In the Kosovo case, the findings showed that Kosovo Albanians do not have strong attachments to the national symbols of the state and identify as Albanians instead of Kosovans, and also have decreased trust in the government. The 2013 survey results showed that Kosovo Albanians were not happy with the national symbols. Based on the in-depth expert interviews the study found support in the dissatisfaction of Kosovo Albanians with the national symbols, where the majority also rejected the idea of "Kosovan" identity.

An alternative explanation with the dissatisfaction in the national symbols and identity would suggest that the domestic versus international context matters. One of the elements that makes Kosovo such a highly unusual case is the historical context of the involvement of the international community in building the local state institutions from ground zero. United Nations became the main trigger for Kosovo choosing its own state symbols, in accordance with Article 1 of U.N.

mediator Martti Ahtisaari's comprehensive proposal for the Kosovo Status Settlement, stating, "Kosovo shall have its own, distinct, national symbols; including a flag, seal and anthem, reflecting its multi-ethnic character."[593]

The international community promoted an inclusive agenda for minorities, primarily the Serbs to feel included.[594] Because the national symbols mostly reflect the minority of Kosovo as opposed to majority, Kosovo Albanians being the majority citizens in Kosovo, do not feel a sense of national pride or cohesiveness towards the national state symbols pushed by the international community. The same sentiment was maintained toward the "Kosovan identity" as the participants felt that it was a made-up identity by the international community.

Although Kosovo as a state is built on democratic structures and principles, it is unique given the two historical conditions: a transitional democratic society stemming from a post-communist context in the Former Yugoslavia and the post-conflict of the 1998-99 war. The transition from non-democratic to democratic rule would indicate that the Kosovo society is moving toward a liberal rule as a country (Huntington, 1991). From the transitional democracy perspective, the Kosovo case supports Inglehart and Baker (2000) who emphasize the notion of generalized trust constricted by "traditional predispositions". Since the values about country hold very strong with the traditional views of Albania for Kosovo Albanians and Serbia for Kosovo Serbs, one would expect a more traditional society such as Kosovo to exhibit lower levels of trust, which corresponds to lower levels of support for democracy (Jamal and Nooruddin, 2010). The data supports the decline of trust in the Kosovo government.

With respect to building trusting relationships across ethnic identities and political participation Godefroidt et al. (2015) believe ethnic identification to weaken trust in institutions. The assumption is that the smaller ethnic groups are better at cooperating than the larger networks across-nationally, due to the traditional predispositions that hold those bonds undermining collective action in a larger scale. This would make it more likely to distrust out-group members (Berg and Hjerm, 2010).

The 2012 results of this study support the notion of ethnic identification weakening institutional trust. Majority of Kosovo Serbs identified as Serb and not as Kosovan. Likewise, majority of the Serbs in the North did not feel that they were Kosovan citizens. Additionally, only a small percentage (less than 9%) participated in local elections. The low participation in voting and the low levels of being-active in the decision-making process would indicate low support for the

---

[593] Kosovo Assembly. (2007, February 2). Comprehensive Proposal for the Kosovo Status Settlement, 2. Retrieved from https://www.kuvendikosoves.org/common/docs/Comprehensive%20Proposal%20.pdf

[594] Thorpe, N. (2007, June 4). Kosovo contest for state symbols. *BBC*. Retrieved from http://news.bbc.co.uk/2/hi/europe/6718105.stm

democratic processes in the country. As the minority groups, including Serbs do not feel a strong sense of belonging to the nation of Kosovo, these low levels of trust are also reflected in the low levels of political and civic participation in the country.

At the macro level, the Kosovo government has taken steps to promote ethnic equality and multi-ethnic tolerance, to the extent that there is positive discrimination, favoring minorities over others in the workplace. However, these efforts have not yet overcome the traditional ethnic barriers at the individual level to make it more likely for participation to increase. Cultural theory considers political participation as a precondition to political trust (Kaase, 2007). And as evident in the Kosovo case, trust, or lack thereof, is key to the relationship between interpersonal trust and trust in the political institutions. The controversial proposed land-swap between Serbia and Kosovo along ethnic lines, is regarded as undermining the building of the multi-ethnic efforts, making it even more difficult for cooperation between the Albanian and Serb communities.[595]

6.3 Institutional Performance Explanations

6.3.1 Trustworthiness in the Political System

Trustworthiness reflects the citizens' judgment of trust in government, politicians, and the political system (regime).[596] The literature on regime-based trust has focused on the relationship between democracy and political trust expecting a positive relationship.[597] The higher the individuals' perceptions towards the level of democracy, the higher the individuals' level of trust in institutions (**hypothesis 5**). Trust is vital to the legitimacy, fairness, and the effectiveness of democratic regimes.[598] Political trust "links citizens with governments and the institutions that represent them, thereby enhancing the legitimacy and stability of democratic government."[599]

To evaluate perceptions of trustworthiness in the broader political system the study asked in the 2012-2013 survey: "*Do you consider Kosovo today as a democratic state?*", with "yes," "no," and "somewhat agree." The results show that only 55% of the respondents consider Kosovo as a democratic state; 19.5% answered "no," and 25% said "somewhat agree." Regarding another posed question, "*Do you consider Kosovo today as a stabilized state?*" the data showed that only 23.5% consider Kosovo stable (35.5% answered "no"; 41% said "somewhat agree"). The results suggest

---

[595] Raxhimi, A. (2019, January 25). Kosovo academics brace for controversial ethnic land swaps. *Nature International Journal of Science.* Retrieved from https://www.nature.com/articles/d41586-019-00293-9

[596] Levi & Stoker (2000), 479.

[597] Mishler & Rose (2001), 36.

[598] Schneider, I. (2017), 963.

[599] Arancibia, C. S. (2008), 2.

that Kosovo Albanians seem reluctant to consider Kosovo as a strong and stable democratic state. (*See Graph 21*)

To better understand the general perceptions of levels of democracy in Kosovo the study asked: "*Do you think the government today in Kosovo is: (1) democratic and fair; (2) democratic but not strong; (3) it does not function; (4) corrupted; (5) not democratic?*". The results show that majority of the Kosovo Albanians consider the government corrupt (37%), only 8% consider it "democratic and fair"; while 30% think it is "democratic but not strong"; 13% said "it does not function"; and 12% consider it "non-democratic" (*See Graph 21*). In 2012, 91% of the respondents preferred a governance change, in response to the question, "*Do you think it is necessary to have a change in the governance of Kosovo?*" In 2018, 80% of the respondents said that they do not trust the Kosovo government. The findings confirm a positive relationship between the perceived democratic functioning of the government and the level of trust in the institution (**confirms hypothesis 5**). The lower the individuals' perceptions toward the level of democracy, the lower the individuals' level of trust in the government (**H5**).

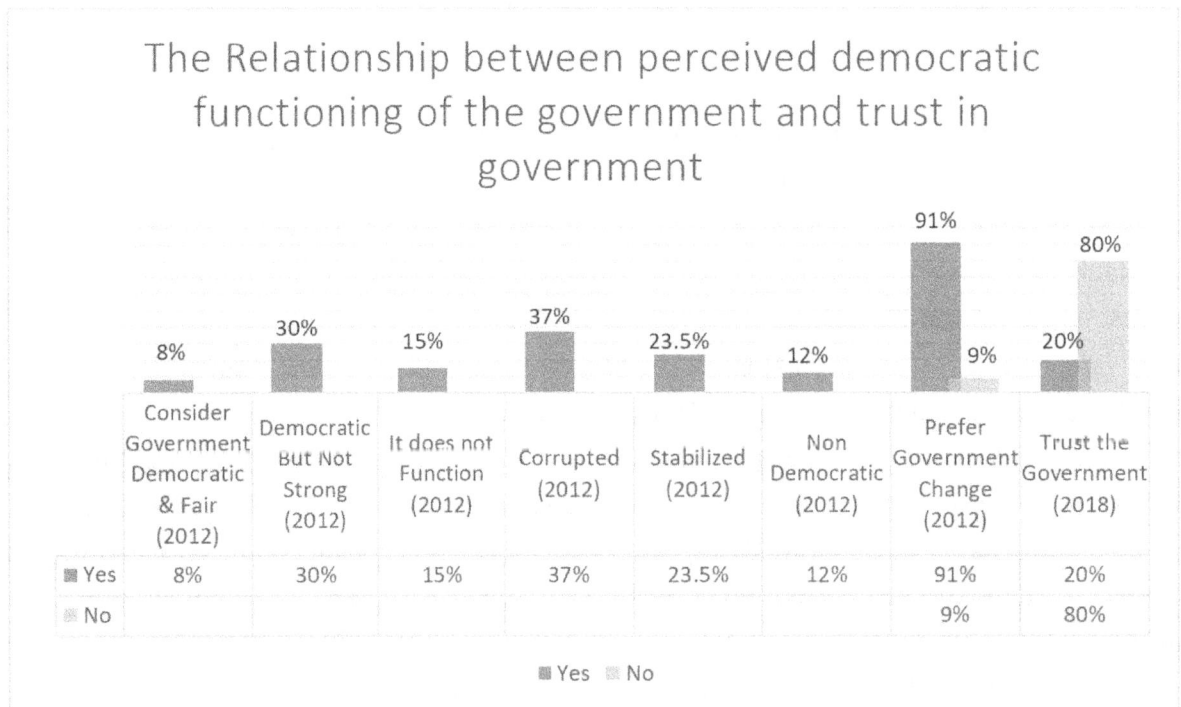

The Relationship between perceived democratic functioning of the government and trust in government

	Consider Government Democratic & Fair (2012)	Democratic But Not Strong (2012)	It does not Function (2012)	Corrupted (2012)	Stabilized (2012)	Non Democratic (2012)	Prefer Government Change (2012)	Trust the Government (2018)
Yes	8%	30%	15%	37%	23.5%	12%	91%	20%
No							9%	80%

Yes   No

Graph 21: The Relationship between perceived democratic functioning of the government and political trust in Kosovo (2012-2018)

The results of this study are in line with the political trust research that shows political trust crisis in former communist countries in Central and Eastern Europe being the lowest as "a signal of crisis of representative democracy."[600] Low levels of political trust pose a threat to emerging democracies.[601] Given the historic and political background of the transition to democracy, Kosovo is no exception to the political trust crisis parts of Europe are also experiencing. During the communist regime under Tito, Kosovo enjoyed some freedoms to a certain degree in terms of constitutional rights and gaining autonomy as a province under Yugoslavia. After Tito's death, with the rise of nationalism in Serbia, that brought to power Milosevic, Kosovo Albanians experienced unfair treatment, discrimination, expulsion, and massive ethnic cleansing. Both the Serbian government policies and the propaganda in the media promoted hatred and discrimination of Albanians as second-class citizens, causing episodes of civil unrest and protests in Kosovo.

The study also found a positive relationship between trust in the media and trust in institutions (**confirms hypothesis 3**). The more trust individuals have in media as the primary source of information, the more trust they have in institutions (**H3**). The lower the trust in media, the lower trust in the institutions. Kosovo Albanians have more trust in foreign media (63%), more trust in the Kosovo Specialist Court (64%) as a source of information about the war crime trials, more trust in the institution of the Kosovo Specialist Court (60%), when compared to the local Serbian and Kosovo courts, and more trust in international actors, namely: the E.U. (67%), NATO (84%) and the United States Embassy (79%). United Nations had low trust ratings of 51% trust score, which could be explained by the administrative performance and mission failure.[602]

---

[600] Van Der Meer, T. W. G. (2018, December). Political Trust and the "Crisis of Democracy". *Oxford University Press*, 2.

[601] Mishler & Rose (1999), 7.

[602] Leopold, E. (2007, July 20). Kosovo pushes independence after UN action fails. *Reuters.*

The relationship between Media and Political Trust

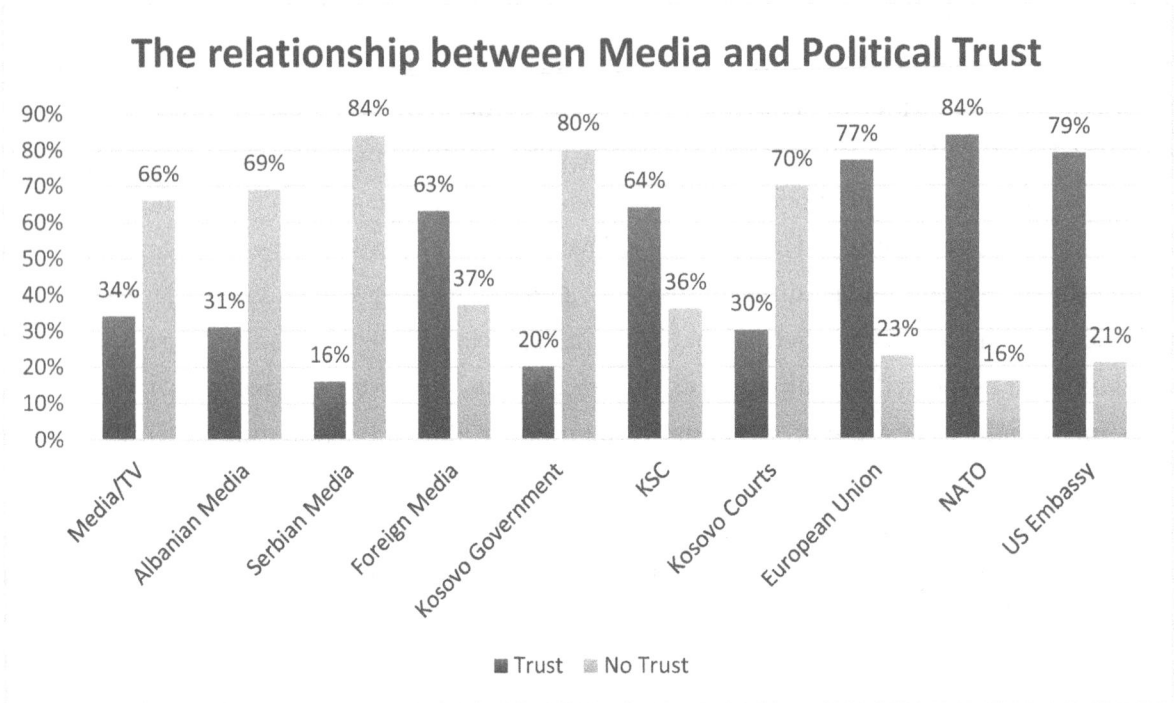

Graph 22: The Relationship between Media and Political Trust in Kosovo (2018)

On the other hand, Kosovo citizens have less trust in media/TV in general (66% no trust); less trust in Albanian media (69% no trust) and Serbian media (84% no trust), less trust in Kosovo Government (80% no trust), less trust in Kosovo Courts (70% no trust), (*See Graph 22*). This suggests that there is a positive relationship between media and political trust (H3), the less trust citizens have in the media, the less trust citizens will have in institutions (**confirms hypothesis 3**).

Visoka (2017) argues that "media can play an important role by taking a constructive, rational and empathetic stance on the importance of speaking the truth, bringing justice and pursuing reconciliation for Kosovo society."[603] The 2012-13 study found that 95% of the respondents believe media/TV had an influence on the image of Kosovo, and 79% said it influenced the image of Serbia. Whereas, 95% said there is anti-Albanian propaganda in the Serb media; and 71% believed there is no anti-Serb propaganda in the Albanian media.

6.3.2 Trustworthiness in the Political Parties

To assess trustworthiness in the larger scale, this study considered the political system and the political parties. Indicators like trust in the political parties, "reflect a broader attitude toward

---

[603] Visoka, G. (2018, February 16), 9.

political institutions,"[604] and the government environment.[605] According to Blind's model used in this study to determine political trust measures, political trust includes both macro-level trust and micro-level trust.[606] At the macro-level, trust in political institutions and the functioning of democracy matter.[607] Studies in Europe have shown that citizens express more trust in government than in political parties, such as in Luxemburg, Finland, Sweden, and Austria; whereas in Denmark trust was at the same level, and in countries with fiscal crisis like Greece, Slovenia, and Spain, political parties are least trusted.[608]

In Kosovo (*Alb: Kosova*), the study found low levels of trust toward the political system, where the government is perceived as not a stable democracy, corrupt and not strong, 91% wanted a change in governance. In 2012 the study asked the respondents: *"Do you trust political parties in Kosovo?"* on a 4-point scale ranging from "strongly agree" (=1) to "strongly disagree" (=4). The results show that majority had no trust in the political parties in Kosovo (58% disagreed), and only 42% had trust. The scores were: 6% said strongly agree; 36% answered somewhat agree; 28% indicated somewhat disagree; and 30% said strongly disagree.

To better understand the reasons why there are low trust levels in the political parties in Kosovo, the study asked whether the political parties represent the citizens' views and interests. The question posed was: *"How satisfied are you with the citizens' interests being represented by the political parties?"* in pre/post-independence, on a 5-point scale ranging from "very satisfied" (=1) to "very dissatisfied" (=5). The results show that during pre-independence only 39.5% were satisfied, and majority 60.5% were not satisfied with their interests being represented by the political parties in Kosovo. After independence, the results showed, 40.5% were not satisfied and 59.5% were satisfied. Pre-independence results: 4% very satisfied, 18% more or less satisfied, 35% neither satisfied not dissatisfied, 21% more or less dissatisfied, and 22% very dissatisfied. Post-independence results: 7% very satisfied, 22% more or less satisfied, 23% neither satisfied not dissatisfied, 19% more or less dissatisfied, and 29% very dissatisfied. (*See Graph 23.1*)

Another question asked was: *"Do you think that the political philosophy of parties is led by (1) Ideology, (2) Ethnic belonging, and (3) Regional belonging?"* The results show that 54% believe that the political philosophy of the parties is led by regional belonging; 33% believe is led by ideology, and only 13% said ethnic belonging. The study also found that 72% believe that there

---

[604] Schneider, I. (2017), 968.

[605] OECD. (2013). Trust in government, policy effectiveness and the governance agenda, in *Government at a Glance* 2013, OECD Publishing, Paris. doi: https://doi.org/10.1787/gov_glance-2013-6-en

[606] Blind, P. K. (2006), 4.

[607] OECD. (2013), 29.

[608] Ibid, 29.

is cooperation between parties, 97% believe that Kosovo needs economic reform, 93% believed Kosovo needs electoral reform, and 91% said Kosovo needs governance change. (*See Graph 23.1*)

Assessing the relationship between trust in political partied and trust in government, Kosovo displays higher levels of trust for political parties by 22% difference. The highest scores were for economic reform (97%). Overall, the trust score for political parties alone is low (only 40% trust), which lines up with the low satisfaction with citizens' interests being represented by the government (42%). This suggests that the lower the satisfaction in the citizens' interests and views being represented by the political parties, the lower the level of trust in political parties. The study concludes that trustworthiness has a positive relationship with political trust (**confirms hypothesis 2**). The results in Kosovo (*Alb: Kosova*) are similar to other countries in Europe facing economic difficulties and have low levels of trust in political parties.

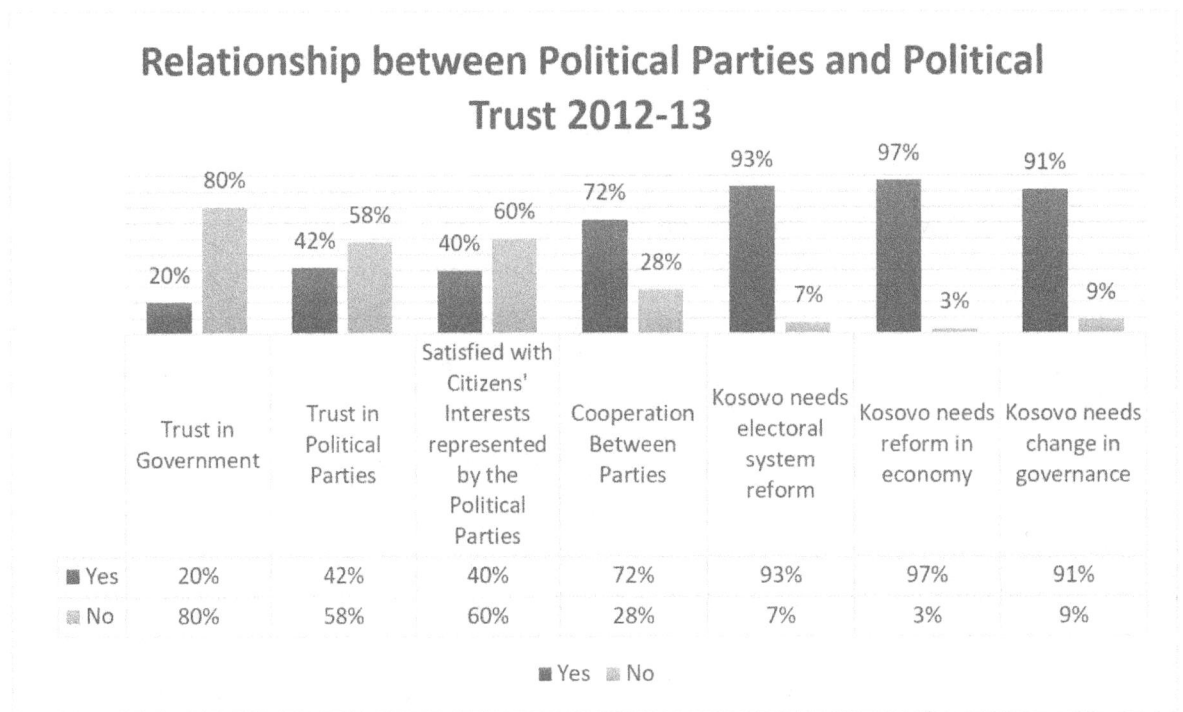

Relationship between Political Parties and Political Trust 2012-13

	Trust in Government	Trust in Political Parties	Satisfied with Citizens' Interests represented by the Political Parties	Cooperation Between Parties	Kosovo needs electoral system reform	Kosovo needs reform in economy	Kosovo needs change in governance
■ Yes	20%	42%	40%	72%	93%	97%	91%
▨ No	80%	58%	60%	28%	7%	3%	9%

■ Yes ▨ No

Graph 23.1: Macro-Level Analysis: The Relationship between Political Parties and Political Trust in Kosovo (2012-13)

The Group for Legal and Political Studies in Prishtina attributes the lack of political trust in political parties with the concerns of financial transparency and accountability of the parties:

"In Kosovo, perceptions of corruption and fraudulent practices relating to the financing of political parties are very high. The misuse of public offices and resources to push forward the agendas of political parties have contributed to this perception. Violations and fraudulent practices range from missing lists of donations to illegal acceptance of foreign donations and incomes. Moreover, gaps in the legal framework for the financing of political parties have allowed for the perpetuation of corruption and fraud relating to the acquisition and use of political party funds. Regular control and monitoring mechanisms must be established to provide a legislative and regulatory framework that allows political parties to legitimately benefit from donations while preventing them from engaging in corruption and illegal bargaining."[609]

For democracies, representation and common interests that channels the citizens' voice are important characteristics of legitimate and effective political institutions. The rational model approach of political trust implies that trustworthiness in the political party is based on the ideological or partisan attachment, justified by citizens' interests included in the party's interests.[610] Blind (2006) argues that citizens follow the political parties and the leaders they identify when their interests are shared in the party's interests (rational reasonings), and when political institutions and leaders are promise-keeping, efficient, fair and honest (psychological evaluation based on morality).[611]

Applying Blind's model to the Kosovo case, both *first-order trust* (rational political trust) and *second order trust* (psychological political trust) are the motivations behind the perceptions of trustworthiness in the political parties and the political system. First-order trust, or the rational political trust is founded in the ideological attachment of the political party, where trust is based on common interests and the rationality of the party, citizens identify with.

The results of this study indicated that 54% of the respondents believe that the political philosophy of the parties is led by regional belonging and 33% believe it is led by ideology (shared interests). And only 40% were satisfied with their interests being represented by the political parties, only 20% trusted the Kosovo government, while 93% wanted reform in the electoral system. This suggests that the rational aspect of trustworthiness in political parties – common interests – plays an important role in the political trust in institutions. Lower perceptions of representation of interests in the political party, indicate lower trust levels in the political system.

---

[609] GLPS. (2013, May). Financing of Political Parties in Kosovo, —can controllability and transparency help? *Policy Report by the Group for Legal and Political Studies,* (5), 6. Retrieved from http://www.legalpoliticalstudies. org/wp-content/uploads/2013/05/Policy-Report-05-2013.pdf

[610] Blind, P. K. (2006), 5.

[611] Ibid.

During my 2013 fieldtrip in Kosovo (*Alb: Kosova*) while meeting with the locals in different regions, most people I spoke with implied that party identification and membership was a crucial aspect to the well-being of their lives as it meant jobs were distributed depending on the party affiliations. This suggests that some members receive preferential treatment to ingroup members, because of the shared interests within the same party (first-order trust); while others could be denied jobs for not being a member of the political party that holds majority seats at the parliament. My observations are also supported by the findings of the 2013 report by the Group for Legal and Political Studies (GLPS) in Kosovo. According to GLPS, public administration politization in Kosovo were a result of "a tremendous decrease in the efficiency in the administration," and corruption manifested in the political parties through "vote buying."[612]

> "One of the ways how corruption is manifested by the political parties is through "vote buying." In transition countries, voters make their decisions to donate based on the amount of gifts and rewards offered by the parties and/or candidates in return. Such manipulations and corrupt practices have been observed in areas considered to be the geographic strongholds of main political parties, such as in the Dukagjini and Drenica regions.
>
> The voter turnout in these regions reached nearly 90%, in most cases because some individuals voted multiple times. Moreover, political parties frequently utilized public resources for their personal enrichment and political campaigns. The most common pattern is the usage of public offices and public procurement means to push forward their agendas."

The report concluded that initiatives have been taken by the Kosovo Agency for Anti-Corruption (KACA) to reduce the rate of corruption in both political parties and institutions. However, they should, "Improve their capacity and expertise in order to better deal with the corrupt practices."[613] Political corruption poses a serious threat to democracy because it has negative effects on democratic politics.[614] Since political trust is considered a necessary precondition to democracy, sources of political trust – corruption, procedural fairness, (economic) performance, inclusive institutions, and socialization matter.[615]

---

[612] GLPS. (2013, May), 32.

[613] Ibid.

[614] Johnston, M. (2005). *Political Parties and Democracy in Theoretical and Practical Perspectives: political finance policy, parties, and democratic Development.* Washington, DC: NDI.

[615] Van Der Meer, T. W. G. (2018, December), 3.

6.3.3 Trustworthiness in the Political Leaders

Political trust in institutions and actors enhances the legitimacy and stability of the democratic functioning of the government.[616] In Kosovo (*Alb: Kosova*), the study found low levels of trust in the broader political system, and distrust in the government. But how much of the distrust is related to the political leaders visa vie the performance of the institutions? Arancibia (2008) identified two key components of trustworthiness in political actors: *fair* and *competent*.[617] The expectation is that trustworthiness has a positive relationship with positive trust (**H2**), expecting democratic institutions that are *fair* and *competent* to positively influence trust.[618] The higher the individuals' satisfaction with the fairness and competence of the political leadership, the higher the political trust in government. (**hypothesis 2a**)

To assess the trustworthiness level the study measured the citizen's perceived fairness and competence in political leadership, using the ANES (American National Election Studies) indicators. ANES measures trust perceptions in the political leaders (incumbent-based trust) using the fairness/competence scale of trust: (1) *honest*, (2) *know what they are doing*, (3) *do the right thing*, and (4) *interest*. Based on Blind's (2006) model of political trust, this study looked at the elite perceptions in the psychological-based factors of trust toward the *political actors* (micro level: individual/person oriented) and *toward policy* (macro level: organizational/ issue oriented). In both micro and macro level, the democratic environment (fairness, competence, efficiency) of the leadership and institutions are expected to be detrimental trustworthiness and have a positive relationship with the levels of political trust.[619] (**hypothesis 2a, 2b**)

To get a clear and accurate understanding of the political leadership in a certain time period, the study did not want to lump pre-independence years as one period. Rather the leadership was separated by specific terms or years of leadership. Pre-independence included 2001 to 2004, and 2004 to 2008. Post-independence included 2008 to 2010, and 2010 till 2012 (end period being the year the survey was conducted in Kosovo). Table 10 gives a detailed history of the political leadership timeline of the presidents and the vice presidents of Kosovo.

The 2012 survey asked questions about following trustworthiness indicators: (1) the trust atmosphere, (2) honesty and moral behavior of the political leaders, (3) clear vision and (4) expectations, (5) responsibility, (6) administrative goals, (7) communicating decisions, (8) responsibility of actions, (9) including others during planning, (10) relationships with the civil servants, (11) tolerance, (12) training in leadership skills, and (12) policy orientations in different areas. The 2018

---

[616] Levi, M., & Stoker, L. (2000), 479.

[617] Arancibia, C. S. (2008), 3.

[618] Mishler & Rose (2001), 35.

[619] Levi, M. (1998), 90.

survey primarily focused on the institutional performance evaluation of the judiciary in Kosovo and the Kosovo Specialist Court in The Hague, based on fairness, efficiency and impartiality indicators.

The 2012-13 study asked the respondents: "Have the leaders created an atmosphere of mutual trust for the people and government?" in pre-independence under two leadership periods (2001-04; 2004-08) and post-independence (2008-10; 2010-12). Overall, during pre-independence scores went down from first period to the second, then the trend goes up. During post-independence, satisfaction increased by 2% when compared to pre-independence period, but still majority is not satisfied.

The results show 49% were satisfied, while 51% were not (2008-10). Additionally, 2010-2012 showed the highest satisfaction score out of 4 periods of creating mutual trust, with 50.5%. While 2004-08 showed the highest dissatisfaction score with 54% compared to all 4 time periods. (*See Table 11*)

Table 11 Questionnaire: Satisfaction Trends in Kosovo Political Leaders

Have the leaders created an atmosphere of mutual trust for the people and government?

Do leaders in Kosovo demonstrate honesty and moral behavior in accordance with the appropriate ethics in all their actions?

Do leaders demonstrate a clear vision with known purposes for the administration and the people?

Do leaders declare their expectations / hopes and confirm understanding?

Do leaders expect people to be responsible and do they provide the necessary support?

Do leaders make the administration goals / priorities practical and understandable to the citizens starting from the most important to the least important ones?

Do leaders communicate their decision, and do they act immediately?

Do leaders communicate effectively and charismatically with various groups?

Do leaders take responsibility for their actions without blaming others?

Do leaders include others during action planning?

Do leaders have good relationships with the civil servants regardless of position?

Do leaders show tolerance?

Do leaders use training that teaches skills in leadership and common work?

Table 10: Timeline of Kosovo Political Leadership

POLITICAL LEADERSHIP IN KOSOVO KOSOVO PRESIDENTS						
Pre-Independence			Post-Independence			
1992–2000	2002 - 2006	2006 - 2008	2008 - 2010	2011	2011-2016	2016-2020
Ibrahim Rrugova *Democratic League* (LDK)	Ibrahim Rrugova *Democratic League* (LDK) (Died in office)	Fatmir Sejdiu *Democratic League* (LDK)	Fatmir Sejdiu *Democratic League* (LDK) (17 Feb 2018) Kosovo Declared Independence	Behgjet Pacolli (Feb. - Apr. 2011) *New Kosovo Alliance* (AKR) Jakup Krasniqi *Acting President* (4 -7 Apr. 2011) (PDK)	Atifete Jahjaga *Independent*	Hashim Thaçi (2016-incumbent) *Democratic Party* (PDK)
KOSOVO PRIME MINISTERS						
1999-2000	2002-2004	2004-2008	2008-2014		2014-2017	2017-2020
Hashim Thaçi *Provisional PM Democratic Party* (PDK) (1999) UN Administered Kosovo	Bajram Rexhepi *Democratic Party* (PDK)	Ramush Haradinaj (2004-2005) (AAK) Adem Salihaj *Acting PM (8-25 Mar. 2005)* (LDK) Agim Çeku (2006-2008) *Independent* Hashim Thaçi (Jan-Feb 2008) (PDK)	Hashim Thaçi *Democratic Party* (PDK) (2012) International Supervision ended		Isa Mustafa *Democratic League* (LDK)	Ramush Haradinaj (2017-inbumbent) *Alliance for Future* (AAK) Albin Kurti (acting VP since Feb. 2020) *Vetëvendosje* (April 2020) 115 countries recognize Kosovo's Independence

Table 11: Satisfaction Trends in Kosovo Political Leaders (Pre/Post-Independence)

Trustworthy Leadership %	Satisfaction Trends in Political Leaders (Pre/Post-Independence)										
Indicators:	2001-04		Trend	2004-08		Trend	2008-10		Trend	2010-12	
	Yes	No		Yes	No		Yes	No		Yes	No
Mutual trust	48%	52%	↓	46%	54%	↑	49%	51%	↑	50.5	49.5
Honesty/moral behavior	41%	59%	↓	39%	61%	↓	29%	71%	↓	23%	77%
Clear vision	44%	56%	↑	81%	19%	↓	46%	54%	↑	66%	34%
Expectations	46%	54%	↑	71%	29%	↓	47%	53%	↑	51%	49%
Provide Support	47%	53%	↓	46%	54%	↑	50%	50%	↑	88%	12%
Admin goals	36%	64%	↑	58%	42%	↑	82%	18%	↓	76%	24%
Communicate immediately	63%	37%	↑	66%	34%	=	66%	34%	↑	76%	24%
Communicate effectively	80%	20%	↑	86%	14%	↑	90%	10%	↓	85%	15%
Responsible/don't blame	46%	54%	↑	77%	23%	↓	52%	48%	↑	56%	44%
Inclusive	64%	36%	↑	70%	30%	↑	77%	23%	↑	79%	21%
Civil relations	54%	46%	↑	88%	12%	↓	77%	23%	↓	69%	31%
Tolerance	86%	14%	↑	87%	13%	↓	84%	16%	↓	82%	18%
Training	91%	9%	↑	95%	5%	↑	99.4	0.6	↓	96%	4%

Conducted in Kosovo (2012-13)   Total Participants: 220

Another trustworthy indicator used in this study is "*honesty.*" The study asked: "*Do leaders in Kosovo demonstrate honesty and moral behavior in accordance with the appropriate ethics in all their actions?*" In pre-independence under two leadership periods (2001-04; 2004-08) and post-independence (2008-10; 2010-12). The results show that satisfaction scores about honesty and behavior show a downward trend, where the scores go down from the highest score of being satisfied 41% (2008-10) to the lowest 23% in the last period (2010-2012). This suggests that the respondents identify with President Rrugova's leadership the most in terms of honesty and ethics. During my field trip in Kosovo many participants I interviewed, shared that President Rrugova was popular and loved by many for his peaceful path to independence. The international leaders, in particular the United States leadership, supported his democratic values. Rrugova advocated for democracy, peace, human rights, inter-ethnic tolerance and was called the "Gandhi of the Balkans."

> "Without a doubt, Kosovo's historic president Ibrahim Rrugova is one of the most respected leaders in the nation. He deserves the merit for establishing the amicable relationship between the Albanian nation and the West, first and foremost with the United States, United Kingdom, Germany, France, Italy, and the Vatican."[620]

The data from this study support the local sentiment, indicating Rrugova's term from 2001 to 2004 having the highest satisfaction scores out of four periods (2001-2012) in terms of demonstrating honesty and great ethics. The study also revealed that the mutual trust scores were the highest out of the four periods, during President Atifete Jahjaga's term. She was the first woman president of the Republic of Kosovo and advocated for empowering women and promoted peace and stability in the Balkans. She came into power when Kosovo was at a constitutional deadlock in 2010 and successfully coordinated justice mechanisms for fair, democratic, and inclusive elections, drawing the political participation of Kosovo Serbs in the North for the first time in the electoral process.

In an interview with Sweden-based professor and writer Xhemajl Shatri, he stated: "President Jahjaga, even though she didn't have political experience, strengthened the image of the nation in the international stage, when Kosovo's politics became deadlocked in December 2010 after President Fatmir Sejdiu's resignation."[621] Considering the challenging conditions of the political system when President Jahjaga came to power, she played a crucial role in resolving the parliamentary crisis and worked with leaders of various political parties to form parliament and a

---

[620] Shatri, Xhemajl. (2013, March 16). Personal Communication. Interview.
[621] Shatri, Xh. (2013, March 16).

government. Jahjaga strengthened the relationships between various ethnic communities and prioritized the visa liberalization plan and European integration for Kosovo (*Alb: Kosova*).[622]

The study also included "*clear vision*" and "*expectations*" as measures of trustworthiness in the political leaders. The posed questions were: "*Do leaders demonstrate a clear vision with known purposes for the administration and the people?*" and "*Do leaders declare their expectations / hopes and confirm understanding?*" in pre-independence (2001-04; 2004-08) and post-independence (2008-10; 2010-12). The results were interesting because the period 2004-2008 stood out significantly having the highest satisfaction scores in both clear vision and expectation out of all four of the time periods. The time-period 2004-2008 corresponds with the leadership of President Fatmir Sejdiu and Vice President Rramush Haradinaj.

The results for demonstrating a clear vision were: 44% satisfied in 2001-04; 81% satisfied in 2001-08; 46% satisfied in 2008-10; and 66% satisfied in 2010-12. The satisfaction trend goes up twice, during 2004-08 (Sejdiu-Haradinaj), as well as 2010-12 (Pacolli/Jahjaga-Thaçi). Regarding declaring the expectations and promoting understanding the satisfaction trend is the same with the clear vision trend: it goes up during Sejdiu-Haradinaj; and again it goes up during the Presidency of Pacolli & Jahjaga, with Prime Minister Hashim Thaçi (now President).

The study also asked: "*Do leaders make the administration goals / priorities practical and understandable to the citizens starting from the most important to the least important ones?*" and "*Do leaders communicate their decision and do they act immediately?*" in pre-independence (2001-04; 2004-08) and post-independence (2008-10; 2010-12). Regarding making the admin goals known and practical, data showed satisfaction trends were up with 2008-10 (Sejdiu- Thaçi) receiving the highest score 82%. This corresponds with the declaration of independence decision, so it makes sense for the public to be satisfied with Kosovo's political agenda. Declaring the independence was both a great desire of the public and a priority of the leadership, which was communicated clearly by the politicians. Communication of decisions and acting immediately also received high scores during both pre/post-independence periods, with 2010-12 (Pacolli/Jahjaga-Thaçi) receiving the highest satisfaction score (76%).

Two other measures were used "*communicate effectively*" and "*inclusive*" to understand cooperation between different political leaders and parties. The posted questions were: "*Do leaders communicate effectively and charismatically with various groups?*" and "*Do leaders include others during action planning?*" Satisfaction scores were very high for both of these measures with the trend going up in all 4 time periods, with 2008-10 (Sejdiu- Thaçi) being the highest score for

---

[622] President of the Republic of Kosovo. (2012, May 24). President Jahjaga received the Minister for European Affairs of Denmark. Retrieved from https://www.president-ksgov.net/en/news/president-jahjaga-received-the-minister-for-european-affairs-of-denmark

communicate effectively and charismatically with 90% satisfaction sore. Whereas 2010-12 (Pacolli/ Jahjaga-Thaçi) was the time period with the highest score for being inclusive or working with others during planning.

Comparing *cooperation* scores in political parties (72%) and satisfaction scores in political leaders, namely "*effective communication*" (80%, 86%, 90%, 85%), "*inclusive*" (64%, 70%, 77%, 79%), and "*communicate and act immediately*" (63%, 66%, 66%, 76%) the findings suggest that trustworthiness has a positive relationship with political cooperation and a negative relationship with trust in political parties and government (**rejects hypothesis 2a**). The study concludes that high satisfaction with the leaders' fairness and competence is positively related with cooperation in political parties. However, it is important to make the distinction that this relationship between cooperation and trustworthiness based on effective communication, inclusiveness, communicate and act immediately, does not hold true for trust in political parties or trust in government. In general, Kosovo Albanians have low trust for political parties (40%), and the lowest trust level for the government (20%). (*See Graph 23.2*) But when comparing trust in political parties and trust in government, Kosovo Albanians have higher trust in political parties, than in government.

The Relationship between Trustworthiness in Leaders and Trust/Cooperation in Political Parties

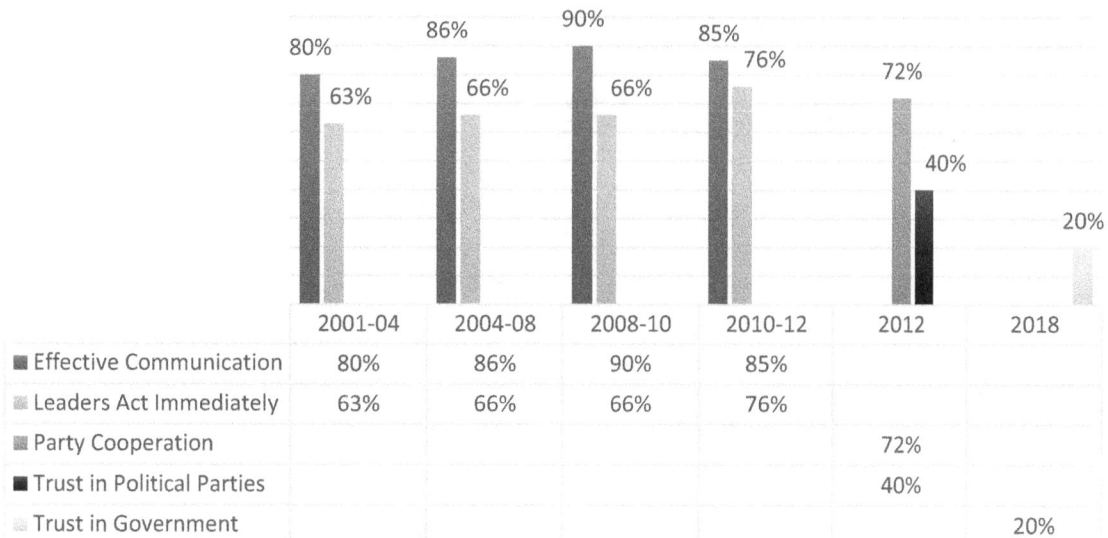

	2001-04	2004-08	2008-10	2010-12	2012	2018
■ Effective Communication	80%	86%	90%	85%		
▨ Leaders Act Immediately	63%	66%	66%	76%		
▨ Party Cooperation					72%	
■ Trust in Political Parties					40%	
▨ Trust in Government						20%

Graph 23.2: Micro-Level Analysis: The Relationship between Trustworthiness in Leaders and Trust/Cooperation in Political Parties (2001-18)

When considering the relationship between the trustworthiness indicator "*honesty and moral behavior*" and political trust, the study finds that the lower the citizen's satisfaction with the moral behavior and honesty of political leaders, the lower the trust in political parties and the government. This suggests that there is a positive relationship between trustworthiness and political trust (**confirms hypothesis 2a**) when considering the measure of "honesty and moral behavior" of trustworthiness. This means that when satisfaction scores go up on trustworthiness, the trust scores will go also up on political trust; and when satisfaction scores go down on trustworthiness, the political trust scores decrease as well.

In Kosovo (*Alb: Kosova*), the satisfaction with leaders demonstrating honesty and moral behavior are quite low, ranging from low 23%, 29%, 39% and 41%. This corresponds with low trust in political parties in Kosovo (40%) and low trust in Kosovo government, only 20%. The study concludes that low trust in political leaders in terms of honesty and morality, means low political trust in government and political parties. (*See Graph 23.3*)

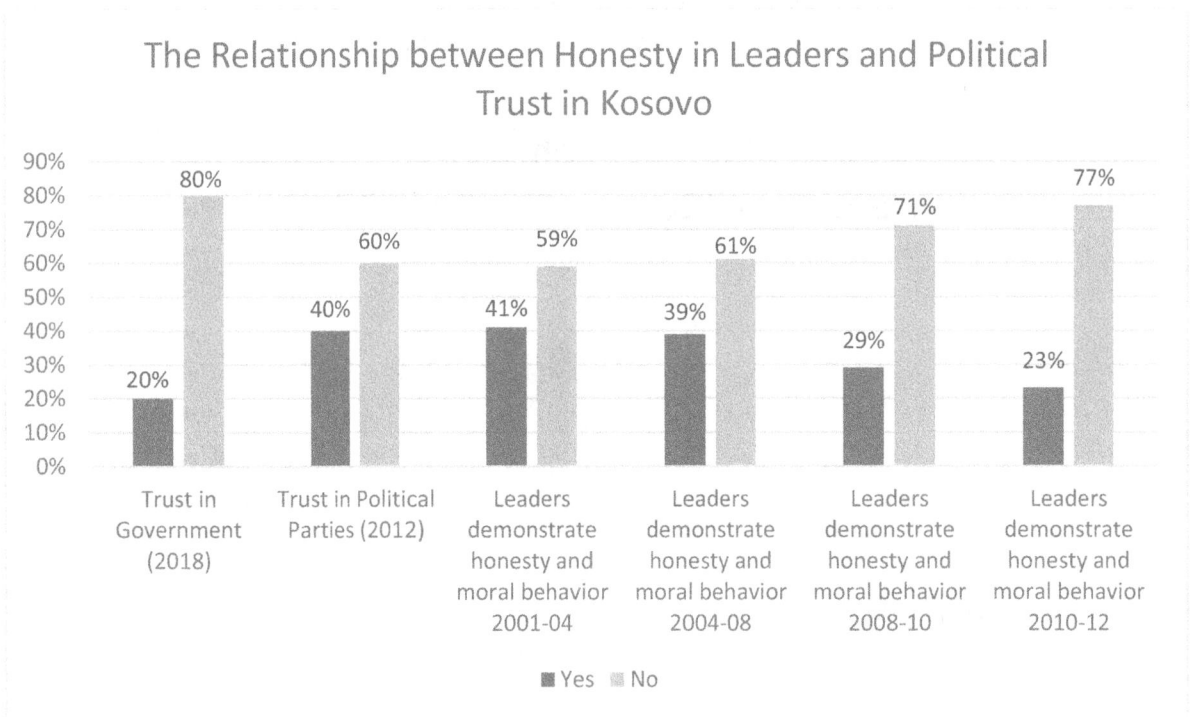

The Relationship between Honesty in Leaders and Political Trust in Kosovo

Graph 23.3: Micro-Level Analysis: The Relationship between Honesty in Leaders and Political Trust (2001-18)

In an interview with award-wining Albanian investigative journalist from Kosovo, Arbana Xharra (winner of the 2015 International Women of Courage Award from the U.S. State

Department), she pointed out that trust in leaders in Kosovo is largely based on the leaders' war involvement to liberate the country, but no vital institutional changes have occurred since the end of the war.

> "In Kosovo, the factors that have led to political institutions to lose their credibility is that they have not undergone any significant changes, even though nearly 20 years have passed since the end of the war. The institutional denigration comes from corrupt politics and nepotism from the political parties that came into power to the central and local government. Clientelist connections that are extended to a broader mechanism have now become the norm.

> The confidence in leaders is largely based on areas divided into two categories: supporters of politicians who have a war-related past and politicians with populous discourse. Since the institutions do not have credibility, then the people's leaders get more support. The topics which are brought to the surface by these politicians are exactly where the institutions have failed: fighting corruption, no perspectives for youth, isolation, etc."[623]

To better understand the factors that have an influence on political trust, the study considered "support for others," "responsible," "relations with civil servants," "tolerance," and "training" as measures of "fair" and "competent" of trustworthiness of leaders. The posed questions were: "*Do* leaders *expect* people to b*e responsible and do they provide the necessary support? Do leaders take responsibility for their actions without blaming others? Do leaders have good relationships with* the *civil servants regardless of position?* Do leaders *show tolerance?* Do *leaders use training that teaches skills* in leadership *and* common *work?*" during pre-independence (2001-04; 2004-08) and post-independence (2008-10; 2010-12).

The findings show that tolerance and training had the highest satisfaction scores. Specifically, 2008-10 (Sejdiu- Thaçi) stood out as the highest satisfaction score for training with 99.4% score, while the other time periods were also high: 91% 200104; 95% 2004-08; 96% 2010-12. The tolerance scores were high as well with 2004-08 (Sejdiu-Haradinaj) being the highest at 87% out of all 4 time periods. Satisfaction with leaders showing tolerance were: 86% 2001-04; 84% 2008-10; and 82% for 2010-12.

Relations between leaders and civil servants improved significantly during 2004-08 (Sejdiu-Haradinaj) with 87% (the highest score out of 4) and 77% during 2008-10 (Sejdiu- Thaçi). In terms

---

[623] Xharra, Arbana. (2018, November 20). Personal Communication. Interview.

of showing leaders taking responsibility without blaming others 2004-08 (Sejdiu-Haradinaj) had the highest score of 77%, followed by 2010-12 (Pacolli/Jahjaga-Thaçi) with 56%, and 52% during 2008-20. Time period 2001-04 had the lowest score of out of four time periods with 46%. (*See Table 11*)

Graph 23.4 shows the organizational environment of political leadership showing the relationship between low levels of mutual trust with low trust in political parties, whereas tolerance and good relations with civil servants show high scores from 2001-2010. The next section will look at the link between trustworthiness in the legal system and political trust.

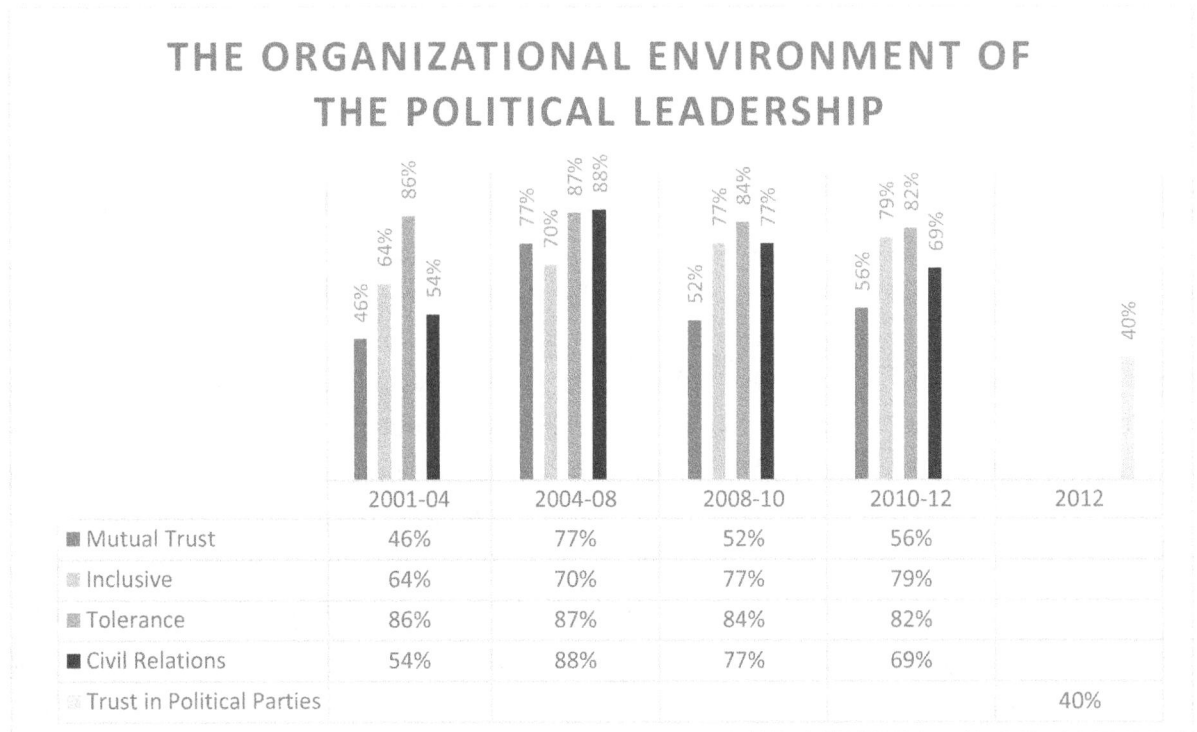

THE ORGANIZATIONAL ENVIRONMENT OF THE POLITICAL LEADERSHIP

	2001-04	2004-08	2008-10	2010-12	2012
Mutual Trust	46%	77%	52%	56%	
Inclusive	64%	70%	77%	79%	
Tolerance	86%	87%	84%	82%	
Civil Relations	54%	88%	77%	69%	
Trust in Political Parties					40%

Graph 23.4: The Organizational Environment of the Political Leadership (2001-12)

6.3.4 Trustworthiness in the Legal System: Kosovo Specialist Court

Trustworthy government institutions, including the judiciary must be fair and transparent. *Fairness* is the "assurance of ethical and legal rights" and *transparency* involves awareness, access, and accountability.[624] The expectation is that democratic institutions that are fair and competent

---

[624] Antues, N. et al. (2018). Fairness and Transparency of Machine Learning for Trustworthy Cloud Services. CISUC, 1. Retrieved from https://dependablesecureml.github.io/papers/dsml2018_trusted_cloud.pdf

have a positive influence on political trust.[625] In this study trust in the *legal system* is linked to *fair* and *impartial* as measures of "*fairness*" and "*competence*" for trustworthy legal institutions.

Fairness

To gage the participants' perceptions of trustworthy legal institutions, the 2018 survey asked respondents their level of confidence in Kosovan and international courts to conduct fair and impartial trials. The posed question was: "*How much confidence do you have in the Kosovan courts to conduct fair trials?*" followed by a 4-point scale "very much," "some," "a little," or "not at all." The results showed that only 5% said "very much," 35% have "some" confidence, 47.5% stated "a little" confidence, and 12.5% said "not at all." This suggests that majority of the Kosovo Albanians have little confidence in the Kosovo's courts to conduct fair trials.

The same question was posed to assess the participants' confidence in international courts: "*How much confidence do you have in the international courts to conduct fair trials?*" using the same 4-point confidence scale. The findings showed that 32.5% have "very much" confidence in international courts; 40% said "some"; 20% said "a little"; and less than 1% said "not at all" (0.75%). Comparing elite perceptions between Kosovan and international courts, there is a significant difference between the two. Kosovo Albanians have more confidence in international courts to conduct fair trials, and lower confidence in the fairness of Kosovan courts.

Considering the relationship between trust in legal institutions and trustworthiness in legal institutions, the findings of the study suggest that the more individuals believe trials are fair, the more trust they have in the legal institutions; reduction in confidence in fair trials means lower trust levels in the judiciary (**confirms hypothesis 2b**). In Kosovo 70% do not trust Kosovan courts, while only 30% trust the local legal institutions. Compared to the levels of trust in the Kosovo Specialist Court, the results show higher trust levels – 60% trust the Kosovo Specialist Court. (*See Graph 24*)

The results suggest that there is a positive relationship between fairness and trust in institutions as well as a positive relationship between trustworthiness in international legal institutions and international political trust. The higher the trust in international legal institutions (i.e. Kosovo Specialist Chambers and Specialist Prosecutor's Office - KSC), the higher the trust in international actors or institutions (the European Uion).

---

[625] Mishler & Rose. (2001).

Confidence in Fair Trials and Trust in the Judiciary

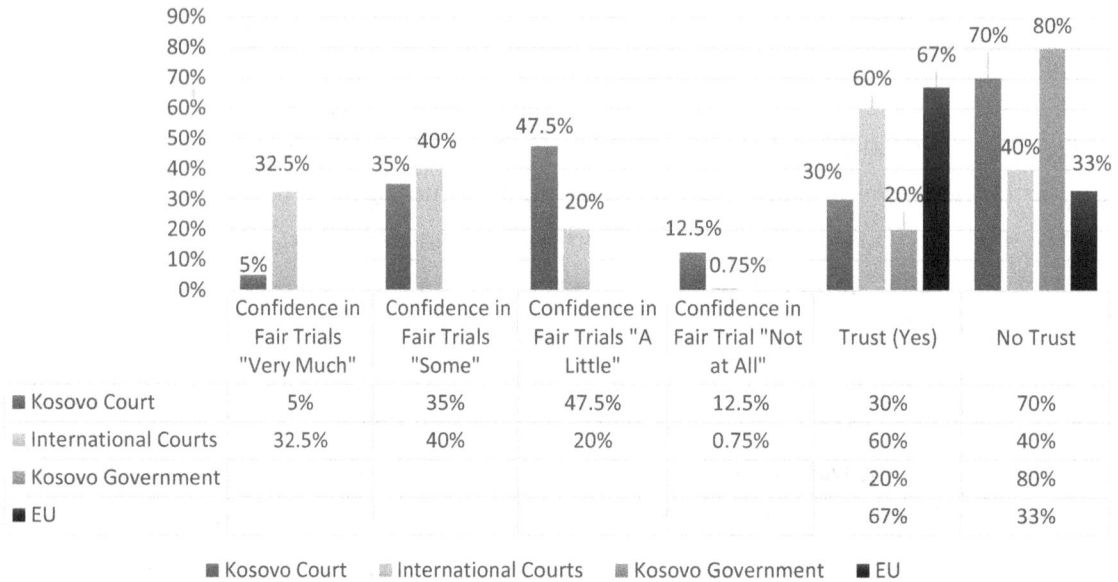

	Confidence in Fair Trials "Very Much"	Confidence in Fair Trials "Some"	Confidence in Fair Trials "A Little"	Confidence in Fair Trial "Not at All"	Trust (Yes)	No Trust
■ Kosovo Court	5%	35%	47.5%	12.5%	30%	70%
▨ International Courts	32.5%	40%	20%	0.75%	60%	40%
▨ Kosovo Government					20%	80%
■ EU					67%	33%

■ Kosovo Court ▨ International Courts ■ Kosovo Government ■ EU

Graph 24: The Relationship between Fairness and Trust in Kosovo's Legal System (2018)

Impartiality

The 2018 also asked: "*Which judges are better able to make impartial decisions in trials of war crimes that took place in Kosovo?*" immediately followed by (1) Kosovo Specialist Court international judges, (2) Kosovan judges, and (3) Serbian judges. Concerning war crimes trials, the overwhelming majority chose International judges of the Kosovo Specialist Court (92.5); whereas only 2.5% chose Kosovan judges, 0% chose Serbian judges, and 5% chose "none." The results suggest that Kosovo Albanians have higher trust in International Judges of the Kosovo Specialist Court in making impartial decisions.

The participants were also asked about violations of human rights and genocide to understand if there was as difference in opinion. The question posed was: "*Which judges are better able to make impartial decisions in trials of genocide /human rights violations that took place in Kosovo?*" followed by (1) international judges; (2) Kosovan judges; and (3) Serbian judges. Regarding impartial decisions of trials involving *genocide or human rights violations*, majority sided with international judges (77.5%); 15% chose Kosovan judges; 5% chose Serbian judges; and 2.5% said "none". Interestingly, the category "none" was added by the respondents who did not feel the given options matched their preferences, to indicate no impartiality of the legal system, or the judges.

Considering the high levels of trust in the international legal institutions such as the Kosovo Specialist Court and the high confidence in the international judges to make impartial decisions, the study concludes that there is a positive relationship between impartial decisions of the judges and high levels of trust in the legal institutions (**confirms hypothesis 2b**). This suggest that there is a direct relationship between trustworthiness in legal institutions and political trust.

6.3.5 The Institutional Perspective

This study also conceptualized institutional trust as a key endogenous determinant of political trust based on the institutional theories. The institutional explanation in this research conceptualized trust as an indicator of two institutional variables: *trustworthiness in institutions and actors* and *perceived government performance*. The expectation is that individuals will be rational, therefore are likely to trust legal and political institutions based on the rational evaluation of the institutions' performance (Huseby, 2000). According to the institutional performance analysis trustworthiness and efficiency in the government are expected to have a positive influence on the levels of political trust.

Another expectation of trustworthiness is that an individual is more likely to trust a legal or political institution if the institution is perceived as fair and competent (Arancibia, 2008). Godefroidt et al. (2015) argued that higher levels of institutional trust could facilitate democratic consolidation based on enhancing the legitimacy, efficiency, and sustainability of the government. Mishler and Rose (1997) maintain that trust is important to the legitimacy and the effectiveness of the democratic regime. In emerging democracies, the institutional design in terms of perceived fairness, transparency, efficiency, and accountability matter to the policy outputs (Mishler and Rose (1997). The assumption is that the higher the satisfaction with fairness and competence of the political leadership or institution, the higher the political trust. Likewise, the higher the individual's satisfaction with the government's performance, the higher the level of trust in institutions. Another expectation of the institutional analysis positively links democratic functioning of the government with institutional trust. The higher the individuals' perceptions towards the level of democracy, the higher the individuals' level of trust in institutions.

This study found support for the democratic regime in Kosovo. The 2012-13 survey found that majority consider Kosovo as a democratic state (55% agree, 25% somewhat agree). However, the study found low support in the quality of the democratic regime. Majority of Kosovo Albanians do not consider Kosovo as a strong and stable democracy, reflected in the low levels of trust in the government. The findings suggest that the quality of the democratic regime matters to the political trust, not just support for democracy. This study argued that corruption is another explanation for the levels of distrust in political institutions. In the 2012 survey, majority of the Kosovo

Albanians considered the government corrupt, while only 8% considered it democratic and fair, with an overwhelming majority opting for a regime change. The 2018 results also reflected the dissatisfaction of the Kosovo Albanians with government performance.

The study found low levels of trust in the broader political system (20%), but slightly higher levels of trust were found towards the political parties (40%). The data showed higher satisfaction scores with the ethics and the moral behavior of the political leaders, as well as leaders demonstrating a clear vision and communicating effectively. The findings confirm a positive relationship between trustworthiness and political trust.

The study found high levels of trust in the law enforcement institutions, particularly in the Kosovo Police in 2012-2013 (75%), with decreasing levels of trust in 2018 (53%). The results showed high levels of confidence in the Kosovo police associated with the higher satisfaction of the Kosovo Albanians with the effectiveness and the competence of Kosovo Police Force. The respondents were also satisfied with the management capacity of the Kosovo police and its competence to achieve the strategic objectives, which was reflected in the high levels of institutional trust. This suggests that political trust in institutions depends on the efficiency and the performance outputs of the institutions, as confirmed by this study.

The data also showed high levels of distrust in the local legal institutions in Kosovo. The 2018 results showed that majority did not trust the Kosovo courts, while 60% trust the Kosovo Specialist Court. The expectation is that democratic institutions that are fair and competent are seen as trustworthy institutions and are likely to have higher levels of trust (Mishler & Rose, 2001). The study found that Kosovo Albanians have more confidence in international courts to conduct fair trials, and lower confidence in the fairness of Kosovan courts. This suggests that there is a positive relationship between fairness and trust in institutions. These results fit with the institutional performance approach of political trust, linking fairness and competence as measures of trustworthy institutions.

The study also used another measure of trustworthiness, impartiality, and the 2018 survey result found support for higher trust in international judges of the Kosovo Specialist Court. Majority of the respondents believed that the international judges were better able to make impartial decisions in trials of war crimes and genocide, compared to local Kosovan judges or Serbian judges. The study found a positive relationship between impartiality and trustworthiness in legal institutions.

Kosovo has made progress in the preparation for the fight against corruption, making progress in the investigation and prosecution for high level corruption and organized crime cases.[626] The

---

[626] European Commission. (2018). Kosovo 2018 Report, 4. Retrieved from https://ec.europa.eu/neighbourhood-enlargement/sites/near/files/20180417-kosovo-report.pdf

2018 European Commission reports finds that Kosovo's judiciary system has made big progress in the integration of Kosovo Serb judges and prosecutors, and regards it as major achievement.[627] However, the report is critical of the slow and inefficiency administration of justice, and the vulnerability to undue political influence.[628]

6.3.6 Kosovo: A Sui Generic Case

Kosovo (*Alb: Kosova*) is a very unique case of transitional democracy given the unusual long-term domestic and international relationship, with EULEX being the largest civilian mission launched under the Common Security and Defense Policy (CSDP) of the European Union.[629] United States and the European Union members also portray Kosovo as unique case, with respect to NATO's decision to use force on humanitarian grounds.[630] NATO's 1999 humanitarian intervention was seen as unprecedented as NATO did not seek or receive U.N. Security Council authorization, given the "unique circumstances and the purposes for which force was used."[631]

The European Council officials also consider Kosovo's declaration of independence as a "sui generis case," making the Kosovo case incompatible and incomparable with other secession cases such as Catalonia and Scotland.[632] The E.U. statement said that Kosovo constitutes a sui generis case because "the Kosovo breakaway was unique, due to the wars in the 1990s that tore Yugoslavia into seven different countries."[633]

The establishment of the Kosovo Specialist Chambers and the Specialist Prosecutor's Office in the Hague is another factor that adds to the uniqueness of the Kosovo case making it a highly unusual case of domestic and international link. The Kosovo Specialist Court was adopted by the Kosovo Assembly in 2015, grounded in Kosovo's constitution, staffed with international judges, with a seat outside Kosovo, in the Netherlands. KSC entered into force in July 2017.

With respect to the judiciary system, Kosovo has undergone a process of transitional democracy in a very unusual way given its historical background. During the Former Republic of Yugoslavia period, Kosovo's judiciary exercised independent competencies within the People's

---

[627] Ibid, 3

[628] Ibid, 3.

[629] EULEX. (2013). Short history of EULEX. Retrieved from http://www.eulex-kosovo.eu/?page=2,44,197

[630] Wippman, D. (2001). Kosovo and the Limits of International Law. *Fordham International Law Journal*, 25(1), 129-150.

[631] Ibid, 136.

[632] Tota, E. (2017, October 5). Kosovo is a sui generis case. *Balkan EU*. Retrieved from https://www.balkaneu.com/kosovo-is-a-sui-generis-case/

[633] Traynor, I. (2008, February 18). Spain exposes EU split as US leads recognition. *The Guardian*. Retrieved from https://www.theguardian.com/world/2008/feb/19/kosovo.serbia

Court of Province, until such competencies were abolished in 1945, giving judicial power to the Supreme Court of Serbia.[634] In 1974, Kosovo was given the status of province within former Yugoslavia and was given the right to establish self-governing courts, the Supreme Court of Kosovo having the highest authority at the time.[635] The Kosovo Assembly had the competence to appoint judges of the Constitutional Court and the Supreme Court. However, this competence was taken away in 1989 by Serbia when Slobodan Milosevic stripped off Kosovo's autonomy and all judicial competences were taken over by Serbia. The Milosevic government "dissolved the provincial government and fired more than 100,000 ethnic Albanian workers."[636]

> "The period 1989 - 1999 finds Kosovo, its citizens and the whole economic, political and legal system in an extraordinary position. With the intention of protecting its citizens, Kosovo Liberation Army fought for an independent and democratic Kosovo, with the purpose of establishing institutional mechanisms in order to first of all guarantee an independent and unbiased judicial system, justice and impartiality in decision making process to the citizens; equal approach and treatment for all, in accordance with the law; honesty and integrity; transparency and accountability; efficiency and effectiveness; professionalism; responsibility and accountability for the use of public means, principles of justice which were violated in the most severe form by Serb genocide."[637]

For the entire decade of the 1990s Kosovo Albanians were banned from the law school at the University of Prishtina and were not permitted to take the bar exam.[638] Ethnic Albanian judges and prosecutors were dismissed, deregistered, and denied the opportunity to practice law.[639] These conditions are reflective of an authoritarian regime. The transitional democracy literature would expect low levels of trust in government and institutions transitioning from an authoritarian rule, and this supported by the data in this study. The 2018 survey results showed low trust levels for

---

[634] Hajdari, A. Ibrahimi, S. & Hajdari, A. (2014, June). Reforming of the Judicial System of Kosovo based on the Law no. 03/L-199 on Courts and its challenges. *ILIRIA International Review*, 4(1), 249-270. doi: 10.21113/iir.v4i1.64

[635] Ibid, 252.

[636] NBC News. (2013) Q&A: The history of strife in Kosovo. Ethnic Albanians, Serbs have tussled over region for years. Retrieved from http://www.nbcnews.com/id/23292619/ns/world_news-europe/t/qa-history-strife-kosovo/#.XE_0G1xKiM8

[637] Hajdari, et al,. (2014), 253.

[638] American Bar Association. (2009, May). Legal Profession Reform Index for Kosovo. Washington DC, 1-73. Retrieved from http://www.americanbar.org/content/dam/aba/directories/roli/kosovo/kosovo_lpri_vol_iii_05_09_en.authcheckdam.pdf

[639] Ibid, 7.

Serbian judges in Kosovo with low confidence in their ability to make impartial and fair decisions. The level of distrust can be explained by the complex historical and institutional background of the judiciary in Kosovo, characterized by decades of oppression by the Yugoslav and Serbian government.

Yet Kosovo, as a transitional democracy has unique features: low trust levels in local legal institutions and judges but high trust levels in international judges and institutions. In Kosovo political trust is higher in well-performing international institutions such as the European Union, NATO, the U.S. Embassy and the Kosovo Specialist Court. The results suggest that performance as well as democratic principles are important to political trust in Kosovo when it comes to the local legal institutions. Perceptions of corruption and low competence undermine political trust in the local legal institutions in Kosovo. The 2009 American Bar Association Index pointed out the judicial corruption in Kosovo, with "more than half of judges accept bribes."[640]

By contrast, perceptions of corruption of the European Union and international judges did not undermine political trust in Kosovo towards the international institutions and judges. In 2017, Malcolm Simmons resigned as president of the judges of the E.U.'s rule-of-law mission in Kosovo, claiming that EULEX was subject to political interference.[641] In 2014, former EULEX prosecutor Maria Bamieh was terminated after accusing the mission of "not thoroughly investigating allegations in wiretaps that an Italian judge had received a €300,000 bribe."[642] The 2018 expert interviews of this study revealed that Kosovo Albanians felt that they are better off under the guidance of international community, particularly the European Union, despite the corruption scandals involving EULEX. This suggests that outcomes are important to political trust. This idea lines up with Blind's model of political trust, involving rational political trust.

According to Blind (2006) rational political trust involves interest-based calculations where the citizens evaluate the actions of the stakeholders.[643] This is based on the first-order of trust known as "encapsulated trust" allowing for trust to exist for "A when he delegates to B control over C in which A has an interest."[644] In the Kosovo case, the Kosovo government (A) has delegated to the European Union rule of law mission in Kosovo (B) control over the Kosovo Specialist Court (C) to uphold international rule of law. If following the first-order of trust based on rational political trust, one would expect trust to exist on the basis of encapsulated interests. Since the common

[640] Ibid, 14.

[641] Saeed, S. (2017, November 16). Top judge quits EU Kosovo mission, alleging corruption. *Politico*. Retrieved from https://www.politico.eu/article/judge-quits-eu-kosovo-mission-alleging-corruption/

[642] Hopkins, V. (2017, November 17). EU courts trouble with Kosovo scandal. *Politico*. Retrieved from https://www.politico.eu/article/malcolm-simmons-eulex-eu-courts-chaos-with-kosovo-scandal/

[643] Blind. (2006), 4.

[644] Ibid, 5.

interest for both Kosovo and the European Union is to maintain international rule of law, the rational logic would allow for maximizing the self-interests in A, because they are also included in B and are "mutually-inclusive."

Blind (2006) argues that the legitimacy and the durability of the democratic system largely depends on the government institutions doing what is right and as well as when they are perceived as fair and efficient.[645] When entering into trusting relationships, Blind (2006) maintains that people combine both rational and psychological trust in order to maximize their interests and ethical perceptions of the actors. As seen in the Kosovo case international judges are perceived as fair and impartial.

Another motivation of trust known as the "second-order or trust" or "psychological trust" in Blind's model, involves the assessment of the moral and ethical attributes associated with the government, institution or the individual leader.[646] This is based on trustworthiness, rooted in psychological reasoning, where sincerity and truthfulness are valued (Blind, 2007). According to Blind (2006) lack of trust towards leaders, could transform to distrust in the institution and the political system as a whole. This is especially true when considering the local courts in Kosovo. Lack of trust in Kosovan judges, based on psychological reasoning, is characterized by distrust in the Kosovo local courts.

Blind (2006) argues that building trust in post-crisis countries is especially unique and challenging. He considers it unique because post-crisis countries allow for different dynamics of social trust and political trust to emerge, when compared to the developed countries.[647] This makes the relationship between social and political trust to be country-specific depending on the attributes of the relationship.[648] Blind (2006) stated that "while the forming of new institutions is relatively easier, their effective functioning and the legitimacy they enjoy are harder to achieve."[649] This proved to be true in Kosovo, as the challenge remains the effective functioning of the democratic institutions, put in place by the international community.

In two other studies, Dominican Republic[650] and Morocco[651] saw increased civic engagement while political trust levels decreased. This assumption does not hold true in Kosovo, which saw

[645] Ibid, 5.

[646] Ibid, 5.

[647] Ibid, 7.

[648] Ibid, 14.

[649] Ibid, 7.

[650] Espinal, R. and J. Hartlyn. (2006, March). Performance Still Matters Explaining Trust in Government in the Dominican Republic. *Comparative Political Studies*, 39, (2), 200-23.

[651] Hazan, P. (2006, July). Morocco: Betting on a Truth and Reconciliation Commission. *United States Institute of Peace Paper*. Washington DC: United States Institute of Peace, 1-16.

low levels of both civic and political participation and political trust. The idea behind this assumption is that civic participation will increase to expose corruption and illegitimacy of the government, motivating the citizens to get involved in the political and democratic processes, as seen in Morocco and the Dominican Republic. The results of this study found low civic engagement in general in Kosovo as well as low political participation of Kosovo Serbs. The relationship between social and political trust differs in Kosovo compared to Moroco and the Dominican Republic.

Blind (2006) attributes corruption and poor economic performances as two key political factors, contributing to the decline in the levels of trust in government in advanced democracies.[652] For instance, Iceland's financial crisis is attributed to the corruption of the banking system.[653] In 2008, Iceland suffered a collapse of the banking system and its economy, followed by increased unemployment. The financial crash led to massive riots and the governing coalition was forced to resign.[654] Prior to the financial crisis, Iceland was a high-performing democracy with high levels of popular support and high levels of legitimacy. After the crisis, the study found that Iceland saw a sharp drop in the levels of support for democracy in 2009.[655]

Blind (2006) concludes that more recently citizens are putting more focus on the psychological and ethical norms of political trust, instead of the rational attributes.[656] According to Blind (2006) the new state in the globalization age, must be able to adopt both psychological and rational norms based on competence, legitimacy, accountability, integrity, professionalism, respect for diversity, and effective communication.[657]

---

[652] Blind. (2006), 11.

[653] Erlingsson, G. Linde, J. & Öhrvall, R. (2015). Distrust in Utopia? Public Perceptions of Corruption and Political Support in Iceland before and after the Financial Crisis of 2008. *Government and Opposition*. 51, 1-27. doi: 10.1017/gov.2014.46

[654] Ibid, 3.

[655] Ibid, 9.

[656] Ibid, 14.

[657] Ibid, 15.

CHAPTER 7

Conclusions and Recommendations

7.1 Key Findings

Analysts of political trust have taken into account both socio-cultural and institutional performance factors influencing trust. What are the factors that influence political trust at different levels of government? What shapes the elite perceptions towards the leaders, the state, and the broader political system? Political trust can be analyzed through various levels: *micro level of analysis* (individual or person-oriented trust)[658] or *macro level of analysis* (organizational or issue oriented),[659] or *diffuse trust* analysis (system-based level).[660] Other scholars have explained political trust through cultural[661] and institutional interpretations.[662] From this context, political trust can be explained by *the social vs. political integrative model* of sources of trust (Blind, 2006; Godefroidt, Langer & Meuleman, 2015) and *the two-factor structure model of trust* – trust in the national and international political trust (Andre, 2014).

Trust in political institutions and political leaders is vital to the democratic functioning of the state. A certain degree of trustworthiness in institutions is a necessary precondition for the legitimacy, fairness and democratic governance. Transitional democracies face lower levels of trust due to corruption, low economic and government performance.[663] In Kosovo (*Alb: Kosova*) distrust in the government is the lowest at 20% in 2018, with higher trust in political parties

---

[658] Miller, A. H. (1974), 951.

[659] Levi, M. (1998), 496.

[660] Easton, D. (1975), 447.

[661] Berg & Hjerm. (2010), 392.

[662] Rothstein & Stolle. (2008), 441.

[663] Catterberg & Alejandro. (2006), 32.

(40%). Moreover, international political trust in Kosovo is very high towards the European Union, NATO, United States and the Kosovo Specialist Court. However, there is a disconnect between international political trust and national political trust. For instance, higher trust in the European Union, also meant higher trust levels for the Kosovo Specialist Court, but not for Kosovo Courts. So, if fairness, impartiality and effectives are desired when considering international civil and legal institutions working domestically in Kosovo, why don't the same performance principals work for the local legal institutions?

Despite Kosovo Albanians being highly against the establishment of the Kosovo Specialist Court, majority have higher trust towards the special court. As the data of this study showed, trust perceptions of the E.U. in 2018 were 60%, and 64.5% for the Kosovo Specialist Court, but very low 32.5% for the Kosovo courts. Whereas trust in international military organizations such NATO/KFO in Kosovo received the highest trust scores in 2012 (84%), along with 80% trust score for the Kosovo police (Kosovo Security Force), the latter declining levels of trust to 53% in 2018.

> "The political aspect has been a major obstacle to not fully functioning of the security and defense scheme. Although the Kosovo Police Service initially and then Kosovo Police had made important strides in profiling and structuring, the consequences of the various experiences from UNMIK for police have been evident obstacles.
>
> As the police institution is an implementing law institution, efforts to intervene and interfere with politics and interest groups have damaged its reputation. The numerous scandals that had followed this institution such as burglaries in the evidence room, the scandal with penetration of the Turks…etc, were never addressed in the field of political and professional responsibility. The control of senior executives from politics is another aspect of citizen dissatisfaction, which affects the continued decline of citizens' credibility."[664]

Institutional theories propose that trust is a function of government performance, based on the rational evaluations of the performance of institutions.[665] While cultural theories offer socio-cultural explanations emphasizing that trust is shaped by cultural values and normative beliefs.[666] Accordingly, "both theories are not mutually exclusive and can reinforce each other in developing

[664] Dugolli, Enver. (2018, December 3). Personal Communication. Interview. Military Attaché of the Republic of Kosovo in Tirana, Republic of Albania (2004-2018).
[665] Newton, K. (2001), 202.
[666] Godefroidt et al. (2015), 4.

more institutional trust."[667] However, data from recently-established democracies such as Kosovo is lacking, absent in many in-between years of pre/post-independence.

This study collected original data from two fieldtrips in Kosovo in 2012 and 2017 to conduct field research and interviews with the political elite and experts of rule of rule of law in Kosovo. Two quantitative surveys were conducted during 2012-2013 in Kosovo (220 participants) and 2018 survey (40 participants). The surveys were modeled after the Chicago Council on Foreign Relations 2004 survey and Katharine Richards' rule of law in Croatia survey (2013). The study identified political trust measures using indicators from: (1) the European Social Survey (ESS) to examine political trust at the institutional level (*fair, legitimate* and *competent*); (2) the American National Election Studies (ANES) for possible factors involving political leaders "incumbents" (*honest, know what they are doing, do the right thing,* and *interest*); and (3) United Nations rule of law indicators to analyze political international trust of the police from the institutional performance approach (*performance, capacity, integrity, transparency* and *accountability*).

In Kosovo (*Alb: Kosova*), the decrease of the political trust level is a great concern for a crisis of representative democracy. The results show that majority of the Kosovo Albanians consider the government corrupt (37%), only 8% consider it "democratic and fair"; while 30% think it is "democratic but not strong"; 13% said "it does not function"; and 12% consider it "non-democratic." This suggests that lower levels of a democratic government show even lower levels of political trust in institutions. Thus, trust in political institutions is detrimental to democracy and the democratic functioning of the state.

In an interview with Aaron Nething, U.S. Air Force Intelligence analyst, he expressed that democratic societies – where media, freedoms and rights are protected, and the citizens' voices are being heard – are preconditions of political trust.

"Like any developing country, trust in political institutions can grow very slowly among civilians, and Kosovo is no exception. Initially, once trust among the people develops in the fact that they feel there are free and fair elections...this ensures that their voices are being heard...also, when they feel there is freedom for the press/media to voice their views and that society as a whole has the freedom of speech, then the foundations of trust are laid.

I do remember the people I talked to in my visits to Kosovo 20 years ago when it was just trying to gain its independence how there was more trust in national institutions as opposed to local. This can be, and to some degree, has lessened due

---

[667] Ibid, 12.

to more confidence in the judicial process. It reminds me of the age-old question, which came first, the chicken or the egg? In this case, which comes first, trust in the political institutions themselves or the politician? Regardless, the variables mentioned, along with a healthy civil society, have to be present..."[668]

In Kosovo (*Alb: Kosova*), satisfaction with democracy and trust in institutions explains the difference in political trust. The variance in political trust between institutions and political parties was significant by 20% more trust towards the political parties. But in terms of satisfaction with institutional performance local institutions including the courts and the government had lower trust compared to international civil and legal institutions.

The study also explored the relationship between trustworthy political leaders and political trust. The findings suggest that lower satisfaction with honesty and moral behavior of leaders decreased mutual trust, while effective communication increased cooperation between political parties.

7.2 Discussion and Conclusions

7.2.1 Why the Kosovo case matters

This study confirms the assumption that post-crisis countries are unique cases due to the different relationships that emerge between social and political trust, that differ from the more developed to transitional democracies.[669] Kosovo (*Alb: Kosova*) fits the profile of being a unique case as it is a nascent state, that emerged from post-conflict and is considered a transitional democracy. The international community considers Kosovo a sui generis case when it comes to the unilateral declaration of independence. Another factor that makes Kosovo an extraordinary case and highly unusual is the way the national and international relationship merges in a variety of ways, including the political, economic, legal and institutional relationships. Therefore, a country-specific analysis of political trust would be beneficial for a thorough understanding of the levels of trust across various political institutions and actors.

---

[668] Nething, Aaron. (2018, November 26). Personal Communication. Interview. Aaron Nething, Intelligence Analyst U.S. Air Force for 23 years, Counterintelligence Analyst with Azimuth Inc. for 20 years, MA in Security Studies with concentration in Terrorism/Counterterrorism from Georgetown University.
[669] Blind. (2006), 7.

The general assumption about developed countries is that government performance is one of the major determinants of trust in stable democracies.[670] Trust in government matters because it has been linked with the legitimacy and the sustainability of the political systems.[671] Satisfaction with government performance "renders government legitimacy, which in turn enhances government's trustworthiness."[672] Does this relationship hold true in post-conflict and transitional democracies? What does the Kosovo case say about the performance-trust relationship?

7.2.2 Political Trust and Democracy

Legitimacy is identified as a foundation of trust because it affects the government's ability to govern, to provide services and to perform its duties.[673] The main argument is that a high level of trust in government might increase the legitimacy, efficiency and the effectiveness of government operations.[674] Blind (2006) argues that high dissatisfaction with democracy and extremely low levels of trust can result in "deleterious consequences for governments and governance."[675] A study of trust in developed democracies showed that advanced industrialized democracies in Europe such as Sweden, Norway, and the Netherlands show high degree of trust in politics and increasing trust in government.[676] While Austria, Germany, Japan, U.S. and New Zealand showed patterns of decreasing trust in institutions and government from mid-1960s to mid-1990s.[677]

The 2005 BBC Gallup International study found Eastern and Central Europe with the highest level of global dissatisfaction in government at 73%, followed by Latin America with 69%, and 65% in Africa.[678] The study also found higher trust in institutions in East Asia and the European Union, but decreased institutional trust in Latin America. Trust in political institutions and political leaders in the developed countries, except the Netherlands, has been in the decline because politicians are perceived as less trustworthy overtime.[679] For instance, citizens in Australia felt that

---

[670] Levi, M. Sacks, A. & Tyler, T. (2009) Conceptualizing legitimacy, measuring legitimating beliefs. *American Behavioral Scientist*, 53(3), 354-375.

[671] OECD. (2013), 21.

[672] Wong, P. (2016). How can political trust be built after civil wars? Evidence from post-conflict Sierra Leone. *Journal of Peace Research*, 53(6), 772-785.

[673] OECD. (2013), 21.

[674] Ibid.

[675] Blind. (2006), 7.

[676] Ibid, 8.

[677] Ibid.

[678] Ibid, 10.

[679] Ibid.

their political officials are loosing touch with the public, while people in Britain, Finland, Norway and Austria felt that politicians care more about votes than the citizens' needs.[680]

The individual case study in Kosovo (*Alb: Kosova*) reveals that there is high level of trust in the law enforcement institutions, in both the Kosovo Police and the NATO's mission in Kosovo "KFOR." Kosovo police saw a drop in the satisfaction levels in 2018 compared to the 2012-13 survey, despite the high scores of effectiveness, competence, and management capacity. The study also found steady high trust levels in European Union institutions, international judges, and the E.U. backed Specialist Court, formally known as the Kosovo Specialist Chambers (KSC) and Specialist Prosecutor's Office. The study found high dissatisfaction with the government, as well as low confidence in the local courts, the local Kosovan judges, Serbian judges, and the United Nations. Additionally, the study found higher levels of trust in political parties when compared to trust levels in the government.

In order to understand the possible causes of the deviation of trust levels in Kosovo compared to stable democracies this study explained the socio-cultural and the institutional factors. Van Der Meer (2018) argues that support for democratic principles and values should not equate to blind trust in political institutions or unconditional trust in politicians.[681] Mishler and Rose (1997) maintain that "democracy requires trust but also presupposes an active and vigilant citizenry with a healthy skepticism of government and a willingness, should the need arise, to suspend trust and assert control over government – at a minimum by replacing the government of the day." While political trust is desirable and necessary to democracy, political cynicism and vigilant skepticism would keep the citizens engaged and would encourage the citizens to monitor the actions of government in terms of compliance of the laws and implementation of policies.[682] In this context, lack of trust stimulates engagement, thus strengthening democracy.[683]

7.2.3 Social and Political Trust

The relationship between legitimacy and trust holds true in Kosovo to a certain extent. Trust literature in developed countries relates government legitimacy with increased trustworthiness.[684] However in post-conflict and transitional countries such as Kosovo, this relationship will depend on the levels of stability, security, legitimacy and capacity. Wong (2016) argues that the satisfactory performance-trust relationship may not hold in post-conflict states due to war

---

[680] Ibid.
[681] Mishler & Rose. (1997), 419.
[682] Van Der Meer, (2018), 6.
[683] Ibid.
[684] Levi, Sacks & Tyler. (2009), 354.

experiences, security situations, and economic hardship.[685] He maintains that "people living in post-conflict countries are likely to have different preferences and priorities than those living in stable democracies."[686]

War experiences affect building of trust by raising insecurity. Due to the war experience, preferences and priorities in Kosovo were reflective of the need for security and state-building. Hajdari, et al. (2014) argue that the oppressing actions of the Serb state institutions over ethnic Albanians in Kosovo, as well as the war, encouraged the international intervention.[687] With the end of the war, the priorities shifted to setting up a new legal system, ensuring security and rule of law, and establishing a multi-ethnic fair and independent justice system. When UNMIK mission began in Kosovo in 1999, there was no functioning court system:

> "Legal order of Kosovo inherited a destroyed judiciary, disappeared case files, lack of technology, etc. One of the primary priorities of this [UNMIK] Mission is presented to be the establishment of multiethnic justice with fair, unbiased and independent judicial processes. All this was as a result of problems and insecurity in which the citizen rights were. A consequence of this situation was parallelism in laws and in competences."[688]

UNMIK was tasked with developing Kosovo's the Emergency Judicial System, which established the Prishtina District Court, with branches in Gjilan, Mitrovica, Prizren.[689] In 1999, UNMIK appointed 36 judges and 12 prosecutors, that included Serbs, Slavic Muslim, Roma and Turks.[690] By June 2000, there were more than 400 judges and prosecutors,[691] and by September 2000, an additional 136 judges and prosecutors were appointed with 309 lay judges.[692] The court system in 2000 consisted of the "Supreme Court, five district courts, 22 municipal courts, one commercial court, one High Court of Minor Offences, 22 minor offences courts and 13 offices

---

[685] Wong. (2016), 772.

[686] Ibid, 772.

[687] Hajdari, et al. (2014), 253.

[688] Hajdari, et al. (2014), 253.

[689] UNMIK Emergency Decree No. 1999/1 (28 June 1999) (providing legal basis for the establishment of the Joint Advisory Council for Provisional Judicial Appointments). Retrieved from http://www.unmikonline.org/regulations/1999/re99_01.pdf

[690] Baskin, M. (2001), 13.

[691] Out of the 400 judges and prosecutors 46 were non-ethnic Kosovo Albanian.

[692] Out of the additional judges and prosecutors 16 were from non-Albanian ethnic groups. By 2001, the Kosovo court system employed 325 judges, 51 prosecutors, 617 lay judges, and about 1,000 support staff in 69 judicial institutions.

of the Public Prosecutor."[693] During the interim government phase of UNMIK administration, people living in the Serb enclaves in the North were not integrated into the Kosovo judicial system because "Serbs have continued to view themselves as part of the Yugoslav system centered in Belgrade rather than as part of the Kosovo governed under the authority in SCR 1244."[694]

Security is an important pillar of trust in society. Perceptions of good security improve trust. This study found that in the Kosovo case, both security and political stability are strong determinants of trust. This holds up with existing trust studies in post-conflict states, where exposure to violence is a determinant of social trust.[695] The Kosovo findings are inconsistent with studies in developed countries and stable democracies, which have found satisfaction with government services to be a strong predictor of trust in government.[696] Therefore, institutional trustworthiness in Kosovo, is not only associated with the evaluation of institutional performance in government, but also with security concerns and political stability. This explains why local courts in Kosovo are perceived less trustworthy (with only 30% trust), when compared to the high trust scores of the Kosovo Specialist Court, stationed outside of Kosovo (70%). There is a clear difference between the trust levels in the local versus international legal institutions of Kosovo.

To account for the security concerns, the Kosovo Specialist Chambers have allocated the Witness Protection and Support Office in the Hague to ensure a protection system during the gathering of evidence and testimonies. Whereas judges and prosecutors in Kosovo continue to face threats, harassments, assaults and intimidation.[697] In their 2010 report, OSCE presented findings detailing the growing trend of insecurity and intimidation of the judiciary.[698]

> "The Organization for Security and Co-operation in Europe Mission in Kosovo (OSCE) is concerned that the lack of adequate security for judges and prosecutors may violate legal framework in Kosovo and international human rights standards. In the course of its monitoring of the justice system, the OSCE has witnessed and recorded a number of acts carried out against judicial and prosecutorial officials which indicate a continuing or even growing trend of insecurity and intimidation

---

[693] Baskin, M. (2001), 13.

[694] Ibid, 14.

[695] Wong. (2016), 772.

[696] Hetherington. (1998), 798.

[697] Report from Group for Legal and Political Studies. (2018, October). Rule of Law Performance Index in Kosovo. *ROLPIK*, 4, 1-32. Retrieved from http://www.legalpoliticalstudies.org/wp-content/uploads/2018/10/RoLPIK-4EN-web.pdf

[698] OSCE. (2010, April). Intimidation of the Judiciary: Security of Judges and Prosecutors. *Department of Human Rights and Communities*, 3, 1-7. Retrieved from https://www.osce.org/kosovo/67676?download=true

of the judiciary... OSCE monitors have reported on security-related incidents against judges, prosecutors and even court support staff, ranging from verbal insults, harassment and threats to severe beatings and bodily injuries. This affects not only the independence and impartiality of the courts, or at least the perception of it, but it also undermines the credibility and authority of prosecutorial and judicial institutions in the eyes of the public."[699]

The 2018 Rule of Law Index in Kosovo reported that courts in Kosovo do not have the means and resources needed to protect judges and prosecutors from threats, harassments, assaults, or intimidations.[700]

An independent judiciary is another important pillar of trust in society. The right to a fair trial by an independent and impartial court, without any improper influence is key to rule of law and human rights. This fosters trust and confidence in the judicial system to perform its duties in resolving disputes. The issue of security of judges and prosecutors and the outside pressures undermine the independent and impartial criteria of the judiciary, set out by the European Commission of Human Rights for democratic societies. The judicial independence problem has a negative impact on the rule of law and access to justice in Kosovo.[701] The findings of this study confirm the security problem being an issue with the effectiveness and the judicial function of the legal system in Kosovo. Only 2.5% chose Kosovan judges, when asked which judges are better able to make impartial decisions in war crime trials, while 92.5% of the respondents chose international judges of the Kosovo Specialist Court as impartial.

Problems of judicial independence and impartiality have an affect on both the justice system and the judges.[702] The 2012 OSCE report pointed out that public perceptions of independence of the judiciary have suffered "partly as a result of cultural factors, including too-easy access by the public to judicial actors, and partly as a result of lax security and a lack of rigor in adhering to ethical precepts."[703] Kosovo has undergone substantial judicial reform to increase the administrative competences. The International Judicial and Prosecutor Commission took over the vetting process for appointment to permanent positions. The new Law on the Courts allowed for judges and prosecutors to focus on aspects of the reappointment process, "to securing the material wellbeing

[699] Ibid, 1.

[700] Report from Group for Legal and Political Studies. (2018), 17.

[701] OSCE. (2012), 4.

[702] Ibid, 4.

[703] Ibid, 4.

of judicial professionals as well as increasing the security of their tenure."[704] Despite the positive developments, the judiciary continues to struggle with high-profile cases.

Another element that makes the case of Kosovo unique and different from other democracies is the existence of parallel structures. At the end of the NATO bombing campaign in 1999, the security concerns in the north made it difficult for Kosovo Serbs and other minorities to travel outside of their enclaves and through the rest of Kosovo.[705] In these enclaves and in the northern municipalities, Serbian parallel structures existed, which operated in the territory of Kosovo, but with de facto authority of the Serbian government in Belgrade.[706] Kosovo Serbs did not recognize the new administration established by UNMIK, nor Kosovo's independence. Therefore, the northern municipalities in Mitrovica region created their own parallel structures, including security structures, courts, schools, hospitals, and other activities of the Serbian government, operating in the territory of Kosovo (*Alb: Kosova*).

The existence of the parallel systems in North Mitrovica raised numerous issues concerning the validity of decisions taken by parallel courts, and the risk of double jeopardy in criminal law.[707] In other cases, individuals carrying invalid driving licenses issued by FRY authorities were convicted for forgery.[708] The UNMIK Department of Justice in 2003 considered the forgery charges as not appropriate for individuals with invalid licenses. But the prosecutors continued to bring the forgery charges under Article 203 of the 1977 Criminal Law of the of the Socialist Autonomous Province of Kosovo.[709]

The parallel systems created a serious problem in the legal system of Kosovo, prompting UNMIK to deal with the challenge of how to ensure a unified and lawful implementation of the applicable law. In August 2015, the European Union and Kosovo signed the Brussels Agreement, a landmark achievement in the EU-Kosovo relations.[710] The Stabilization and Association Agreement (SAA) included the dismantling of the parallel structures in North Kosovo, the establishment of Association of municipalities with Serb majority in Kosovo and normalization of relations in the

---

[704] Ibid, 4.

[705] OSCE. (2003, October. Parallel Structures in Kosovo. Department of Human Rights and Rule of Law, 1-44. Retrieved from https://www.osce.org/kosovo/42584?download=true

[706] OSCE. (2003), 5.

[707] Ibid, 5.

[708] Ombudsperson Institution in Kosovo Report. (2004, July). Kosovo Ombudsperson of Kosovo Fourth Annual report 2003-2004, 1-54. Retrieved from http://www.ombudspersonkosovo.org

[709] Ibid, 2.

[710] European Council. (2015, October 27). Stabilization and Association Agreement (SAA) between the European Union and Kosovo signed. Retrieved from https://www.consilium.europa.eu/en/press/press-releases/2015/10/27/kosovo-eu-stabilisation-association-agreement/

Mitrovica region. Other aspects of the SAA focused on key democratic principles pertaining to free trade, energy, justice, political dialogue, regional cooperation, and stabilization.[711]

The process of transition of the judicial system of Kosovo has allowed for all courts to be part of a unified legal and judicial system.[712] The European Union insists on the importance of multi-ethnic character of the Kosovo society. EULEX sought to assist Kosovo's institutions to reinforce a multi-ethnic justice system and multi-ethnic police services.[713] Although the Kosovo legal system has benefited from the intensive international support, it has not led to a functioning rule of law society.[714] The dominance of the international influence "has led to stresses and tensions and to a high, unsustainable dependence on the international community."[715]

Corruption reduces trustworthiness by decreasing performance and legitimacy. Corruption increases dishonesty and unethical behavior, contributing to the decrease of trust levels in political leaders and institutions. Judge Bekim Sejdiu of the Constitutional Court of Kosovo stated that the overall progress in Kosovo has been challenged by corruption and organized crime, having a negative effect on the efficiency of the justice system in Kosovo:

> "Despite the achievements, there is an apparent discrepancy between the energy and resources invested; the results achieved and the expectations of the Kosovar society, in terms of the standards of rule of law and efficiency of the justice system.
>
> Kosovo resembles an average European country, when it comes to statistical measurement of public safety and the crime rate. However, similarly with the regional countries, Kosovo's overall progress is challenged from the corruption and organized crime. The general perception among the Kosovar society is that first UNMIK, then EULEX, together with the Kosovo courts and other institutions, have had much more modest achievements than expected, when it comes to fight against organized crime and corruption.[716]

---

[711] Ibid.

[712] International Commission of Jurists. (2016). Uncharted Transition: the "Integration" of the Justice System in Kosovo. *Ministry of Foreign Affairs of Finland*, 1-28. Retrieved from https://www.refworld.org/pdfid/57ee8b074.pdf

[713] Zupančič, R., Pejič, N., Grilj, B., & Rodt, A. (2018) The European Union Rule of Law Mission in Kosovo: An Effective Conflict Prevention and Peace-Building Mission?, *Journal of Balkan and Near Eastern Studies*, 20(6), 599-617, DOI: 10.1080/19448953.2017.1407539

[714] International Commission of Jurists. (2016), 23-24.

[715] Ibid, 23-24.

[716] Sejdiu, Bekim. (2018, November 28). Personal Communicating. Interview.

Corruption is a widespread problem and Kosovo is at its early stages in fighting corruption and organized crime.[717] Progress has been made in the investigation, prosecution, and conviction of high-level corruption. However, law enforcement agencies "struggle to effectively fight organized crime in the north of Kosovo."[718] The 2018 European Commission Report stressed the need for Kosovo authorities "to be more effective in their efforts to fight money laundering and the relevant law should be brought in line with EU acquis and international standards."[719]

This study confirmed the link between corruption and support for democracy. The 2012 survey results showed that majority of the Kosovo Albanians consider the government corrupt, while only 8% consider it democratic and fair. Fighting corruption and administration effectiveness are important to institutional theories.[720] The macro theoretical approach emphasizes the importance of institutional performance, versus the micro level that focuses on the individual's experiences in the past.[721] The traditional institutional view is that the quality of governance is important to democracy.[722] Blind (2006) argued that fighting corruption contributes to the enhanced transparency and accountability of the political system.[723] According to Blind (2006) "there can be no trust or good governance devoid of transparent and accountable underpinnings."[724]

Additionally, corruption is linked with reducing trustworthiness, because it reduces fairness[725] and worsens institutional competence.[726] This study made the argument that corruption can lead to distrust in the government. The 2018 results also reflected the level of dissatisfaction of the Kosovo Albanians with the government performance. The study confirmed that corruption undermines political trust, which is consistent with studies in established democracies in in North America and Western Europe,[727] as well as democratic regimes in East Asia.[728]

"The fact that UNMIK (before 2008) and EULEX (after 2008) have prioritized political stability over the rule of law and fight against corruption has nurtured a

---

[717] European Commission. (2018), 3.

[718] Ibid, 4.

[719] Ibid, 4.

[720] Pula, E. (2017), 6.

[721] Ibid, 6.

[722] Jamal & Nooruddin. (2010), 48.

[723] Blind. (2006), 19.

[724] Ibid, 19.

[725] Arancibia. (2008), 38.

[726] Della Porta. (2000), 154.

[727] Van Der Meer. (2018), 18.

[728] Chang, E. C., & Chu, Y. (2006). Corruption and trust: Exceptionalism in Asian democracies? *Journal of Politics*, 68(2), 259-271.

negative perception in the public about the achievements, and even the objectives of these missions, in terms of the justice and the rule of law. This has been exacerbated by the scandals within the missions, particularly within the EULEX (such as the cases when the EULEX judges and prosecutors accused one another for serious misconduct and corruptive behavior).

These facts have blurred the image of the international justice institutions in Kosovo and this has overshadowed their achievements. This does not mean however, that the Kosovo institutions, particularly the justice system, can escape their part of the responsibility."[729]

The findings of this study illustrate that the relationship between social trust and political trust in a transitional democracy will depend on the context. The case of Kosovo (*Alb: Kosova*) has unique and unusual features that may not allow findings of this study to be generalized to other post-conflict democracies. Firstly, the dominance of the international influence is directly related with the success of the state-building experience. Secondly, the creation of the temporary independent judicial institution, the Kosovo Specialist Court in the Hague speaks to the complex domestic-international intervention nature, that may not be present in other post-conflict societies combating war crimes. The effect of the explanatory factors of building trust relationships in post-crisis democracies, based on government performance, should be examined further in future research.

Past research has shown that political trust in democracies is a relatively more rational attitude associated with the assessment of government performance. According to Blind (2006) rational political trust involves interest-based calculations and evaluations of the political institutions and leaders. The main idea is that high levels of satisfactory performance is expected to yield high levels of political legitimacy and increase government's trustworthiness. In the case of Kosovo, it appears that performance satisfaction is not enough to build political trust. Trust in the government may require a combined psychological and rational political trust, where war experiences, security, corruption, media and legitimacy play an important factor.

The findings of this study imply that, although legitimacy of the democratic government will depend on the fairness and efficiency of the government institutions, the ethical qualities of the institutions are equally important. This study contributes to the trust literature in transitional democracies and adds to the knowledge of the elites within Kosovo. The Kosovo case study is

---

[729] Sejdiu, Bekim. (2018, November 28). Personal Communicating. Interview.

valuable because it contributes original data and it provides an in-depth country specific analysis of political trust in a post-conflict society and transitional democracy.

7.3 Recommendations

This study found that Albanians in Kosovo (*Alb: Kosova*) have lost faith in politics as shown by the low levels of trust in government, supported by another study,[730] finding women to be the least trustful in politics. Results suggest that Kosovo Albanians living inside the country have the same level of distrust in the government (95%) as Kosovo citizens living outside the country. While foreign nationals expressed slightly a higher level of trust in Kosovo's government (37.5%) when compared to ethnic Albanians (only 10.92% trust).

Considering the high level of support and nationalism from the Albanian diaspora in general and the success of Kosovo's public diplomacy in the independence and the European Union integration path, the role of the diaspora should be reevaluated. Organizing the Albanian diaspora more effectively to institutionalize their engagement formally within different levels of government would address the need for promoting cultural and economic ties for Kosovo. Effective engagement, "Almost always requires a concerted effort towards capacity building."[731] This means developing an effective policy at the state level that is implemented on a meaningful scale.

Albanian diaspora has gained momentum in the United States, especially in New York, Michigan, Washington DC, Connecticut, Boston, Florida, etc. Engaging the diaspora at the bilateral, regional, and local levels could shift the focus on development and cooperation. Most migrants maintain family ties and exhibit a continued interest in their place of origin. Thus, keeping the diaspora active at the local level is important in developing a two-way working relationship. Having additional diaspora offices in Kosovo other than the capital in Prishtina, would encourage productive networks.

Additionally, tourism could foster greater trust and facilitate new economic growth. Tourism can be used as vehicle for cultural diplomacy that leads to building trust. The Consulate General of Kosovo in New York has recently tried to export Albanian cultural products to the United States attracting Albanian businessmen and produce from Kosovo (*Alb: Kosova*). Albania and Kosovo are known for superb quality of wine and cheese in the Balkans. However, they lack trust and name brand on the global market, making it difficult for local Kosovo businesses to enter the

---

[730] Pula, E. (2017).

[731] Agunias. D. R. (2013, February 20). How to improve diaspora engagement. *The Guardian*. Retrieved from https://www.theguardian.com/global-development-professionals-network/2013/feb/20/improving-asian-diaspora-insitutions

market or to compete with existing household trusted brands. Establishing the Albanian brand name on the global market is important not just to economic growth, but to building trust about the Albanian cultural identity at the international level.

Many of the finest restaurants in New York are Albanian but advertised as "Italian," where waiters are given Italian names, because the American public does not know or trust what is "Albanian." Considering that many Albanian immigrants come from Italy to United States for a better life, it is no surprise that Albanians identify as Italian and speak the language. However, this undermines national identity and trust. The social cohesion is threatened by lack of trust and has greater repercussions that lead back to political distrust.

Security concerns and ethnic tensions still remain sensitive given the war past and ethnic divide between Albanians and Serbs. While ethnic disturbances remain beneath the surface they could be brought back anytime. There is a need for building constructive-interethnic relations. Kosovo has fulfilled the European Union standards for minority rights, by favoring ethnic communities in many aspects of political, social, and economic life. However, Serbia needs to meet Kosovo halfway and move beyond the negative propaganda. Normalizing bilateral relations is not just about European Union membership. It is about the broader regional stability at the international level.

When the Greek financial crisis occurred in 2008, it caused a ripple effect across Europe and the United States resulting in the market crash. Brexit, U.K.'s decision to leave the European Union will have a profound impact on the movement of E.U. citizens within its borders and access to the European Union market on a cross-border basis.[732] Therefore, it is important that both Serbia and Kosovo make significant progress both bilaterally and locally, to not undermine the security, stability and the economy of Europe.

Creating meaningful change in the state's legal justice system is pivotal to Kosovo's democracy and political trust. Citizens need to feel the need that they are protected by the law, and their needs are met in a fair and just way at the institutional level. Trust in Kosovo's police (Kosovo Security Force) is a great step forward to state-building and could trigger democratic transition processes. In an interview with Enver Dugolli, former Kosovo's Military Attaché in Albania, he emphasized that the democratic organizational culture of NATO was detrimental to the citizen's positive perceptions and the high levels of trust in the agency.

> "The security aspect along with justice is one of the main pillars that the citizens
> face daily. Unlike justice, the area of security and defense is a field with more

---

[732] Barigazzi, J. (2018, January 8). Where Brexit will hurt most in Europe. *Politico*. Retrieved from https://www.politico.eu/article/brexit-impact-on-european-regions-revealed-by-eu-report-phase-2-negotiations/

investments. As NATO's mission, KFOR was the first to be placed in post-war Kosovo, security and defense were always the positive perceptions of the citizens. Although this mission, like UNMIK, has the source from UN Security Council Resolution 1244, it has changed in organization and approach.

KFOR is still led by military leaders who come from developed countries but also with the tradition of states ruled with democratic organization. It is very indicative of the situation that even now, 20 years after the end of the war and 10 years after the declaration of independence of Kosovo, KFOR continues to have satisfactory citizens' credibility, in comparison to UNMIK's mission which consistently had a decline of confidence to disregard."[733]

Kosovo, as an independent country, should be able to resolve citizen's personal conflicts in the civil and criminal justice system inside its borders. The establishment of the Kosovo Specialist Court (KSC) outside of its borders in The Hague, but grounded in Kosovo's constitution, suggests that Kosovo's justice system does not function properly or that it has not matured yet, thus prompting international intervention. Kosovo citizens expressed higher levels of support for the Kosovo Specialist Court and the European Union, compared to the citizens' low trust scores in Kosovo's judiciary.

Kosovo (*Alb: Kosova*) has taken some steps towards the independence of the judiciary, but the justice system is not yet up to par with international standards. Corruption, nepotism, and political interferences were the main concerns expressed by Kosovo citizens. To achieve justice the elements of rule of law are important: access to justice, impartiality, effectiveness and efficiency, integrity, transparency and accountability. These rule of law standards should be upheld by both the Kosovan and international judges and prosecutors. Former U.K.'s Defense Attaché to Albania, Mark D. Vickers expressed the need for the Kosovo Specialist Court and the Specialist Prosecutor's Office "to remain completely neutral in their deliberations."[734]

"Somehow these issues have to be dealt with and justice must be done and be seen to be done. However, there is such a polarization and strength of opinions about the Balkans that I have little faith that anyone from any country which might have historical links to either Serbia or Albania can be fair and open minded.

---

[733] Dugolli, Enver. (2018, December 3). Personal Communication. Interview.

[734] Vickers, Mark, D. (2018). Personal Communication. Interview. British army officer for 33 years, including 7 years with diplomatic status and 3 years as the U.K.'s Defense Attaché in Albania.

I saw this very clearly in my role as a Defense Attaché where few diplomats were clearly neutral. Some from countries which were traditionally more aligned with Serbia had nothing good to say about Albania or Albanians, and vice versa. I must also say however that historically many of the Powers which might be considered more neutral do not have a great track record in dealing with Balkan issues, whilst others clearly have a very poor understanding or interest of the historical context."[735]

Kosovo (*Alb: Kosova*) is both a transitional democracy and undergoing transitional justice. Twelve years after the independence progress has been slow, however initiatives have been taken to address Kosovo's needs and concerns. Coalition RECOM, comprising of five Western Balkan states – Bosnia and Herzegovina, Kosovo, Macedonia, Montenegro and Serbia, seemed promising in the reconciliation efforts to address war atrocities, education reform, and missing persons.[736] RECOM is part of the Berlin Process (2014), a diplomatic initiative by Germany to empower the integration of the Western Balkan Six (WB6)[737] into the European Union.[738]

Western Balkans proposed the creation of the Regional Commission for the Establishment of facts, "About victims of war crimes and other serious human rights violations committed in the former Yugoslavia between 1991 and 2001" (RECOM).[739] Ana Marjanovic Rudan from the RECOM initiative stated that "fact-finding is a prerequisite for preventing manipulation of the 1990s conflicts for political purposes."[740] Government leaders of Kosovo, Macedonia, Montenegro, and Serbia had promised the signing of the declaration on the establishment of RECOM.[741] However the RECOM agreement failed to be signed in the EU-Western Balkans Summit in

---

[735] Ibid.

[736] Haxhibeqiri, N. (2018, February 14). Transitional justice in Kosovo, 10 years after independence. *Prishtina Insight.* Retrieved from https://prishtinainsight.com/transitional-justice-kosovo-10-years-independence/

[737] Western Balkans Six (WB6) refers to Albania, Bosnia and Herzegovina, the former Yugoslav Republic of Macedonia, Kosovo, Montenegro, and Serbia. Leaders of the six Western Balkan countries met in Berlin in 2014 to increase regional cooperation, and to improve links between the Balkans and the European Union, known as the "connectivity agenda". See European Commission. (2018, June 12). International Relations: Western Balkans. retrieved from https://ec.europa.eu/transport/themes/international/enlargement/westernbalkans_en

[738] BIRN. (2018, January 29). Balkan States 'Expected to Sign Truth Commission Agreement'. *Balkan Insight.* Retrieved from http://www.balkaninsight.com/en/article/recom-announces-state-forming-agreement-soon-01-29-2018

[739] *European Western Balkans.* (2018, May 30). Reconciliation and Good Neighbourly Relations in the Western Balkans: A Continuing Dilemma? Retrieved from https://europeanwesternbalkans.com/2018/05/30/reconciliation-good-neighbourly-relations-western-balkans-continuing-dilemma/

[740] BIRN. (2008), 1.

[741] Stappers, M., & Unger, T. (2018, July 16). How the Balkans Summit Failed on Truth and Justice. *Recom.* Retrieved from http://recom.link/how-the-balkans-summit-failed-on-truth-and-justice/

London (July 2018), thus failing to establish the regional truth-seeking committee.[742] The Western Balkans Summit in London ended without representatives of Kosovo, Macedonia, Montenegro and Serbia signing the agreement, and the signing ceremony was removed from the summit's agenda.

According to the 2018 report of the Impunity Watch of the Western Balkans, impunity for crimes committed 20 years after the conflict remains widespread across the region.[743] Promoters of transitional justice for post-conflict countries operate on national ideologies, and, "include former war criminals in their ranks."[744]

> "Measures taken in the area of transitional justice have by and large failed to tackle these structures of impunity. More specifically, prosecutions are on the decline, truth-seeking is challenged by a one-sided public discourse of denial and revisionism, and reparations have been largely selective and politicized.
>
> At the institutional level, the judiciary and other oversight bodies are too weak to fulfil their function in guaranteeing the non-recurrence of violations. Civil society, as well as the media, lacks strength or is too compromised to make a difference in society. Education is segregated, and history manipulated to tell nationalist narratives that go against any serious attempts to deal with responsibility for the past. The Western Balkans continues to be a battleground of conflicting narratives, in which each side claims victimhood and blames the other for past abuses. These are all indicators that are concerning and can, if not addressed, become root causes for future conflict."[745]

The reconciliation agenda should be brought back to the European Union agenda to address impunity and prevent future crimes and human rights abuses. Both Kosovo and Serbia must focus on reconciliation. Bringing justice to the war victims and survivors of war rape is an important part of the retributive and restorative justice and maintaining peaceful multi-ethnic relations in the country. Further steps need to be taken to ensure that all victims, regardless of ethnicity, deserve protection of human rights and justice served.

---

[742] Milekic, S. (2018, July 18). Balkan Govts Dodge Signing Truth Commission Declaration. *BIRN*. Retrieved from http://www.balkaninsight.com/en/article/west-balkans-states-not-singing-recom-declaration-07-09-2018

[743] Unger, T. (2018, May). Keeping the Promise Addressing Impunity in the Western Balkans. *Impunity Watch*, 1-48. retrieved from https://www.impunitywatch.org/docs/Keeping_the_Promise_%5bFINAL%5d.pdf

[744] Stappers & Unger (2018), 1.

[745] Ibid, 4.

REFERENCES

Aarts, Kees, Fladmoe, Audun, and Strömbäck, Jesper. (2012). Media, Political Trust, and Political Knowledge: A Comparative Perspective, 98-118.

ABC News. (2018, June 22). World Cup: Albanian eagle celebration controversy as Switzerland beats Serbia 2-1. Retrieved from www.abc.net

Academy of Justice. (2017). Kosovo Judicial Institute has been transformed into Academy of Justice. Retrieved from https://ad.rks-gov.net

Agunias, Dovelyn, R. (2013, February 20). How to improve diaspora engagement. *The Guardian*. Retrieved from www.theguardian.com

AIK. (2012, February 24). Sa Shqiptare ka në botë? *Presheva Jonë*. Retrieved from www.preshevajone.com

Almond, Gabriel, and Verba, Sidney. (1963). *The Civic Culture: Political Attitudes and Democracy in Five Nations*. Princeton: Princeton University Press.

American Bar Association. (2009, May). Legal Profession Reform Index for Kosovo. Washington DC, 1-73. Retrieved from www.americanbar.org

American Public Media. (1999). War Crimes Indictment against Milosevic. Justice For Kosovo. Retrieved from www.americanradioworks.publicradio.org

Andre, Stephanie. (2014). Does Trust Mean the Same for Migrants and Natives? Testing Measurement Models of Political Trust with Multi-group Confirmatory Factor Analysis. *Soc Indic Res.*, 115:963-982. doi: 10.1007/s11205-013-0246-6

Anderson, Christopher J., and Tverdova, Yuliya, V. (2003). Corruption, Political Allegiances, and Attitudes Toward Government in Contemporary Democracies. *American Journal of Political Science*, 47(1), 91-109.

Antues, Nuno, Balby, Leandro, Figueiredo, Flavio, Meira, Wagner, and Santos, Walter. (2018). Fairness and Transparency of Machine Learning for Trustworthy Cloud Services. *CISUC*, 1-6.

Arancibia, Carolina, S. (2008). Political trust in Latin America. *University of Michigan*, 1-197.

Ariely, Gal. (2015). Trusting the Press and Political Trust: A Conditional Relationship. *Journal of Elections, Public Opinion and Parties*, 25(3), 351-367, doi: 10.1080/17457289.2014.997739

Arrow, K.J. (2000). *Observations on Social Capital*, in P. Dasgupta & I. Serageldin (Eds.), Social Social Capital: A Multifaceted Perspective, 3-5. Washington, D.C.: The World Bank.

Assembly of Republic of Kosovo. (2010). On Courts. Law No. 03/L-199, *Republic of Kosovo*. Retrieved from www.assembly-kosova.org

Associated Press, (2018, November 22). Tensions Soar Between Kosovo and Serbia Over Trade Tax. *New York Times*. Retrieved from www.nytimes.com

AFT. (2020, Feb. 24). First indictments are filed before the Kosovo Specialist Chambers. *Justice Info*.

Avdyli, Brahim. (2015, January 14). Personal Communication. Interview.

Aylmer, G. (1975). *The Levellers in the English Revolution*. Ithaca, NY: Cornell University Press.

Babamusta, Ermira. (2008, January). *Kosovo Status Talks: A Case Study on International Negotiations*. (Master's Thesis). Long Island University, NY, 1-254.

Babamusta, Neki. (2018, November 26). Personal Communication. Interview.

Baldwin, Clive. (2006). Minority Rights in Kosovo under International Rule. *Minority Rights Group International*, 1-40. Retrieved from www.refworld.org

Baskin, Mark. (2001, June 5). Lessons Learned on UNMIK Judiciary. *Pearson Peacekeeping Center*, 1-35.

Bauer, Paul, C. and Fatke, Matthias. (2014, February 05). Direct Democracy and Political Trust: Enhancing Trust, Initiating Distrust–or Both? *Swiss Political Science Review*, 20(1), 49–69.

Barigazzi, Jacopo. (2018, January 8). Where Brexit will hurt most in Europe. *Politico*. Retrieved from www.politico.eu

BBC News. (2018, June 23). 'Double eagle' celebration provokes Serbs. Retrieved from www.bbc.com

BBC. (2006, May 22). Timeline: Break-up of Yugoslavia. Retrieved from www.news.bbc.co.uk

Berg, L., and Hjerm, M. (2010). National Identity and Political Trust. *Perspectives on European Politics and Society*, 11(4), 390–407. doi:10.1080/15705854.2010.524403.

Berman, E. M. (1997). Dealing with cynical citizens. *Public Administration Review*, 57(2),105-112.

Betts, Wendy, S. Carlson, Scott, N. and Grisvold, Gregory. (2001). The Post-Conflict Transitional Administration of Kosovo and the Lessons-Learned in Efforts to Establish a Judiciary and Rule of Law. *Michigan Journal of International Law*, 22(3), 1-20.

Bilefsky, Dan. (2008, February 18). Kosovo Declares Its Independence From Serbia. New York Times. Retrieved from www.nytimes.com

BIRN. (2018, January 29). Balkan States 'Expected to Sign Truth Commission Agreement'. *Balkan Insight*. Retrieved from www.balkaninsight.com

Blind, Peri, K. (2006). Building Trust in Government in the Twentieth Century: Review of Literature and Emerging Issues. UNDESA, 1-31. Retrieved from www.unpan1.un.org

Blakaj, Lumturie. (2015, January 5). Opozita Nuk e Voton Gjykatën Speciale. *Zëri*. Retrieved from www.zeri.info

Bota Sot. (2015, March 3). Hapet rruga nga Qeveria për themelimin e Gjykatës Speciale. VV-ja, kjo Gjykatë është mbi shtetin e Kosovës. Retrieved from www.botasot.info

Buchanan, Allen. (2002). Political Legitimacy and Democracy. *Ethics*, 112, 689-719.

Bouckaert, Geert, and Steven Van de Walle. (2003). Comparing measures of citizen trust and user satisfaction as indicators of 'good governance': difficulties in linking trust and satisfaction indicators. *International Review of Administrative Sciences 69*(3), 329-343.

Boyce, Carolyn and Neale, Palena, (2006). Conducting In-Depth Interviews: A Guide for Designing & Conducting In-Depth Interviews for Evaluation Input. *Pathfinder International Tool Series*, 1-16.

Brehm, J. and Rahn, W. (1997). Individual-Level Evidence for the Causes and Consequences of Social Capital. *American Journal of Political Science*, 41, 999-1023.

Brewer, P. R., Gross, K., Aday, S., and Willnat, L. (2004). International trust and public opinion about world affairs. *American Journal of Political Science*, 48, 93–109.

BTI. (2018). *Kosovo Country Report*. Retrieved from www.bti-project.org

Cai, R. (2004). Interaction between trust and transaction cost in Industrial Districts. *Virginia Polytechnic Institute*, 1-64. Retrieved from www.cholar.lib.vt.edu

Call, Charles. (2007). *Constructing Justice and Security After War*. Washington DC: United States Institute of Peace.

Catterberg, Gabriel, and Moreno, Alejandro. (2006). The Individual Bases of Political Trust: Trends in New and Established Democracies. *International Journal of Public Opinion Research*, 18(1), 31-48.

Chang, E. C., and Chu, Y. (2006). Corruption and trust: Exceptionalism in Asian democracies? *Journal of Politics*, 68(2), 259-271.

Chicago Council on Foreign Relations. (2006). Global Views 2004: American Public Opinion and Foreign Policy. Ann Arbor, MI: *Inter-university Consortium for Political and Social Research*.

Chicago Tribute. (1999, March 30). Milosevic increases ethnic cleansing. Retrieved from www.chicagotribune.com

Choi, E., and Woo, J. (2016). The origins of political trust in east Asian democracies: Psychological, cultural, and institutional arguments. *Japanese Journal of Political Science*, 17(3), 410-426. doi: https://doi.org/10.1017/S1468109916000165

Christon, Van. (2008, December). The Four Albanian Vilayets During the Ottoman Empire. *Frosnia*. Retrieved from www.frosina.org

Cierco, Teresa, and Reis, Liliana. (2014). EULEX's Impact on the Rule of Law in Kosovo. *Revista De Ciencia Politica*, 34(3), 645-663.

Citrin, Jack. (1974). Comment: The Political Relevance of Trust in Government. *American Political Science Review*, 68(3),973–988.

Clark, Wesley, K. (2018, April. 11). Don't wait for the western Balkans to blow up again. The U.S. and the E.U. must act. *The Washington Post*. Retrieved from www.washingtonpost.com

Collis, J., and Hussey, R. (2003). *Business Research: A Practical Guide for Undergraduate and Postgraduate Students*. Palgrave Macmillan Houndmills: Basingstoke, Hampshire.

Council of Europe. (2010, May 31). Second Opinion on Kosovo. Advisory Committee on the framework convention for the protection of national minorities, 1-52. ACFC/OP/II(2009)004

Cook, K.S. (2001). *Trust In Society*. New York: Russell Sage Foundation.

Cook, K., and Hardin, R. (1998). *Trust and Governance* (Braithwaite V. & Levi M., Eds.). Russell Sage Foundation, 9-27.

Cook, Timonty, E., and Gronke, Paul. (2001, April). The Dimensions of Institutional Trust: How Distinct is Public Confidence in the Media? *Midwest Political Science Association*, Chicago, 1-26.

Cooper, Christopher A., H Gibbs Knotts, and Brenna, Kathleen, M. (2008). The Importance of Trust in Government for Public Administration: The Case of Zoning. *Public Administration Review*, 68(3), 459-468.

Corrin, Chris. (2003). Developing Policy on Integration and Reconstruction In Kosovo. *Development in Practice*, 13(2), 189-207.

Crepaz, Markus, L. and Polk, Jonathan. (2012). Democracy in crisis? An analysis of various dimensions and sources of support for democracy. *Joint Research Project*, University of Georgia and University of Gothenburg, World Values Survey, 1-30.

Creswell, J. (1998). *Qualitative Inquiry and Research Design; Choosing Among Five Traditions*. London, New Delhi, Thousand Oaks, Sage Publications.

Dalton, R. J. (2004). *Democratic challenges, democratic choices: The erosion of political support in advanced industrial democracies*. Oxford: Oxford University Press.

Della Porta, Donattella. (2000). *Social Capital, Beliefs in Government, and Political Corruption.* In Disaffected Democracies. What's Troubling the Trilateral Countries?, edited by S. J. Pharr and R. D.Putnam. New Jersey: Princeton University Press.

Demekas, Dimitri, G., Herderschee, Johannes, and Jacobs, Davina. (2001). Progress in Institution-Building and the Economic Policy Challenges ahead. *IMF Report,* 1-35.

Department of Peacekeeping Operations. (2011). The United Nations Rule of Law Indicators: Implementation Guide and Project Tools. United Nations Publication, 1-137.

Derks, Maria, and Price, Megan. (2010, November). The EU and Rule of Law Reform in Kosovo. Conflict Research Unit, *Netherlands Institute for International Relations,* 1-62.

Deutsche Welle. (2012, September 12). International Steering Group passes sovereignty to Kosovo. Retrieved from www.dw.de

Devenport, Mark. (1999, July 1). Analysis: UN Faces Kosovo Challenge. *Global Policy Forum.*

Dezfuli, César. (2018, February 16). 51st state: Kosovo's bond to the US. *The Guardian.* Retrieved fromwww.theguardian.com

Dobbs, Michael. (1981, April 3). Yugoslavs Take Emergency Steps In Face of Ethnic Disturbance. *Washington Post.* Retrieved from www.washingtonpost.com

Doyle, Nicholas, and Morina, Engjëllushe. (2013, October). The United Kingdom's Foreign Policy towards Kosovo - A policy perspective. *Group for Legal and Political Studies and Prishtina Council on Foreign Relations,* 7, 1-22.

Duch, R.M. (2001). A development model of heterogeneous economic voting in new democracies. *American Political Science Review,* 95, 895-910.

Duck, S. (1997). *The Handbook of Personal Relationships: Theory, Research and Interventions.* New York: Wiley.

DW. (2018, November 21). Kosovo slaps 100 percent tariff on Serbian goods after Interpol bid failure. Retrieved from www.dw.com

Easton, D. (1965). *A System Analysis of the Political Life.* Chicago, IL: The University of Chicago Press.

Easton, David. (1975). A re-assessment of the concept of political support. *British Journal of Political Science,* 5(4), 435-457.

Easterbrook P. J, Berlin J. A, Gopalan R, et al. (1991). Publication bias in research. *Lancet,* 337, 867-72.

Elshani, Hafize. (2018, September 20). Personal Communicating. Interview.

Elsie, Robert. (2010). *Independent Albania (1912-1944): Historical dictionary of Albania.* Lanham: Scarecrow Press.

Erlingsson, Gissur, Linde, Jonas and Öhrvall, Richard. (2015). Distrust in Utopia? Public Perceptions of Corruption and Political Support in Iceland before and after the Financial Crisis of 2008. *Government and Opposition*. 51, 1-27.

Espinal, R. and J. Hartlyn. (2006, March). Performance Still Matters Explaining Trust in Government in the Dominican Republic. *Comparative Political Studies*, 39, (2), 200-23.

European Rule of Law Mission. (2018). EULEX Kosovo. Retrieved from www.eulex-kosovo.eu

European Commission. (2014). Serbia Membership status, candidate country.

European Commission. (2014). Kosovo Progress Report.

European Commission. (2018). Kosovo 2018 Report. *SWD*, Strasbourg, 156, 1-86.

European Commission. (2018, April 17). Key findings of the 2018 Report on Kosovo. Brussels, 1-3.

European Commission. (2018, June 12). International Relations: Western Balkans.

European Commission. (2018, July 18). Visa Liberalization: Commission confirms Kosovo fulfils all required benchmarks.

European Commission Report. (2018, July 18). Update on the implementation of the remaining benchmarks of the visa liberalization roadmap by Kosovo. Brussels, 18.7.2018 COM (2018) 543, 1-12.

European Commission. (2014). Serbia membership status, candidate country.

European Council. (2015, October 27). Stabilisation and Association Agreement (SAA) between the European Union and Kosovo signed. Retrieved from www.consilium.europa.eu

European Union. (2008, June 11). Council Decision on amending Joint Action on the European Union Rule of Law Mission in Kosovo. *Official Journal of the European Union*, L 146/5.

European Union Office in Kosovo. (2017, July 3). Stabilization and Association Agreement between EU and Kosovo. Retrieved from www.eeas.europa.eu

European Union Mission in Kosovo. (2018). Executive Division. Retrieved from eulex-kosovo.eu

European Western Balkans. (2018, October 10). Getting to an Agreement between Serbia and

European Western Balkans. (2018, May 30). Reconciliation and Good Neighbourly Relations in the Western Balkans: A Continuing Dilemma? Retrieved from europeanwesternbalkans.com

Fang, Songying, and Stone, Randall. W. (2010). Trust and International Organizations. *Political Science*, University of Rochester. 1-41.

Federal Foreign Office. (2018, November). Kosovo: Political Relations.

Fison, Maryrose. (2011, October 30). Tensions between Serbs and Albanians flare up in Kosovo. *The Independent UK*. Retrieved from www.independent.co.uk

Focus News Agency. (2015, April 22). Hashim Thaçi to Be Arrested If He Enters Serbia. Retrieved from www.focus-fen.net

Freedman, D. A., Pisani, R., and Purves, R. A. (2007). *Statistics*. 4th ed. New York: W. W. Norton & Company.

Fukuyama, Francis. (1996). *Trust: The Social Virtues and The Creation of Property*. Free Press Paperbacks.

Fukuyama, Francis. (1999). The Great Disruption: Human Nature and the Reconstitution of Social Order. *The Atlantic Monthly*, 272, 55-80.

Gashi, Adem, and Musliu, Betim. (2013). Justice System Reform in Kosovo. *Kosovo Law Institute*, 1-37.

Gazeta Express. (2015, April 16). The 16th Anniversary of Kosovo Albanians Exodus. Retrieved from www.gazetaexpress.com

Gazeta Express. (2014, April 20). Vetëvendosje përsëri kundër EULEX'it dhe Gjykatës Speciale. Retrieved from www.gazetaexpress.com

Gardner, Andrew. (2014, December 9). Kosovo Forms New Government. *Politico*. Retrieved from http://www.politico.eu/article/kosovo-forms-new-government

Giddens, Anthony. (1984). *The constitution of society: Outline of the theory of structuration*. Berkeley and Los Angeles: University of California Press.

GLPS. (2013, May). Financing of Political Parties in Kosovo,—can controllability and transparency help? *Policy Report by the Group for Legal and Political Studies*, (5), 1-39.

Godefroidt, A., Langer, A., and Meuleman, B. (2015). Developing political trust in a developing country. *Centre for Research on Peace and Development (CRPD)*. KU Leuven, 1-19.

Gordy, Eric. (2018, October 10). Why Borders Are Not the Problem or the Solution for Serbia and Kosovo. *Foreign Affairs Magazine*. Retrieved from www.foreignaffairs.com

Gray, Andrew. (2018, August 13). Angela Merkel: No Balkan border changes. *Politico*.

Green, M., Friedman, J., and Bennet, R. (2012, July 18). *Rebuilding the Police in Kosovo. Foreign Policy*. Princeton University. Retrieved from www.foreignpolicy.com

Gripshi, Genc. (2014). *Historia e Peqinit*. Tiranë, Albania: Shtëpia Botuese "8 Nëntori."

Griffiths, Phil. (2015). The "Necessity" of a Socially Homogeneous Population: The Ruling Class Embraces Racial Exclusion. *Labour History*, 108, 123-144.

Hajdari, Azem, Ibrahimi, Shpresa, Hajdari, Albulena. (2014, June). Reforming of the Judicial System of Kosovo based on the Law no. 03/L-199 on Courts and its challenges. *ILIRIA International Review*, 4(1), 249-270.

Haxhibeqiri, Njomza. (2018, February 14). Transitional justice in Kosovo, 10 years after independence. Prishtina Insight. Retrieved from www.prishtinainsight.com

Hazan, P. (2006, July). Morocco: Betting on a Truth and Reconciliation Commission. *United States Institute of Peace Paper*. Washington DC: United States Institute of Peace, 1-16.

Hetherington, Marc, J. (1998). The political relevance of political trust. *American Political Science Review*, 92, 791-808.

Hetherington, M. J. (2005). *Why Trust Matters: Declining Political Trust and the Demise of American Liberalism*. Princeton: Princeton University Press.

Hooghe, M., and Marien, S. (2010). Does political trust matter? An empirical investigation into the relation between political trust and support for law compliance. *European Journal of Political Research*. 50(2), 267–291.

Hopkins, Valerie. (2017, November 17). EU courts trouble with Kosovo scandal. *Politico*.

Hosmer, L. T. (1995). Trust: the connecting link between organizational theory and philosophical ethics. *The Academy of Management Review*, 20(2), 379-403.

Human Rights Watch. (2014, April 11). Kosovo: Approve Special Court for Serious Abuses.

Huntington, Samuel, P. (1968). *Political Order in Changing Societies*. New Haven: Yale University Press.

Ian, Bache, and Taylor, Andrew. (2003). The Politics of Policy Resistance. Reconstructing Higher Education in Kosovo. *Journal of Public Policy*, 23(3), 279-300.

Independent International Commission on Kosovo. (2006). *The Kosovo Report*, 1-107.

Inglehart, Ronald. (1977). *The Silent Revolution Changing Values and Political Styles Among Western Publics*. Princeton, NJ: Princeton University Press.

Inglehart, Ronald F., and Wayne E. Baker. (2000). Modernization, Cultural Change, and the Persistence of Traditional Values. *American Sociological Review*, 65, 19-51.

International Commission of Jurists. (2016). Uncharted Transition: the "Integration" of the Justice System in Kosovo. *Ministry of Foreign Affairs of Finland*, 1-28.

International Court of Justice. (2010, July 22). Accordance with international law of the unilateral declaration of independence in respect of Kosovo. *Advisory Opinion of 22 July 2010*, 1-54.

International Crisis Group. (2013, February 19). Serbia and Kosovo: The Path to Normalization. Europe Report 223, Brussels, ii. Retrieved from www.crisisgroup.org

Jamal, Amaney, and Nooruddin, Irfan. (2010). The democratic utility of trust: A cross-national analysis. *Journal of Politics*, 71, 45-59.

Jansson, Frederik, and Eriksson, Kimmo. (2015). Cooperation and Shared Beliefs about Trust in the Assurance Game. *PLoS One*. 2015; 10(12), e0144191. Retrieved from www.ncbi.nlm. nih.gov

Jelavich, Barbara (1999). *History of the Balkans: Eighteenth and nineteenth centuries*. Cambridge University: Cambridge University Press.

Jelavich, Charles and Jelavich, Barbara. (1986). *The Establishment of the Balkan National States*. Vol. III. London and Seattle: University of Washington Press.

Johnston, Michael. (2005). *Political Parties and Democracy in Theoretical and Practical Perspectives: political finance policy, parties, and democratic Development.* Washington, DC: NDI.

Judah, Tim. (2011, February 17). Yugoslavia: 1918 – 2003. BBC. Retrieved from www.bbc.co.uk

Kaase, Max. (2007). Interpersonal trust, political trust and non-institutionalized political participation in Western Europe. *West European Politics,* 22(3),1-21.

Kaase, Max, and Newton, Kenneth. (1995). *Beliefs in Government.* Vol. 5 of Beliefs in Government. Ed. Kenneth Newton. Oxford: Oxford University Press.

Kaufman, Joyce P. (1999, September). NATO and the Former Yugoslavia: Crisis, Conflict and the   Atlantic Alliance. *Journal of Conflict Studies,* 19(2), 1-30.

Kazmer, Michelle, M., and Xie, Bo (2008). Qualitative interviewing in internet studies: Playing with the media, playing with the method. *Information, Communication, and Society,* 11(2), 257-278.

Kelley, Kate, Clark, Belinda, Brown, Vivienne, and Sitzia, John. (2003, May 1). Good practice in the conduct and reporting of survey research. *International Journal for Quality in Health Care,* 15(3), 261–266.

Keukeleire, Stephan, Kalaja, Arben, and Çollaku, Artan. (2011, February). The EU and Kosovo: Structural Diplomacy in Action, but on the basis of one-sided paradigm? *The Center for the Study of International Governance,* 1-7.

Koha Ditore. (2014, April 14). Borg Oliver: Special Court Against KLA will Damage Kosovo. Retrieved from http://koha.net/?id=27&l=6264

KoSSev. (2018, August 27). Thaci: No partition of Kosovo, no land swap. *N1 News.*

Kosovo Assembly. (2007, February 2). Comprehensive Proposal For the Kosovo Status Settlement, 1- 59. Retrieved from www.kuvendikosoves.org

Kosovo Specialist Chambers & Specialist Prosecutor's Office. (2018). Background. Retrieved from www.scp-ks.org/en/documents

Kosovo Specialist Chambers. (2018, March). Kosovo Specialist Chambers and Specialist Prosecutor's Office – First Report 2016-2018, 1-64. Retrieved from www.scp-ks.org

Kosovo Police. (2018). History. Retrieved from http://www.kosovopolice.com/en/history

Kosumi, Vebi. (2018, November 14). Personal Communication. Interview.

Kosumi, Vebi. (2014, May). Can the European Union Resolve the Life-Cycle of the Conflict in Kosovo? *Queens Political Review,* 2(1), 59-76.

Krasniqi, Gëzim. (2016). Rising up in the world: Kosovo's quest for international recognition. *Prishtina Insight.* Retrieved from www.prishtinainsight.com

Krasniqi, Gëzim. (2015, January). Country Report on Citizenship Law: Kosovo. *European University Institute,* 1-37.

Krishna, A. (2000). Creating and Harnessing Social Capital, in P. Dasgupta & I. Serageldin (Eds.), Social Capital: A Multifaceted Perspective, 71-93.

Kuchenkova, A. V. (2017). Interpersonal Trust in Russian Society. *Sociological Research*, 56(1), 81–96.

Kuenzi, Michelle. (2008). Social capital and political trust in West Africa. *Afrobarometer*, 96, 1-32.

Kurteshi, Sami. (2012, December 26). In Person Interview.

Lameck, Wilfred Uronu. (2013, July). Sampling Design, Validity and Reliability in General Social Survey. *International Journal of Academic Research in Business and Social Sciences*, 3(7), 212-2018.

Law No. 03/L-047. On the protection and promotion of the rights and communities and their members in Kosovo. Assembly of Kosovo. Retrieved from www.assembly-kosova.org

Lehne, Stefan. (2012, March). Kosovo and Serbia: Toward a Normal Relationship, 1-16.

Leopold, Evelyn. (2007, July 20). Kosovo pushes independence after UN action fails. *Reuters*.

Lemay-Hébert, Nicolas. (2009). State-building from the outside-in: UNMIK and its paradox. *JPIA*, 65- 86. Retrieved from https://jpia.princeton.edu/sites/jpia/files/2009-4.pdf

Lewicki, R. J., McAllister, D. J. and Bies, R. J. (1998). Trust and distrust: new relationships and realities. *The Academy of Management Review*, 23(3), 438-458.

Levi, Margaret. (1996). Social and Unsocial Capital: A Review Essay of Robert Putnam's Making Democracy Work. *Politics & Society*, 24(1), 45-55.

Levi, Margaret. (1998). *A State of Trust. In Trust and Governance* (V. Braithwaite and M. Levi Eds). New York: Russell Sage Foundation.

Levi, Margaret, and Stoker, Laura. (2000, June). Political Trust and Trustworthiness. *Annual Review of Political Science*, 3(1), 475-507.

Levi, Margaret, Sacks, Audrey, and Tyler, Tom. (2009) Conceptualizing legitimacy, measuring legitimating beliefs. *American Behavioral Scientist*, 53(3), 354-375.

MacDowall, Andrew. (2018, August 22). Could land swap between Serbia and Kosovo lead to conflict? *The Guardian*. Retrieved from www.theguardian.com

Maliqi, Reshat. (2016, June). Corruption, the Challenge for Kosovo Institutions. *European Journal of Multidisciplinary Studies*, 1(2), 204-209.

Mabillard, Vincent and Pasquier, Martial. (2015). Transparency and Trust in Government: A Two-Way Relationship, *Yearbook of Swiss Administrative Sciences*, 23-34.

Maloy, J. S. (2009, April). Two concepts of trust. *The Journal of Politics*, 71(2), 492-505.

Malpas, J. (2012). *The Stanford Encyclopedia of Philosophy* (Edward N. Zalta Ed.). Stanford: Center for the Study of Language and Information.

Martin, Philip L., Martin, Susan Forbes, and Weil, Patrick. (2006). *Managing Migration: The Promise of Cooperation*. New York: Lexington Books.

Manzetti, Luigi, and Wilson, Carole, J. (2007). Why Do Corrupt Governments Maintain Public Support? *Comparative Political Studies,* 40(8), 949-970.

Mayer, R., Davis J., and Schoorman F. (1995). An integrative model of organizational trust. *The Academy of Management Review,* 20(3), 709–734.

Matebesi, Sethulego. (2017). *Civil strife against local governance: Dynamics of community protests in contemporary South Africa.* Toronto: Barbara Budrich Publishers.

McLaughlin, Daniel. (2017, November 24). New EU-backed court for Kosovo war crimes awaits its first case. *Irish Times.* Retrieved from www.irishtimes.com

Milekic, Sven. (2018, July 18). Balkan Govts Dodge Signing Truth Commission Declaration. *BIRN.*

Mill, John, Stuart. 1861. *Considerations on Representative Government.* London: Parker, Son, and Bourn.

Miller, A. H. and O. Listhaug. (1990, July). Political Parties and Confidence in Government: A Comparison of Norway, Sweden and the United States. *British Journal of Political Science,* 20(3), 357-386.

Miller, A. H. (1974, September). Political Issues and Trust in Government, 1964-1970. *American Political Science Review,* 68(3), 951-972.

Miller, Arthur, H. (1974b). Rejoinder to 'Comment' by Jack Citrin: Political Discontent or Ritualism? *American Political Science Review,* 68(3), 989–1001.

Ministry of Foreign Affairs. (2018). Kosovo's New Foreign Policy Roadmap. From www.mfa-ks.net

Mishler, W., and Rose, R. (1997). Trust, distrust and skepticism: Popular evaluations of civil and political institutions in post-communist societies. *The Journal of Politics,* 59(2), 418-451.

Mishler, William, and Richard, Rose. (2001). What are the Origins of Political Trust? Testing Institutional and Cultural Theories in Post-Communist Societies. *Comparative Political Studies* 34(1), 30-62.

Mishler, William, and Richard, Rose. (2005). What Are the Political Consequences of Trust? A Test of Cultural and Institution al Theories in Russia. *Comparative Political Studies,* 38(9), 1050-1078.

Mistzal, B.A. (1996). *Trust in Modern Societies: The Search for the Bases of Social Order.* Cambridge: Polity Press.

Molla, Admir. (2018, October 2). Personal Communication. Interview.

Morelli, Vincent, L. (2018, August 13). Kosovo: Background and U.S. Relations. *Congressional Research Service,* 1-17.

Morina, Die. (2018, January 18). Push to Scrap Special Court Fails Again in Kosovo. *BIRN.*

Mulaj, Klejda. (2008). Resisting an Oppressive Regime: The Case of Kosovo Liberation Army. *Studies in Conflict & Terrorism,* 31(12), 1103-1119.

Mušanović, Meris. (2020, March 31). Kosovo Specialist Chambers: Providing compensations for victims. *European Western Balkans.*

Nahzi, Fron. (2020, April 7). Applauding Kurti's Fall, the US is Testing Kosovo's Loyalty. *BIRN.*

National Council for European Integration. (2015). National Strategy for European Integration: Kosovo 2020, 1-64. Retrieved from www.kryeministri-ks.net

NATO. (2018). NATO's role in relation to the conflict in Kosovo. Retrieved from www.nato.int

NATO. (2009, April 9). NATO's role in Kosovo. Retrieved from www.nato.int

NATO. (2014, January 14). Secretary General's Annual Report 2013, 1-45. Retrieved from http://www.nato.int/cps/en/natohq/opinions_106247.htm?selectedLocale=en

NBC News. (2013) Q&A: The history of strife in Kosovo. Ethnic Albanians, Serbs have tussled over region for years. Retrieved from www.nbcnews.com

Nething, Aaron. (2018, November 26). Personal Communication. Interview. Newton, Kenneth. (2001). Trust, Social Capital, Civil Society, and Democracy. *International Political Science Review,* 22 (2), 201–214.

Newton, Kenneth. (2013). Social and Political Trust. *Norwegian Social Science Data Services*, 1-13.

Norman, Laurence, and Hinshaw, Drew. (2018, August 31). U.S., Germany at Odds Over Serbia-Kosovo Land Swap. *The Wall Street Journal.*

Norris, Pippa. (1999). Critical Citizens: Global Support for Democratic Government. Oxford: Oxford University Press.

Nye, Joseph. (1967). Corruption and Political Development: A Cost-Benefit Analysis. *American Political Science Review*, 61, 417-427.

Ocampo, J. A. (2006, September 6-8). "Congratulatory Message," The Regional Forum on Reinventing Government in Asia. Seoul, Korea: United Nations Department of Economic and Social Affairs and the Ministry of Government Administration and Home Affairs, Republic of Korea.

OECD. (2013). Trust in government, policy effectiveness and the governance agenda, in *Government at a Glance* 2013, OECD Publishing, Paris.

Office of the Prime Minister. (2009). Prime Minister Thaçi: Our commitment and our dedication to a multi-ethnic society will not stop – this is for the good of Kosovo.

Ombudsperson Institution in Kosovo Report. (2004, July). Kosovo Ombudsperson of Kosovo Fourth Annual report 2003 – 2004, 1-54. Retrieved from www.ombudspersonkosovo.org

Osmanli Atlasi: XX, Yüzyil Başlar. (1970). Harta zyrtare e Vilajetit të Kosovës nën osmanët gjatë viteve '70 të shek. XIX! Retrieved from http://www.njekomb.com/?p=6069

OSCE. (2018, October 10). Profile of Mitrovica/Mitrovicë North. *Organization for Security and Co-operation in Europe*. Retrieved from https://www.osce.org/mission-in-kosovo/122119.

OSCE. (2012, January). Independence of the Judiciary in Kosovo: Institutional and Functional Dimensions, 1-29. Retrieved from https://www.osce.org/kosovo/87138?download=true

OSCE. (2010, April). Intimidation of the Judiciary: Security of Judges and Prosecutors. *Department of Human Rights and Communities*, 3, 1-7.

OSCE. (2003, October. Parallel Structures in Kosovo. *Department of Human Rights and Rule of Law*, 1-44.

OSCE. (2001, November 19). First official results in Kosovo election announced.

Pahumi, Nevila. (2007). The Consolidation of Albanian Nationalism: The League of Prizren 1878-1881. (Master's Thesis). *University of Michigan*,1-91.

Parker, Suzanne, L., Parker, Glenn, R., and Towner, Terri, L. (2014). Rethinking the Meaning and Measurement of Political Trust. *Political Trust and Disenchantment with Politics*, 59-82.

Patton, Michael Q. (2002). *Qualitative research and evaluation methods* (3rd ed.). Thousand Oaks, CA: Sage.

President of the Republic of Kosovo. (2018). The KSF a professional force ready for every challenge.

President of the Republic of Kosovo. (2018). President Thaçi received a letter of congratulations from the US President, Donald Trump. Retrieved from www.president-ksgov.net

President of the Republic of Kosovo. (2012, May 24). President Jahjaga received the Minister for European Affairs of Denmark. Retrieved from www.president-ksgov.net

Pineles, Dean B. (2018, August 19). War Crimes Indictments Could Wreck Kosovo-Serbia Talks. *Balkan Insight*. Retrieved from www.balkaninsight.com

Pula, Erëza. (2017, October). Determinants of Trust in Institutions in Kosovo: An empirical perspective. *Group for Legal and Political Studies*, 4, 1-27.

Putnam, Robert (1993). Making democracy work. Princeton, NJ: Princeton University Press.

Putnam, Robert (2000). Bowling Alone: The Collapse and Revival of American Community. New York: Simon and Schuster.

Radio Free Europe. (2008, February 18). Kosovo Celebrates A Decade Of Sovereignty.

Radosavljevic, Zoran. (2018, September 10). Kosovo-Serbia talks break down as tensions mount again. *EURACTIV*.

Rapoport, Anatol. (1998). *Decision Theory and Decision Behavior*, 2nd edition. London: Macmillan Press.

Raxhimi, Altin. (2019, January 25). Kosovo academics brace for controversial ethnic land swaps. *Nature International Journal of Science*.

Raynard, Mia & Johnson, Gerry, and Greenwood, Royston. (2015). *Institutional Theory and Strategic Management*. (3r Ed), Palgrave Macmillan.

Report from Group for Legal and Political Studies. (2018, October). Rule of Law Performance Index in Kosovo. *ROLPIK*, 4, 1-32.

Republic of Kosovo. (2018). Justice System. Retrieved from www.rks-gov.net

Republic of Kosovo Ombudsperson (2018). The Mission of Ombudsperson Institution. Retrieved from https://oik-rks.org/

Resolution 1244. (1999, June 10). *United Nations Security Council*. S/RES/1244 (1999).

Richards, Katharine. (2013). International Trials, Rule of Law & Local Legal Consciousness in Croatia: Can International Justice Transform Local Norms? *University of Connecticut-Storrs*, 1-210.

Riker, William H. (1980). Political Trust as Rational Choice. In: Lewin L., Vedung E. (eds) Politics as Rational Action. Theory and Decision Library (An International Series in the *Philosophy and Methodology of the Social and Behavioral Sciences*), 23, 1-24. Springer, Dordrecht.

Ristic, Marija. (2017, January 4). Hague Tribunal Prepares for Shutdown in 2017. *Balkan Insight*.

Robinson, E. Scott, Stoutenborough, James W, and Vedlitz, Arnold. (2017). *Understanding Trust in Government: Environmental Sustainability, Fracking, and Public Opinion in American Politics*. New York: Routledge.

Rossi, Michael. (2018, September 19). Partition in Kosovo Will Lead to Disaster. *Foreign Policy*.

Rothstein, Bo. (2003). Social capital, economic growth and quality of government: The causal mechanism. *New Political Economy*, 8(1), 49-71. d

Rothstein, Bo, and Eek, Daniel. (2009). Political Corruption and Social Trust: An Experimental Approach. *Rationality and Society*. 21, 81-112.

Rothstein, Bo, & Stolle, D. (2008). The state and social capital. An institutional theory of generalized trust. *Comparative Politics*, 40(4), 441-467.

Rrecaj, Besfort. (2018, September 26). Personal Communication. Interview.

RTK Live. (2015, April 22). Serbia Lost a Chance Of Reconciliation with Kosovo. Retrieved from http://www.rtklive.com/en/?id=2&r=1679

Rudic, Filip. (2017, May 16). Rabid Anti-Albanian Sentiment Grips Serbian Media. *Balkan Insight*.

Saeed, Saim. (2017, November 16). Top judge quits EU Kosovo mission, alleging corruption. *Politico*.

Sahatqija, Teuta. (2018, December 4). In Person Interview.

Sahatqija, Teuta. (2014, October 2). Beyond "soft" issues: The Women's Caucus of Kosovo speaks up. *Chicago Policy Review*.

Salihu, Hyzri. (2018, November 26). Personal Communication. Interview.

Samuels, Kirsti. (2005). Sustainability and Peace Building: A Key Challenge. *Development in Practice*, 15(6), 728-736.

Saracini, Klotilda. (2015, April 21). Kosovë, aktivitete në kuadër të "Javës për Personat e Zhdukur". Agjencia Telegrafike Shqiptare. Retrieved from www.ata.gov.al

Schelling, T. C. (1957). Bargaining, Communication, and Limited War. *Conflict Resolution*, 11, 19-36.

Schneider, Irena. (2017). Can We Trust Measures of Political Trust? Assessing Measurement Equivalence in Diverse Regime Types. *Soc Indic Res*, 133(3), 963–984.

Schiffman, Leon, Shawn Thelen, and Sherman, Elaine. (2010). Interpersonal and political trust: modeling levels of citizens' trust. *European Journal of Marketing*, 44(3/4), 369-381,

Scorgie, Lindsay. (2003). Kosovo and the International Community: The Prolonging and Exacerbation of a Crisis. *A worldwide Journal of Politics*, 1-40. Retrieved from

Security Council Report. (2003, December 10). Standards for Kosovo, 1-16.

Sejdiu, Bekim. (2018, November 28). Personal Communicating. Interview.

Seligson, Mitchell. (2002). The Impact of Corruption on Regime Legitimacy: A Comparative Study of Four Latin American Countries. *Journal of Politics*, 64(2), 408-433.

Senèze, Nicolas. (2018). Diocese for Kosovo. *La Croix*.

Shao, R., Aquino, K., and Freeman, D. (2008). Beyond moral reasoning: A review of moral identity research and its implications for business ethics. *Business Ethics Quarterly*, 18(4), 513–540.

Shatri, Xhemajl. (2013, March 16). Personal Communication. Interview.

Shi, Tianjian. (2001). Cultural Values and Political Trust: A Comparison of the People's Republic of China and Taiwan. Comparative Politics, 33(4), 401-419.

Shepsle, Kenneth, A. (1995). Studying institutions: some lessons from rational choice. In James Farr, John S. Dryzek, & Stephen T. Leonard (Eds.), *Political science in history* (276-285). Cambridge, UK: Cambridge University Press.

Skendi, Stavro (1967). *The Albanian National Awakening*. Princeton: Princeton University Press, 1967.

Smolar, Piotr. (2013, April 30). Serbia and Kosovo sign historic agreement. *The Guardian*.

Sopjani, Enver. (2011). *Military Policies and Policing in Kosova since 1999.The Role of the International Community*. Berlin: Internationale Politik.

Silverman, David. (2005). *Doing qualitative research: a practical handbook* (2nd ed.). London: Sage.

SRA and MRS. (2005, October). Data Protection Act 1999: Guidelines for Social Research. *Social Research Association*,1-63.

Stake, Robert, E. (1995). *The Art of Case Study Research: Perspective in Practice*. London: Sage.

Stake, Robert, E. (2005). *Qualitative case studies*. In N.K. Denzin & Y.S. Lincoln (Eds.) The Sage handbook of qualitative research (3rd ed.), 443-466. Thousand Oaks, CA: Sage.

Stappers, Marlies, and Unger, Utrecht, Thomas. (2018, July 16). How the Balkans Summit Failed on Truth and Justice. *Recom.*

Susila, Ihwan. (2014). Conceptualizing trust in electoral behavior in a transitional democracy: an intergenerational perspective. *University of Hull*, 1-263.

Tamilina, Larysa, and Tamilina, Natalya. (2017). Explaining the impact of formal institutions on social trust: A psychological approach. *Munich Personal RePEc Archive*, Paper No.84560.

Tariq, Shema, and Woodman, Jenny. (2013). Using mixed methods in health research. JRSM short reports, 4(6), 2042533313479197.

Tawil, Edward. (2009, February). Property Rights in Kosovo. A Haunting Legacy of Society in Transition." *International Center for Transitional Justice*, 1-69.

Tendler, Judith. (1997). *Good Governance in the Tropics.* Maryland: Johns Hopkins University Press.

The Independent, UK. (2018, February 17). Leading article: Kosovo: a triumph for intervention.

Thorpe, Nick. (2007, June 4). Kosovo contest for state symbols. *BBC.*

Torgler, Benno. (2007). Trust in International Organizations: An Empirical Investigation Focusing on the United Nations. *School of Economics and Finance* Discussion Papers and Working Papers Series 213, School of Economics and Finance, Queensland University of Technology, 65-93.

Tota, Elton. (2017, October 5). Kosovo is a sui generis case. *Balkan EU.*

Traynor, Ian. (2008, February 18). Spain exposes EU split as US leads recognition. *The Guardian.*

Tyler, Tom, R., and Yuen J. Huo. (2002). *Trust in the Law. Encouraging Public Cooperation with the Police and Courts.* New York: Russell Sage Foundation.

Wheeless, L. R., and Grotz J. (1977, March). The Measurement of Trust and Its Relationship to Self- Disclosure, Human Communication Research, 3 (3), 250-257.

Weiss, R. (1994). *Learning From Strangers; The Art and Method of Qualitative Interview Studies.* New York, The Free Press.

Wilson, P.A. (1997). Building Social Capital: A Learning Agenda for the Twenty-first Century. *Urban Studies,* 34(5-6), 745-760.

Unger, Thomas. (2018, May). Keeping the Promise Addressing Impunity in the Western Balkans. *Impunity Watch*, 1-48.

United Nations. (1998, March 11). Items relating to the situation in Kosovo, Federal Republic of Yugoslavia.

United Nations. (1998, March 31). Security Council imposes arms embargo on the federal republic of Yugoslavia.

United Nations. (1999). UNMIK background. United Nations Interim Administration Mission in Kosovo. http://www.un.org/en/peacekeeping/missions/unmik/background.shtml

United Nations Interim Administration Mission in Kosovo. (2003). Standards for Kosovo.

United Nations Security Council, UN Resolution 1244 (1999). June 10, 1999, S/RES/1244, Security Council official minutes of its 4011th meeting in New York.

UNMIK Emergency Decree No. 1999/1. (28 June 1999) (providing legal basis for the establishment of the Joint Advisory Council for Provisional Judicial Appointments).

USAID. (2018, February 12). Kosovo: Rule of Law and governance. Retrieved from www.usaid.gov

US Department of State. (2018, April). Kosovo Report. *Bureau of Democracy, Human Rights and Labor*, 1- 35. Retrieved from http://www.state.gov/j/drl/rls/hrrpt/2017/eur/277181.htm

United States Department of State. (2013). Kosovo 2013 Human Rights Report. Country Report for Human Rights Practices. *Bureau of Democracy, Human Rights and Labor*, Washington DC.

Vajdich, Daniel, P. (2018, October 11). Let Serbia and Kosovo define their own peace. *Washington Post*.

Van Der Meer, Tom, W. G. (2018, December). Political Trust and the "Crisis of Democracy". *Oxford University Press*, 1-23. DOI: 10.1093/acrefore/9780190228637.013.77

Vasa, Pashko. (1999). *The Truth on Albania and Albanians: Historical and Critical Issues*. London: National Press Agency, 1879. Reprint introduction by Robert Elsie. Centre for Albanian Studies. London, 1999.

Vickers, Mark, D. (2018). Personal Communication. Interview.

Visoka, Gëzim. (2018, February 16). Becoming Kosovo: Independence, legitimacy, future. *Kosovo 2.0*. Visoka, Gëzim (2017, September). Assessing the potential impact of the Kosovo Specialist Court. *PAX*, 1-48.

Walker, Sh. (2020, March 26). Kosovans look on aghast as government falls while coronavirus bites. The *Guardian*. Retrieved from www.theguardian.com

Walker, Shaun and MacDowall, Andrew. (2018, September 3). US-backed Kosovo land-swap border plan under fire from all sides. *The Guardian*. Retrieved from www.theguardian.com

Walter, Roberts, R. (1973). *Tito, Mihailović, and the Allies, 1941-1945*. Rutgers University Press.

Wang, C. (2016, June). Government Performance, Corruption, and Political Trust in East Asia. *Social Science Quarterly*, 97, 211-231.

Wippman, David. (2001). Kosovo and the Limits of International Law. *Fordham International Law Journal*, 25(1), 129-150.

Wong, Pui-Hang. (2016). How can political trust be built after civil wars? Evidence from post-conflict Sierra Leone. *Journal of Peace Research*, 53(6), 772-785.

Xharra, Arbana. (2018, November 20). Personal Communication. Interview.

Yang, Qing. (2012). A political story of political trust: Institutional settings, political performance, and political trust in East Asia. *Social Science Quarterly*, (97), 211-231.

Zaheer, Akbar, Bill McEvily, and Vincenzo Perrone. (1998). Does trust matter? Exploring the effects of interorganizational & interpersonal trust on performance. *Organization Science*, 9(2), 141-159.

Zainal, Zaidah. (2007, June 9). Case study as a research method. *Jurnal Kemanusiaan*, 9, 1-6.

Zivanovic, Maja. (2018, November 27). Serb Mayors in Kosovo to Resign Amid Tensions.

Zupančič, Rok, Pejič, Nina, Grilj, Blaž & Rodt, Annemarie Peen. (2018) The European Union Rule of Law Mission in Kosovo: An Effective Conflict Prevention and Peace-Building Mission?, *Journal of Balkan and Near Eastern Studies*, 20(6), 599-617.

APPENDICES

2018 Kosovo Survey

Doctoral Research September 19, 2018 – Special Court of War Crimes - Kosovo Case study

Part I: Statistical Questions – Anonymous answers (Pages 1-2)
Part II: Expert Interviews – Open ended questions (Page 3)

Part 1: The fill in the blank with X. Part 1 answers are anonymous, as they will be converted into percentages.

Q1: Rate how much you trust the following as sources of about the Kosovo Special Court on war crimes? *(Write an X next to your answer)*

	No Trust				*Complete Trust*
A. Newspaper / TV	1	2	3	4	5
B. Albanian Media	1	2	3	4	5
C. Serbian Media	1	2	3	4	5
D. Foreign Media	1	2	3	4	5
E. Kosovo government	1	2	3	4	5
F. Kosovo Specialist Court	1	2	3	4	5

Q2: Rate how much trust do you have in the following institutions? *(Write an X next to your answer)*

	No Trust				*Complete Trust*
A. Kosovo government	1	2	3	4	5
B. Kosovo police	1	2	3	4	5
C. UN	1	2	3	4	5

D. EU	1	2	3	4	5
E. NATO	1	2	3	4	5
F. Kosovo Specialist Court	1	2	3	4	5
G. Kosovo courts	1	2	3	4	5
H. US Embassy in Kosovo	1	2	3	4	5

Q3: Do you feel that you are a victim of war crimes?

Yes _____   No_____

Q4: How much do you care about the decisions the Specialist Court makes in war crimes trials?

Very Much _____   Some _____   A Little _____   Not At All _____

Q5: Do the decisions of the Specialist Court affect how safe you feel to live/work in Kosovo?

Very Much _____   Some _____   A Little _____   Not At All _____

Q6: Do you think the Specialist Court is effectively achieving justice for the war crimes that occurred during the 1998 Kosovo war?

Yes _____   No _____

Q7: How much confidence do you have in the Kosovan courts to conduct fair trials?

Very Much _____   Some _____   A Little _____   Not At All _____

Q8: How much confidence do you have in the international courts to conduct fair trials?

Very Much _____   Some _____   A Little _____   Not At All _____

Q9: Which judges are better able to make impartial decisions in trials of war crimes that took place in Kosovo?

A. Kosovo Specialist Court International judges _____

B. Kosovan judges _____

C. Serbian judges _____

Q10: Which judges are better able to make impartial decisions in genocide /human rights violations trials that took place in Kosovo?

A. International judges _____

B. Kosovan judges _____

C. Serbian judges _____

Q11: Do you think the EU has the best interest of Kosovo in mind when making decisions in the special court?

Yes _____   No _____

Q12: If a person committed an act of genocide in Kosovo, what is the best way to address the crime?

A. Kosovo court _____

B. Serbian Court _____

C. Kosovo Specialist Court _____

D. ICTY Hague Tribunal _____

Q13: If a person committed war crimes in Kosovo, what is the best way to address the crime?

A. Kosovo court _____

B. Court in country where the criminals came from _____

C. Kosovo Specialist Court _____

D. ICTY Hague Tribunal _____

Q14: If a KOSOVAN committed war crimes in Kosovo, what is the best way to address the crime?

A. Kosovo court _____

B. Serbian court _____

C. Kosovo Specialist Court _____

D. ICTY Hague Tribunal _____

Q15: If a SERBIAN committed war crimes in Kosovo, what is the best way to address the crime?

A. Kosovo court _____

B. Serbian court _____

C. Kosovo Specialist Court _____

D. ICTY Hague Tribunal _____

Demographics:

What is your age _____   **Are you Male**_____ **or Female** _____

What is your religion _____   **Country of Current Residence** _____

What is your ethnicity _____   **City, Country of Birth** _____

Your current job? *(Indicate answer with an X)*

____ Government	____ Military/Police	____ University
____ Administrative	____ International Organization	____ Author
____ Local NGO	____ Media/TV/Journalist	____ Business

Part II: <u>EXPERT INTERVIEWS</u>

If you work in government, police, journalist, university, NGO, agency, courts, embassy/consulate please answer any of the questions. Answer as many as you like.

1. What are your thoughts about the creation of the Kosovo Specialist court on war crimes?
2. What do you think will be the biggest challenges facing Specialist Court International Judges?
3. What difficulties do you envision the international judges will encounter when dealing with allegations of war crimes from KLA members, organized crime and other violations from 1998-2005?
4. What are some of the major problems today facing Kosovo Albanians who have immigrated outside the country?
5. What do you believe are currently some of the major challenges of the Specialist Court?
6. What about the current & future challenges of Kosovo people/government in dealing with the Specialist Court?
7. Do you think that the Kosovo Specialist Court has strengthened rule of law in Kosovo? Why? Why not?
8. How would you describe accountability, fairness and transparency of the Specialist Court in Hague, Kosovo courts and Kosovo government?
9. What are some local or international initiatives to strengthen rule of law in Kosovo?
10. What are the biggest obstacles to achieving justice for the violations of human rights /war crimes that occurred in the 1998 Kosovo war?
11. What are rule of law successes in Kosovo?
12. Safety and security in Kosovo today. Obstacles /factors that have improved the sense of security.
13. UK's role in training judges/prosecutors in Kosovo & combating organized crime in Kosovo & Albania.
14. US's role in strengthening rule of law in Kosovo.
15. Any additional comments? Any final thoughts about Kosovo/transitional Kosovo?
16. How do you define national identity?
17. How is national identity characterized among Albanians?
18. What connects the shared identity between Albania and Kosovo?
19. What has been United States in Kosovo's independence?
20. Which key factors influence political trust in government, the political elite, and the governmental institutions?

2012-2013 Kosovo Survey

Field Research conducted in Prishtina, Kosovo

INTRODUCTION

This research is being prepared for Ermira Babamusta, a PhD candidate at the University of West Virginia, in USA, Political Science / International Relations Major. The scientific study relates to the issue of Kosovo's independence in regard to a) the direction of the country, b) local concepts to other states and the image of Kosovo, c) the role of the international community, d) the process towards the EU, e) decisions of the leadership, f) decisions in regard to international relations, etc.

In 2007 Ermira completed her first research in Kosovo during her second Master's in Political Science and United Nations Diplomacy in New York. The conclusion of Ermira's scientific research recommended the 'declaration of independence' as the only alternative for Kosovo. The research was published in New York two weeks before independence was declared.

Title of scientific research I:
Ermira Babamusta, "Kosovo Status Talks: A Case Study on International Negotiations", Long Island University, The Brooklyn Center, 2008.

Title of scientific research II:
Political Trust in Kosovo: The Effects of Cultural and Institutional Factors on Trust

Ermira's contact: Ermira Babamusta   **Email**: ermirab@yahoo.com

Thank you for your participation and contribution in this scientific research. This study does not include the general public, but only experts involved directly with the Kosovo issue.

Please recommend the survey to your colleagues in the following fields:

a- Government/institutional post (in Kosovo, Albania and Diaspora).
b- Employed in foreign organization in the country (such as UN, EU, Red Cross, USAID, etc).
c- Academics: University professors (particularly in the fields of Politics/History).
d- Religious leaders.
e- Newspaper and TV journalists (in the role of media and public opinion).
f- Writers/Authors in relation to Kosovo.
g- Lawyers, Police officers.

Thank You,
Ermira Babamusta
New York

CONTENT

<u>Clarification:</u>

"Pre-Independence" includes the period before the war and independence (1999-2008).
"Post-Independence" includes 2008 and to date.

* This paper involves two phases:

   Phase I – ANONYMOUS – <u>Answering the survey</u> (pages 1-20)
         Fill in the survey with yes/no answers, evaluate, list according to importance.

   Phase II – Face-to-face Interviews with select experts.

DEMOGRAPHICS OF PARTICIPANT

(Insert X in ___ or write the appropriate answer based on the question)

*1 **Your gender** ___ Male ___Female

* 2 **Your age** (years old)_____

*3 **Your nationality**_____

* 4 **Place of birth** _____**Residence (town, country)**_____

*5 **What is your level of work/post?**

___ Government	___ Police/Army/Military
___ Institutional/Administrative	___ Foreign organization
___ Local organization	___ Corporation/Business/Agency
___ Higher education/University	___ Media/TV
___ Writer/Author	___ Religious group

* 6 **Are you currently employed in a leadership/director position?**

___ Yes ___ No ___ If yes for how many years?

* 7 **Your education:**

___High School ___University (BA) ___Master (MA) ___Post graduate (Ph.D.)

* 8 **Reference** (Please recommend other people that are suitable for this research)

	Name, Surname	Contact: E-mail	Tel
1.			
2.			
3.			
4.			
5.			

SURVEY- PHASE I (ANONYMOUS)

I: SITUATION IN KOSOVO: PRE- AND POST-INDEPENDENCE
(Pre-independence means 1999-2008 and post-independence means 2008-to date)

Q1. Do you consider Kosovo today as a *(insert X in the ___)*

1. multi-ethnic state   Yes ___   No ___   Somewhat agree ___
2. stabilized state   Yes ___   No ___   Somewhat agree ___
3. democratic state   Yes ___   No ___   Somewhat agree ___
4. independent state   Yes ___   No ___   Somewhat agree ___

Q2. Your view regarding Kosovo's national symbols (flag, emblem, hymn)

(insert X in ___)

1. Very satisfied   ___
2. More or less satisfied   ___
3. Neither satisfied nor dissatisfied   ___
4. More or less dissatisfied   ___
5. Very dissatisfied   ___

Q3. After declaring independence in 2008, has Serbian government changed its attitude towards Kosovo?

(insert X in ___)

1. Definitely not   ___
2. Probably not   ___
3. Probably yes   ___
4. Probably not   ___

Q4. What are the options / priorities of the Albanian party before and after the declaration of Independence?

Pre-Independence (pre-2008):   Post-Independence (post-2008):
1.   1.
2.   2.
3.   3.

Q5. What are the options / priorities of the Serb party before and after the declaration of Independence?

Pre-Independence (pre-2008):   Post-Independence (post-2008):

1.   1.

2.   2.

Q6. What do you think about the alternatives presented by the Kosovars? Do you think they are feasible?

(insert X in ___)

1. Strongly agree   ____

2. Somewhat agree   ____

3. Somewhat disagree   ____

4. Strongly disagree   ____

Q7. Do you think there will be division in Kosovo?

(insert X in ___)

1. Strongly agree   ____

2. Somewhat agree   ____

3. Somewhat disagree   ____

4. Strongly disagree   ____

Q8. Do you think Kosovo was safer

1. Pre-Independence   ____

2. Post-Independence   ____

Q9. The tension between Albanians and Serbs in North has *(insert X in__)*

Pre-Independence (pre 2008)   Post-Independence (post 2008)

1. Increased   ____   1. Increased   ____

2. No change   ____   2. No change/same   ____

3. Decreased   ____   3. Decreased   ____

Q10. Do you think there is safety currently in Kosovo?

(insert X in ___)

1. Strongly agree   ____

2. Somewhat agree   ____

3. Somewhat disagree   ____

4. Strongly disagree   ____

Q11. Do you think the issue in the North has a solution?

(insert X in ____)

1. Strongly agree   ____
2. Somewhat agree   ____
3. Somewhat disagree   ____
4. Strongly disagree   ____

Q12. How do you consider the Situation in the North pre- and post-independence? *(insert X in ____)*

Pre-Independence (pre-2008)

1. Not Stabilized   ____
2. Grave and Serious   ____
3. Stabilized but delicate   ____
4. Stabilized   ____
5. Needs to Improve   ____

Post-Independence (post-2008)

1. Not Stabilized   ____
2. Grave and Serious   ____
3. Stabilized but delicate   ____
4. Stabilized   ____
5. Needs to Improve   ____

Q13. Do you think that the minorities in Kosovo are protected?

(insert X in ____)

1. Strongly agree   ____
2. Somewhat agree   ____
3. Somewhat disagree   ____
4. Strongly disagree   ____

II: KOSOVO LEADERSHIP UNDER THE LOCAL LEADERS

Q14. Please rate the priorities (selected by the Ministry of Foreign Affairs) by relevant importance on a scale of 1 to 5, with 1 being the most important and 5 the least important:

(Rate 1-5)

Create diplomatic relations   ____

Promote political interest   ____

Promote economic interest   ____

Protect citizens' rights (women, minorities) ____
Maintain Law and Order ____

Q15. What priority is missing on the above list that should be added?
1.
2.
3.

Q16. Has there been fundamental change how the local leaders perceive foreign policy pre- and post-independence?   (*insert X in* ___)

    Yes ____   No ____   Somewhat agree ____

Q17. Has there been fundamental change in foreign policy in terms of the priorities of Kosovo's Foreign Ministry?

    Yes ____   No ____   Somewhat agree ____

Q18. What are the three most important agreements *Pre-Independence*? Initially write the three agreements, then rate them on a scale of 1 to 5, with 1 being failure and 5 success.

1) List the agreements (includes the most important documents for Kosovo):
1.
2.
3.

2) Rate the agreements   (*Rate 1-5 each of the agreement*):

Agreement	1	2	3
1. Failure	____	____	____
2. More or less failure	____	____	____
3. Neither success, nor failure	____	____	____
4. More or less success	____	____	____
5. Success	____	____	____

Q19. What are the three most important agreements *Post-Independence*? Initially write the three agreements, then rate them on a scale of 1 to 5, with 1 being failure and 5 success.

1) List the agreements (includes the most important documents for Kosovo):

1.

2.

3.

2) Rate the agreements   (*Rate 1-5 each of the agreement*):

Agreement	1	2	3
1. Failure	___	___	___
2. More or less failure	___	___	___
3. Neither success, nor failure	___	___	___
4. More or less success	___	___	___
5. Success	___	___	___

Q20. Rate cases of violations against property (for all citizens)   (*insert X in ___*)
PROPERTY RIGHTS

	Pre-Independence	Post-Independence
1. Increased significantly	___	___
2. Higher	___	___
3. Neither higher nor lower	___	___
4. Lower	___	___
5. Decreased significantly	___	___

Q21. Rate cases of violations of minority rights   (insert X in ___)
PHYSICAL ABUSE:

	Pre-Independence	Post-Independence
1. Increased significantly	___	___
2. Higher	___	___
3. Neither higher nor lower	___	___
4. Lower	___	___
5. Decreased significantly	___	___

Q22. DISCRIMINATION: (*insert X in ___*)

	Pre-Independence	Post-Independence
1. Increased significantly	___	___
2. Higher	___	___
3. Neither higher nor lower	___	___

	Pre-Independence	Post-Independence
4. Lower	____	____
5. Decreased significantly	____	____

Q23. RETURN OF MINORITIES IN KOSOVO: (insert X in ___)

	Pre-Independence	Post-Independence
1. Increased significantly	____	____
2. Higher	____	____
3. Neither higher nor lower	____	____
4. Lower	____	____
5. Decreased significantly	____	____

Q24. RETURN OF ALBANIANS TO KOSOVO: (insert X in ___)

	Pre-Independence	Post-Independence
1. Increased significantly	____	____
2. Higher	____	____
3. Neither higher nor lower	____	____
4. Lower	____	____
5. Decreased significantly	____	____

Q25. FREE MOVEMENT OF MINORITIES IN KOSOVO: (insert X in ___)

	Pre-Independence	Post-Independence
1. Increased significantly	____	____
2. Higher	____	____
3. Neither higher nor lower	____	____
4. Lower	____	____
5. Decreased significantly	____	____

Q26. Rate cases of violation of women's rights   (*insert X in ___*)

ABUSE/DOMESTIC VIOLENCE:

	Pre-Independence	Post-Independence
1. Increased significantly	____	____
2. Higher	____	____
3. Neither higher nor lower	____	____
4. Lower	____	____

5. Decreased significantly   ____   ____

Q27. RAPES: (*insert X in ___*)

	During war	Pre-Independence	Post-Independence
1. Increased significantly	____	____	____
2. Higher	____	____	____
3. Neither higher nor lower	____	____	____
4. Lower	____	____	____
5. Decreased significantly	____	____	____

Q28. DISCRIMINATION: (insert X in ___)

	Pre-Independence	Post-Independence
1. Increased significantly	____	____
2. Higher	____	____
3. Neither higher nor lower	____	____
4. Lower	____	____
5. Decreased significantly	____	____

Q29. SUPPORT OF THE GOVERNMENT FOR WOMEN: (*insert X in ___*)

	Pre-Independence	Post-Independence
1. Increased significantly	____	____
2. Higher	____	____
3. Neither higher nor lower	____	____
4. Lower	____	____
5. Decreased significantly	____	____

Q30. FREE MOVEMENTS OF ALBANIANS IN KOSOVO.   (insert X in ___)

	Pre-Independence	Post-Independence
1. Increased significantly	____	____
2. Higher	____	____
3. Neither higher nor lower	____	____
4. Lower	____	____
5. Decreased significantly	____	____

Q31. Have there been changes in foreign investment?   (insert X in ____)

	Pre-Independence	Post-Independence
1. Increased significantly	____	____
2. Higher	____	____
3. Neither higher nor lower	____	____
4. Lower	____	____
5. Decreased significantly	____	____

Q32. Have there been changes in local development by local investors?   (insert X in ____)

	Pre-Independence	Post-Independence
1. Increased significantly	____	____
2. Higher	____	____
3. Neither higher nor lower	____	____
4. Lower	____	____
5. Decreased significantly	____	____

Q33. How do the local political leaders perceive the image of Kosovo?   (*insert X in ___*)

	Pre-Independence		Post-Independence	
	(2001-04)	(2004-08)	(2008-10)	(2010-12)
1. Strong and stabilized	____	____	____	____
2. Strong but not stabilized	____	____	____	____
3. Weak but stabilized	____	____	____	____
4. Weak and destabilized	____	____	____	____

Q34. Have the leaders created an atmosphere of mutual trust for the people and government?

	Pre-Independence		Post-Independence	
	(2001-04)	(2004-08)	(2008-10)	(2010-12)
1. Very satisfied	____	____	____	____
2. More or less satisfied	____	____	____	____
3. Neither satisfied Nor dissatisfied	____	____	____	____
4. More or less dissatisfied	____	____	____	____
5. Very dissatisfied	____	____	____	____

Q35. Do leaders in Kosovo demonstrate honesty and moral behavior in accordance with the appropriate ethics in all their actions? (*insert X in ___*)

	Pre-Independence		Post-Independence	
	(2001-04)	(2004-08)	(2008-10)	(2010-12)
1. Very satisfied	___	___	___	___
2. More or less satisfied	___	___	___	___
3. Neither satisfied Nor dissatisfied	___	___	___	___
4. More or less dissatisfied	___	___	___	___
5. Very dissatisfied	___	___	___	___

P36. Do leaders demonstrate a clear vision with known purposes for the administration and the people? (*insert X in ___*)

	Pre-Independence		Post-Independence	
	(2001-04)	(2004-08)	(2008-10)	(2010-12)
1. Very satisfied	___	___	___	___
2. More or less satisfied	___	___	___	___
3. Neither satisfied Nor dissatisfied	___	___	___	___
4. More or less dissatisfied	___	___	___	___
5. Very dissatisfied	___	___	___	___

Q37. Do leaders declare their expectations / hopes and confirm understanding? (*insert X in___*)

	Pre-Independence		Post-Independence	
	(2001-04)	(2004-08)	(2008-10)	(2010-12)
1. Very satisfied	___	___	___	___
2. More or less satisfied	___	___	___	___
3. Neither satisfied Nor dissatisfied	___	___	___	___
4. More or less dissatisfied	___	___	___	___
5. Very dissatisfied	___	___	___	___

Q38. Do leaders expect people to be responsible and do they provide the necessary support?

	Pre-Independence		Post-Independence	
	(2001-04)	(2004-08)	(2008-10)	(2010-12)
1. Very satisfied	___	___	___	___
2. More or less satisfied	___	___	___	___
3. Neither satisfied Nor dissatisfied	___	___	___	___

4. More or less dissatisfied   ___ ___   ___ ___
5. Very dissatisfied   ___ ___   ___ ___

Q39. Do leaders make the administration goals / priorities practical and understandable to the citizens starting from the most important to the least important ones? (*insert X in* ___)

	Pre-Independence		Post-Independence	
	(2001-04)	(2004-08)	(2008-10)	(2010-12)
1. Very satisfied	___	___	___	___
2. More or less satisfied	___	___	___	___
3. Neither satisfied Nor dissatisfied	___	___	___	___
4. More or less dissatisfied	___	___	___	___
5. Very dissatisfied	___	___	___	___

Q40. Do leaders communicate their decision, and do they act immediately? (*insert X in* ___)

	Pre-Independence		Post-Independence	
	(2001-04)	(2004-08)	(2008-10)	(2010-12)
1. Very satisfied	___	___	___	___
2. More or less satisfied	___	___	___	___
3. Neither satisfied Nor dissatisfied	___	___	___	___
4. More or less dissatisfied	___	___	___	___
5. Very dissatisfied	___	___	___	___

Q41. Do leaders communicate effectively and charismatically with various groups?

	Pre-Independence		Post-Independence	
	(2001-04)	(2004-08)	(2008-10)	(2010-12)
1. Very satisfied	___	___	___	___
2. More or less satisfied	___	___	___	___
3. Neither satisfied Nor dissatisfied	___	___	___	___
4. More or less dissatisfied	___	___	___	___
5. Very dissatisfied	___	___	___	___

Q42. Do leaders take responsibility for their actions without blaming others? (*insert X in* ___)

	Pre-Independence		Post-Independence	
	(2001-04)	(2004-08)	(2008-10)	(2010-12)
1. Very satisfied	___	___	___	___

2. More or less satisfied   —— ——   —— ——

3. Neither satisfied Nor dissatisfied   —— ——   —— ——

4. More or less dissatisfied   —— ——   —— ——

5. Very dissatisfied   —— ——   —— ——

Q43. Do leaders include others during action planning? (*insert X in* ___)

	Pre-Independence		Post-Independence	
	(2001-04)	(2004-08)	(2008-10)	(2010-12)
1. Very satisfied	——	——	——	——
2. More or less satisfied	——	——	——	——
3. Neither satisfied Nor dissatisfied	——	——	——	——
4. More or less dissatisfied	——	——	——	——
5. Very dissatisfied	——	——	——	——

Q44. Do leaders have good relationships with the civil servants regardless of position?

	Pre-Independence		Post-Independence	
	(2001-04)	(2004-08)	(2008-10)	(2010-12)
1. Very satisfied	——	——	——	——
2. More or less satisfied	——	——	——	——
3. Neither satisfied Nor dissatisfied	——	——	——	——
4. More or less dissatisfied	——	——	——	——
5. Very dissatisfied	——	——	——	——

Q45. Do leaders show tolerance?   (*insert X in* ___)

	Pre-Independence		Post-Independence	
	(2001-04)	(2004-08)	(2008-10)	(2010-12)
1. Very satisfied	——	——	——	——
2. More or less satisfied	——	——	——	——
3. Neither satisfied Nor dissatisfied	——	——	——	——
4. More or less dissatisfied	——	——	——	——
5. Very dissatisfied	——	——	——	——

Q46. Do leaders use training that teaches skills in leadership and common work? *(insert X)*

	Pre-Independence		Post-Independence	
	(2001-04)	(2004-08)	(2008-10)	(2010-12)
1. Very satisfied	___	___	___	___
2. More or less satisfied	___	___	___	___
3. Neither satisfied Nor dissatisfied	___	___	___	___
4. More or less dissatisfied	___	___	___	___
5. Very dissatisfied	___	___	___	___

Q47. The Dayton Agreement in 1995 did not place Kosovo on the international agenda because the war in Bosnia was a priority. Would such an inclusion have stopped the fighting and the genocide of Albanians in Kosovo?

(insert X in ___)

1. Strongly agree   ___
2. Somewhat agree   ___
3. Somewhat disagree   ___
4. Strongly disagree   ___

Q48. The former President Ibrahim Rugova took a peaceful and multi-party consent stance to the achievement of independence. Do you think that the peaceful politics of Rugova brought independence?

1. Strongly agree   ___
2. Somewhat agree   ___
3. Somewhat disagree   ___
4. Strongly disagree   ___

Q49. What effect did Fatmir Sejdiu's resignation from office have in Kosovo's political image?

1. It weakened it very much   ___
2. It weakened it somewhat   ___
3. No effect   ___

Q50. Are you in favor of the unification of Kosovo with Albania?

Yes ___   No ___

III: INTERNATIONAL AND DIPLOMATIC RELATIONS WITH OTHER COUNTRIES

Q51. How do foreign political leaders perceive the image of Kosovo? (*insert X in* ___)

	Pre-Independence	Post-Independence
1. Strong and stabilized	____	____
2. Strong but not stabilized	____	____
3. Weak but stabilized	____	____
4. Weak and destabilized	____	____

Q52. Are you in favor or against of having trade ties with the following states (*insert X in* ___)

Serbia	In favor ____	Against ____
Greece	In favor ____	Against ____
Macedonia	In favor ____	Against ____
Albania	In favor ____	Against ____
Montenegro	In favor ____	Against ____
Russia	In favor ____	Against ____

Q53. Are you in favor or against of having diplomatic ties with the following states   (*insert X in* ___)

Serbia	In favor ____	Against ____
Greece	In favor ____	Against ____
Macedonia	In favor ____	Against ____
Albania	In favor ____	Against ____
Montenegro	In favor ____	Against ____
Russia	In favor ____	Against ____

Q54. Which country has had stronger ties with Kosovo and shown stronger support for its Independence? Rate them on a scale of 1 to 5, with 1 being the strongest link and 5 the weakest one:

	(*Rate from 1-5*)
USA	____
UK	____
Germany	____
Albania	____
France	____

Q55. In February 2012, Serbia recognized a diplomatic agreement which clarifies the conditions under which Kosovo could be representative at international meetings, but it does not use the word "Republic" for Kosovo (footnote). Do you think this agreement is a tactic for Serbia to gain membership in the European Union (EU)?

(insert X in ___)

1. Strongly agree   ___
2. Somewhat agree   ___
3. Somewhat disagree   ___
4. Strongly disagree   ___

Q56. Do you think that the Ahtisaari plan is a barrier for Kosovo?

(insert X in ___)

1. Strongly agree   ___
2. Somewhat agree   ___
3. Somewhat disagree   ___
4. Strongly disagree   ___

Q57. Under the Ahtisaari plan, the northern part of Kosovo remains part of Kosovo to preserve the territorial and political integrity of Kosovo, whilst Serbia aims for the North to be part of Serbia. Should the North be divided from Kosovo?

1. Strongly agree   ___
2. Somewhat agree   ___
3. Somewhat disagree   ___
4. Strongly disagree   ___

Q58. How is an Albanian from Kosovo identified?   *(insert X in ___)*

Albanian ___   Kosovan ___   Kosovan Albanian ___   Other (explain)_____

Q59. How is a Serb from Kosovo identified   *(insert X in ___)*

Serb___   Kosovan ___   Kosovan Serb ___   Other (explain)_____

Q60. The United States has played a key role in Kosovo. Are you in favor of the US continuing to support Kosovo?

(insert X in ___)

1. Strongly agree   ___

2. Somewhat agree   ____
3. Somewhat disagree   ____
4. Strongly disagree   ____

Q61. Do you think that: (*insert X next to the appropriate answer*)
    1. Coordination with the US is necessary   ____
    2. Coordination with the US is somewhat necessary   ____
    3. Kosovo itself should be a leader in the world   ____

Q62. Do you think Kosovo today can govern itself?

                                                (*insert X in* ____)

    1. Strongly agree   ____
    2. Somewhat agree   ____
    3. Somewhat disagree   ____
    4. Strongly disagree   ____

Q63. Do you think that Kosovo still needs support from other countries?

                                                (*insert X in* ____)

    1. Strongly agree   ____
    2. Somewhat agree   ____
    3. Somewhat disagree   ____
    4. Strongly disagree   ____

Q64. Do you think Kosovo meets the condition for membership in the EU?

                                                (*insert X in* ____)

    1. Strongly agree   ____
    2. Somewhat agree   ____
    3. Somewhat disagree   ____
    4. Strongly disagree   ____

Q65. Do you think Serbia meets the condition for membership in the EU?

                                                (*insert X in* ____)

    1. Strongly agree   ____
    2. Somewhat agree   ____

3. Somewhat disagree   ____
4. Strongly disagree   ____

Q66. British Prime Minister Tony Blair and England have played a key role in supporting Kosovo's independence. Do you think that England and the US should put more pressure on Serbia?

Yes ____   No ____

Q67. Do you think the government today in Kosovo (*insert X for all points that you agree*)
1. Democratic and fair   ____
2. Democratic but not strong   ____
3. It does not function   ____
4. Corrupted   ____
5. Non democratic   ____

Q68. Do you think it is necessary to have a change in the governance of Kosovo?

Yes ____   No ____

Q69. What are the main problems in Kosovo? Sort by relevance from 1-15, with 1 being the biggest problem and 15 the smallest problem.

(*List from 1-15 based on the importance*)

Legal order, public safety   ____
Transparency in government decisions   ____
Corruption   ____
International recognition   ____
Protection of Minorities   ____
Protecting women's rights   ____
Unemployment   ____
Economic welfare   ____
Better relations with Serbia   ____
EU Membership   ____
Strengthening institutions   ____
Crime   ____
Free movement of the population within the country   ____
Protection of cultural and religious places   ____
Fair and democratic elections   ____

Q70. Do you think Kosovo needs reforms in the   (*insert X in ____*)

    1. Legal system   Yes ____   No ____

    2. Electoral system   Yes ____   No ____

    3. Economic system   Yes ____   No ____

Q71. Do you think that civil society is active in the decision-making process?   (*insert X in__*)

    1. Yes ____   2. No ____   3. Partially ____

Q72. Do the Serbs in the north feel they are Kosovan citizens?

    1. Yes ____   2. No ____   3. Partially ____

Q73. Do Serbs take part in local elections?

    1. Yes ____   2. No ____   3. Partially ____

Q74. Is there cooperation between political parties in Kosovo?

                                       (*insert X in ____*)

    1. Strongly agree   ____

    2. Somewhat agree   ____

    3. Somewhat disagree   ____

    4. Strongly disagree   ____

Q75. Do you trust political parties in Kosovo?

                                       (*insert X in ____*)

    1. Strongly agree   ____

    2. Somewhat agree   ____

    3. Somewhat disagree   ____

    4. Strongly disagree   ____

Q76. Do you think that the political philosophy of parties is led by

    1. Ideology ____   2. Ethnic belonging ____   3. Regional belonging ____

Q77. Give examples of parties led by:

    1. Ideology:

    2. Ethnic belonging:

    3. Regional belonging:

Q78. How satisfied are you with the citizens' interests being represented by the political parties?

	Pre-Independence	Post-Independence
1. Very satisfied	____	____
2. More or less satisfied	____	____
3. Neither satisfied nor dissatisfied	____	____
4. More or less dissatisfied	____	____
5. Very dissatisfied	____	____

Q79. Are you satisfied with the relations between Kosovo-Serbia?

	Pre-Independence	Post-Independence
1. Very satisfied	____	____
2. More or less satisfied	____	____
3. Neither satisfied nor dissatisfied	____	____
4. More or less dissatisfied	____	____
5. Very dissatisfied	____	____

IV: ROLE AND FUNCTION OF INTERNATIONAL COMMUNITIES

Q80. Do you think the UN has played a positive role in Kosovo?

(insert X in ____)

1. Strongly agree ____
2. Somewhat agree ____
3. Somewhat disagree ____
4. Strongly disagree ____

Q81. Do you think the civil presence of the international community is needed in Kosovo?

(insert X in ____)

1. Strongly agree ____
2. Somewhat agree ____
3. Somewhat disagree ____
4. Strongly disagree ____

Q82. Do you think that UNMIK has fulfilled the conditions of the mission for Kosovo? (*insert X in* ___)

	Pre-Independence	Post-Independence
1. Very satisfied	____	____
2. More or less satisfied	____	____
3. Neither satisfied nor dissatisfied	____	____
4. More or less dissatisfied	____	____
5. Very dissatisfied	____	____

Q83. Do you think that the role of the European Union has been efficient in Kosovo? (*insert X in* __)

	Pre-Independence	Post-Independence
1. Very satisfied	____	____
2. More or less satisfied	____	____
3. Neither satisfied nor dissatisfied	____	____
4. More or less dissatisfied	____	____
5. Very dissatisfied	____	____

Q84. How do you evaluate the role of the EULEX? (*insert X in* ___)

1. Efficient	____
2. Efficient and powerful	____
3. Partially efficient	____
4. Not efficient	____
5. Poor	____

Q85. How do you evaluate the role of UNMIK? (*insert X in* ___)

	Pre-Independence	Post-Independence
1. Efficient	____	____
2. Efficient and powerful	____	____
3. Partially efficient	____	____
4. Not efficient	____	____
5. Poor	____	____

Q86. How do you evaluate the role of NATO?   (*insert X in* ___)

	Pre-Independence	Post-Independence
1. Efficient	____	____
2. Efficient and powerful	____	____
3. Partially efficient	____	____
4. Not efficient	____	____
5. Poor	____	____

Q87. Do you think that NATO's intervention stopped the genocide in Kosovo?

Yes ____   No ____

Q88. Do you think that NATO's intervention is the cause of the declaration of independence?

Yes ____   No ____

Q89. How do you evaluate the role of international community including here UNMIK, EULEX, ICO, KFOR, OSCE, etc.   (*insert X in* ___)

	Pre-Independence	Post-Independence
1. Efficient	____	____
2. Efficient and powerful	____	____
3. Partially efficient	____	____
4. Not efficient	____	____
5. Poor	____	____

Q90. Which foreign organizations have played the most important role in Kosovo? List according to importance where no. 1 means the strongest role.   (*insert X in* ___)

Pre-Independence		Post-Independence	
UNMIK	____	UNMIK	____
KFOR	____	KFOR	____
OSCE	____	OSCE	____
Red Cross	____	Red Cross	____
		EULEX	____
		ICO	____

Q91. How do you evaluate the decisions of the leaders of these states in foreign policy towards Kosovo?

Evaluation:

1. Very poor   2. Poor   3. Somewhat poor   4. Neutral   5. Good   6. Better   7. The best

Pre-Independence   *(Rate from 1-7 for each country)*

Serbia	Russia	USA	UK	France	Germany	Albania
___	___	___	___	___	___	___

Post-Independence   *(Rate from 1-7 for each country)*

Kosovo	Serbia	Russia	USA	UK	France	Germany	Albania
___	___	___	___	___	___	___	___

Q92. How do you evaluate the decisions of the leaders on internal politics in Kosovo?

(Insert X ___)

	Pre-Independence	Post-Independence
1. Very poor	___	___
2. Poor	___	___
3. Somewhat poor	___	___
4. Neutral	___	___
5. Good	___	___
6. Better	___	___
7. The best	___	___

Q93. In which areas has Kosovo progressed? List them from 1 to 10 with 1 being the most developed area and 10 the least developed area.

	(List from 1-10) Pre-Independence	*(List from 1-10)* Post-Independence
1. Politics	___	___
2. Economy	___	___
3. Diplomacy	___	___
4. Legal system	___	___
5. Police and security	___	___
6. Internal affairs	___	___
7. Foreign affairs	___	___

8. Business and commerce ____ ____
9. Human rights ____ ____
10. Religious rights ____ ____

Q94. Rate from 1-7 the work of the leaders in each field with 1 being Very poor.

1. Very poor   2. Poor   3. Somewhat poor   4. Neutral   5. Good   6. Better   7. The best

	Rate 1-7 Pre-Independence	Rate 1-7 Post-Independence
1. Politics	____	____
2. Economy	____	____
3. Diplomacy	____	____
4. Legal system	____	____
5. Police and security	____	____
6. Internal affairs	____	____
7. Foreign affairs	____	____
8. Business and commerce	____	____
9. Human rights	____	____
10. Religious rights	____	____

Q95. Your opinion on Serbia-Kosovo talks, how do you evaluate them:

	Pre-Independence	Post-Independence
1. Very satisfied	____	____
2. More or less satisfied	____	____
3. Neither satisfied nor dissatisfied	____	____
4. More or less dissatisfied	____	____
5. Very dissatisfied	____	____

Q96. Your opinion on multilateral talks, how do you evaluate them:

	Pre-Independence	Post-Independence
1. Very satisfied	____	____
2. More or less satisfied	____	____
3. Neithersatisfied nor dissatisfied	____	____
4. More or less dissatisfied	____	____
5. Very dissatisfied	____	____

V.   KOSOVA TOWARDS EUROPEAN UNION

Q97. Is Kosovo in the path towards EU?   Yes ____   No ____

Q98. Is Serbia in the path towards EU?   Yes ____   No ____

Q99. Do you see Kosovo in the future as a member of the EU?   Yes ____   No __

Q100.   Rate the steps the leaders have taken towards the membership of Kosovo in the EU
1. Very satisfied
2. More or less satisfied
3. Neither satisfied nor dissatisfied
4. More or less dissatisfied
5. Very dissatisfied

(Based on the above-mentioned explanation, rate 1-5 each of the areas in the following list)
1. Economic integration   ____
   a. Feasibility study (short term + long term obligations)   ____
   b. Visa liberalization   ____
   c. Trade agreements with the EU   ____
   d. Dialogue on the stabilization association process (free trade)   ____
   e. Functioning of the economic courts   ____
   f. Fulfilling the short-term economic criteria   ____
   g. Economic development   ____
   h. Medium Term Expenditure Framework   ____

2. Political integration   ____
   a. Legal and legislation aspect   ____
   b. The rule of law and order in Kosovo   ____
   c. Efficient functioning of the courts   ____
   d. The distribution of responsibility to the institutional officials   ____

3. Social and Democratic integration   ____
   a. Fighting corruption   ____
   b. Bureaucratic structures   ____

   c. The necessary procedures in business and different areas   ____

   d. Encouraging reports of cases   ____

   e. Reform of public administration   ____

   f. Cultural heritage   ____

VI. KOSOVO POLICE AND INTERNATIONAL CIVIL / MILITARY PRESENCE

Q101. Do you think the military presence of the international community is needed in Kosovo?

Yes ____   No ____

Q102. Do you think that the Kosovo Police is effective in implementing its strategic objectives?

Rate: *(Insert X in ____)*

1. Very satisfied   ____
2. More or less satisfied   ____
3. Neither satisfied nor dissatisfied   ____
4. More or less dissatisfied   ____
5. Very dissatisfied   ____

Q103. Is Kosovo police effective in the following tasks?

(Based on the above-mentioned explanation, rate 1-5 each of the steps in the following list)

	Pre-Independence	Post-Independence
1. Protecting life and property	____	____
2. Maintaining public order and peace	____	____
3. Preventing and detecting crime	____	____
4. Protecting people's rights and freedoms	____	____
5. Treating people equally regardless of race, color, religion, gender and age.	____	____

Q104. Do you trust the Kosovo police?   Yes ____   No ____

Q105. Do you think Kosovo police is competent in achieving the strategic objectives described above?   Yes ____   No____

Q106. Do you trust the foreign military forces in protecting Kosovo?   Yes ____   No ____

Q107. Do you think the following show responsibility and professional integrity?

Kosovo Police	Yes ___	No ___
Eulex	Yes ___	No ___
UNMIK	Yes ___	No ___

Q108. Do you think that the international civil and military presence is effective in Kosovo?

(*Rate 1-5*)

1. Very satisfied ___
2. More or less satisfied ___
3. Neither satisfied nor dissatisfied ___
4. More or less dissatisfied ___
5. Very dissatisfied ___

Q109. Kosovo aspires to join NATO. Do you think Kosovo is ready from an institutional perspective?

Yes ___   No ___

Q110. Do you think that KFOR has played an effective part in defending the Northern part of Kosovo?   (*insert X in ___*)

	Pre-Independence	Post-Independence
1. Efficient	___	___
2. Efficient and powerful	___	___
3. Neither efficient nor powerful	___	___
4. Not efficient	___	___
5. Not efficient and poor	___	___

Q111. Do you think that the number of international civil and military troops should be reduced?

Yes ___   No ___

Q112. Kosovo Security Force (KSF) is created based on NATO's military system. Do you think that this force will be the successor of the international military presence in Kosovo?

Yes ___   No ___

Q113. Are the two new international organizations operating in Kosovo competent?

1. European Union Special Representative (EUSR)   Yes ___   No ___
2. European Union Rule of Law Mission in Kosovo (EULEX)   Yes ___   No ___

Q114. Do you think there is sufficient coordination between the Kosovo Police and EULEX?

Yes____   No ____

Q115. How do you evaluate the management of the Kosovo Police?   *(insert X in ___)*

	Pre-Independence	Post-Independence
1. Efficient	____	____
2. Efficient and powerful	____	____
3. Neither efficient nor powerful	____	____
4. Not efficient	____	____
5. Not efficient and poor	____	____

Q116. How do you evaluate the management of EULEX?   *(insert X in ___)*

	Post-Independence
1. Efficient	____
2. Efficient and powerful	____
3. Neither efficient nor powerful	____
4. Not efficient	____
5. Not efficient and poor	____

VII. ROLE AND FUNCTION OF MEDIA/TV

Q117. Has media / tv had an influence in the image of Kosovo?   Yes ____   No ____

Q118. Has media / tv had an influence in the image of Serbia?   Yes ____   No ____

Q119. Which side do you think has the Albanian media supported?

	Pre-Independence	Post-Independence
1. Albanian side	____	____
2. Serb side	____	____
3. Both sides	____	____

Q120. Which side do you think has the Serb media supported?

	Pre-Independence	Post-Independence
1. Albanian side	____	____
2. Serb side	____	____
3. Both sides	____	____

Q121. What role did the media / TV play?

	Pre-Independence		Post-Independence	
	Positive	Negative	Positive	Negative
Albanian	____	____	____	____
Serb	____	____	____	____
Foreign	____	____	____	____

Q122. Which media source do you think is the most reliable in Kosovo? List the numbers in each option below, rating them from 1 to 5, with 1 being most reliable and 5 the least reliable.

	List 1-5 Pre-Independence	List 1-5 Post-Independence
Albanian	____	____
Serb	____	____
American	____	____
British	____	____
Foreign (other)	____	____

Q123. Which areas in the media / tv in Kosovo have progressed?

	Pre-Independence	Post-Independence
Defamation law	Yes ___ No ___	Yes ___ No ___
Copyright law	Yes ___ No ___	Yes ___ No ___
Public broadcasting law	Yes ___ No ___	Yes ___ No ___

Q124. Do you think there is anti-Albanian propaganda in the Serb media?

Yes__   No____

Q125. Do you think there is anti-Serb propaganda in the Albanian media?

Yes __   No ___

PHASE II – OPEN CONVERSATION ADDITIONAL QUESTIONS

TOPIC I: SITUATION IN KOSOVO: PRE- AND POST-INDEPENDENCE

TOPIC II: KOSOVAN LEADERSHIP UNDER LOCAL LEADERS

TOPIC III: INTERNATIONAL AND DIPLOMATIC RELATIONS WITH OTHER
                COUNTRIES

TOPIC IV: ROLE AND FUNCTION OF INTERNATIONAL COMMUNITIES

TOPIC V: KOSOVO TOWARDS THE EUROPEAN UNION

TOPIC VI: KOSOVO POLICE AND INTERNATIONAL CIVIL / MILITARY
                PRESENCE

TOPIC VII: THE ROLE AND FUNCTION OF MEDIA/TV

TOPIC VIII: LEADERSHIP AND THE FUTURE OF KOSOVO

ADDITIONAL QUESTIONS   (Topic I: Explain the political situation in Kosovo)

Q126. How can you describe the current political situation in Kosovo?

Q127. What does the independence of Kosovo mean for the state? Citizens? What about neighboring countries?

Q128. What is the most effective strategy to:

1. Achieve stability in Kosovo?
2. Reduce violence between ethnic communities?
3. Reduce the presence of foreign military forces in Kosovo?

Q129. What are the reasons for the increase / decrease of the tensions between the two communities in Kosovo?

Q130. What were the peak years for the increase of tension Pre- and Post-Independence?

Q131. What actions are being taken to ensure the safety of citizens in Kosovo?

Q132. What actions are not taken for the safety of citizens in Kosovo and what else should be done in order to achieve this goal?

Q133. Kosovan governments attitude towards minorities (such as Roma, Serbian, Bosnian Ashkali, Gorani, etc.), the protection of their rights and what programs are available for their support?

Q134. What is Kosovo's stance in regard to the internal affairs to ensure peace, stability and the rule of law?

Q135. The issue of North / Mitrovica: What is Belgrade's official stance towards North?

Q136. How much control has got the government of Kosovo in the North? What about the Serbian government in the North?

Q137. What solutions do you see for the North? Your recommendations for resolving the issue.

ADDITIONAL QUESTIONS (Topic II: Explain the leadership in Kosovo and decisions of the leaders)

Q138. What was the involvement of Kosovan leaders in building state institutions?

Q139. Do you think that this current government differs from the previous one? What values does the current leadership offer and what improvements should be made in terms of leadership?

Q140. Compare the political situation in Kosovo before independence with today: what are the accomplishments, developments, changes: 1) legal, 2) economic and 3) electoral system?

Q141. Your opinion for Albanian and Serbian leaders: (qualities, principles and decisions)

President:
1. Ibrahim Rugova
2. Fatmir Sejdiu
3. Behxhet Pacolli
4. Atifete Jahjaga

Prime minister:
1. Bajram Rexhepi
3. Bajram Kosumi
4. Agim Çeku
5. Hashim Thaçi
2. Ramush Harajdinaj

President
1. Slobodan Milošević
2. Boris Tadić
3. Tomislav Nikolić

Prime minister
1. Zoran Đinđić
3. Vojislav Koštunica
4. Ivica Dačić
2. Vojislav Koštunica

Q142. How's the progress of the independence? The impact on the economy, politics, etc. Why is it difficult for a country to gain independence? What is the process / steps to be taken by a country to be recognized by the world?

Q143. Role of Diaspora on the issue of Kosovo and local development.

Q144. The role of culture: What role does the local culture play in the residents' attitudes in terms of its influence on what citizens expect from government leaders?

Q145. What new agreements were signed in 2012 and which should be signed in the future? What does the achievement depend on?

Q146. What new laws are formulated for the protection of women, minority, property, security, and legal order?

Q147. Talk broadly about the minorities and women's rights. What programs are designed to promote/ protect their rights? Where did they have improvements, where do they still have problems?

Q148. Talk broadly about the local elections and the role of political parties in Kosovo.

Q149. Your recommendations for Kosovo's leadership.

ADDITIONAL QUESTIONS (Topic III: Explain Kosovo's relations with other countries)

Q150. What bilateral relationship should be strengthened more?

Q151. How do you foresee the relations of Kosovo with Belgrade in the future?

Q152. How can you describe the role of Albania and what do you think about the idea of reunification with Albania?

Q153. What is Kosovo doing in terms of international recognition in relation to countries that have not recognized her yet?

Q154. How have the consular missions developed with the countries that have recognized Kosovo as a state?

Q155. Explain further Ahtisaari plan about the Albanians and Serbs in Kosovo.

Q156. Under what circumstances /what areas need more support from other countries?

Q157. What is the effect of the international administration in the functioning of political parties?

Q158. How do you envision the future of Kosovo?

Q159. Your recommendations for the development of Kosovo's foreign policy and strengthening its ties with other states.

ADDITIONAL QUESTIONS (Topic IV: the role and function of international organizations)

Q161.   What political and military organizations have played a role in Kosovo?

Q162.   Talk broadly about the role of NATO, UN, and EU missions in Kosovo? What is their impact? In which aspects have they had a positive role, in which a negative role?

Q163.   Talk more about institutional coordination between foreign Organizations.

Q164.   What mechanisms has Kosovo created in order to facilitate its entry in the EU? Your recommendations.

Q165.   Talk about the role of the media and some of the prejudices of local and foreign media.

Q166.   What are the aspects that need more protection of the press and what aspects have already seen improvements?

Q167.   What was the influence of the foreign missions? In which aspects have they had a positive role, in which a negative role?

ADDITIONAL QUESTIONS (Topic V: leadership and the future of Kosovo)

Q168.   Do you think Kosovo is headed the right direction? Yes or No

Q169.   Grade the President, the Prime Minister, the Minister of Foreign Affairs, and the Minister of Internal Affairs (excellent, good, weak, bad).

Q170.   Political Profile of each leader.

2012 Kosovo Field Trip Agenda

November 09 – December 23, 2012, Prishtina, Kosovo

Monday, November 12:

    11:00am   Meeting with Journalist Ilir Berisha.

Tuesday, November 13:   *Ministry of Diaspora Visit*

    2:00pm   Meeting with Naim Dedushaj, Director of Diaspora Investment.

    2:30pm   Meeting with Shani Hamitaga, Ministry of Diaspora.

    3:00pm   Meeting with Naim Gashi, officer research and investment support for diaspora members, Ministry of Diaspora.

    3:30pm   Meeting with Minister Ibrahim Makolli, Ministry of Diaspora.

Thursday, November 15:   *Kosovo Assembly Visit*

    1:00-3:00pm   Meeting with Assemblyman Mehmet Hajrizi, Chief of Cabinet, Kosovo Assembly, former Deputy Prime Minister of provisional government.

    3:00-5:00pm   Meeting with Luz Balaj, *Instituti për Studime Kushtetuese dhe Parlamentare* (ISKP) / University of Prishtina, Faculty of Law.

    5:00-6:00pm   Meeting with Dr. Bajrami, University of Prishtina, Faculty of Law.

Friday, November 16:

10:00am	Meeting with Naser Rrugova, Deputy of the Kosovo Assembly.
11:00am	Interview with Mehmet Hajrizi, Deputy of the Kosovo Assembly.

Saturday, November 17:

11:00am	Interview with Naser Rrugova, Deputy of the Kosovo Assembly.
1:30-3:00pm	Meeting with LTC Enver Dugolli, Head of Cooperation with Agencies CIMIC Department, Ministry for the Kosovo Security Force.
	Site Visit to the Marble Cave, in the village of Gadime e Ulët in Lipjan.
3:30pm	Meeting with journalist Bardha Shpuza Azari.

Sunday, November 18:

7:00-10:00pm	Meeting with Gëzim Kunoviku, Emine Emini, Valbona Hajredini at Shtëpia e Vjetër.

Monday, November 19: *Kosovo Assembly Visit*

12:00-2:00pm	Interview with Glauk Konjufca, Vice President of the Assembly.
2:30-4:00pm	Interview with Journalist Ilir Berisha, at Aurora.
6:30-8:00pm	Meeting with Florent Gorca.
8:00pm	Meeting with Egzon Bunjaku, Shtëpia e Vjetër.

Tuesday, November 20: *Ministry of Culture and Ministry of Foreign Affairs Visit*

11:00-1:00pm	Interview with Mirushe Emini, Head of Section, Ministry of Culture, Youth and Sport.
12:30-1:00pm	Lunch at Aurora restaurant.
1:00pm	Meeting with Vjosa Osmani, Deputy of the Kosovo Assembly.
2:30pm	Meeting with Zoja Krasniqi, Department of Prishtina Municipality and Valbona Hajredini.

| 3:30pm | Meeting with Fatmir Rrahmanaj, Senior Officer for Economy Integration, Ministry of Foreign Affairs. |

Wednesday, November 21:

| 1:30pm | Visit at the Institute of Albanology. |
| 2:00pm | Meeting with Kosovare Krasniqi, Institute of Albanology. |

Thursday, November 22:

11:30-12:30pm	Interview with Dr. Memli Krasniqi, Institute of Albanology.
12:30-1:00pm	Meeting with Kosovare Krasniqi, Institute of Albanology.
1:00-2:00pm	Meeting with Lulzim Laici, Professor Sali Bytyqi and Arbnora Dushi.
2:00pm	Interview with Teuta Haxhiu, Deputy of the Kosovo Assembly.
3:00pm	Lunch at Aurora.
3:30-5:00pm	Interview with author Naim Kelmendi at Aurora.
5:30-7:30pm	Meeting with Bujar Vehapi at Shtëpia e Vjetër.

Friday, November 23:

11:00-1:00pm	Meeting with Fatmir Rrahmanaj, Ministry of Foreign Affairs.
1:00pm	Conducted Phase 1 of 2012 Surveys at the Kosovo Assembly.
2:00pm	Interview with Luz Balaj.
3:00pm	Pick up completed Stage 1 Surveys from the Kosovo Assembly.
3:00pm	Meeting with Glauk Konjufca, Vetëvendosja.
5:30pm	Meeting with Arben Gashi and Bahtije Vllasaliu.
6:00-7:00pm	Interview with Visar Duriqi.

Saturday, November 24:

| 2:00pm | Meeting with Naim Kelmendi. |

Sunday, November 25:   *Peja and Rrugova Site Visits*

11:00am   Left Prishtina to Peja trip. Travelled through Drenica, Malisheva Klinë.

12:30pm   Semitronix Café in Peja, owned by Shemsedin Zeka.
               Site Visit Rrugova Mountain, Bjeshkët e Rrugovës.

2:30pm   Lunch at Bregu restaurant in Rrugova, traditional Albanian restaurant owned by Xhevdet Dreshaj.

3:00pm   Guri i Kuq in the village of Lecinat, Selim Dreshaj.

Monday, November 26:

9:30am   Meeting with Mirushe Emini, Ministry of Culture, Youth and Sports.

11:00am   Meeting with Memli krasniqi and Fadil Grajcevci, Institute of Albanology

3:00-4:00pm   Meeting with Kushtrim Binaku, On Air.

6:00-7:30pm   Meeting with Visar and Adili, Center of Journalism.

Tuesday, November 27:   *Mitrovica Site Visit*

3:00pm   Visiting the city center of Mitrovica and the Statue of Isa Boletini.
               Meeting in Café Flat 137, Mitrovica.

6:30pm   Ibri Restaurant in the neighborhood of Kushtove, Mitrovica.

8:00pm   Dinner at Pandora Restaurant.

Wednesday, November 28: *Macedonia Site Visit*

1:00pm   Site Visit to Skopje, Macedonia, Kacanic, Komuna Hani i Elezit.

6:00pm   Meeting with Albanian female entrepreneur and designer Mila Kadriu
               Site visits to downtown Skopje, Ura e Gurit, Macedonia Square, Alexander the Great monument, the Macedonia Gate, Museum of Macedonian Struggle, the National Theatre of Macedonia, Mother Theresa Memorial House.

Friday, November 30: Site Visits to the ethnic Serbian community in Gracanica, KFOR, and the Church visit which was previously a mosque.

Monday, December 3: Film Festival, National Theater of Kosovo, Prishtina.

Wednesday, December 5:

1:30pm	Meeting with Naim Kelmendi, Metropol restaurant.
4:00pm	Meeting with Law professor, Bekim Kadriu, University of Iliria.
8:00pm	Theatre show "Burrneshat", Oda Theater.

Thursday, December 6: *Gjilan Site Visit*

12:00pm	Visit at the Ministry of Trade, Meeting with Minister Mimoza Kosari Lilaj and Rina Domi.
	Site Visit in Gjilan, Gracanica neighborhood, Serb communities, Padova Lake.
1:00pm	Vila Valboni Café in Mramor village, owner Enver Gashi (18 km from Prishtina).
	Site Visit to Novo Brdo Fortress, medieval fortress, 20 km from Prishtina.
3:00pm	Arrived in Gjilan, visited the city center, the Theater of Gjilan, Café Bar Palace.
4:30pm	Dinner at Vali Ranch, owned by Fehmi Fetau, Behar Maleci gave a tour of the horse stables, llamas, rabbits, winery, and the resort spanning to 15 acres.
6:00pm	Restaurant Bujana in Gjilan, owned by Naser Shabani, known for the Bujan Conference and the Prizren League.
7:00pm	Kalaja Krujës, on the way to Gjilan-Ferizaj, owned by Nazmi Shala.

Friday, December 7:

6:00-7:00pm	Dit e Nat Café in Prishtina.
8:30pm	Skena Up Festival, "Mësimi" theatre play directed by Bekim Lumi, featuring Astrit Kabashi as lead actor, Dodona Theater.

Monday, December 10: *EULEX Mission Visit*

3:00pm   Interview with EULEX Police.
4:00pm   Meeting with Marc Tartière, EULEX.

Wednesday, December 12:

1:30pm   Meeting with Minister of Security Forces, Agim Çeku.
4:00pm   Meeting with Law Professor Bekim Kadriu, Iliria University.

Thursday, December 13:

7:00pm   Interview with Dr. Zymer Neziri, University of Prishtina.

Friday, December 14:

9:00am   Meeting with Mehmet Hajrizi, Deputy of the Kosovo Assembly.
10:00am   Meeting with Zoja Krasniqi, Komuna (Municipality of Prishtina).
11:00am   Interview with Irina Gudeljevic, EULEX Spokesperson.
2:00pm   Visit at the Prime Minister's Office (Prime Minister Hashim Thaçi).
2:30pm   Visit at the President's Office (President Atifete Jahjaga).
3:00-4:00pm   Visit at the Ministry of for the Kosovo Security Force, Meeting with Lieutenant Colonel Enver Dugolli.
5:00pm   Meeting with Bahtije at Komuna (Municipality of Prishtina).
5:30-6:00pm   Meeting with Adili at Aurora.

Saturday, December 15:

9:00am   Meeting with Meeting with Mehmet Hajrizi, Deputy of the Kosovo Assembly.

Saturday, December 16:

5:00-8:00pm   Interview with Naser Rrugova, Deputy of the Kosovo Assembly.

Monday, December 17:

9:00am	Visit at the Ministry of European Integration.
12:00pm	Interview with Robert Wilton, International Civilian Office (ICO).
1:30-3:00pm	Interview with Ismail Kastrati, former Head of the Kosovo Chamber of Commerce.
3:00-4:00pm	Meeting with Xhemail Mazrekaj, Director of Department of Finance and General Services, Ministry of European Integration.
4:00-5:00pm	Meeting with Dr. Zymer Neziri, Shabani and Xhevahire, Institute of Albanology.

Tuesday, December 18:

11:00-12:00pm	Interview with Agron Gashi, Legal Advisor of the Prime Minister.
12:00-1:00pm	Interview with Pëllumb Kallaba, Foreign Policy Advisor, Ministry of Foreign Affairs. Meeting with Zana Daka, Executive Assistant to Deputy Minister, Ministry of Foreign Affairs.
1:30pm	Interview with Nora and visit at the UNDP Office.
2:00pm	Visit at the British Council.
2:30-4:00pm	Visit at the Kosovo Protection Corps (TMK) with LTC Enver Dugolli. Meeting with Ali Uka, Musa Zenuni, Agron Durmishi, Hajrush Kurta and LFC CRLT Lars Aage Knudsen, Advisor and Mentor DNK Army.
4:30-6:30pm	Meeting with Halil Gashi, Arben Gashi.
7:00pm	Meeting with police officer, Isuf Vrapci.
8:00pm	Meeting with Eroll Maxhuni, Egzon Bunjaku, Egzone Idrizi (Journalist), Halil Gashi (artist/performer) and Arben Gashi.

Wednesday, December 19:

11:00am	Interview with Ombudsperson Sami Kurteshi.
3:00pm	Interview with lawyers Florim Gashi and Afrim Kosumi.
4:30pm	Meeting with Law Professor Bekim Kadriu, Iliria University.
6:30pm	Meeting with Robert Wilton, ICO.
8:30pm	Meeting with Dr. Zymer Neziri, at Ringsi.

Thursday, December 20:

	Phone Call Correspondence, Valentina Saraci, journalist.
10:00am	Meeting and interview with Basri Murati, Deputy Prime Minister of the Local Government.
12:00pm	Meetings at the Kosovo Assembly.
1:00pm	Meetings at the Ministry of Foreign Affairs.
3:30pm	Meeting with District Attorney Imer Beka.
	Meeting with lawyers Florim Gashi and Afrim Kosumi.
4:00pm	Meeting with Zana Daka and Pëllumb Kallabaj, Ministry of Foreign Affairs.
5:30pm	Meeting with Ismail Kastrati, author, and Chief of Finance Commission.
9:00pm	Dinner at Pëllumbi Restaurant.

Friday, December 21:

8:00am	Meeting with Arbër Vllahiu, Ambassador of Kosovo in Prague.
9:00am	Correspondence with the President of Kosovo Office, Atifete Jahjaga.
10:00am	Interview with Edita Tahiri, Deputy Prime Minister.
11:00pm	Interview at Vetëvendosje Movement.
	Picked up surveys from the Kosovo Assembly.
	Picked up surveys from the Institute of Albanology.
12:00pm	The Kosovo Force (KFOR) / Komanda e Forcave Tokësore, Visit at the Adem Jashari Barracks. Meeting with Hajrush Kurtaj, Director of Department for Civil-Military Cooperation.
1:00pm	Interview with Dr. Hajredin Kuci, Deputy Prime Minister and Minister of Justice.
3:00pm	Meeting with Mirushe Emini, Ministry of Culture, Youth and Sports.
3:30pm	Meeting with District Attorney Imer Beka, Florim Gashi (laywer) and Afrim Kosumi (lawyer).
4:30pm	Visit with ethnic Albanian and ethnic Serb communities.

Interview with Judge Bekim Sejdiu,
Judge of the Constitutional Court of Kosovo and former Consul General of the Republic of Kosovo in New York

(November 28, 2018, Kosovo)

Biography:

Bekim Sejdiu, PhD, serves as a judge of the Constitutional Court of Kosovo and teaches at the Faculty of Law of the University of Prishtina and the University for Business and Technology - UBT, in Prishtina. He has served as Ambassador of Kosovo to Turkey and Consul General to New York. Bekim Sejdiu has completed his law studies at the Law Faculty of the University of Prishtina.

He has completed two master studies: in the area of international relations at the University of Bilkent, Ankara and in the area of democracy and human rights at the University of Sarajevo and University of Bologna. He has earned doctoral degree in International and Diplomatic Studies, at the Faculty of Government and European Studies – Nova Univerza, in Slovenia. Bekim Sejdiu has conducted study visits to different universities in Europe and USA. He has published book chapters and numerous articles in various academic journals.

Bekim Sejdiu was part of the founding group and at the same time a member of Professional Researcher Council of the Kosovo Institute for Policy Research and Development – KIPRED (2002-2008). In the period 2000-2002 he was also a program director at the Kosovo Foundation for Civil Society – KCSF.

During his public activity, Bekim Sejdiu has been awarded a number of decorations and appreciations, including the Decoration of the Assembly of New York State (USA), Key to the City of Worcester (Massachusetts, USA) and a medal from the Minister of Foreign Affairs of the Republic of Turkey.

Rule of Law and Legal System in Kosovo

Bekim Sejdiu: With the ending of the war in Kosovo and deployment of international administration, a new legal system was erected from scratch. This huge enterprise involved two fundamental dimensions: First, creation of the new legal order through adopting of new legal acts. Second, establishment of the new justice system, which entails organization of the court system, public prosecutorial system, correction service, etc.

From 1999/2000, when the UNMIK was deployed, and up to 2008 when Kosovo became an independent country, the entirely new legal system was established. This, in itself, is a remarkable success of the joint efforts of the Kosovar institutions and the international missions (EU, UN, NATO). Furthermore, the legal order created in Kosovo has been shaped within the normative framework of the EU standards. In other words, the Constitution and the laws adopted in Kosovo, particularly after the independence in 2008, reflect the legal standards generated from the EU acquis communautaire as well as the highest international standards on human rights and protection of ethnic minorities.

These remarkable achievements notwithstanding, there is an apparent discrepancy between the energy and resources invested; the results achieved and the expectations of the Kosovar society, in terms of the standards of rule of law and efficiency of the justice system.

Kosovo resembles an average European country, when it comes to statistical measurement of public safety and the crime rate. However, similarly with the regional countries, Kosovo's overall progress is challenged from the corruption and organized crime. The general perception among the Kosovar society is that first UNMIK, then EULEX, together with the Kosovo courts and other institutions, have had much more modest achievements than expected, when it comes to fight against organized crime and corruption.

The fact that UNMIK (before 2008) and EULEX (after 2008) have prioritized political stability over the rule of law and fight against corruption has nurtured a negative perception in the public about the achievements, and even the objectives of these missions, in terms of the justice and the rule of law. This has been exacerbated by the scandals within the missions, particularly within the EULEX (such as the cases when the EULEX judges and prosecutors accused one another for serious misconduct and corruptive behavior).

These facts have blurred the image of the international justice institutions in Kosovo and this has overshadowed their achievements. This does not mean however, that the Kosovo institutions, particularly the justice system, can escape their part of the responsibility.

APPENDIX 5

Interview with LTC Enver Dugolli,
Former Kosovo's Military Attaché in Albania

(December 3, 2018, Kosovo)

Biography:

Enver Dugolli was born on 01.27.1963 in Nekoc of Drenica, Kosovo (*Alb: Kosova*). was persecuted and sentenced for political activities by the Serbian regime. Because of his political beliefs he was sentenced twice and spent over 10 years of difficult imprisonment in Serbia. He is a victim of the biggest Serbian massacre which took place in Dubrava Prison (near Istog) in May 1999, where over 150 Albanian prisoners were executed without trial.

Work experience:

2001-2009 – Media Officer (Public Relations) in the Kosovo Protection Corps.
2009-2014 – Senior Officer at the Kosovo Security Force.
2014-2018 – Military Attaché of the Republic of Kosovo in Tirana (Republic of Albania).
2018 – Retired with the Rank of the Active Colonel and the Honorary Grade of Reserve Colonel.
2018 – Currently politically engaged, member of the General Council of the Self-Determination Movement!

Education:

Enver Dugolli graduated from University at the Faculty of Philosophy in Prishtina, where he earned a master's degree in Sociology. He has attended and completed numerous specialized training in the field of Defense and Security.

Justice, Security, and Defense System in Kosovo

Enver Dugolli: There is a broad public perception that the justice and security system is affected by the phenomenon of corruption and external political influence and interference. Unfortunately, this perception even though it may be exaggerated, a fact that cannot be overlooked is that these two areas are crucial to the quality of life for all citizens. Since the people of Kosovo emerged from the war, with a lot of suffering and trauma, they had rightly expected that with the freedom they gained, things would be improved and the lack of freedom would be compensated with certainty and justice above all else.

The installation of UNMIK's temporary administration at its beginnings was seen as a real rescuer because it was thought that a mission directed by United Nations would be guided by the principles of universal rights and laws by setting standards of security, freedom, and substantial justice. Kosovo even under captivity had a justice system that did not enjoy credibility of over 90% of the population in Kosovo, because it led by a system which treated Albanians as second-rate citizens.

The initial failure of UNMIK Administration to set the foundations for justice and security for citizens was related with the fact that it was a great mission but mixed composition where judges and persecutors came from many different countries of the world.

The practices implemented by the mission of UNMIK were in conflict with the tradition and different systems of judges, prosecutors and also the police which was the indisputable backbone of building the justice. Considering that since the beginning of setting the initial fundamentals it was wrong, there was no standard of a Western democratic country, but it was a system where the police applied the practices of a country, unknowingly whether came from Africa or the east, and whereas the Prosecutor could have been from Asia, and judges came from different countries who as well had substantial problems about principles and practices.

The beginning of recruitment of local judges and prosecutors had its own shortcomings because UNMIK's mission was led by the established criteria of the proven experience from other countries and did not give an opportunity for establishment experience of new judge and prosecutor. Almost all the recruited judges and prosecutors had a past in the earlier system of selective justice in Serbia and being so they had their mortgages of the past, which as such does not guarantee a proper justice.

The situations created after the war were very contradictory because they had to deal with people on totally two different poles. The war-torn people whom also had form political parties and other governmental and nongovernmental organizations, and a part of them had been involved in security institutions, had often been the victims of persecution and punishments that they had received from the former system of justice in Serbia, and now those judges and prosecutors were infiltrated into the system of justice. Based on the principle of justice, that it should be applied to whoever and in front of law we are all are the same, here we have the initials problems that followed Kosovo for a long time. There was not how to apply justice from a judge or prosecutor of a past system when people from the scene of politics and society (the majority), had been victims of persecution from the same system. This phenomenon was producing adverse effects to justice because the actors being called to set justice, were interested in being personally rehabilitated and not being interested in confronting their former victims, now powerful, even when these violated the law.

The growth of the political power of some powerful people who are on the scene even today has caused damage injustice even though formally separate powers. Crime, corruption, and insecurity did not decrease, but only increased and structured. Although various progress reports, as well as numerous recommendations coming from states and credible world organizations, addressed these phenomena, there was never any improvement since there was no political will. Initially, prosecutors and judges were compromised by the former system and then the political class cared for the recruitment of obedient and close people to the party and interest groups, bypassing the professionalism and courage of the people who wanted to be part of the justice system. The extent of the absolute influence on the judiciary has made the credibility of the citizens on this judiciary bodies result in very low level of trust.

Various scandals in this system have continued at the same pace and there was never willingness and will to improve the situation. The point where this justice system is mostly focused on is trials of war crimes, but here it has also consistently failed. Starting with the premise of a justice with political agenda, it left no justice for war crimes, but the worst proved the opposite. The establishment of a Special Court headquarters in the Hague is evidence of lack of credibility for a credible and unbiased local court. The establishment of the Special Court has damaged the reputation of Kosovo, but above all, by only targeting war crimes supposedly committed by the Albanians has only damaged the trust of people and victims for a proper justice.

Security

Enver Dugolli: The security aspect along with justice is one of the main pillars where the citizen faces daily. Unlike justice, the area of security and defense is a field with more investments. As NATO's mission, KFOR was the first to be placed in post-war Kosovo, security and defense were always the positive perceptions of the citizens. Although this mission, like UNMIK, has the source from UN Security Council Resolution 1244, have changed in organization and approach. KFOR still is led by military leaders who come from developed countries but also with the tradition of states ruled with the democratic organization. It is very indicative situation that even now 20 years after the end of the war and 10 years after the declaration of independence of Kosovo, KFOR continues to have satisfactory citizens' credibility, which marks 60% according to the latest measurements by the Kosovo Center for Security Studies, in comparison to mission of UNMIK which consistently had a decline of confidence to disregard.

The political aspect has been a major obstacle to not fully functioning of the security and defense scheme. Although the Kosovo Police Service initially and then Kosovo Police had made important strides in profiling and structuring, the consequences of the various experiences from UNMIK for police have been evident obstacles. As the police institution is an implementing law institution, efforts to intervene and interfere with politics and interest groups have damaged its reputation. The numerous scandals that had followed this institution such as burglaries in the evidence room, the scandal with penetration of the Turks...etc., were never addressed in the field of political and professional responsibility. The control of senior executives from politics is another aspect of citizen dissatisfaction, which affects the continued decline of citizens' credibility, and according to recent measurements by the Kosovo Center for Security Studies, marks a 42% quota citizen credibility.

Unlike this institution, again measurements of the Kosovar Center for Security Studies, the citizens of Kosovo, according to this publication, mostly expressed satisfaction with the work of Kosovo Security Force, with a quote of 72%. This high percentage of citizens coincides with the desire and the need for Kosovo to have an army of its own, which would guarantee the protection of the sovereignty and territorial integrity of the country. The KSF, having the various stages of its development had its difficulties but has managed to maintain a great credibility among the citizens, even by becoming a model for its communication skills and minorities integration. Beside its professional achievements of KSF, helped by NATO and KFOR, especially in the fields of training and education, achieved to integrate successfully even other minorities in Kosovo, and particularly Serbian minorities. This is a great accomplishment when we consider the pressure and the consistently attacks by Serbian institutions whom they see KSF as continues Kosovo Liberation Army (KLA).

Now when we are in the final steps of finalizing changings of KSF mission, the political pressure from Serbia keeps increasing. On the other hand, within the political spectrum in Kosovo, including every different civil society category, there is a full consensus for this organization which is seen as one of the best success stories of the Kosovo country.

APPENDIX 6

Interview with Neki Babamusta,
Historian, Writer, Professor of History and Literature
(November 26, 2018, London)

Biography:

Neki Babamusta served as a world history and literature professor for over 40 years in Albania. Neki has contributed to the development of education in Albania and Kosovo (*Alb: Kosova*). He has been awarded many honors during his life, including: "Teacher of Merit" and "Exemplary Teacher." Neki Babamusta was honored by the United States Congress for his International Advocacy of Diplomacy (2013), and for his continued efforts to strengthen US-Albanian relations and further democratic values (2003 & 2004).

How do you define national identity?

Neki Babamusta: National identity is determined by personal identity and common identity. National identity includes hometown, residence, date of birth, citizenship, language, traditions, and religious affiliation. For Native Albanians, traditions and ancestors are of great importance. The birthplace for Albanians is the pride of their ancestors, parents, grandparents, and forefathers, it is the place where you are raised, brought up by the family, educated, with the care of your family home. The birthplace is the place of your relatives, friends, society, the place where you prepare for life.

Albanians, wherever they are, preserve their native country traditions as the pride of their national identity. The Arbëresh of Italy is an excellent example of preserving national identity, by preserving their Albanian language, traditional dresses, weddings, dances, and songs for many centuries. In their traditional wear, the Arbëresh reflect the emblems of the birthplace, with the embroidery of the eagle and the flag.

The religious affiliation to Albanians is not primary in terms of national identification. For Albanians, traditions are more important, such as faith, generosity, humanity, bravery, and hospitality. An Albanian feels proud of being Albanian, for having Albanian blood, and Illyrian origin.

What connects the common identity between Albania and Kosovo?

Neki Babamusta: The national consciousness and the Illyrian genesis of the population naturally connects the common identity between Albania and Kosova. Albanians in Albania, Kosova, and in all the Albanian speaking lands have a common history, meaning descent and origin from Illyrian tribes. In addition to history, they have the same Albanian language, common lands, and their traditions inherited by their predecessors. Also, Albanians in Albania and Kosova have a common identity based on ancient traditions such as faith, generosity, love for the homeland and the Albanian language, respect for the forefathers of the country who fought for freedom and Albanian education.

National symbols are celebrated and valued by Albania and Kosova. To preserve national pride, Albanians have carved the portrait of Scanderbeg and representatives of the Albanian Renaissance in statues in various central squares, have named schools, neighborhoods, and institutions with their names.

At the same time, scientific symposiums are organized in Kosova and Albania dedicated to high Renaissance figures in order to preserve the national identity. In my 40-years working as a history teacher, I have spread Albanian language education in Albania and in Kosova. Meanwhile, in Kosova, teaching in Albanian was prohibited by the Tito regime, where many professors were dismissed and imprisoned. Teachers who spread the Albanian language in Kosova were persecuted, ill-treated, imprisoned, by shutting down the schools for the Albanian students, who were forced to learn in secret.

Another factor that connects the common identity between Albania and Kosova is the creation of a new European and democratic identity. Both countries want to integrate into the European family, with great assistance from America, England, Germany, and the European Union. European and democratic identity means meeting standards, having stability and economic growth, market economy, quality products for trade exchanges, respect for cultures and other minorities, political stability, functioning of the rule of law and the legal state with democratic structures in the service of the people, and not political clans.

What factors influence political trust in government, the political elite, and government institutions?

Neki Babamusta: In Albania and Kosova, the highest level of trust is with NATO and the EU, whilst the judicial system and political parties are the least trusted institutions. In general, the local education and law enforcement institutions have stable trust regarding accountability and transparency.

Democratic institutions become more trusted when they function on the basis of values, norms, and laws, and are transparent and accountable in their work. Some of the factors that influence the reduction of political trust in the government and the political elite are: abuse of power, corruption, political influence on the work of public institutions which then become the cause of people's revolt.

Increasing prosperity and economic investment boosts people's confidence in the government when financial state budgets are not given to non-businessmen and corrupted clans linked to crime, but to honest and foreign businessmen on the basis of mutual benefit, according to the law.

Our great Renaissance patriot Mit'hat Frashëri has emphasized, "Our party is Albania." All reforms in the economy, justice and policy changes are necessary to strengthen democracy in Kosovo and Albania and to increase political confidence. Vetting (justice reform) should hit corrupt segments in politics and economy.

Common factors that determine the identity of the Albanian nation

Neki Babamusta: The Albanian population living in the Albanian lands in Europe forms a nation with a common national identity because within its body and origin they share these values: language, territory, origin (historical ethnogenesis), traditions, customs, archaeological-historical, cultural-artistic heritage, educational, emblems with national representative symbols such as the flag and eagle, high moral patriotic values, love to live freely, desire for knowledge, faith, bravery, humanism, and religious tolerance.